MW01675298

Wisdom Of The Rays

The Masters Teach

Volume II

Copyright © 1999 by America East Publishers, Inc.

All rights reserved. No part of this text may be reproduced or transmitted in any form, by any means, without prior written consent of the publisher, except for brief, unedited extracts or quotations for inclusion in a magazine, newspaper, or broadcast media review or other presentation.

Also available in French

For more information, please contact:

America East Publishers, Inc.
Post Office Box 794
Champlain, New York 12919-0794

ISBN: 0-9661921-1-7
Library of Congress Catalog Card Number: 97-77792

Cover photography
© 1998 Index Stock Photography, Inc.

Printed in Canada

TABLE OF CONTENTS

DEDICATION

The Guiding Hand of God

and His Angels

can make any one a Teacher

and

any event a Lesson.

This book is dedicated to ALL

who are Guided to cross our paths,

sharing their Lessons

for our Awakening.

May the thoughts gifted herein

help YOU to help another!

PUBLISHER'S FOREWORD

In my Foreword to volume I of this series, I said: "What so impressed me with this collection of writings was the mastery of the written word and the fluent simplicity of style being made use of to explain otherwise difficult-to-grasp concepts of the human condition. Within the rich and intricate tapestry of the lessons presented, there also weaves a thread of timeless Wisdom that reaches ever-so-knowingly past the curiosity of the searching mind, to gently soothe the yearnings of heart and soul."

The messages offered in this present collection—gifted by Master Teachers from the Higher Realms of Creation who care dearly about our future and who wish to see our lives enriched from within—continue from and build upon those presented in volume I. The perceptive reader will notice that the sophistication of that which is discussed herein has incremented up a notch, such as one would experience from moving up a grade in school.

There is an Excitement stirring in the air these days which the lessons herein address from many points of view. Why are we here in the first place? Is it simply to acquire a paycheck and impress some friends, play with our toys, and then provide fertilizer for cemetery horticulture?

Hardly! This is schoolroom Earth, a most challenging environment which provides the ultimate "university" education in important fundamental areas of mastery of the creative process. We are *all* unique "sparks" of Creator Source, learning to be like our Father. Our prayer is that these messages help to unlock *your* unique gifts, for in you sharing what is uniquely yours to give, we all grow, and Creation unfolds in awesome majesty!

Dr. Pierre Cloutier
America East Publishers

PREFACE

My mother, almost into her 84th year in this life, is part of a small team of eight ladies who feed almost 700 children every day at my old grade-school cafeteria. This seemingly routine activity is repeated in thousands of schools around the world every day.

I'm reminded of it here because, upon closer inspection, one actually finds "the macrocosm in the microcosm"—just as the entire Creative Process that lovingly builds awesome galaxies and universes is displayed in the tiny bloom of a single roadside wildflower or conveyed through the interactions that these angel-ladies have with the children each school day.

Some of the children are latch-key kids who seem to see their money-focused, yuppie parents only by appointment. Others look to the school cafeteria for their only decent meal for the day. Very few are growing up in the kind of stable, loving, two-parent environment I took for granted when I walked that same path, at that same school, forty-some years ago now.

Especially in such a "modern" social environment, where so many kids are casualties of a condition over which they have no control, Mom says that rarely does a day go by wherein she is not called upon to hug a lonely or scared or crying child, or help with the calamity when some child spills something all over themselves—or worse yet "looses their cookies" so to speak, maybe all over Mom or an unfortunate kid sitting innocently nearby the sick child.

Never a dull moment since kids will be kids—right?

Well, maybe the more important underlying point is that *human beings will be human beings!* And THAT is the many-faceted thought I find running loud-and-clear through volume II in this ongoing series of messages gifted to us by Master Teachers from the Higher Realms of Creation.

If anything, this is a theme that could use some positive PR (public relations), don't you think? When you first read the phrase *"human beings will be human beings!"* above—come on now, admit it—what went through your mind?

Was it something wonderful like the thought of the little child who walked up to my Mom with a big smile and gave her a crinkled-up, handmade (crayon drawing, on a table napkin) thank-you note with a tiny little teddy bear taped inside, because Mom helped her find her lost mitten on a bitter cold day.

Or did your thoughts go to that "inconsiderate jerk" sporting purple hair and a ring through his nose, driving the old trashmobile with broken windows and blaring heavy-metal rock, who stole YOUR parking space the other day at the grocery store?

See what I mean? This world is not exactly a place overflowing with paragons of the Golden Rule these days. If anything, I feel the messages herein from the Master Teachers are designed to remind us of our TRUE potential as HUman Beings, where HUman means "Higher Universal man" who exists throughout the universes at many different levels of maturity, mostly well beyond us kindergartners.

This is the time of the Great Awakening of the residents of this planet to that True Potential within each of us. It is a time when some will feel, with great hand-wringing trepidation, that the sky is falling, while others will feel, with great sparkling excitement, that a new world is being born.

Both of these views—and all the levels of perception in between—are swirling all around us as I write this. Some sense deeply what is happening, while others, mesmerized by distraction or paralyzed by fear, won't consciously become aware of (or finally have to face) the situation until they are, maybe literally, knocked out of their TV-watching couches or basement bunkers.

I think that is why more of the writings in this volume-II collection are from Geophysical Commander Ceres Anthonious "Toniose" Soltec than from the other 13 Authors who more equally contributed to volume I in this series. (Go back to the Introduction to volume I for important background material on

Soltec and the others. As well, the design of this volume assumes you are familiar with all of the background information and earlier messages assembled in volume I. There seems to be a purposeful "flow" to the lessons, chapter after chapter after chapter.)

Yes, Soltec is in charge of the geophysical aspects of this Earth Transition Mission. But, as part of the Hosts of God here at this time, his primary job necessarily overlaps with the people-education effort that has come to be called "The Great Awakening".

He is a highly evolved scientist, yes, but he is equally well versed in the spiritual laws that govern *all* of God's creation. Thus, as a Higher Teacher and Guide, he often efforts to help us see the DIRECT connection between OUR thoughts and emotions and actions, and the Earth changes happening now and a-comin' 'round the corner like a speeding freight train—as great Mother Earth, herself a sentient being of enormous compassion and patience (as our Native American brothers and sisters have been trying to teach us for centuries), "sneezes" and "fevers" the man-generated poisons out of her body on HER way to cleansing, rebalancing, and rebirth into a higher-frequency, higher-dimensional level of existence.

Related to the theme I like to call "The Hug From Above" that runs throughout the writings herein to effort to awaken our True Potential as HUman beings, there is also the recurring urging to "go within" and discover (awaken) the DIRECT CONNECTION we all have with our Creator, as unique sparks of His Light.

Is that the same as prayer? Something like that, but more developed along the two-way street. Does it require our meeting head-on the major-stumbling-block issue of PERSONAL RESPONSIBILITY? You bet! Nobody else to blame. It reminds me of the old Murphy's Law quip that goes: "Teamwork is essential—it allows you to blame someone else." Right. Remember: *human beings will be human beings!* Meanwhile, our Higher Teachers are efforting to help us to see that: HUman beings will be HUman beings.

It's tough to break the drug-like dependency upon so-called "expert authority figures" and their "religions" that we have been trained to defer to—whether they be politicians (who are mostly all #*@%!! lawyers), doctors (especially psychiatrists), celebrities, or churches. That urging of *personal communication* with God, with its attendant adult *personal responsibility* clause, greatly threatens the sneaky mind-control/people-control agenda that historically drove (and continues to drive) the very creation of organized "religions" in the first place—whether they be the familiar establishments we've grown up with, including "churches" like the American Medical Association, or the newer, secret-government designer-type of operation like a Heaven's Gate cult.

After all, if God is truly within *each* of us, then why do we need to be so dependent upon, say, the God-"expert" reverends and their churches (with—dare I say it—their ever-present collection plates) to intercede between us and God? Why indeed! Is God really so inept a Creator that we need these "specialists" as go-betweens to reach Him? I don't think so.

But that subject is only one of many volatile topics that shall be confronted—and largely recognized for what it truly is—at this time of the planetary Great Awakening. In other words, "earthquakes" are going to be happening on MANY fronts, and not just literally shaking the ground under our feet. That "jelly" between our ears is also about to get quite a ride!

How can we, here on planet Earth, possibly join in society with our more advanced relatives from elsewhere in God's Vast Creation until we at least wake-up to the most basic truths of reality and the Golden Rules of coexistence—and shed the limiting beliefs that have been ever so skillfully imposed upon our thinking, over many centuries, by dark puppets of The Adversary, whose agenda has always been to attempt to control, and thus derail, God's Lighted HUmans, on this testing, schoolroom planet, from achieving their magnificent True Potential?

Exactly how we residents of the surface of planet Earth were seduced to spiral downward, over the centuries, into our present state of darkness, is a larger theme than the focus of this book and requires dealing with such uncomfortable, mind-stretching information as is contained weekly in the *CONTACT* newspaper.

CONTACT is also the forum in which the uplifting "spiritual" messages, collected herein, first appeared—as a kind of balancing "refreshment" to offset sometimes heavy, shocking reading.

So you will see mention of *CONTACT* sprinkled throughout the messages collected in this book. Sometimes my original editor's notes are retained, or modified to suit this volume, or other notes have been added to guide the reader who may be encountering this kind of material for the first time herein.

You will often also find reference made to "Ground Crew" by the Authors of the writings. This is a respectful expression of acknowledgment by the Teachers "up there" for those ones "down here" who feel a genuine connection to the great Planetary Transition Mission underway at this time. There are *many* of you out there! I know this, if for no other reason than from the many incredible letters and other messages which arrive all the time at the *CONTACT* offices that speak loud-and-clear on the subject.

For those readers of this volume who are unfamiliar with references made in the various writings herein to either the Phoenix Journals or the *CONTACT* newspaper, or to the sometimes unique health products offered by New Gaia Products, I here provide contacting information:

For more information about the Phoenix Journals or *CONTACT* newspaper, call: 1-800-800-5565 during normal West Coast business hours, or write for information about the Phoenix Journals to: Phoenix Source Distributors, Inc., P.O. Box 27353, Las Vegas NV 89126, and for information and/or a sample copy of *CONTACT*, write to: CONTACT, Inc., P.O. Box 27800, Las Vegas NV 89126; for more information and/or a catalog about the offerings of New Gaia Products, Inc., call: 1-800-639-4242 during normal West Coast business hours, or write to them at: P.O. Box 27710, Las Vegas NV 89126.

The *CONTACT* newspaper also has an Internet address for the growing numbers of you who can access the 'net. That address is: **http://www.contactnews.com** and freely provides all current issues of the paper (which does not accept advertising revenues) as well as a growing collection of sometimes infamous back issues.

Now, with that bookkeeping message out of the way, let me

next mention that the response to volume I was so buoyant and warm that we who had a hand in the production constantly fight feelings of inadequacy and responsibility to match the exhilarating notes of thanks that have poured in.

It is one thing to simply share some "spiritual" writings with you; it is quite another to get back, over and over again, such completely unexpected appreciation as: "Your book gives me new reasons to keep on living!" or "You must have written that *just* for me!" or "It's amazing how the book just seems to open to the page I need!" or "I'll buy copies for others, but I *won't* part with MY copy!"

Well, thank you very much, and know that those notes of appreciation greatly fuel this present labor of love, too. We hope you feel the same way about volume II, which continues with the same kind of messages where volume I left off. You might herein notice, however, that the messages have gotten a little more challenging—maybe like going up a grade in school. And that's how it should be, for after all, aren't we here on schoolroom planet Earth to learn and be tested and grow?

It's the learning and the testing and the growing that life here is really all about. This interchange begs, more than anything else, for the sharing of talents—which, in turn, implies, first, the discovery and unfoldment of the *unique* talents within each of us, talents gifted to us by virtue of our beingness as *unique* sparks of the Light of Creator Source, the One who created us.

Or, as Sanat Kumara (the Silver Ray, or Grandfather to the Native Americans) put it in the chapter fifty-nine writing which closes out this volume:

"The sum total of ALL who partake in this interaction brings forth a constant, forever evolving growth interchange wherein ALL grow in some way. We [*from the Higher Realms*] are as much thankful for those of you who elect to play the physical game of 'life' as you are who frequently express your gratitude for our Higher assistance.

"This circle of interaction is infinite in its possibilities and without end in its extension, and often, as ones leave behind the physical and re-emerge into the nonphysical, YOU become the

Guides for those who are entering into the physical arena. WE ARE ALL BOTH TEACHER AND STUDENT!"

Since we *all* have something unique to bring to the party, life takes on a most amazing dimension when we realize that. I mean *truly* realize—actualize, manifest—that! Which gets back to my Mom and the cafeteria angel-ladies.

How important is the pizza served that day to the kids? How about the smiles and the hugs and the wiped-away tears? How may those seemingly "small and insignificant" interactions affect not just the later development of those children but—egads—THE WHOLE OF CREATION?!

Well, that's where I stop and let the true Master Teachers take over. I know when I'm out of my depth!

In my Preface to volume I, I began with the statement: "You have begun to read a most unusual book. It defies easy explanation. But for those of us who have had a hand in its development, it has been a labor of love, mixed with no small amount of excitement, for the messages you are about to read are gentle (well, sometimes NOT TOO gentle!) guidance from Advanced Ones who have progressed further along the evolutionary path which ALL Lighted Souls must travel in their growth."

Volume II is a continuation of those provocative messages. It still amazes me, when re-editing the writings again for this book, how beautifully these Master Teachers seem to be able to knit together connections and examples illustrating very powerful Higher Spiritual Laws which span the entire Omniverse of universes, yet include the tiniest roadside wildflower—or those lost and scared little children in the school cafeteria who may need a hug of encouragement to re-sparkle their day.

But don't we *ALL* need some kind of a "hug" sometimes? That's how I see the underlying flavor of the messages gifted to us in this book.

Within a longer, private message on November 28, 1998, to the main receiver of the writings contained within this collection, Commander Soltec made some unexpected general comments that we feel are most appropriate to share here in this Preface:

"Allow for the forthcoming [*public*] messages, for they are sent in response to the heart's call for balance and peace. Many are crying out and many are seeking that which brings forth *inner satisfaction.* The old ways of doing things are beginning to prove quite inadequate these days, and many are left in a semi-confused state—not knowing exactly why their lives and world are falling apart.

"We have come so that there can be a stabilizing factor injected into the equation, so that ones can *KNOW* that what they are experiencing is a natural evolutionary process—and not some sort of punishment from a vindictive god. Our primary concern is to get a remnant through the changes, so that there can be the added value of experience added unto the collective consciousness of God and Creation.

"The efforts you put forth at this time will greatly aid many a person in the upcoming years, and many will draw great inner strength from applying the principles of that which you offer forth and share with them.

"No, God's word *CANNOT* be silenced, and you may indeed step down from the task of receiver if you so choose. Be aware that we know your heart, and we have chosen you for many reasons, not the least of which is the fact that we know the depth of your desires to help your fellow traveler and to understand for yourself the greater reasons for all that has been a part of your current life experience.

"Those things which cause you the most inner conflict are the very experiences that will cause you to continue to seek answers. The more answers you find, the greater clarity you will have, and the easier the task becomes. It is a win-win situation you find yourself in. It is only you who places the perceived burden of responsibility upon your own shoulders.

"Beyond the intent for clarity and accuracy within Truth, you need not accept any further burden of responsibility. There will always be ones who misinterpret our words. Likewise, there will always be ones who are frightened by the implications of personal responsibility, and they will effort to tear down and discredit our words. This is not your problem, nor is it something you need to worry about.

"You hear us just fine, and though you worry a great deal over the accuracy of your receiving, be assured that you are doing more than an adequate job for us at this time. Let go of these fears and worries, for they serve no purpose. We see that your intent is one of clarity and accuracy. This intent is all that is needed in your case, for it runs so deep as to touch the heart core of your being.

"We will guide you through your current challenges, and you will recognize the Hand of God at work. You cannot hurt another with our words if the intent is to truly help them to see. Light will always absorb and transform the darkness and broaden the experiences of all beings, everywhere.

"You cannot get your part wrong, and you will never be asked to do something that you are not capable of doing. Reasonable Guidance will always be offered in response to a sincere petition. Let not the distractions of day-to-day living accumulate to the point of utter confusion. Let the past serve as marker points so that you may determine the general direction of your travels. Beyond that, it is merely a distraction.

"Create a better future for yourself and others! Find peace within yourself and accept who you are. Let not the overwhelm of the 'possible' implications distract you. You are who you are, and denying self only serves to limit self. Accept your role and embrace the opportunities that come your way.

"I am Toniose Soltec, come as Teacher and Friend. Salu!"

How much more compassionate and understanding of a Professor can we hope to experience at this time of the Great Awakening upon schoolroom Earth? All of the lessons offered herein provide that underlying "hug" as even the most profound of topics are discussed with great skill and simplicity by these most loving Master Teachers and Guides.

As Esu "Jesus" Sananda explains in chapter five:

"You each wish to explore the various aspects of your being and test your own uniqueness in your own unique way. One major aspect of Creator's desires is to expand and grow. *You* are part of His desire to do so, and when you grow individually, He is growing alongside of you.

"As a 'genetic' subset of The One Whole, you must first come into understanding of the impact of that which you are capable of manifesting. You have INFINITE potential within. Potential is the same for each—infinite!

"Each individual is at a different level of understanding of HOW to responsibly direct and control this infinite potential. There have been structured various schoolrooms so that ones can come into detailed understanding of the various aspects of harnessing and controlling this infinite creative potential.

"The physical (third dimension) is but one, small, yet important, classroom or laboratory in which to explore. You will find yourselves surrounded by ones facing similar challenges upon any one level of experiencing."

I am left considering, as we approach the ending of this century and the dawn of a New Age for Mankind upon planet Earth, the stunningly appropriate picture that author and gifted social commentator of the last century, Charles Dickens, so exquisitely put into words as you begin his *A Tale Of Two Cities*:

It was the best of times, it was the worst of times;
it was the age of wisdom, it was the age of foolishness;
it was the epoch of belief, it was the epoch of incredulity;
it was the season of Light, it was the season of Darkness;
it was the spring of hope, it was the winter of despair;
we had everything before us, we had nothing before us;
we were all going direct to Heaven,
we were all going direct the other way.

Actually, where we are "going" is of our own choosing. And the messages collected together for this volume help us not just to grow comfortable (yet responsible) in the driver's seat, but also to remember just how much there is "out there" to explore.

Have fun—and keep an eye out for the Angels in God's many "cafeterias" dispensing those all-important "hugs" along the way!

Dr. Edwin M. Young
Editor-In-Chief, *CONTACT* Newspaper

The Messages

CHAPTER ONE

Allow For The Balance Of Taking Responsibility

Ceres Anthonious Soltec
April 5, 1997

Good morning, my friend. It is I, Toniose Soltec, come in the Radiant Light of Creator God. Thank you for sitting this day, for we have messages that need to get written.

Change is inevitable and NO ONE ever remains completely the same from moment to moment. Your thoughts today are different from those of yesterday, even if the difference is slight and hardly noticeable. Your surroundings such as the temperature, atmospheric pressure, weather conditions, position of the Earth in relation to other celestial bodies, or less noticeable changes such as electromagnetic pulses, are constantly impacting and affecting you in a relentless manner.

As you move through your experience in the physical, we notice from our position of Higher Understanding that many are resisting change. By this I mean that ones are constantly efforting to go against the natural flow of Creation. It is quite contrary to the EVOLUTIONARY nature of your being to stagnate, and not evolve and move forward. Yet, we see many stuck in and paralyzed by fear, or living in the past where there is usually great emotional pain constantly being reflected upon.

Many of you would be wise to go back and re-read Phoenix Journal #27, called the *Phoenix Operator-Owner Manual,* for therein lie many of the insights that have been offered so that you can learn to recognize the subtle nature of the adversary and come to appreciate and more fully understand the TRUE Laws of Creation and God.

In the Introduction to that Journal, Aton says: "MY LAWS and those of THE CREATION were given unto you of physical experience to honor total simplicity and gain wondrous fulfillment and joy from your relationships with your brethren, to pass the journey of experience in learning, and then make passage into Higher Levels of understanding and knowledge. You have now bound yourselves by shackles of lies into the endless rotation of the wheel of experience, worsening with each experience until you have forgotten all the Truth of LIFE. Most of you have wasted your experience and are the moving DEAD searching after bits of physical dregs to pass the journey."

And in the Foreword, Esu Sananda says: "Herein you shall find The Laws clearly outlined. There is no room for misunderstanding the message. There are no little grey areas for you to move around in. If you violate The Laws after completing this document, you shall do so willingly, knowingly, and therein shall be CONSEQUENCES FOR THOSE ACTIONS. God is most forgiving for actions done in ignorance. Willful violations of The Laws is entirely a different matter. It is the better part of wisdom to heed this warning for it is most grave indeed.

"We are at the final hours of the planetary cycle. Choices will be made by man that shall affect him for eons in your future counting. Be most cautious when seeking the momentary thrill, for the excitement you seek shall not satisfy you in the countless generations of recycling and rebirths before you as you learn well the lessons you so carelessly refused to learn *this time around*."

There is not time here to re-write all the lessons over and over again. We will, however, direct you to that which is often overlooked, for it has been over six years since the release of that Journal and many of you Ground Crew members would do well to refresh the memory with these TIMELESS words. They are just as important today as they were the day they were first written to help in the guiding of you ones through the many experiences and challenges of the third-dimensional path.

As you evolve and grow, you will see that your experiences are NEVER without challenge. In fact, the more you grow in responsibility, the greater the challenges become! So when you are feeling overwhelmed with the never-ending barrage of greater and greater pressures, know that these are a sign of your growth and that you need all the combinations of challenges that you are being faced with so that you can truly evaluate your abilities.

The greatest difference between those who seem to "have it easy" and those who appear to be the constant "victim" is the viewpoint or ATTITUDE of the individual and their reaction to each challenge. Those who can keep the Larger Picture in mind while going through the experiences of challenging growth, will naturally see that fear and anxiety need NOT be part of the experience. Those who are resisting their lessons (opportunities) for growth, and are constantly focusing on the pain or hurt, will pull into themselves more PAIN and HURT!

Step outside the inner world of your mind and see the unfolding drama from a Higher Perspective: You are on a small planet in a small solar system circling around your Sun. Your solar system is part of a galaxy (the Milky Way Galaxy) of trillions of stars. Your galaxy, in turn, makes up a very small part of what you refer to as your universe. There are MANY universes out there, all of them full of life. This is only a third-dimensional (physical) point-of-view of the truly infinite expanse of Creation of which you are a part and to which you contribute.

Begin to see that your personal challenges in the physical, though they are important to experience, are but the baby steps of awakening the inner potential of your responsible awareness of the enormity of your true self. When you can see that you NEED the experiences that cause the emotional responses that generate pain, anxiety, grief and such, so that you can learn to control same with responsibility and knowledge of the fact that you have created the conditions (either deliberately or by default) that have led to the situation with which you are now faced, then you will begin to realize that there is NOTHING you cannot handle in terms of emotional control. It is only your current beliefs that limit you in this regard.

You may feel grief over loss of a loved one, but let me put this into a slightly different perspective: How do you think God feels when one of His free-will planets degrades to the point of destruction of the entire planet? In His moment of great sorrow, if He did not realize the value of the experience for all involved (both physical and non-physical), and instead only focused on one very small aspect of the event, rather than on the larger reasons for such a challenge, there would be such a GREAT unbalance in The Creation as to cause every living entity, everywhere, to experience an overwhelming condition of grief and sorrow.

This situation God would view as unjust and unbalanced. You in the physical often focus on "getting even" or "I'll show them what pain really is" and go forth in an emotionally unbalanced state of irresponsibility that will only garner more pain for yourselves.

This is a vicious cycle once it has started and is very difficult to get oneself out of, for you are often too much focused on the inner world of your mind to take a larger viewpoint and forgive self and those whom you have allowed to be a part of your experience.

YOU ARE **NOT** A VICTIM! You have created your

emotional state, and when you can take personal responsibility for your condition and stop blaming others, you will have then taken the first major step toward finding the balance that you have been pushing away from yourself.

It will not be instantaneous. Like a person with a drug addiction, you will have a lot of habitual thoughts and beliefs that will cause you to want to react emotionally, without thinking. You will have to modify your thoughts and monitor your emotional reactions so that you can allow for the balance of taking responsibility—not just once but ALWAYS!

When RESPONSIBILITY becomes the habit, instead of the excuses or blame of another for your condition, then you will have the balance and general happiness that you want, for you will be now thinking ahead as to the consequences of a thought or action and not just living a reactionary life. This is to say that a by-product of truly learning responsibility is control over your life.

To sum this up: With knowledge (understanding) applied in a deliberate, responsible manner, you WILL create with deliberate control over your experiences. Remove the responsibility from the equation and you will find that your deliberate control will be removed as well.

Please see that you are fast entering a time wherein you will need to allow those who continue to turn away from The Laws, or otherwise enter into a state of shutdown or overwhelm, to experience the unfolding events as they so choose. This means that if ones do not want to face the responsibility for their experiences, then let them to their self-imposed misery and move on with your experiences. You do NOT have to make another's pain YOUR pain!

No souled being likes to see another person in pain, and I tell you now, those of you who go through this Transition will see ones in great, great emotional confusion and pain. And you will then see that, if YOU are to survive, you will have to learn to allow these ones their experience without taking on the responsibility for their care. If they cannot see value in helping themselves, then why should you force your viewpoint upon them? They will either come to this realization on their own or they will not. It is each individual's choice.

Offer always a helping hand, but do not "carry the donkey", lest you both perish in ignorance! This is not to frighten; it is to offer a reminder of WHY you are there and WHAT you should be preparing yourselves for mentally.

The mental part of you is far more important than the physical, for the mind controls the physical. The physical part of you would be a motionless blob if it were not for the mind to give it direction. Note: I did NOT say brain! I said MIND!

These words are offered in Love and with the intent to educate and remind you ones of WHO you are and WHY you are there. Keep the Large Picture in focus and, for your own sake, keep your thoughts centered in Light (GOD) and keep the dark ones out of your sacred temple—your MIND!

I am Toniose Soltec, come at this time with the Hosts, as a Guide and Wayshower, in the Light of OUR Creator. Thank You!

Soltec to clear until we next can have time for a writing session in which to continue this subject.

April 12, 1997

Good morning, and thank you for sitting this day. It is I, Toniose Soltec, come in the Radiant One Light of Creator God. Let us please continue with the subject of responsible, balanced choice.

This is a time of great challenge and opportunity. Look forward to the upcoming experiences with excitement!

Worrying over events that have not happened yet serves no real purpose. Having the intention to prepare for any and all challenges will allow for the manifestation of WHAT you need WHEN you need it. Worry will only serve to cause those events which will feed the worry and it will grow. If you redirect that focus of energy toward joy and fulfillment, then you will, likewise, feed the joy and fulfillment and it will grow. The choice is yours. This is free will!

This challenging time is an experience that is meant to be fulfilling and full of great value. Value, in this case, is as it would be perceived from your Higher Self viewpoint. From this viewpoint you would perceive great value in the growth of your being and not in anything of a physical nature. Money and such are but a symbol of value as viewed from a third-dimensional standpoint. There is nothing of lasting value from the time spent down there except for that which you gain in the way of experience and knowledge.

Continue to seek out that which has true, lasting value and you will find the fulfillment that the Infinite You desires. Expect the joy to be there along the journey and it will be so!

There is no such thing as a complete waste of time, for all experiences will give you feedback in the form of emotional feelings. Those things that are not of great value to your overall growth will leave you feeling less than alive and, in time, you will learn that there are better ways of spending the moments of "now" and you will gravitate toward those experiences of greater and greater inner fulfillment.

Yes, restrictions from your current beliefs are usually limiting your experience. But, this too has value in that only those who are ready to accept the responsibility of CREATING IN BALANCE will be given those experiences that will allow them to transcend the crowds of disbelievers.

This is a natural self-testing process that is in place, so that only when ones have grown enough mentally to accept this level of responsibility will they be able to put the information gathered in any one experience together in such a manner as to see that they themselves are solely (soul-ly) responsible for their creations and that they create EVERY FEELING that they experience.

This is the point when one can deliberately create the life of excitement and joy. Prior to this, ones will simple continue to believe that "life is hard" and thus continue to create a "hard" life for themselves.

Life is what you decide it will be! Nothing more and, indeed, nothing less! As you begin to realize the implications of this message, you will begin to see the value in NOT dwelling upon the emotionally hurtful experiences, but focusing more upon those experiences that allow your heart to soar with laughter and joy.

YOU CHOOSE WHAT YOU DWELL UPON.

YOU CHOOSE AS TO WHAT AND WHERE YOU PLACE YOUR VALUES.

YOU CREATE THROUGH YOUR CHOICES THAT WHICH IS YOUR EXPERIENCE.

If you are feeling pain (emotional or physical), sadness, boredom, frustration or whatever, then it is because YOU have allowed those thoughts to persist within your mind and YOU feed and nurture them to the level they hold at this moment. When you change your focus to thoughts that are positive, you will create more of that which will cause you to feel good. What could be simpler?!

The answer to ALL of your emotional "problems" lies within. Seek for your happiness within yourself. Another may be able to offer a short-term comfort to you, but unless and until YOU change the mental programming, you will find the old tapes resurfacing and those old seeds planted long ago will still be bearing fruit. Whether the fruit is bitter or sweet depends upon the seeds YOU have planted.

Perhaps it is time to weed the garden and plant again anew? With the gained value of the past you can, if you so desire, make a more educated and deliberate choice about what seeds you will plant and grow, and what weeds you will no longer tolerate.

Thank you. I am Toniose Soltec, come in Light and in Love.

Salu!

CHAPTER TWO

Auditioning Tips For Your Part In The Play

Ceres Anthonious Soltec
April 23, 1997

Good afternoon, my friend. It is I, Toniose Soltec, come in the Radiant One Light of Creator God. Be at peace and be still. Let us write this day that many who earnestly ask may have answers.

All is unfolding in Radiant perfection! You shall soon see where your path is heading and the Larger Picture will be more evident. The past is written and cannot be changed. The present moment will dictate the future unfolding of your desires.

The play is written, though not all of the individual roles have been assigned. Each participant in the play will add his or her uniqueness to the drama, thus there will be the spontaneity of the experience!

When one chooses not to participate, then that is their choice. This choice shall be honored. This "selection" process will cause delays to some extent, though very small in most cases. When and where we can, we will effort to work with those expressing a desire to participate. Though, just as a casting director must evaluate abilities and skills, so too must we, and our subsequent testing of those skills will determine the selectee for any particular role. There will always be a selection and "auditioning" process for each task.

As ones PROVE their abilities and suitability for any given assignment, these ones are then put through RIGOROUS training and practice for their given role. Many will get too involved in the physical experience, with family or career distractions, to realize that they have come into this experience in order to participate in a much broader manner than what they may even be able to perceive themselves capable of at this time.

We know the potential of each and we also can see the given probability of circumstance that will unlock the potential of each. From our vantage point, we orchestrate, with the personal Guides of each, scenarios that are quite objective in presenting opportunities to each souled creation so that each will be presented with optimum opportunities in which to grow.

Many have come to participate at this planetary transition time so that they can experience same and grow in awareness and abilities. Some have returned at this time for very specific and focused reasons. These ones are the ones who will be called upon in the event that no one else arises to the occasion. These ones are working on their primary reason for coming into the physical and will continue to do so throughout their journey regardless of their "collateral" assignments.

In some cases they will only fill in as long as it takes for another to be brought up to speed in order to accept the challenges of any particular assignment. This is the reason for a lot of the fatigue that you ones are feeling and the burden of "not enough time" that seems to be haunting you constantly. Have faith in the play's perfection.

As the play continues to unfold, you will see that there WILL be just compensation for your efforts. Nothing goes unnoticed from the Higher-Dimensional Perspective of

Creator. Nothing! All will circle back into balance and each will be given to understand the reasons for their frustrations. Be aware that THE limiting reason is, almost without exception, due to your own inner viewpoints and beliefs.

If your perception is that of confusion and disbelief, then you will find great inner conflict and a sense of overwhelm. This is because you are resisting the very opportunities that you have come down there to experience for your own personal growth. Your foot's on the gas pedal AND brake!

No one of the Lighted Hosts will force you to grow; the choice will have to be yours. Our place is to offer you guidance and instruction in the form of suggestions made in reason. We will never coerce you into doing anything, nor will we insist that you do anything. We may very well offer nudges, even in a nagging sort of way, in order to get your attention from time to time, but we will NEVER force you to do anything.

Your growth is YOUR responsibility and you will do it of your own free will—or you will stagnate of your own free will. I will offer here and now that it is my suggestion that you CONSIDER CAREFULLY your intent.

Consider all of your actions and whether or not you would consider them worthy and Godly. When you can live in such a state that you do not have to feel regret for an action taken in anger or in a state of emotional instability, then you will begin to turn yourself around and you will see the balance coming back into your life.

Let go of the past for it is GONE! Forgive yourselves and move forward. What and who you were yesterday is insignificant compared to what and who you are today! No one in the physical is without error. You all make mistakes and you all grow from your mistakes. Stop expecting perfection from yourself—and most certainly from others—else you will find yourself in a state of frustration that will consume and confuse you.

Start fresh this day and move forward in TRUTH and

HONESTY with yourself. When you can stop lying to yourself, you will find it much easier to be honest with those around you. Think how it makes you feel when someone is honest with you! You are all Godly creations and you can, if you so desire, reflect this at any time.

We offer these messages in Love, Compassion, and Understanding. We know, in most cases better than you, what will bring forth the inner balance and joy that you desire. Ask honestly with the Heart and you will be given to know.

Please keep in mind that those things which you are hiding from are the things which cause you the most pain and are often the things you will need to confront in order to find the balance you desire. This is to say that your emotional state may appear to be getting worse (rather than better) at first, but with persistence you will be freeing yourself from the pains and traps of your mind, and the end result will be a more balanced and harmonious state.

Keep in mind that I said we would help and offer you that which you need. I did not say that it would be easy! It will, however, be quite valuable to you in your overall growth. And the experience, in retrospect, will be quite fulfilling.

As you work through your fears, you will gain great knowledge and insight into the workings of the mind. This experiential knowledge will grow at an exponential rate—slow at first but, with persistence of effort, it will garner you great knowledge. This knowledge will help YOU to free yourself, as well as help you to help others to understand and, in turn, help themselves.

Keep inner balance as your goal and you will draw the resources and experience to you so that you can see where your fears are residing. When you can identify the TRUE cause of your fears, they will no longer be able to control you.

The adversary is a master at exploiting ones' fears.

This is how he can distract and divert those who effort to "do the right thing" from reaching their goals.

Judge not the person, but rather, the actions, for you may be calling a person into your experience and not even be aware that you need the lesson that this one can offer—even if it is a harsh lesson. Be thankful for those ones who show you where your fears are, because how else would you know that those fears are there and controlling you and to what extent?

This is where you would be wise to monitor yourself and learn to recognize when you are in a state of REACTION! The reaction is most often due to a fear (belief) that you hold as true that has NO real substance.

When you truly understand WHO you are and from WHERE you come, you will KNOW that you have NOTHING to fear!

When you doubt your own reality, you are denying truth and you are usually in a state of fear—fear of responsibility! We watch as you ones go through your various colorful and elaborate justification processes as you try to convince yourselves (and often others) that you are justified in your running from responsibility (TRUTH)! These are your fears controlling you and you see this not! Deny all you want; it changes NOT one bit of the truth of the matter.

Have faith in yourself and have faith in that which you KNOW to be true! If you must hold onto one truth, then find one small truth to hold onto and move forward from there.

For example: Let us say that you are in a situation where you have been avoiding telling someone how you truly think and believe regarding spiritual matters because you are afraid they will not understand and will somehow think less of you. Let us say that this person is your spouse or "significant other" and that you know they are very fundamental in their beliefs and have stated as much. So, you go about avoiding the subject, though it nags at you, because you cannot allow yourself to express the joy that the information and thinking brings you, and you are afraid of offending the other or being rejected for your beliefs.

As time goes by, you notice that you are making excuses about what you have been doing, such as telling a story (like, "I went to the library...") instead of telling the truth that you were reading one of the Phoenix Journals or the *CONTACT* newspaper. This continues, and the guilt grows, and the subsequent tension between the two of you builds and builds. You are feeling worse and worse every time you tell a half truth or lie in order to avoid confronting your fears.

This is where you would be wise to find a simple truth about which you have great certainty, such as: "I believe that everyone deserves to know the TRUTH, no matter how embarrassing or difficult it is for me to confront!" If YOU hold this to be true, then act upon your truth and have faith in your judgment.

The person to whom you show this level of honesty will, in time, appreciate your honesty—even if it is several years after the fact and your honesty leads to a divorce or separation. This may sound harsh, but if you consider the alternative—continual lying—the consequence will be even harder to deal with as the guilt consumes you. What do you think the end result of the relationship will be after four or five years of dishonesty?

When you confront your fears, you will find discomfort as the ego tries to justify the need for the fear in the first place. You may experience a "whirlwind" of emotional confusion as the truth settles in and the subsequent realization of "reality" settles in for the one with whom you are being honest. Again: hold onto YOUR truth and act accordingly. It may be the only thing you will be able to hold onto as your world appears to be falling apart and your ego tries to avoid the pain.

Let me reiterate here that the truth you hold onto must be something YOU hold as true with great certainty, else this will not work, because when you first lie to yourself, then you cannot be honest with others. Your truth will anchor you in a position that will allow you to weather through the emotional upheavals as The Truth (honesty with self) sets you free!

This is how you begin to turn around the reactionary cycling of the mind and begin to project from a position of power (truth). Consider carefully that which you hold onto as truth, for if what you are clinging to is NOT completely true for you and you have doubts, then you will not be projecting from a position of power, but rather from a position of inner conflict and dishonesty with yourself!

Consider these words "auditioning tips" which will allow you to overcome the stage fright that might be keeping you from fulfilling your reason and purpose for being there. There are Great Potentials within each unique Lighted Being—awaiting realization and actualization in manifested reality. The only thing standing between where you are this day and the realization of this Potential is YOU and YOUR self-imposed limitations (beliefs)—your fears!

I am Toniose Soltec, come as a Messenger of Truth, in Light and Service to the One Light Source—ATON. May this magnificent play include YOUR unique contribution!

Salu.

CHAPTER THREE

Further Signs Of Pacific Plate Tensions

Ceres Anthonious Soltec
May 7, 1997

Thank you for taking the time this evening to sit and write. Thank you for listening and hearing my call. Yes, it is I, Toniose Soltec, come in and with the Light of Holy God of Light, God of Creation, and with the golden-white Christ Light. Do not struggle with your thoughts; allow my energy to flow. Thank you for clearing your space and for lighting the white candle. This is a symbol for yourself, and it will, if you allow, help you to focus upon the task at hand.

I am with you this day to tell you that we at Command sit at an extremely high state of alertness. The agitation, the ear ringing, the nervousness you and others are experiencing now is due to the stresses which are present RIGHT NOW upon your planet, for many of you are "sensitives" and are experiencing physical reactions to the stresses and changes of your planet.

Do not be distressed over these things, for you are MEANT to be in tune with your planet! Over time, those upon your world have become desensitized to the "nature" of things, and only recently are so many becoming once again attuned to your planet's inner workings.

In a writing on 2/11/97, I called to your attention to watch Japan for clues to impending further pressure build-ups around your tectonic plate called the Pacific Plate. [*Editors's note: That writing, titled* Watch Japan For Earthquake Timing Clues, *is chapter 52 in volume I of this series and was originally presented in the 2/25/97 issue of the* CONTACT *newspaper.*] At that time I said:

"Watch Japan VERY closely during the next several weeks. Watch for POSSIBLE activity to occur in this place—beginning with many small quakes, followed by an earthquake which could well register up to 9.5 on your present scales.

"As the Pacific Plate continues to grind against all adjacent plates, watch next for POSSIBLE quake activity to begin along the coastlines of the Americas—both South and North. There is indication at this time that, should quakes occur in Japan, there would follow, within three to five days time, some significant shaking along the coastal areas of the Americas."

Now, so far that "big one" has not yet struck Japan. However, as that writing was going to press, there WAS quite a swarm of smaller quakes in the general area of the Japanese Islands and these, in turn, continue to cause many repercussions.

Extreme pressure has built on the eastern edge of your Pacific Plate, and though this place has been experiencing many small-to-moderate earth tremors in the past several weeks, the pressures are but slightly relieved in that place. The ground there is in a brittle state, which means that rather than being in a state of flexibility, it acts more like a dry piece of timber, and the pressure present now could easily cause it to snap, which would result in a most violent earthquake.

This is not a prediction, and it is, of course, not carved

in stone; however, the state of alertness under which we are operating is in part due to this state of high tension all along that eastern border of the Pacific Plate. There are several points at which the plate is in a locked state—that is, the plate is attempting to move, and movement is not possible and, therefore, more pressure is building at these critical points.

I realize that we have been down this road many times before, and each time a large, devastating quake has been averted. However, it is our agreement with you ones that we will inform you at any time this area is in a state as critical as at present.

The preparations should already be in place for those of you who are going to prepare. We are not going to go over that one again, except to say to be ready, for the potential for SEVERE activity is there, right now.

There are also other activities present now which we need to bring to your attention.

The volcano 43 miles southeast of Mexico City, Mount Popocatepetl, whose summit is almost 18,000 feet high, is showing signs of building to a massive eruption. Those who live near this place are living in GREAT danger.

Several small eruptions have already taken place, but these only work to make people complacent about a massive eruption. Though warnings have gone out, there are those who say that this mountain has been erupting for eons, and thus are not concerned.

Many have already fled the area, for they have been forewarned; others have heard the warnings before, only to have them never pan out. These ones are remaining and refusing to leave the area. If the volcano should really blow its top, these ones will not have a chance for survival.

And, yes, there is a definite correlation between the tremendous swarm of "UFO" activity in Mexico (especially in the area of Mexico City) and the impending, explosive state of the volcano. As usual, much information on this subject has been suppressed by your controlled news media outlets. However, avenues such as Art Bell's late-night talk-radio program have provided much factual reporting on this lively "UFO" activity being observed around Mexico.

Is this activity increasing? Of course, and it shall continue to do so. That, however, is all I shall say about that, except that these craft are NOT from your planet.

There will be many more of these types of "natural disasters" which you ones are going to experience in your time. Do not allow selves to be so overwrought with worry, fear, or grief that you find yourselves unable to function. You knew, before coming into this lifetime, that these were the times and challenges for which you incarnated, and it is NOW that you ones are most needed.

We must have channels through which to get the messages out, and though the free-will human element of choice always exists, we must continue to use those channels who have come to your place at this time for this purpose. It is not always an easy task, for either you or us, for while you ones want to participate and assist in the mission at hand, there is always that human element, prone to fears and other distractions, which can and does intrude.

Though it can, at times, be a handicap for the task of messaging, it is also that human element—the "Spark of Life" or Light from Creator, so to speak—which makes it all possible. So it is somewhat of a "Catch 22" situation for both of us. We will adjust frequencies on both ends of the spectrum whenever necessary and whenever possible, so that the messages can flow with the highest possible "fidelity". This is not possible with ALL third-dimensional humans, for first must come the desire to serve, and to serve selflessly, and that, dear ones, is a most rare quality amongst those on your planet today!

Very few are they who have determined to work and serve without worrying about personal compensation, for you live in a world filled with greed and lusts for material possessions and power. It may come as a surprise to you ones, but power is more sought after than even monetary gain.

As your world grows more and more crowded, and more and more impersonal, there is the desire within the third-dimensional ego to be recognized, thus the impetus to generate something through which to call attention to oneself, for these ones are fearful of being lost in the crowd, so to speak. So, ultimately, these ones strive to achieve more and more recognition through many different sources. For some it is career, for others it is outrageous actions, but the ultimate goal is the same—recognition.

It is all due to the fact that each of you feels as though you are losing your individuality. And, as you continue down the accelerating path toward your planet's transition, these tendencies will continue to increase, until at last the transition is completed. Then, and only then, will balance begin to return to your now very much out-of-balance planet.

All the political games of power are, in the long term, for naught, and the struggles in which your world finds itself embroiled at the current time are but that—games, and these too shall, one day, come to a halt, when finally the transitional process has been completed.

However, see that you pass not judgment upon these ones, for they are but acting out their roles in this play. Each has their own lessons to experience, and you know not another's agreement prior to entering into this life.

Karmic retribution is in full swing, and that which is sown is also being reaped. But the germination time has much shortened, and what might be called "instant karma" is occurring. There is not much time left for your world in the third-dimensional framework, so many ones upon your planet are experiencing that karma in their current life streams. You have but to watch what goes on around you to see that this is truth.

Be cautious, however, for not all is of The Light; in fact, very little upon your planet now is of The Light, and that is why it is all the more important for you ones to gather about you your protection of Light, and maintain it at all times. It does not hurt to reinforce your protection several times throughout the day, if you feel it necessary. Better to call it in more than needed, than to not call upon it and leave selves exposed and vulnerable.

The darkness is very subtle and very enticing, and sometimes will even APPEAR, at first, to be of Light; however, it is not Light, and will flee from your presence when you bring The Light about you. The darkness cannot and will not stay where The Light is. So, to stave off the darkness, keep yourselves in The Light at all times!

I will here again emphasize that your world is in a very grave state at present. Can the process be reversed? I do not see how, and the only way to the other side is to go through what is on the horizon. There is no turning back now, for you have come too far. Once you have reached the other side, you will see that the trip was all worth it.

The numbers of those who shall make it in their present physical state will be few. It is a hard truth to hear, but you need to hear it, and not lose sight of your goal once the REAL turmoil begins.

As another useful direction in which to keep watch for clues to the upcoming turmoil as Mother Earth efforts to reclaim her balance and shake off the poisons, I again return to my earlier writing of 2/11/97. Therein I suggested that you pay attention to the anomalies around you. That is:

"I would like to urge all of you who have animals near you to watch them very closely. They are telling you that the Earth is about to give a great heave. Watch for abnormal migrations and animals showing up in odd places. Watch your house pets, as well, for many of them are exhibiting odd symptoms of apparent illness or they may be just acting 'weird'.

"You see, these creatures are more attuned to the frequencies of the planet than are their two-legged counterparts, and they will begin to react long before earthquakes and other geophysical events take place. Watch them also for out-of-the-ordinary behavior, such as dogs biting who normally don't bite—that sort of thing. Those of you at the coastal edges, watch the tidal activity, for there are many, many small earthquakes occurring within the depths of your oceans and the tidal activity will reflect these occurrences."

It is NOW that you ones must make yourselves ready, for time has run out. Prepare yourselves quickly, and then be watchful, for it is coming. Keep your eyes upon the skies and your ears to your planet. Be mindful and attuned to our calls, for they shall be on the increase. Remember, this is why you have come to Earth-Shan, and you are about to come into your fullness of purpose in this mission!

Many will there be coming unto you and asking for help. DO NOT TURN THEM AWAY, BUT LIKEWISE DO NOT ALLOW THEM TO SHIRK *THEIR* RESPONSIBILITIES TOWARD SELF AND OTHERS. IF THEY ARE TO MAKE IT THROUGH, THEN THEY MUST PICK UP AND CARRY THEIR OWN LOADS. NONE SHALL MAKE IT ON THE BACK OF ANOTHER! Each one will, of his own, make it or not make it, and there will be no victims in this transition—only personal choices.

Be not in fear of the changes that are upon you, for they are a very necessary part of the transition. The Earth will heave to and fro, and many wondrous things will you experience, but lose not your sight upon the final goal. We will *always* be there with you, and we are but a call away.

Now, let us close this writing, and allow the information to settle within each of you. The Light is about you—keep it there and stray not from that which you know to be The Truth. We of the Heavenly Hosts are very near you, and we are in the service of Holy God of Light. We thank you for your time, and for your determination to see it through the upcoming changes.

I leave you, as always, in the Light of Holy God.

Toniose Soltec to clear. Salu.

CHAPTER FOUR

Understanding Your Bio-Electric Sensing Machine

Master Hilarion
May 17, 1997

Good afternoon, my friend. Please release of the emotional charge and allow the energy to flow naturally and smoothly. It is I, Hilarion, of the Fifth Aspect of Creator's Spectral Expression. I come in the Light of Holy God of Lighted Creation. I come as the Cohan (Master Teacher) of the Emerald Ray.

Ones on your planet are greatly concerned with the physical well-being of the body in which they are housed. Here we shall give forth some insights that will help to clarify the causes of the conditions that ones are experiencing. For most this will not be "comfortable" reading because the reasons for illnesses are most often other than what a person wants to hear, let alone accept.

The physical body is "merely" a conduit for the interaction into and the interfacing with the physical experience. I say "merely" because that body is a most exquisite creation indeed and poorly understood by your current level of so-called medical science.

It is a self-contained bio-electric machine that is quite suited to handle a wide array of energy patterns and frequencies that allow for the animation and coordination between the physical and the non-physical. The body's electrical system is quite sensitive and balanced in such a manner as to have the capability to respond and alter according to emotional desires of the one controlling the mechanism.

YOU ARE NOT YOUR BODY! "You" are the one inhabiting the mechanism and it responds to your desires. There is similarity between "you" inhabiting and operating your body, and the process of sitting behind the wheel and driving your automobile.

The body, for the most part, is self regulating and will tend to run quite well in an "autopilot" mode. However, there come times of experience where the body is subjected to threat, such as physical injury, when it will offer a reactionary response to the danger and bring focus to the impending physical condition.

An example of this reactionary impulse would be to quickly remove one's hand from a hot stovetop. The body will retain information that will help one to avoid future damage and will offer a cautionary warning to the host (YOU) when the hand even gets close to a warm object.

This mechanism is part of the design of the body so that more primitive (lesser aware spiritually) users will be able to persist long enough in the physical without demise so that there will be adequate time sequence for growth.

This is the situation wherein one will tend to live instinctively and obey the signals of the body such as hunger, thirst, and rest. Ones will seek out the satisfaction of these basic needs so that they can experience as fully as possible.

As entities begin to grow more and more aware spiritually, they will begin to come out of the fog and into a more reasoning condition wherein mental anticipation of the future need for food will be recognized and planned for through storage.

This is the point where ones begin to awaken enough to realize that there is something more to the experience than to just exist and search out survival needs. This is where ones begin to reason with others the value of working together with one another in order to quiet the distractions and concerns of the body. This is where there occurs the first spark of sensing that man is more than a reactionary animal and that there is an inner desire to explore this awareness.

As cultures and beings evolve, there comes the need for Guides and Wayshowers to interject more and more of the true nature of the physical experience. While Esu "Jesus" Sananda is a good example of one such Wayshower who came to your planet 2000 years ago, MANY have come at this present time. These more advanced ones will volunteer for the challenge of fulfilling this task and will choose to take on a body in the physical to bring forth the all-important messages concerning the non-seen-but-felt spiritual connectedness of mankind.

These awakening nudges will often cause great emotional stirrings in the body. Ones will not know how to handle these energy surges at first, because they are subtle yet strong in their grip upon the physical apparatus. The surges will cause an array of sensations within the physical which, in turn, can provide the physical entity with guidance as to what is right versus what is wrong.

Much like the reactionary impulses to avoid physical danger, the body will offer reactionary impulses in response to other kinds of situations, which can nudge you to go toward that which will offer comfort and warmth. And in the case of the presentings of spiritual truth, the body will offer the best it can in the way of "gut felt" responses to that which is being offered.

"How", you may ask, "does the body do this?"

The physical part of the body is but "only" one small part of the entire apparatus that makes up the entire, functioning, bio-electric machinery. Just like in a computer, you have all the physical components—the main processor, the memory modules, the peripheral (audio and video) circuit boards, and the interconnecting wiring. And yet, more fundamentally, the computer still requires electricity (energy) operating in very focused ways in order to function and come to life at all.

In the case of the body, there are various electrical counterparts associated with each physical part of the body, including each organ and each individual cell. More fundamentally, there is a coordinated electromagnetic (LIGHT) energy field that encompasses the entire physical body. Some can actually see this "luminous" electromagnetic field under the proper conditions and call it the aura.

Your body's electromagnetic field interacts with the electromagnetic fields emanated by others and will respond to the various frequencies of these fields.

This is when you ones will say that you KNOW you can trust a person immediately; you don't know why but you can just "feel" it. This is why, when another comes offering true spiritual knowledge, you "feel" it within your "gut". You are responding to the higher-frequency energies flowing into the electromagnetic field of your body. The body then responds with a desire to find more of what causes this reaction.

This is also the reason why some ones will be frightened of you. They will know that you hold truth and they cannot hide their trickery from you and that you will, in time, see through their games. These ones have resisted the spiritual path, having not yet learned to recognize that there is value in the experience. These ones have an energy signature that is much lower in frequency. They are usually the ones clinging to the physical-material for their comforts and security. They are much like the animal who has to horde and hide food from others who might take it away—not realizing that there are infinitely abundant sources of nourishment for both the physical apparatus and, more importantly, the soul (the non-physical, God-like, thought projection of Creator Source).

When ones turn from their purpose, there come the "STRESSES" of the life experience. This unbalanced condition is a signal to you so that you can stop to evaluate where you are heading and compare that to where your heart tells you that you should be heading. The heart knows the direction which will garner fulfillment.

More accurately, it is the emotional (electromagnetic) energy center associated with the heart that is attuned to both your purpose from Creator Source and the impinging emotional currents of the ever-changing electromagnetic pulse-wave universe in which you exist. This heart energy center responds by instinctively offering that which will help you to discern your most satisfying path in life.

When you first start heading in a direction that is not fulfilling to the purpose for your being down there, you may or may not notice the subtle annoyance that you feel. But be assured that it is there. This causes slight distortions in the energy field of the body as you resist the natural flow of your experience. These distortions are what you ones refer to as "stress" and the corresponding worry and frustration is a by-product of the electromagnetic distortions in the non-physical part of the body.

If these distortions are allowed to persist, they will cause physiological malfunctions within the body. The physical body will respond to the out-of-balance (out-of-phase electrical impulses) condition of the electromagnetic energy field of the body. This will result in negative physiological changes within the body if the condition persists—such as colds, flu, cancers, and especially that #1 cause of death: HEART dis-ease.

Please be aware that the direction of the individual always starts with a thought and a decision. When ones are considering choices of action is when ones should really make an effort to monitor the response of the heart or "gut" while evaluating their choices. Some do this automatically and may cause frustration in others because there will be times when the only reason they can offer for an action is: "I don't know; it was 'just' a feeling." These perceptive ones have learned to recognize and utilize the "bio-feedback" that is being offered to them.

When there is illness of any sort in the body, you can be assured that the one experiencing the illness was not paying attention to the signals offered through the heart energy center. There are choices and decisions associated with the condition that allowed for the stress to persist on and on until there is great unbalance within the physical, causing improper coordination between the various energy centers, and thus the body will not regulate itself properly.

When ones can isolate that which causes them "stress", they will be looking for that which has a decision or choice associated with it and would be wise to perhaps re-evaluate or look for that which they are resisting. Usually those things that the heart desires by way of growth have responsibility associated with them, and ones know analytically that there are often "growing pains" associated with such responsibility—as the primitive, ego-based, reactionary mode of living is replaced with a freer, more personally responsible mode of living.

Many will go through many life experiences without ever recognizing the connection between the physical condition and the non-physical stress—only to cast blame upon another for *their* lack of physical balance. YOU each are creator of YOUR experience, either through deliberate action or passive reaction. Your physical condition is no exception!

Ponder upon these words, for they are offered in love and NOT with the intent to be offensive or hurtful. At this time many are crying out for assistance with the physical condition of the body. You will see that there is great value in finding within yourselves the TRUE cause(s) of any unbalanced situation.

The subject matter discussed here is far from complete. It is offered as a general overview so that ones can come into awareness of self in a general, yet more balanced, manner. There shall be more coming forth on this subject of the physical body's functioning. Please be patient and understanding. Thank you!

I am Master Hilarion. I represent the Heart Center of God. In Light and Love, Salu!

May 24, 1997

Good afternoon, my scribe. It is I, Master Hilarion, of the Emerald Ray of Creator's Spectral Desires. I come within the Wholeness of The One Light, Creator Source. Let us please continue from last we wrote, for there is great interest and desire for this information at this time.

We last spoke about the general overview of the basic functioning and interactions of the physical body. The various energy centers of the body function in a harmonious and balanced interchange in carrying out the regulation of the various physical-functioning organs and cellular matter that make up the entirety of the body. There must be two-way communication, in a timely manner, between the physical body and the non-physical counterpart we will refer to as the light-body (light being electromagnetic pulse-wave energy) in order for the body to respond to the delicate fluctuations of the electrical impulses generated by each cell of the body.

This exquisite communication is accomplished through what you ones would call superconductivity. We will here broadly define superconductivity as the conduction of electrical energy without resistance to that flow of energy.

In the world of "science", ones are having trouble achieving this superconducting state utilizing just basic metal and ceramic compounds, even at temperatures just slightly above where the conditions are most favorable (very cold). Yet, in Nature (God manifest), it is happening all the time right before your eyes. (In fact, it is happening IN your eyes, for that matter!) And in the body, this superconductivity occurs at temperatures averaging 98.6° Fahrenheit—and higher when the body is fighting foreign invaders.

The problem is that the current perceptions of "physics" are based upon assumptions which would appear to be true, but actually only include half (at best) of the picture. This is why your typical mainstream scientists are having so much trouble duplicating (or even realizing the true physical nature of) the world in which they live. But here I am digressing from the lesson for today, so let me return to that subject.

Each individual type of cell is attuned to very specific frequencies and will respond to the regulating currents of the light-body energy pulses. There is an underlying unique frequency signature associated with EACH individual on the planet that will keep each of you, to some extent, electrically isolated from one another, so that the direct electrical functioning of your body will not interfere with the direct functioning of another person's body.

This is the "genetic signature" of the body, unique to the DNA structure or blueprint of each cell. This is a "plasma shielding" that the body exists within. It will allow physical matter to pass through, while shielding out specific frequencies and wavelengths.

Without this shielding, ones would empathically alter the state of one another. There are ones who can tune into the various frequencies associated with this energy field, and if not careful, make themselves quite sick (unbalanced) if they are tuning into one who is out of balance.

When ones are in an out-of-balance condition, the energy field tends to be compromised in that it will lower in frequency and in intensity. This is a condition wherein you ones become more susceptible to manipulations by those who specialize in the "black arts". These dark ones will alter their frequency to match the lower-frequency state that you enter when in these "stressed" states. Know that these dark ones operate ONLY in the lower spectrum of the physical range of existence.

When you move up in frequency, you are moving beyond the range of their influence. This is why we of the Lighted Hosts of God will urge you to keep your Light shielding in place and fortified.

While each physical body is isolated in certain frequency ranges, each entity is also connected in other HIGHER frequency ranges that will allow for the communication with the rest of the universe (God's infinitely creating Mind). As we spoke about in last week's writing, the creative desires are projected out from the heart energy center and are focused with the mind. The greater the desire, the quicker the physical manifestation of the desire.

This mode of creation exists and works outside of the limitations of moral and ethical beliefs of the individual. This is to say it works for everyone regardless of their morals or beliefs. This is a basic Law of Creation: Go forth and CREATE, expand, and GROW!

There are ones on your planet who will manifest money and power without regard for who they step on, in order to reach their goals. Their desires often manifest quickly because they are not easily distracted with the Conscience that the average person has to contend with.

These ones, who are so physically focused and self-isolated from their Conscience (inner guidance from their Higher Self), will achieve a state where they get to the top of the mountain and will have everyTHING (physical) that they desire—only to find that there is still an inner lacking that is not satisfied. These ones are taking to extremes, one aspect of creating, and will, in time, either disintegrate their souls completely, or rebound back into the Light Source that created them—then wiser, for they know then where value IS NOT!

You focus your desires and send them out through the heart, and then the universe responds. Yet you never seem to get what it is you are wanting. Therefore you dismiss these words as fanciful delusions of a lost soul.

NO! They are NOT!

You ones fail to monitor your thoughts CAREFULLY! You will send out conflicting signals, and thus negate the energy pulses. You will say, "I want more money!" And then, in the next breath (or thought) you will say, "But, I never get it." Do you see that the one thought cancels out the other? Your vacillating heart will send out both, and the net sum will be zero—or quite a bit less than you "thought" you were creating!

The seeming lack of clarity and single-mindedness of thought and focus usually comes from a conflict between what you consciously desire and what your Higher Self is desiring in the way of growth. And that Higher Self is doing battle with the ego-based self which desires comfort and satiation of physical desires.

This causes the kinds of stress that you ones feel usually in the heart area of your chest. While this lower, ego-based self serves a self-preservation purpose in the primitive cultures, it must be overcome if you are to ever move beyond the limitations that hold you from reaching through to Higher levels of realization.

The ego's reactionary impulses will serve you physical "warnings" to obey, by offering physical reactions or pains if you do not follow what it desires. Much like the warning sensations felt when your hand comes into close proximity to a hot object, the ego-based reactionary self will attempt to cause you to avoid situations that could lead you to override the ego's functioning. This war is perhaps the greatest challenge you ones face in the physical experience because there are great efforts on the part of the dark ones to hold you from progressing through that physical classroom.

When you live in fear, you live in a reactionary state that will, at best, only serve the ego's desire for self preservation. However, your Higher Self knows the functioning of the ego and will offer to you challenges that will shed light upon this fact. Most often the "clash" which results from encountering the lessons of this learning process will cause physiological changes and unbalanced conditions within the body. These reactions could manifest in many different ways, from sudden weight gain or loss, to colds and flus, or even cancer.

Most elderly people in poor health are in that deteriorated condition due to years and years of ignoring the "small" stresses and allowing them to build and accumulate into conditions of cancers or other various dis-ease ailments. These ones will often be very unhappy in general, and will reflect this in their physical demeanor, appearance, and voice.

Middle-aged people on this same path will often exhibit physical symptoms of old age (such as prostate troubles or menopause) at an "early" age. The individual always has a choice to turn around the physical conditions of the body, for it will respond miraculously to a re-balanced mental state wherein the head and heart can live in harmony.

Teenagers and younger adults tend to act irrationally to their inner conflicts and will lash out and hurt those around them in both physically and mentally abusive manners. When they realize that this behavior is not acceptable, they will begin to internalize their frustrations and hide them from the world. Meanwhile those stresses begin to manifest in the body, in later years, as degenerative malfunctions like cancers and organ failures.

You may be asking, "How can one avoid this, or turn it around?"

First there must be a desire for inner balance. This means that you have to either confront the garbage that the ego-self holds onto, and see it for what it is, and come to grips with the fact that you are responsible for your condition, and accept the responsibility for that which you have created. Or, you can (and this is possible though difficult) simply insist on balanced physical health, and focus the mind and heart on that singularity with the entire passion of your heart, and don't listen to those who would hold you down, for they are the puppets and tools of the adversary.

Particularly within the framework of policing controls set up by those dark ones who own the drug companies and make great profits from a drug-based "health" business, medical "science" has yet to (be allowed to) discover the correlation between the various electromagnetic energy fields of the body and the body's physical functioning—let alone perceive the connection between (and the true impact from) this "clashing" of the mental reactionary ego with the Higher Self or soul connection. Therefore there is, more often than not, misdiagnosis of the cause for a condition that is manifesting in the body.

These ones trained in your so-called medical schools (again under the control of those drug companies) can prescribe electrochemical mixtures (drugs) which will cause reactions and responses in the physical as your body tries to deal with the chemical invader. They can offer electromagnetic radiation treatments to kill living tissue (both cancerous and non-cancerous). But these "medical professionals" do not understand the non-physical effects that their treatments have on the light-body part of the human apparatus. Therefore they, for the most part, end up treating the symptom(s) instead of the TRUE cause(s).

These ones are usually well intending and well educated in the physical structure of the body (to a point), yet they would need to study fundamental electrical science and molecular physics to great depths in order to come into a more complete understanding of what is taking place around the body. And even then, they would still need special abilities and talents in order to directly perceive these all-important energy fields of the body.

You will have to follow your own Guidance, and be responsible for the choices and decisions that affect both the quality and length of your stay in the physical. Do keep in mind that what you voice with your mouth is often in conflict with what you radiate from your heart. You may be able to hide behind words, but the heart will give you away every time. And for those who tune into the heart energy emanations, they will know you and they will know when you are out of balance and off purpose.

And for those of you who like to deny this to yourselves, you can look to that which manifests in your life: Is your current state of "living" this life's experience something that is fulfilling to you, or is it full of stress and frustration?

May your heart be your guide, and may you learn to listen with the heart and project forth from those inner satisfying desires that bring forth balance. I am Hilarion, Master Teacher and Healer, come in the Radiant One Light of Creator Source so that His promise to you be fulfilled—and so that I, too, may grow in wisdom of experience.

Salu!

CHAPTER FIVE

Your Destiny Is Growing Toward The Infinite

Esu "Jesus" Sananda
June 7, 1997

Good morning, my scribe. Thank you for sitting this day. There is great desire coming forth from many for understanding of who they are and why they have chosen this path at this time. I am Esu Immanuel "Jesus" Sananda come in the Radiant golden-white Light of Creator Source.

It has all been written prior and you ones would be wise to review your past lessons (our discourses on these various subjects). There are many new readers and participants awakening at this time and many who simply need a gentle reminder of these lessons.

Let us begin with WHO you are. You, the non-physical YOU, are an infinite thought projection of the One who created you (God!). You are the product of His desire. You are, in effect, Desire manifest in uniqueness of purpose.

In the creating of YOU, you were given, in balance, all that you need in perfect proportions so that you could fulfill the purpose of your being. This is to say that you were each given part of Creator's Light Essence in perfect proportions that will allow for your own uniqueness to manifest. No two were given the exact same proportions of the various aspects of Creator's Infinite Spectral Range.

This is NOT to say that some are better than others. It is simply stating that all are unique in purpose and yet come from One Source.

God is infinite creativity. You are each a product of His creativity manifest in the form of Light Essence. Please keep in mind that we are still referring to the INFINITE you, NOT the physical body that many erroneously perceive as being the entity of themselves. You each are electromagnetic (LIGHT) thought projections of Creator and you carry His "genetic" signature within your being. This is to say that you are created in His image—LIGHT! YOU ARE GOD MANIFEST!

You carry within you ALL of the infinite creative potential of the One who created you. This leads us to the subject of WHY are you there.

You each wish to explore the various aspects of your being and test your own uniqueness in your own unique way. One major aspect of Creator's desires is to expand and grow. *You* are part of His desire to do so, and when you grow individually, He is growing alongside of you.

As a "genetic" subset of The One Whole, you must first come into understanding of the impact of that which you are capable of manifesting. You have INFINITE potential within. Potential is the same for each—infinite!

Each individual is at a different level of understanding of HOW to responsibly direct and control this infinite potential. There have been structured various schoolrooms so that ones can come into detailed understanding of the various aspects of harnessing and controlling this infinite creative potential.

The physical (third dimension) is but one, small, yet important, classroom or laboratory in which to explore. You will find yourselves surrounded by ones facing similar challenges upon any one level of experiencing.

Each is efforting to understand, and thus unlock, the doors of the mind that will lead to ever greater and greater understanding and ability to utilize this INFINITE potential. Each will do so in a unique manner and approach according to who they are and the purpose that God has projected forth into their being. No two will have the exact same path in reaching the answers that unlock this potential, and in the searching comes the creativity of experience.

Now I wish to speak about a certain subset of all those experiencing here on Earth-Shan at this time of the Great Transition. And here I mean those who we of the Hosts refer to as Ground Crew.

Most of you who are Ground Crew have chosen to come into the physical to explore during a time of great shift in planetary awareness. This shift will present unique opportunities for you each to experience in conditions most favorable to forward growth and realizations that will help you to unlock doors that were closed and bolted by YOU, out of fear and/or overwhelm, long ago.

This does not mean that you will somehow grow and expand by default. It simply means that the opportunity is there and that you have all the tools you will need to RECOGNIZE and OVERCOME your current limitations.

Many of you have left behind talents and abilities so that you would have a "real" challenge, and so that you would not be easily distracted by the attention that your talents would bring. This is to say that many of you are experiencing without the benefit of your whole self so that you will "fit in" and so that you would be more focused on your personal growth in very specific areas.

If that were not enough, you have also chosen to take on the responsibility of assisting your younger brothers through a turbulent time—as they are, for the most part, resistant to change. You are, in effect, part of the team that is fulfilling God's promise to send forth His Hosts and to spread The Word to any and all who will hear and hopefully listen.

Many of our Ground Crew are under severe attack at this time. Many are dropping out and not keeping up with the messages that will educate them about how to survive the upcoming Planetary Transition. Many are going through a cleansing period that will cause them to confront the very demons which caused them to stumble in the past. These are indeed trying, yet quite valuable, opportunities to grow past the fears and move forward into understanding and knowing.

Be thankful for ALL of your challenges, for even the smallest of annoyances will provide you with insights about the self-imposed limitations that you have placed upon yourselves. Take time to look at and analyze even these smallest of annoyances, for when you truly understand what is causing the annoyance within you, you will no longer manifest the need for the annoyance and it will be gone from your experience. This is not to say that ALL annoyances or challenges will be gone. It is to say that great value and insights can be gleaned from understanding even the smallest of bothers.

You shall be finding that the challenges you experience from here on out will continue to grow, and you will have to keep up with the ever intensifying pressures of survival—both mentally and physically. If you find yourself in an overwhelmed state, then I, Sananda, suggest that you call upon The Light for balance and guidance.

For some of you, the challenge of focusing a thought is quite difficult, and many feel as though they are simply not connecting with the inner Light Source.

I will here offer a suggestion that will help you to focus upon The Light. This is NOT in any way a necessary thing to do, but it can be quite helpful:

Light a white candle.

White because it symbolizes purity. The flame represents energy and it produces a natural white light—and it will dance around with a life of its own.

See the flame and know that, with each flicker, the

darkness is expelled from your space. Know that all you have to do is look at the light from the candle, and it will reaffirm your Light shielding and support your mental intention that the darkness be gone from your space. This is but a helpful suggestion to any who feel that they are having difficulty clearing, or keeping cleared, their space.

Allow for the challenges of this life's experiences to present themselves to you. Know that you need each in order to fulfill your goals and manifest the true joy that comes from inner personal growth.

Remember, please: YOU are the Light Workers who are manifesting God's promise to the world—even if "all" you do at the present moment is quietly read that which is offered.

There shall come a time in this life experience when you will be inspired to offer that which will quell the confusion of your neighbors when their world and reality are being shattered.

Right now, persistence and patience are the keys to success because "sequence of events" (not the ticking of a clock) dictates progression and unfoldment of this Planetary Transition event. For many, that which is about to manifest in your physical experience will indeed SEEM to come upon them "as a thief in the night", for these ones continue to sleep in their state of ignorance and illusion.

I am Esu Immanuel Sananda, One with Creator Source, come as promised. In Light and in Love, blessings to you all.

Salu!

CHAPTER SIX

Putting the Adversary's Trickery To Good Use!

Ceres Anthonious Soltec
June 21, 1997

Good afternoon, my friend. It is I, Toniose Soltec, come in the Radiant One Light of Creator Source. There is work to be done—thank you for attending the call.

Your world is in a heightened state of agitation and the energy is becoming quite unstable. The illusionary tactics of the adversary are failing more and more each day as ones are waking up, and more importantly—SPEAKING UP! The TRUTH BEARERS (Light Workers) are hearing the call and are responding in a timely manner. You will be pleasantly surprised to see who all arises to the challenge and will not sit still for more and more lies.

Be careful, for there is the allowance by the global "elite", at this time, for the introduction into the world consciousness of the realization that there IS extraterrestrial life visiting your planet and on your planet. This is to prepare you-the-people for the next phase of unification under a one-world dictatorship as these ones will try to convince you that these "aliens" are attacking you.

The adversary will always give some truth and accompany it with the lies that will cause ones to be sucked into a reactionary impulse to respond in a programmed manner. Be thankful, for there has been sufficient groundwork laid here, in TRUTH, that the adversary's plans will indeed backfire for the most part. Ones will not stand for the lies, especially when they are given the whole truth.

There has been such a complete effort to hide the truth about extraterrestrial life over the years that it will not be an easy task to convince the American public that there are, in fact, extraterrestrials. This should stand as a testimonial to thc effectiveness of the mind-control techniques in use by those who wish to enslave you-the-people of the Earth. AND THESE SLAVE-MASTERS ARE *NOT* THE EXTRA-TERRESTRIALS!

We are offering this information, AGAIN at this time, so that you who effort to understand what is truly taking place on you planet will be able to get your confirmations as to what is truth versus what is lie. Watch your media sources for the clues and you will see that there will come more and more controversy over the cover-ups and lies about extraterrestrial visitors. You are being primed to accept the possibility of a massive war that will cost the lives of many innocent people. Do NOT buy into these lies for they will destroy you if you do!

Keep your heads squarely upon your shoulders and learn to trust your Inner Guidance. You will be given to know what to do when the opportunity and sequence of events are appropriate. Keep your space cleared and keep a discerning eye on all the information that you will be inundated with. There will be a deliberate effort to flood your minds to overflowing with controversy after controversy wherein both sides of the debate will, in fact, be controlled by the same ones who are efforting to enslave you.

As always, question all data that you take in, and discern for YOURSELF what it is that YOU believe deep within

YOUR heart. Let not your excuse be that you were tricked into believing the lies. YOU choose that in which you believe or disbelieve. If you choose to believe in lies, then be responsible for your choices. And when you come into the realization that you have been had, do not cast blame upon another, for no one else is responsible for you except YOU!

All will come to a point of inner conflict as you-the-people will be shown things that you cannot explain. And when the so-called "experts" offer up an explanation, most will be quick to accept that which is offered, for such will provide a comforting (even if misleading) focus of thought and thus give a semblance of alleviating confusion. Prepare now and remember these writings for they are tools to help you to traverse these trying times of confusion and trickery.

There is much in the way of trickery that can be accomplished with the toys of the adversary. These ones have perfected, to a large degree, holographic projection technology. This technology has tricked and fooled even some of the most avid readers of *CONTACT* who consider themselves well informed and astute. You ones are not beyond the influence of these illusionary tactics!

If you find yourself in a state of confusion as a result of what you have seen—whether it be from a television broadcast or first-hand experience—you would be wise to seek within the answers to your confusion. Monitor closely how the event affects you personally.

Were you frightened? Excited? Or, perhaps, overwhelmed? This is the first clue to you as to what it is that you have actually witnessed.

Your Inner Guidance is plugged into Higher Knowledge and Awareness. This connection cannot be fooled, for it is YOUR connection to Creator—who most certainly cannot be fooled! Learn to trust that which the heart is offering you in the way of emotional FEELINGS.

You are not usually taught in your schools or churches to do this, for if you were, you would be most difficult to control and you would become quite resistant to the "habit-modifying techniques" (that is, the mind control) of those who effort to keep you in a state of fear and confusion.

When ones can get you to go run and seek OUTSIDE yourself for answers, then they have succeeded in accomplishing the first step toward controlling you. This is where all the so-called "experts" fit into the picture.

Please note here that it is wise to look for confirmations to that which you are discerning for self. It is also wise to effort to educate yourself, especially when there seems to be contradictory information regarding the same subject. Take in the data, and then go within to discern for yourself what is right for YOU!

You do not have to follow the crowds, but likewise you do NOT always have to go against the crowds either. There is always a balance point of intelligent choice that can be reached when the data you are trying to digest is merged with the nudges of your Inner Guidance.

Be strong in your convictions and do not waver from that which you KNOW in your heart to be true. Be open to those things which provide clues and otherwise offer insights into the workings of the adversary, for you will in turn learn to see within self where you have allowed the adversary a foothold. When you can spot and isolate a fear that is dictating to you how you should or should not live your life, you can be assured that it is the adversary exploiting a weakness that you have not sufficiently attended.

Be thankful when such a fear is recognized, for you then will have the conscious ability to spot and overcome personal limitations (such as beliefs) that are holding you back from the growth you seek. In the overcoming of the fears comes the personal growth and fulfilling satisfaction that you ones are constantly seeking.

Every time the adversary lashes out, he is, in effect, providing you with an opportunity to spot personal weaknesses within self. He is thus giving you an

opportunity to focus on your self-imposed limitations so that YOU can experience for self the inner conflict (usually confusion or frustration) that results when you are caused to confront that which is uncomfortable to you.

Again, be thankful for these opportunities to recognize, and thus grow beyond, who you are this day. Everyone has something to learn and each has plenty of room to grow.

May your path never be without challenge!

We of the Higher-Dimensional Realms await your call for guidance and assistance. We shall never do a thing for you, but we can help to guide experiences and teachers across your path.

Look carefully at the so-called "coincidences" which are brought to your conscious attention. You can KNOW that there are NO coincidences. Rather, such gifts are your Guides working with you to help you to see that you are indeed on the right path.

I am Ceres Anthonious "Toniose" Soltec, come as Guide and Wayshower, in service to the One Light, Creator Source. Blessings to you all!

Salu.

CHAPTER SEVEN

Being Well Through Efforting Toward Well Being

Master Hilarion
June 29, 1997

Good evening and thank you for sitting to write for many who enquire by petition that they might help their brothers more effectively. I am Master Hilarion, come in the Light of Creator Source. I am most closely associated with the Emerald (green) Ray of Creator's Spectral Expression. Take a moment to find peace within your heart.

Many these days have what they label as "health" concerns of the physical. Health is! Health is neither good nor bad, it simply IS. What many actually ask for (and many others only give lip service to, for reasons of sustained attention-getting) is a state of "well being" over that of illness or unbalance.

We see many efforting to fix or cure an unbalanced body with all sorts of physical remedies. This is fine—as long as the patient BELIEVES in the remedy, for the mental state is key to the re-balancing of the body.

To truly understand and heal, one must realize the TRUE cause or nature of a condition. First and foremost is the fact that YOU are NOT your body, and YOU (the NON-physical you) manifest (create) your own reality AT ALL TIMES.

You ones will say, "I do NOT want to feel sick!" But at the same time you will dwell upon (pump energy into) the feeling of sickness, and for most it will last until you either get bored enough or distracted enough to stop dwelling upon that which is causing the unbalanced state.

Likewise, illness is often utilized by you ones as a tool for getting the attention of others and keeping that attention focus as something to fill perceived voids of loneliness. In this case, you don't really want your health to be in balance.

Rather, focus your thoughts upon that which brings forth inner fulfillment and not upon that which causes you to get upset or frustrated. You can try to carry the burden of an entire family, country, or even planet, if you wish. But I will tell you here and now that your reason for coming into the physical experience at this time was NOT to alleviate another's responsibility. It is, in fact, to learn to become a more responsible co-creator, ultimately with the One who created you.

You each have strengths and weaknesses. You each must learn to focus not upon that which is lacking in your life, but rather, be thankful for what you have and what you have accomplished thus far. In this way the energy patterns you radiate attract that which leads to fulfillment.

Many of you are efforting to get family members to see and hear The Truth as offered forth in this publication. [*Editor's note: This statement originally was referring to the* CONTACT *newspaper. See the Preface to this volume for more information about* CONTACT.] This is indeed fine and noble—and usually involves quite a bit of heart energy on your part. When your enthusiasm is met with the negative responses that are so common these days, you ones are left feeling somewhat frustrated and drained.

In this drained or fatigued (low-energy and low-frequency) state, you are most vulnerable to the influences of the adversarial forces. This is when doubt creeps in and you ones will question your "reality" as to what is truly REAL. You each must go through this discernment exercise for self, for it is YOUR reality that is in question—not mine, and certainly not God's!

Let us back up a bit and examine some of the more typical causes for arriving at the point of doubt. For many it will be inner anxiety of going against the "norm" of that which society dictates as being acceptable. For many of you, your hearts soar when you hear Truth, and you want to share this inner enthusiasm with any and all who will listen.

Again, I say to you that this is fine. But, let me add that YOU cannot actually shift another's reality. You can offer insights and data for evaluation, but each must discern for themselves what is the correct path for them.

Now, when another rejects your reality (beliefs), you do not have to take it personally. However, we of the Hosts see that many of you carry this "rejection" response as a burden of guilt—that you erroneously view as responsibility for your family, friends, and loved ones.

You cannot "short circuit" the lessons of another. When you try to take on this role, the logical response from the other will often be anger and even disgust.

Allow each to find their own way. And, more importantly, learn to release the inner GUILT that weighs on your heart.

Now, why have I introduced this subject of guilt? Because, for most of you who are sick, there is a primary cause that will be at the root of nearly any unbalanced condition. That cause is guilt, in one form or another.

Many of you of Ground Crew have a tremendous capacity for compassion within your being and this can predispose you to carry quite a large amount of unnecessary baggage for your brethren. Balancing out this tendency is, in fact, why some of you were compelled to become part of the awakening efforts of the Earth's population at this time.

Please remember that there is wisdom in approaching any and all situations with balance. Sometimes the most giving action you can take concerning loved ones is to allow them to simply walk off the spiritual path altogether and find their own way in their own unique manner.

This is perhaps the hardest thing for you ones to do. In the searching to understand, you can know that there is only One Ultimate Truth and ALL shall, in the end, find their way Home (back to Source).

God monitors heart intent. When you effort to assist another, it is noted. When you beat-up upon self for some perceived failure, this too is noted, for it is an indicator of your progress with respect to TRUE understanding of who you are and why you are there.

There is absolutely NO need to punish self. You may do so, as you wish, in utilization of your gift from Creator of free-will choice, but there is truly no need.

Seek within for understanding of that which is offered here in LOVE. Choose for yourself the path you will take, and know that each path will be filled with its unique challenges so that YOU may test YOUR reality and YOUR awarenesses.

If you choose a harsh path, then so be it, for that is YOUR choice. Look not for sympathy from those who tried to offer to you wisdom that you then rejected.

On the other side of the issue, remember that YOU are not required to concern yourself past the point of offering a helping hand, if the help is rejected. You did your part in the offering. Release the emotional pressures associated with the rejection, and look forward to the next opportunity that will come your way to assist. **These emotional pressures are the seeds that grow into illness and physical degeneration if allowed to accumulate.**

Most of you who are guided to read these messages are not just emotional beings, but emotional beings with a highly attuned sense of compassion for your fellow travelers along the paths of life. Because of a Higher Sense of

Connectedness regarding this effort—that "all is connected to all" and "as one grows, so grows all"—you each want to help those whom you perceive as having need.

Learn to move through each experience and not get stuck in those seemingly negative emotional "micro-realities" that can seem to invalidate your reality—and you as a being, IF YOU ALLOW SAME.

It is perfectly fine to feel the invalidating emotional emanations of a "rejection" experience, but it is quite unwise to allow them to build into a state of doubt and frustrating "reality" shifts FOR YOU. Move through the experience and leave behind the garbage and take with you the knowledge gained from having the experience.

You cannot be held responsible for the "reality" or choices of another. If your intent is goodly (Godly) and you KNOW that you have acted from or spoken from a position of love, then please realize that there is truly nothing more you can do for another.

Release the guilt that you hold onto!

Allow for the liberation of your heart and you will find that a brighter reality does exist and that the physical body will respond to the newer, lighter (en-Light-ened) you.

This exercise in balance is also a key to releasing the unwanted insulation (fat) that you ones place around yourselves in order to buffer the emotional impact of negatively focused energy pulses.

Perfect "health"—whether it be "good" or "bad"—is what you already have. So quit asking for health, and start asking for that which will bring forth inner balance and understanding of the TRUE cause of your un-balanced physical state.

Seek first WITHIN to find the answers to that which ails you, and you will be well—well on your way to achieving physical rebalance of the body.

I am Master Hilarion of the Healing Emerald Ray. I come at this time as Elder Brother and Teacher so that you who seek will have insights and tools to use, if that be your choice.

In the Light and in Service to Creator Source, may these words find understanding within, for as understanding leads to peace and balance, so shall your body reflect same.

Salu!

CHAPTER EIGHT

You Are *Never* Alone Who Recognize My Presence

Aton, The One Light
June 19, 1997

I am Aton, The One Light, come to instruct for these closing chapters of The Great Play now upon your world. Much is set to unfold in rapid sequence and many are those who will be shocked into a state of paralysis (because of their lack of awareness and preparation) by the turbulence of that which they shall witness and experience in this unfolding of events.

Be at peace, you who acknowledge and take within these messages of Higher Guidance, for you are being given that which you will need, in the way of instruction, to meet and surmount these challenges ahead. Many will be those who then ask YOU for guidance in the moments of desperation amidst the chaos.

You are not alone who feel restlessness, unease, and uncertainty in a confused world. Many are the ones who are about expressing their inner turmoil in ways destructive to the enhancement of en-Light-ened man of the next century. Therefore, many there will be who will thereby bring upon themselves the decay and degeneration and destruction of body, mind, and possibly even soul, out of self-created choosings amidst an existing technology base which indeed does allow for the dissolution of soul material itself.

How do you avoid or counteract the state of confusion? Be ever at peace with your inner core. In doing so, you can better hear and receive of Higher Guidance which shall most personally be given from WITHIN.

This is essentially an effort to maintain a condition of Love, in harmony with oneself, though this usage of the word (love) is admittedly foreign to the general conceptual vocabulary of late-twentieth-century man on Earth. This state of attunement can be likened to having one foot planted solidly on hard ground, and the other anchored in etheric space, where physical matter ceases to exist. BALANCE between the things of Earth-matter, and those of the Spirit non-matter, must be sought.

Ones continually get caught-up in the temptations which lure ones from their chosen path. This is fine, until the Higher Self begins to enforce the sometimes painful lessons needed to overcome self-imposed spiritual stagnation. This state of spiritual stagnation pervades your planet (that is, the people on your planet) as a whole at this time, and thus the great currents of rebalancing swell up to manifest that which must play out. Otherwise, man becomes so lost in the material that forward soul movement is replaced with either stagnation or, worse yet, retrograde development.

Ones rarely access Me, within, to soothe their emotional and mental states, preferring to seek that which is exterior or outside of themselves for the balanced upliftment that can only be found within. Such is the plight of man and such is the free-will choosing that shall manifest much that shocks many into recognition of their errors. As your Earth saying puts it: There are no atheists crouched among the terrified behind a bunker or in a foxhole. Indeed! Yet such is the "pound of cure" that Earth-man often chooses over the "ounce of prevention" route.

I say to man of Earth: release of thy fears and insecurities. Seek to find Me, within the center of your being. I am *ever* with you, waiting for the moment you shall return to the sanctity of your Source.

Life physical MUST be counter-balanced with movement toward soul advancement. Otherwise, man will perish for lack of sustenance.

Many ones are now intuitively seeking wholeness in various departments of life. Health and fitness, meditation, and self-help seminars are just a few of these pursuits. However, soon the discovery of the Inner Connection shall be made. And once this comes about, a revolution in thinking will likewise also come about.

As ones get nearer and nearer to this unconscious goal that is within ALL, then an outer extension of this inner connection will manifest in the world. You may liken this to a condition of Radiant Peace—manifest and bathing all of Earth-life with a most electrically intense and tangibly physical impact. The dynamics and consequences of such a global condition the "elite" of your planet fear greatly, as they cannot function (or control YOU, in their Earth-bound, fear-predicated ways) when you are functioning under such a radiant intensity of Peace, manifest FROM WITHIN!

Such is what is SOON to take place. This will begin the turning around of your beloved planet. This is precisely the mechanism involved in the upliftment of a civilization undergoing a cyclic shift toward the higher-frequency ranges.

This, too, is what the Photon Belt denotes. That is a term for the steady but gradual intensifying of Light—My Light. At first this Light shall enter the periphery of your solar system. Then, later on, by 2010, such will begin to bathe and saturate all that is on and within your planet with high-frequency Light.

Under such a high-frequency condition, the materially-oriented (low-frequency) "elite" of your world hope to somehow survive. This will not be the case!

Only ones who can match and mesh with the incoming elevated frequencies will survive into the next century. None can sustain who belong to the lowest frequency ranges that describe the evil (that which is not of God) on your planet. Such was My promise to the people of Earth, stated many centuries ago! And so shall it become the dawning reality.

Many are the events that will take place leading up to the millennium and beyond. I come to caution ones of the final days, as prophesied, that you may prepare selves on the inner spiritual level in order to see you through the approaching tribulations.

Many are the ones who will seek falsely, outside of themselves, for that which only I can provide from within. Man of Earth has yet to re-connect with his inner Divinity that will enable him to find the balance, harmony, and inner peace which he so passionately seeks. That is where these lessons fit into the play of unfolding events at this time.

Recognize the value of these lessons.

Discover your connection to Divine Source.

Seek within for answers.

Cultivate and maintain a strong connection with your Source as you enter the final days of chaos on your planet before the turnaround to Glory.

Seek and ye MUST find.

Know it!

I am the One who IS your Source.

I AM THE LIGHT WITHIN *YOU* AND WITHIN *ALL*. Adonai.

CHAPTER NINE

Recent Volcanic Clues To What's On The Way

Ceres Anthonious Soltec
July 12, 1997

Good morning, my friend. It is I, Toniose Soltec, come in the Radiant One Light of Creator Source. Find peace within and let us continue.

Your planet is convulsing and very few seem to be paying attention to the clues that are unfolding all around you. The masters of distraction have, indeed, done their jobs well.

Approximately six weeks ago, I asked that *CONTACT* re-run my "Tutorial On Volcanos And Related Geophysics" from writings I delivered in 1990 and 1993. [*Editor's note: This information appeared in the May 20, 1997 issue of the* CONTACT *newspaper; see Appendix A at the back of this volume.*] That review was for a specific purpose and I believe those of you who are paying attention to the geophysical news of late can appreciate why.

Since the beginning of 1997, there have been approximately 20 significant volcanic eruptions worldwide on your planet. As I have lectured at length in the past, there is a close connection between volcanic eruptions and the tectonic plate motions that produce major earthquake activity. Both the frequency and violence (magnitude) of these volcanic eruptions are good indicators of Mother Earth's rising "blood pressure" condition.

One of the most important recent events was the newest series of explosive eruptions of 18,000-foot-high Mount Popocatepetl in Mexico, starting about April 24, 1997. According to reports by your own geologists studying that volcano: "Explosions at Popocatepetl from April 24-28 destroyed the lava dome inside the throat of the volcano. The lava dome had been growing since January 1997. An explosion on April 24 sent ash 13,000 feet above the summit." And then, on June 30, 1997: "Popocatepetl threw ash **7.5 miles** into the air on Monday, June 30, during its **largest eruption since 1925**. Lava was also thrown **1500 feet** into the air. This event led to the **first ash fall in Mexico City**, 45 miles from the volcano, **in over 70 years**.... At least **15 small towns are planned to be evacuated** including about 300,000 people who live on the flanks of the volcano."

The second significant volcanic event happened this past week near Italy. Watch closely the recent (and still ongoing) eruption of 11,000-foot-high Mount Etna, in eastern Sicily, on July 8, not very far from 4,000-foot-high sister volcano Mount Vesuvius, near Naples, Italy (which buried the city of Pompeii in a thick layer of volcanic ash in the twinkling of an eye in 79 A.D.). Recall, please, the timing clues for major Earth changes connected to these sister volcanos as given forth by ones such as Edgar Cayce.

There are many pieces of the puzzle now coming together and a more complete picture is beginning to unfold. As you watch these volcanos come to life, feel compassion for a very longsuffering and patient Mother Earth as she begins the process of rebalancing in earnest.

You who are there on the Earth now will witness the great changes prophesied through many sources. There is NO avoiding this inevitability.

PREPARATION IS THE KEY TO SURVIVAL!

We, of the Hosts, have said over and over to prepare, yet we see many who sit and wait for another to somehow do it for them. We can do much more to help you—IF you take action and focus your energies on helping yourselves, FIRST!

For example, in my first public writing through this receiver, on 6/13/96 [*Editor's note: That writing is chapter 15 in volume I of this series, and is a writing which was, by the way, scribbled on some old, chemical-stained scraps of laboratory notepaper, as that receiver was interrupted by "the call" right in the middle of some chemical analyses work at the receiver's then place of employment.*], I emphasized:

"Dream time is long over and those still running around in La La Land shall wish they had awakened to find out what all the commotion was for. Indeed, the changes shall come: 'Like a thief in the night', as far as the general masses are concerned.

"But, for those who have heard the 'alarm clock', you shall see much of what we, of the Hosts of Lighted God, have told you, time and time again, shall come to pass. There shall be much excitement for those of you who have prepared. God truly helps those of you who make efforts to help selves.

"Even if you do not notice all the subtle clues along the way, know in your heart that He is there and is helping you along your way. Pay attention to the seeming coincidences, for NOTHING HAPPENS BY CHANCE—especially now, and from here on out."

When you take action in the physical, you are reinforcing the mind's desires and amplifying the creative energy necessary for the manifestation of the thought or desire. As the desire begins manifesting in physical space, ones around you, either directly or indirectly, will be adding their energy to that which you are creating.

We, of the non-physical realms, can add our energy to that which has already been set into motion, in many direct and indirect ways. The key is to solidify your intent WITH ACTION, and ask for Assistance and Guidance while DOING your part.

We have helped many to produce the "miracles" that defy mere coincidence or luck. Yet, many will still view it as mere "luck" or "coincidence", not realizing the true nature of the dynamics set in motion when they first take sincere and determined action in the physical.

Also, some more aware ones will realize that there is a Higher Guidance assisting them. These ones will rightfully and humbly give thanks for the assistance that manifests in their lives. You ones are fond of an expression that goes something like: "Luck favors those who help themselves." You might take a moment to ponder on the possibilities of that elusive thing called "luck"!

Our main concern in this regard is that we see many of you just sitting around and worrying over the upcoming Earth changes and economic collapse. We see that you are either too frightened, or too easily distracted by the daily matters of living, to take serious actions in preparation.

Many ones have great excuses, such as: "I have a family to take care of and not enough extra money for such things." Or another good one: "My family thinks I am crazy and they resist my reasoning with them on the subject of survival preparation." And then there's the perennial fall-back position: "I only have to take care of myself and I can survive on very little; therefore why should I prepare?"

I think you ones get the idea here. There are many other colorful, yet sad, excuses that are given. Many of you who have not yet prepared, will not prepare, and such is YOUR choice.

If money is your excuse in any way, then I would suggest you look carefully at that upon which you spend your money—that is, what has value to you. What is it you buy that is truly necessary? What are the not-so-necessary items that are more for your immediate pleasures?

It is wise to have balance in all things. When you can

prioritize, with responsibility, you will find that you can have the best of both worlds.

When you can learn to prepare not only for self and your immediate family, but perhaps ALSO for your neighbor, then you will find that you will draw into your experience the creative energies necessary to manifest all of the things you truly desire. The basic Law of Giving and Regiving operates quite well here.

A large bag of beans or rice is truly inexpensive, as is a large container of peanut butter. If you make the effort to shop around, you can stretch a dollar QUITE far when you focus your energy upon doing so.

Going to fast-food restaurants will deplete your funds faster than you may realize. When you pay a dollar or more for a single cup of carbonated, flavored, sugar water, you would be wise to reflect upon your health, as well as upon what you COULD buy with the money that you spend, on a regular basis, on such nutritionally empty items.

The point here is NOT to tell you how to live your lives or how to spend your money. The point here is to get you to take a look at the day-to-day robotic actions (actions taken with little or no thought) that you ones seem to not notice.

The mind-control experts have done their jobs very well through the media machinery of advertising campaigns. Do you really NEED that cup of sugar water or that cigarette or that beer? How about the fourth one of the day? Do you really NEED a new car every few years? Do you really NEED those expensive vacations?

When the Earth changes or the economic collapse impact your lives, you will then know what you truly NEED versus that which you "think" you need. You WILL figure it out, one way or another—sooner OR later! This is where Mother Earth's "school of hard knocks" comes into the picture!

There is great wisdom in diligently going about the business of preparation, and all of the contrite choruses of

"I should have listened" that many will be singing AFTER the fact, will not ease those empty stomachs—whether such be your family's stomachs, or those of your neighbors and their children.

We, of the Hosts, have been sent at this time to give forth the warning messages that were promised to you at this time so that your excuse cannot be that you were not warned and that you did not know.

In that same 6/13/96 writing, I also warned:

"That which has been prophesied is at hand. You are in the Ending Times of the current cycle of humanity on that orb. This is a time when chaos reigns supreme, for the confusion of change is overwhelming to the masses.

"All things continue in a revolving, evolving spiral of never-ending cycles of birth-growth-decay-rebirth. Out of the old harshness of chaos shall spring forth the peace and balance that you ones constantly seek.

"These are grand times for experiencing. The Light shall reign supreme. The awakening masses shall overcome or succumb to their ignorance. It is always their choice."

I will ask you here and now: What causes you to read these messages in the first place? What part of yourself allows you to accept these messages, even when others are laughing at you or are antagonistic toward your beliefs? Learn to consciously connect with who you really are and from where you come, AND KNOW THAT IT IS BECAUSE YOU ARE GROUND CREW!

Ground Crew is part of the team sent to assist in the awakening of the ones on this planet at this time. You lead by example. That means that when you are compelled to tell another that they should prepare, then they, in turn, are most likely to ask you: "Do YOU have food supplies stored up?" Now, if the honest answer is "No", then how effective do you think your efforts are going to be toward convincing others of the seriousness of that which is offered here?

Live your life AS AN EXAMPLE for others to follow and you will be doing a great service to those who cross

your path! There is a phrase on your planet which goes something like, "Nothing is more annoying than a good example." Indeed!

If you invite someone over to your dwelling, and you have to ask them to excuse the cases of canned food in your living-room area because that is the only available space in which to store the overstock, this will speak a certainty and conviction of who you are and how serious you are. Remember—ACTIONS ALWAYS SPEAK LOUDER THAN DO WORDS! ALWAYS!

Please know that the resisting family members will be thankful to have food to eat and candles to light the darkened hours of the night, or the unhybridized seeds to plant that will symbolize hope for the coming months. The greatest teaching can and will be done when there is no distraction from the television or such!

There will come a resurgence of community. Ones will again come to know who are their neighbors and what it means to be neighborly. The man-made distinctions of race, color, creed, or religious conviction will also drop away. You will all be faced with a common reality: DAY-TO-DAY SURVIVAL!

Please take whatever action is necessary to prepare yourselves for the extreme possibilities. You will be thankful that you did and you may save many lives.

Thank you for taking the time to read this message.

Call upon We, of the Lighted Brotherhood, for assistance along the way.

BUT—YOU take the first step and build the momentum! FEEL, in your heart, the connectedness to those around you, and **KNOW that your actions will teach, where your words fall onto deaf ears.**

I am Toniose Soltec. I come as the Geophysical Commander for your planet at this time. I am sent by Our Father, as are many of YOU! Face your challenges with His Light in your heart, and create the miracle.

In Light and Love, blessings to you ALL! Salu.

CHAPTER TEN

True Value Is A Matter Of The Heart

Lord Michael, Archangel
July 19, 1997

Good afternoon, my friend, and thank you for sitting this day. This is Michael, of the Archangelic realms, come to briefly commune with you this day so that there may be greater understanding of what it is you ones are experiencing at this time. I come IN and OF The Light! Thank you for asking and reaffirming the connection.

As Messengers of God's desires, we of the Hosts will continue to give forth the promised Guidance that is part of the third-dimensional experience. You EACH, prior to entering into this experience, knew that there would be Guidance offered to you along the way. This Guidance has always been part of the third-dimensional experience and shall always be a part.

For many at this time, it is quite a stretch to accept such writings as authentic or "real". This is fine, for the promise is that they be offered, NOT shoved down anyone's throat! There are many who are seeking to connect and find that which seems to be lacking in their lives. These ones are hungry for that which gives a sense of genuine value and meaning to their lives.

Each must find their own way through the challenges before them at this time. Each must choose, for themselves, that which is of value and act accordingly. Many place great value on money or a high-paying job. This is fine, if it be your choice. I will, however, ask you to consider the lasting value of a TRUE friend? Or, the value of the smile that comes to the face of ones when you offer them HONEST praise for that which they have completed. What is the value of these things that make you FEEL alive and connected?

You EACH are part of The Oneness that many refer to as God. When you do something for or to another, you are doing same for or to yourself AND God. EVERYTHING in the physical is a result of God's creative thinking. There is an inner-connectedness of all things in the physical, by way of a non-physical counterpart that is as much a part of your experience as is the chair upon which you sit or the air that you breathe.

This non-physical counterpart is the electromagnetic (Light) energy that animates the body and causes the apparent motion of electrons around the atom. It is the energy which causes all substance to have a frequency and vibration. It is, simply put, God expressing Himself!

This is not new information, nor is it brought to you in some sort of mystical manner. Every culture on your planet has ones who will bring forth these messages of Inspired Truth. Each will be unique in style and limited, in some ways, by the language base into which the messages are translated.

The individual examples may vary, but the general message will never change. For example, it would make very little sense to talk about atoms to a primitive culture that has just discovered fire. However, when you talk about the "warmth" of the fire, they can understand the concept and may be able, on a FEELING level, to relate it to the idea that it is of God—as are the trees that grow around these primitive ones, or the food that is taken within for nourishment.

Look to the messages of ancient philosophies and you will see the same ideas recurring over and over again. Whether the concept, for instance, be "angels" or "spirit guides", there is little difference except for terminology of translation into the physical. Learn to let go of the prejudices and conceptual frameworks which limit you to so-called "modern" ideas.

There are many ANCIENT teachings that are again being brought forth to you ones. Some of these were written many hundreds of thousands of years ago, yet they state the same basic message.

You have the tools and information before you at this time to discern what has value and what does not. There is that which will fill the void within or fuel the desire to FEEL an inner sense of worth or value. Inner fulfillment comes from understanding who you really are and why you are here at this time.

The answers are simple. However, there are ones (especially in positions of authority, and most especially in your churches) who would keep you from recognizing this fact. You are led to believe that these questions cannot be readily answered, especially by "lowly" YOU, and certainly not from such a personal and direct process as going within.

REMEMBER: YOU ARE *INFINITE* BEINGS EXPERIENCING WITHIN A BODY. THAT BODY IS BUT A SHELL THAT YOU UTILIZE SO THAT YOU CAN COME INTO A MORE FOCUSED STATE OF AWARENESS, AND THUS CONCENTRATE UPON CHALLENGING SITUATIONS SO THAT YOU CAN GROW IN UNDERSTANDING OF WHAT IT MEANS TO BE A CO-CREATOR WITH GOD!

You are in a schoolroom called Earth. The overall purpose is so that you can have opportunity to expand

your awareness and ability to RESPONSIBLY create. The value comes in an ability to handle more and more of the Infinite Creative Potential that is within.

This only comes when you prove your understanding of the Laws of Cause and Effect. This is to say that you must learn to be RESPONSIBLE for the effects of that which YOU create. This goes for any and all creations, regardless of size or magnitude. If you create an unbalanced situation in your home life by lying to your family members, and then denying same when confronted by them later, then how can you be trusted with the responsibility of creating a third-dimensional solar system, let alone a universe, yourself?!

We are talking here of *INFINITE* CREATIVE POTENTIAL! That is why you ones have chosen to come into the physical and go through the challenges of life with only a limited conscious connection to that with which you are connected—ALL (everything, everywhere)!

You are efforting to expand your awareness of WHO you are, as well as become more skilled in the utilization of your abilities to manifest and create. Now, while you will only be given that which you can handle, you can be assured that it will be a challenge to you, so that if you so choose, you can maximize the rate at which you grow.

Notice also that you always have the option to quit. However, it is then far more difficult to be responsible for that which you have set in motion in the first place. And, though you can always run away from a situation when it gets uncomfortable, it is quite another thing to see a challenge through to completion.

Each time you are faced with a choice to continue or to quit, you must examine what it is upon which you place value, and what it is that will fulfill, within you, the desires of the heart. The heart is given to know what is right and what is wrong. The mind is given to reason all data and evaluate and place importance upon things.

It is often the case that the mind and heart are in

conflict because the reactionary impulse of the mind is to avoid pain while the Innate Knowing of the heart is to seek out growth, which often leads to—PAIN (that is, growing pains!).

This is where discernment of value comes into play. You each must decide for yourselves what has personal value to you. Is the emotional pressure so great that you cannot persist another moment? Do you HAVE to run away? Is there NO other choice? Would being homeless on the street be better than going to work just one more day? These are questions of value and balance.

While there are no wrong choices, there ARE better choices! And be assured that, when you run away from a challenge, it will be coming back around to impact your experience again. It may not be in this lifetime, or even on this particular planet, but you WILL have to again face that which you could not presently overcome—if you are ever to get through the third-dimensional schoolroom. Though you may not be able to see it from your current vantage point, there is great value in ALL—EACH AND EVERY ONE—of the experiences that you are now faced with at this time.

We, of the Hosts, know quite well what it is that you are faced with, for we have walked the physical path MANY times while we too learned our lessons and earned our current positions of responsibility—as eventually shall YOU, too! If you feel as though no one could possibly understand what you are going through in your life, then go back and read this message again, for you surely missed the fact that ALL IS CONNECTED TO ALL! What YOU experience is the experience of ALL, for we all exist within the One who created us.

These are the ideas that the "holy" men of your world would rather you not listen to, for such are the ideas that make these ones unnecessary and thus they would be out of a job.

You have within you a direct connection to God. You do not need another to tell you what YOU feel in your heart. Learn to trust your Inner Guidance and learn to follow your heart, and such will guide you to the experiences that will cause you to grow in awareness, and thus in ability to create better SOUL-UTIONS!

I am Lord Michael, of the Archangelic Realms. I am your Elder Brother, just a bit further along the path that you are now walking. I come as Messenger of Truth, within the Light of the One who is ALL!

Salu!

CHAPTER ELEVEN

Just Being Aware Is *Not* Being Prepared!

Master Hilarion
August 2, 1997

Good morning and be at PEACE! It is I, Master Hilarion, come to briefly commune with you this day so that you who ask with sincerity will have a greater understanding of that which is flowing into your experience.

Yes! I do come within the Light of Aton, The One Light. Thank you for asking. I represent the Emerald Ray of His Spectral Desire. This is to say that I have chosen to specialize in one aspect or area of Creation's infinite frequency spectrum. Emerald is but a harmonic correlate to a particular area of specialization—an area that you would recognize as "heart energy". I utilize this term so that you, in the third-dimensional experience, can more closely relate to that which is my focus.

The heart of mankind on your planet is in for quite a jolt. There are actually far fewer ones who are *truly* prepared for the great change, which is in the process of unfolding, than most realize.

We, of the Lighted Hosts of God, are working ever

diligently to awaken any and all who will hear. We come through in many forms and in many ways. We work with and through ANY who will allow—whether they be scientist or politician, medicine man or priest. We WILL get the message through! That is indeed God's very promise to mankind.

Our concern at this time is the impact that the upcoming events will have upon many of you who consider yourselves prepared. Being aware of an event is NOT the same as being prepared for an event—though it surely helps and is indeed the first step to true preparation.

Let us consider several points of action and attention that should be a part of your mental and spiritual preparation effort.

First and foremost—**BE *NOT* AFRAID!**

Fear will only serve to limit the creative energies that would otherwise naturally flow through you. This is why ones will become "paralyzed with fear". In a technical sense, it is because they have shifted their frequency and vibration down to such a low level that they have disconnected almost completely from the creative flow of Source—or at least choked it down so that it is but a mere trickle of what it could or should be.

This is also why the adversary exploits your fears—because in a state of fear you become less and less connected with who you really are, and thus you are much more easily controlled and manipulated.

The upcoming events will indeed be shocking, for they are designed to cause this fear reaction within you. We will not be more specific as to how, exactly, the events will unfold, for there are always variables that will change as more and more of you awaken and speak out, or take up a pen and voice your awareness of the games that your "elite" controllers are playing. For now, just keep in mind that your connection to Source is most worrisome to these ones. Thus these events are designed to induce fear and get you off balance so that you can be more reliably controlled by them.

Remember this most important point: These dark ones cower in the Light of exposure of any kind and, in response, they will simply change their plans if they think that they cannot get away with any particular scenario.

However, as more doors close on their plans, these ones are also becoming more and more desperate. Thus, like trapped animals, they are becoming more and more aware that they cannot win. Therefore, they will eventually arrange for "all hell to break loose" regardless of the amount of prior exposure. And this is the dangerous situation that warrants our work with you toward becoming truly prepared.

Look back upon that which has been offered prior, through this information source and others, and you will find sufficient clues as to that which these ones are attempting to "pull off". But do keep in mind that there are as many variations on the main themes as there are avenues of possibilities to keep you guessing.

So, the first important point to keep in mind at this time is to NOT become overwhelmed by fear—and thus become disconnected from Source—else chaos rules the scene.

And speaking of chaos, the second important point is to get centered and balanced—that is, firmly connected with your Higher Consciousness. This is a very powerful position of stability.

This centering and balancing is not necessarily as difficult as it may at first appear. Any of you who are drawn to (and implementing the lessons within) these messages are already connecting and will continue to do so—as long as you can maintain the intent and desire to be centered and balanced.

As the fear-inducing events begin to unfold more and more in the physical awareness of your experience, you may begin to feel a sense of overwhelm as the reality breaks through as to what is happening. This is natural, but it is also within your abilities to control the emotional currents that result.

Let us use for example, again, a possible scenario of horrendous intent. Let us say that New York City has just been bombed by a thermonuclear device.

If this announcement was to come across your news media TODAY, what would you do?

How would you respond?

How would such affect your priorities?

Will you simply sit there in disbelief or denial, in a state of being "frozen with fear"?

Will you check to see that your shelter is in a state of readiness?

Do you even have a shelter?

Will you just give up?

OR—will you stop and take a moment to get centered within the Light, and find peace in recognizing that even an event such as this can serve as an opportunity for growth?

Preparation is done AHEAD OF TIME so that you can more effectively maintain a God-connection-fostering state of "peace of mind" by releasing such considerations or worries as whether or not your family will have food and shelter.

With preparation comes peace of mind, so you can go about your days without carrying around the crippling burden of worrying about whatever does happen, for you have that which will enable you to survive and rebuild if necessary. Recognize that, in eliminating this worry drain, you strengthen your God connection and thus intensify your flow of creative solutions.

All preparation begins first with mental desire for safety and well being. Those who are prepared will NOT likely be the ones who are overwhelmed with fear or grief.

While compassion about tragic events is a natural reaction for Lighted Beings, those who are TRULY prepared will likely also experience an emotional response similar to that of exhilaration as they, especially if they are Ground Crew, realize that their life's challenge is unfolding. These ones will be the ones who will step-in to organize those, who do not just give up, into the working parties that will enable whole communities to survive in the event that ones are cut off from usual food supplies, utilities, and such. These social units can mean the difference between survival or perishment for many as tumultuous events unfold.

Learn to recognize what your heart is telling you, when you read messages such as this, and you will have your first clue as to whether or not you are prepared.

Does this message annoy you?

Is your response: "Yeah! Yeah! I've heard it before, and nothing ever happens!"?

Do you find yourself making excuses, such as: "I don't have enough money" or "It is too expensive"?

Or, do you feel clear and connected with the intent of the message and say, "I better go check my supplies and make sure they are still in a state of readiness!"?

This is how you know whether or not you are prepared. As always, actions speak louder than words.

In a state of balance, your heart will give you clear messages of guidance as to what is the right decision for you. When you follow your heart, you will never regret the experiences of your life and you will find that you will be fulfilling your purpose, either directly or indirectly, at all times.

Your heart does NOT know fear! Yet, it will offer you a sensation of discomfort when your ego-self reacts (and thus vibrates) in a state of fear. Fear is not your purpose! Fear is not of God! You are a Lighted Fragment of God!

Likewise, your heart will let you know when you are off course—if you pay attention!

When you feel discomfort regarding such as the discourses which have comprised this ongoing series of messages, but you do not really know why, it would be of great benefit to take the opportunity to look at what you are resisting, for the discomfort only comes when you are going against that which would otherwise be the “natural flow”.

When you continually ignore these feelings, the manifestation of discomfort will continue to grow and grow, and this negative accumulation will begin manifesting more and more in the physical, until you make yourself sick. And if you are still resisting the message, eventually your vibration will sink so low that you will not be able to sustain a functioning body.

What are YOU resisting?

What are YOU pushing against that causes you “stress”?

Does it really matter to you that much what the rest of the world thinks about you, that it is worth walking around, year after year, in a state of depression or anxiety?

Let go of the past and focus on the joyous experiences that you are wanting—and THEY WILL COME! This is the natural process of creating. This is God working through you!

The vibrations within you are the energy signals you send out to ALL of Creation. These will cause, through resonance, more of those vibrations to circle around and manifest back in your life.

Changing your vibration will bring about change in your life. FEEL the joy that you want and it WILL come! Expect it!

Words are empty without the FEELING that the heart gives to them! So, mouthing your desires is not enough; you must FEEL the joy and radiate that feeling to the universe and it (ALL OF CREATION) will send back to you, AMPLIFIED, the joy which you are radiating. Likewise, if you radiate boredom or anger, then all of Creation will return to you more of the same.

You can know what you are radiating at any given moment by taking a moment to monitor HOW you are feeling. What you are feeling is what you are radiating, and thus creating.

For those of you who have not enough money, then be aware it is because you are radiating lack! Those of you who have plenty of money or resources, have same because you are radiating abundance!

GOD IS ABUNDANCE!

God is NOT lack!

Where are you radiating?

Ponder these words, for they are in response to the call of the heart for the answers that can help you to heal and help you to survive. As always, it is YOUR choice to do that which you will with the information that is offered, and it is YOUR choice as to what you radiate out into the universe and thus to all of Creation.

I am Master Hilarion, Cohan (Teacher) of the Emerald Ray, sent forth to help you find the answers that your heart calls out for. In Light, and in service to Creator and Creation, I bid you the joy of creating that which your heart truly desires.

Salu!

CHAPTER TWELVE

More Lessons On The Fundamentals Of Creating

Master Hilarion
August 10, 1997

Good morning and be at peace, my scribe, for all IS well! Master Hilarion present to continue where we left off at the end of last week's lesson. I come within the Light of Creator's magnificent and infinite spectral expression. I represent the Emerald Ray, as you would perceive same in the visible frequency range. You know me well.

We last spoke of the basics of preparation and following one's internal guidance system. We monitor the response from those of you who are taking in the information as given. We see the need to offer more upon the subject of connecting to your Higher Self.

You each are connected at all times to the higher energy of Source. However, when you are in a lower-frequency state, say due to emotional "stress", your ability to consciously connect is greatly diminished.

When you are feeling boredom, frustration, anger, or any of those states that debilitate, then you can know your frequency has lowered and the otherwise-free-flowing connection has been diminished or choked off. These feelings are, for most of you, associated with the heart energy center.

Many of you have experiences in your life where you were extremely excited and happy, and had a feeling there was nothing in the world that could stop you. This is when the heart is soaring and you are vibrating at a frequency that more closely matches who you REALLY are!

When the heart energy center (your Guidance center) is radiating the higher-frequency emotions of joy, excitement, and enthusiasm, you will cause the solar plexus energy center (just below the heart center) to respond in like manner. It begins to "rev-up" and thus you begin to radiate with greater and greater intensity. All of your energy centers are connected in a coordinated and complimentary manner. The heart center and the solar plexus are closely linked, and many will say that they have a "gut" feeling regarding a particular experience when, in fact, more of that "gut" feeling may be emanating from the heart.

There is a great amount of lower-frequency energy being radiated at this time on your planet. However, due to the nature of the energy associated with this lower-frequency state, it is such that ***ONE*** **who is radiating in a joyous state puts out more energy than a million who are radiating in the lower-frequency state!** Therefore, a balance can be achieved and the process of turning around the "mess" on your planet is truly not as difficult as it may at first appear.

As has been stated many times prior: IT ONLY TAKES *ONE* TO RECOGNIZE THEIR TRUE POTENTIAL AND THE GAME IS OVER!

This means that, from the point of view of energy dynamics, if there is just ONE who functions in the physical from a position of being truly connected to Higher Source, then that ONE can so greatly tip the scales back into balanced Radiance that the dark "elite" controllers of your planet would shrivel to a point of insignificance.

This is the reason for the mind control of the masses—especially as you ones spoon-feed yourselves by way of your news media and television programing. Even the seemingly harmless "comedy" shows give forth subliminal (programing) suggestions which can cause you to feel helpless or ineffectual or dispersed (from an energy perspective), and induce attitudes that may distract you from a focus which would allow you to connect more fully with your true Potential of Being.

Please do not take the above statement in the wrong way. Understand that laughter is a most wonderful frequency vibration and is beneficial to your well-being. However, the "elite" controllers are utilizing your media for programming your minds, and through such means have corrupted the potentially good to achieve their ends. This corruption is centered around the power of suggestion.

Therefore, it is the subtle nature of suggestion which will get you, for instance, to a point where you will find humor in something that is truly twisted and not humorous at all. Moreover, when you find yourself all wrapped up in some of the modern "bad guy" movies, then you may want to ask yourself: "Is there truly joy in this sort of violence, or am I that desensitized to actual violence that I have become numb to it?"

Recognize that the "numbness" of mind keeps you off balance and in a mode of seeking something of even greater "shock" value in order to register the slightest charge of emotional stimulation. This desensitizing situation has been built-up to such a level in recent years that the movie producers are finding it more and more difficult to pack enough violence and/or sex into a film so that the public will even want to see it! Meanwhile the desensitization causes you to lose touch with your Spiritual Center, your Guidance, your Source of Being.

We monitor many who say with the mouth that they want to feel more connected to the spiritual nourishment of

Higher Self. Yet all the while these same ones sit in front of their television screens, day after day, in ritualistic fashion, filling their heads with programing that will eventually lower their frequency to such a level that they will surely be among the first to "jump through the hoops" whenever the "elite" controllers say to jump through those hoops.

Large companies like Pepsi Cola, Anhauser-Busch, Colgate-Palmolive, or General Motors do not pay millions of dollars for 15-second spots of advertising (brainwashing) during events like the Super Bowl because they are ineffectual. Rather, the power of suggestion is most commanding over the largely-brain-dead masses of vidiot-box junkies.

Many of you would be far wiser to spend more of your time focusing on strengthening your Inner Connection and Guidance System. And then, when you can truly FEEL your connection and KNOW you can pull yourself out of the negativity of the world, THEN go back and watch the programing and monitor your response. It will be quite different—and instructive in its revelations!

Raising your frequency, and thus connecting more fully with your Higher Self, is as simple as visualizing a time when you were feeling really good and resonating again with that situation as if you were there. Now hold that feeling and begin to feel it radiating from within you, out to the whole universe.

This is what it FEELS like to be connected at a higher frequency. You can do this anytime you desire.

Now, while maintaining this high-frequency vibration, focus your thoughts upon your desires, with that feeling of joy in your heart, and you will be a million times more powerful in manifesting your desires in the physical!

If you find it difficult to hold these higher emotional frequencies, then take a moment to look at what you are resisting and simply let go of it. Then, again, focus on those thoughts from times that bring forth joy you have known. Soon you will find that what you are radiating is the higher-frequency energies, and you are connecting with who you REALLY are—a Being of Light who has been endowed by God with INFINITE capabilities of creating!

Now, when you have done this, and you KNOW you can feel this joy anytime you like, and there is no situation wherein you cannot pull yourself up out of the lower frequencies and into the higher frequencies, then it is time to focus your thoughts upon that which causes these creative energies to intensify. That is, FOCUS on the way you would like your life to be; FEEL what it will be like; RADIATE your heart's desire with the power of joy and enthusiasm—and you will be amazed at how fast change will manifest and the joy will flow into your experience like never before. Then you will know, with Inner Certainty that IS the God Source within, that you cannot be stopped or dragged down or contained within another person's drama—unless YOU so choose same!

A CAUTION: As I gave for background in last week's lesson, seek first a condition of balance—else you will find that you are actually more focused upon what you do NOT want, and you will miss a very fundamental dynamic of creation. If you do NOT want poverty, then don't dwell upon a perceived condition of poverty, but upon abundance!

The fundamental point here is that YOUR Higher Self connection is YOUR guidance system. And when you are properly focusing your desires, your Higher Self will offer high-frequency emotional support, and well-being WILL manifest.

Always try to follow and sustain the high-frequency signals. When you encounter lower-frequency situations, look at what you are doing (or thinking) which has caused this encounter. Find a better way to meet the challenge. Often this means letting go of that which you are resisting (that is, change your focus). Be thankful for the experience, for you now know better where to focus your thoughts and energy.

Your Higher Self will naturally guide you through your challenges, and the resulting growth will enable you to more fully recognize your true potential. In this way you will be doing your part to turn around the low-vibration condition on your planet. If not YOU, then who?

Stop waiting for another to do it for you and you will eventually come to understand that the reason you were so disconnected in the first place was because you were not following the Guidance within that says: "TAKE ACTION!" In the larger perspective, there are no wrong actions, only better choices of action. If the result of an action taken leaves you feeling worse than you felt prior to the action, then change the focus (now that you are wiser) and TAKE MORE ACTION! This is why you are there on that third-dimensional playing field!

If you do not have a job, or you are unhappy with the one you now have, then get focused on what it is that you are wanting, and go interview with as many companies as you can. Do it with enthusiasm radiating from your being, and you are likely to get the job that you are not even qualified to do!

Worry and fear will only serve to lock you into a mundane existence with little about which to truly feel good. JOY and ENTHUSIASM are the signals from Higher Self which tell you that what you are focused on is in alignment with who you really are. If you are feeling otherwise, then you can know that your focus could be better.

There is no limit to the joy you can create; it is truly infinite. When you are connected and aligned in joy, your physical condition (whatever it is) will naturally return to complete balance and perfection, given enough time and persistence. Resist the alignment with Higher Self for any continued length of time, and your physical condition is likely to suffer. Why do you think that "stress" has been observed to cause so many physical illnesses?

You ones are entering a higher-frequency area of planetary travel (Photon Belt area of space), and as the upward frequency-shifting of your space continues, there will be less and less tolerance for out-of-balance, lower-frequency energies. Negative physical manifestations in the body will come more rapidly to you who have the tendency to dip down into the lower-frequency emotions for any length of time.

Know that you can turn around your emotional state instantly by simply changing your focus of thought. When you are feeling down, take a moment to look at what you can be thankful for, and know that what you are experiencing is what you have created for yourself, and you can change it anytime you like by simply focusing the mind on those things which cause the HEART to soar.

There is more stated here than what words alone can convey. Go within and seek your own clarity. Resist not the simple answers, for many will find that the simple answers are the RIGHT ones—so much so that you may find yourselves slightly embarrassed for having missed these simple (NOT simplistic!) points all these years.

There is great joy awaiting you all! Get clear; get focused; and carry out your Inspired actions with JOY! The dark ones cannot control you who live in this en-Light-ened way.

I am Master Hilarion, come as Teacher and Lightworker, here to assist those who would desire insights and tools for spiritual awakening. I am but a heartbeat away; call upon my energy and I will respond.

In Light and Love, Salu!

CHAPTER THIRTEEN

One Person *Can* Make A Difference!

Ceres Anthonious Soltec
August 23, 1997

Good morning, and be at peace. Geophysical Commander Ceres Anthonious "Toniose" Soltec here in the Radiant Light of Aton, the One Light. Get centered within the energy and let us commune a bit in addressing matters about which many are curious who are watching and following the clues.

There is much taking place worldwide, as we speak, in terms of weather manipulations and other kinds of so-called "natural" disasters. Let us just take a quick look:

• Intense fires are devastating thousands of acres of beautiful Nature, especially in dry, remote (and thus hard to reach) areas of the western U.S. and parts of Europe.

• Flash flooding is causing entire cities to be immersed under water, cities which have never seen such problems before.

• High winds and tornados are touching down from "nowhere", with pinpoint destructive accuracy, and are disappearing just as quickly.

• Violent hurricanes are stacked up like bowling balls, just off your southeastern U.S. coastal waters, ready to strike on a moment's instruction.

• Your western United States is readying for supposedly "the worst" El Niño in fifteen years—these, of course, caused by the large number of active volcanos under your Pacific Ocean as part of the upsurge of activity around what you refer to as the "Ring of Fire"—all of which you are not being told about.

• Earthquake activity is escalating worldwide—so much so that there is now tighter control (through consolidation) of the Internet-available data sources, thus facilitating further attenuation of the activity frequency and magnitude numbers.

• Unusual tsunami waves are catching coastal areas by great surprise and causing unpredictable "tidal" activity in many locations.

• Volcanos (above-ground) are causing mass relocations of people—such as occurred about six weeks ago near Mexico City with Popocatepetl, and more recently with Montserrat in your West Indies.

Yes, some of these were once "merely" quite natural occurrences on your planet. It is thus difficult for ones to accept that what is going on now could be deliberate manifestations by those who are efforting to manipulate and control you-the-people.

Why, you may ask, would anyone go to such lengths to control anyone? There are ones on your planet who have a personal agenda to become, so to speak, the "king" of the world—in a most literal way! These ones cannot possibly control ALL of the masses, completely, at this time, due to both the sheer numbers of people on the planet, and those few percent who have not fallen for (or are waking up from) the rampant mind control. These so-called "elite" ones literally view you "common" people as mere "useless eaters" and consumers of natural resources which they consider their private property.

The use of "natural" disasters (and herein should be included the various "designer" biological micro-viruses) to outright kill-off large numbers of people, either directly or indirectly (by destroying food supplies, contamination of drinking water, and destroying shelter), is their primary goal.

The secondary goal of these would-be-kings is to make those "common folk" who survive such disasters so dependent upon this self-appointed "royalty" for survival that they (the survivors, regardless of race, color or religion) literally become the "slave" class for these "elite".

These would-be-kings, if left unchecked, would most certainly destroy your entire planet. This is most unacceptable in the Higher Order of the universe!

This is where you who come into "The Knowing" make the greatest impact, for the dark ones CANNOT stand the Light of exposure. They will change their plans, again and again, in order to avoid being found out, and also to try to make the Truthbringers seem crazy and thus not worth listening to.

Those of you who are daring enough to speak out in a resourceful fashion (that is, who make it difficult, maybe just through sheer numbers, for ones to discount what you have to say) and voice your knowledge of what IS, are the ones who are literally changing the course of history on your planet, and are diverting the destruction of your planet!

This is no small task and no one person could expect to do it alone. However, ONE person CAN organize teams of like-minded players into information hubs that "tell it like it is" and voice their accumulated knowledge to any and all who will hear. There is great power in combining such energies, especially in conjunction with calling in Lighted Help from we of the Higher Realms, here at this time for, among other tasks, this very reason!

Those of you who hold back that which you know to be TRUTH, do a disservice to your fellow man. In your state of fear or false allegiance, you are simply among

the many controlled puppets actually working FOR the "elite". Surely a few moments of quiet reflection would counsel the folly of such a path!

Let us consider the proportions of this matter: For every one person who speaks out, there are at least ten others who have the same knowledge, but who quiver in their shoes with the fear of some sort of retribution from the "elite" controllers. I say, here and now, that the ONLY way to regain ANY true freedom is to speak out and turn this mess around. Call upon God for assistance and protection AND YOU *WILL* HAVE IT! If you dwell upon fear, it will consume your life and, moreover, expedite the death of your physical body.

Dwell upon that which you know to be true, and share your unique knowledge with the world. Many wait until they are literally on their deathbed to speak out, for in their final moments they finally feel that they haven't anything left to lose.

Speak out NOW and do something TRULY meaningful with your life! Then, when you do finally transition from this testing and learning environment back to the non-physical, evaluative side of life, you will savor a great feeling of KNOWING that you have contributed a greater awareness of what IS to all of humanity.

There are MANY out there who can confirm for you the "unbelievable" technologies that we have spoken about for so many years now in the pages of this information source [*that is, the* CONTACT *newspaper*]—technologies that control the masses through the likes of weather modifications and other "natural" disasters, through direct electromagnetic mind-control techniques, and through well-placed misinformation.

BUT—ONE PERSON *CAN* MAKE A DIFFERENCE!

Take Rev. Louis Farrakhan as a good example. He knows that the world is corrupt. He knows that the solution (Soul-ution) is not through violence, but rather through education of the masses. He does not discriminate against anyone, and teaches the African-American community to unify in a peaceful and civilized manner. He teaches that education is the answer.

He is one man—and yet was able to galvanize WELL OVER a million people into a peaceful demonstration to the world! He is not afraid and efforts to not keep around him those who try to divert his attention using subtle fear tactics. Of course he must be on constant guard, for those closest around him may be the most susceptible targets for the adversary's attacks.

Is this one man better than any other man on your planet? NO!

Does he have mystical powers over people? NO!

He is truly educated and focused on freeing not only his people, but also upon setting an example for all to see—that the power of The One Light can manifest greatness within anyOne and everyOne.

Mr. Farrakhan KNOWS the suppression of the media. As well he KNOWS the diabolical tactics of mis-information and dis-information utilized by the controllers of that media to program the minds of the public.

Meanwhile, he has a standing, open invitation to get his message heard, here in this forum [*the* CONTACT *newspaper*] **any time he may choose to do so, without distortion or even the changing of a single word of a communication. God promised an avenue for Truth to reach the "four corners of the world" at this time—and so shall it be!**

I say now, to those of you who can offer confirmations to what is, in fact, Truth: **IT IS NOW TIME TO SPEAK OUT!** This kind of sharing will release the inner concern and "stress" that is building within.

Your brothers on this planet are in need of the confirmations of what has become of your world, and how it is that such has happened. Shed the fears and take a stance for Truth, else there will not be a world left for your children or grandchildren.

I am Ceres Anthonious "Toniose" Soltec, come as a Messenger of Truth so that you ones might have awareness of what IS the current state of your planet's health in this time of a major dimensional transition.

I come in Light and in Service to that One Light, Creator Source. May YOU find the strength to do YOUR part. And remember: you are NEVER alone so long as you call upon The Light for assistance.

Salu!

CHAPTER FOURTEEN

Answering The Higher Call To Serve

Violinio Saint Germain
August 23, 1997

Good afternoon, my scribe. Violinio St. Germain here in the Light of Creator's magnificent One Light. I represent the Violet Ray of transmutation and I work closely with my brother, El Morya, the First Ray of new beginnings.

Out of that darkness and chaos which is your present world, there shall spring forth in newness a time of Radiance and Peace. There is need to see the contrast between where you (and your planet) are now, and where you are wanting to be. Out of the chaos and confusion of a world gone mad, there is being borne a DESIRE within the hearts of many for balance and peace. It is this desire which is the key ingredient that drives change and transmutation.

You ones ask how this works. I shall explain for the sake of those awakening to their God-power, that you may choose to add yours to the overall chorus of Lightworkers coordinating the manifestation of Creator's will-be-done on Earth.

Thus, I say again: desire drives change. As more and more awaken to an awareness of the chaos and confusion, the impetus for change grows, and the transformation begins. More and more are coming into a similar alignment of desire-energies that summons forth the change.

There are now far more wanting this change than resisting the change, and it is only a matter of sequence of events (basically, intensity of energy flow) that determines the rate of manifestation of the New Dawn of mankind. Thus you can see the wisdom in our focus upon sequence of events, and not upon "time" as you perceive same.

When you each make effort to pull yourself out of the confusion of the day-to-day world built around the lust for material gain, and focus more fully upon inner balance and growth of self, then you are connecting more fully with (and conducting into the physical) the energy that will bring forth the desired change upon your world.

Take personal inventory of that upon which you place importance, and what actions you allow to take priority in your life: Is money a primary concern? How about the so-called (false) "security" and "freedom" and "importance" it seems to provide? Are "social pressures" a preoccupation? Do you worry more about what other people think of you than about what you can feel (know) within to be correct and act upon same with courage?

When measures of material or social "status" become more important than finding a point of inner balance and peace, then you have lost sight of what has lasting value. The distractions of the material arenas may, perhaps, allow you to feel better in the moment, but such will do little to help you find LASTING inner peace and knowing!

Seek first to find that Higher Connection which guides you toward finding inner peace and balance, and then take action according to that which takes priority in the moment. That which crosses your path each moment, happens for a reason. ALWAYS! Recognize that this is so—that "life is what happens while you make other plans"—and be attentive to the clues and nudges which will help you make the active choices that both indicate and determine your most deeply seated priorities.

We of the Hosts are always looking for ones who can stay centered, focused, and connected. We are particular about who we choose. ("MANY are called; FEW are chosen!") If you are drawn to this information source, and messages like this, then consider yourself CALLED.

You answer the call by disciplining yourself to stay centered and balanced and connected. We shall NEVER force you to do anything! However, we DO have a myriad of resources at our disposal to help you, who ask with the heart, and we WILL respond to a sincere plea for help. Count on it!

Many in the U.S. and Canadian cultures spend far more time watching television than focusing upon that which will facilitate spiritual growth. The choice is always left up to the individual, and so too is the responsibility of each choice.

Dis-ease, dis-comfort, health problems, and addictions will be cleansed from the planet. If you cannot overcome these things, then you will be below the frequency range which your environment will support. You will simply leave the "new Earth realm" and go elsewhere to experience.

Cleanse thyself of the inner emotional pain. Let go of what was. Focus your energy upon the Perfection of what is taking place all around you on a grand scale—a planet returning to Balance and Radiance.

Consider this an invitation to become a more active participant in The Solution. Commit to yourself, in the form of a heartfelt desire, time to spend consciously connecting to Higher Self (your inner Godself) every day. Disallow the negative energies from entering into your experience.

Consider your connecting to Higher Self like the operation of a light switch in a darkened room. When you turn on the switch, you make connection, and the light comes on, and the darkness is gone.

Now, let us imagine the switch as a dimmer-type switch (one that allows the intensity of the light to vary). As YOUR emotional state changes, so too does the illumination level in the room.

For example, let us say you find that you are currently in a state of stress-filled doubt and unrest and chaos. Your room is thus pretty dark and it does not feel very pleasant.

Now you focus upon clearing your space and finding balance. As you begin to focus on this, and hold the thought, the room becomes brighter and brighter. As a result of this, metaphorically, you begin to see more clearly the details of the environment in which you find yourself. The things around you take on a more understandable (less vague) form; you find yourself less "in a fog". You can deal much better with that which confronts you due, again metaphorically, to all the now-visible clues for proceeding with the given challenge.

Now you feel more focused and clear about what perhaps is standing in your way. You may even appreciate that the only REAL reason you were afraid to move forward was simply because you were not connecting with your Inner Source.

If you are feeling satisfaction and certainty with who you are and where you are heading, then you can be assured that you ARE connected and, more likely than not, that the light switch is cranked up to full! You know such ones; dispense of thy envy toward these Lightworkers and become similar hands and feet for Creator!

We cannot stress ENOUGH the importance of staying connected and centered at this time. The natural flow of the planetary system is into a high-frequency state. The very body of your globe will transform and change, and as she does, those who are in harmony with her shall thrive, while those who are not will find the experience quite harsh and even unbearable.

You all live within the magnificent, nurturing energy field(s) of your planet. You all knew, prior to coming into this experience, that this planetary transformation (energy shift) would take place. Moreover, you understood that it would provide you with a tremendous opportunity to meet and grow through challenges that have faced some of you for thousands of years, lifetime after lifetime.

Think of it this way: Your planet is turning up HER "dimmer switch" and is fast approaching a position of being fully connected, with her light at full intensity. This is what is meant by the "State of Radiance" into which your planet is fast evolving.

This is a time for paying close attention to ALL the clues around you, and then discerning for YOURSELF what is the correct path for YOU! Your connection to Inner Guidance is thus an imperative part of your "tool kit" at this time! Your Inner Guidance will direct you toward what is perfect for YOU.

It is not anyone else's prerogative, business, or responsibility to tell you what to do, where to do it, when to do it, or even how or why to do a thing. You must learn to not rely upon another for YOUR personal choices and decisions.

This is not to say that consultation with those around you, whose wisdom you consider valid, should not be a part of your decision-making. The key here is in the asking and the heart intent, for "the call compels the answer" and you can never be sure of what possible avenues may be employed by We of God's Hosts to get your answers to you in a form you can recognize and appreciate. Yet, the burden of responsibility still rests squarely upon YOUR shoulders to take-in all solicited information, and then make YOUR OWN decisions about YOUR course(s) of action.

Many, all around your world, in every culture and language, are receiving this type of message and Guidance. This message is intended to serve as a reminder of that which you already know, within your heart, to be true.

Get centered and learn to trust your own Inner Guidance. Keep The Light on and stay connected. When your Light is on, then the adversary will go elsewhere to find an easier target.

If you slip, and the doubts and fears come back, then simply turn The Light back on and proceed forward. Do not worry about making mistakes, for EVERYONE in the physical makes mistakes. Be thankful for what you have learned from ANY mistake and move forward. In doing so, you will be transforming yourself into a role-model for others to follow, and therein you will also be fulfilling your Higher Purpose. You will then know the satisfaction which your heart is longing to feel and maintain.

I am Violinio St. Germain, come as Teacher and Guide in response to the heart-directed petitions of those at this time who are desiring clarity within the Light of Truth.

Salu!

CHAPTER FIFTEEN

Take Responsibility *Now* For Connecting Within

Esu "Jesus" Sananda
August 30, 1997

Good afternoon, little one. It is I, Esu Sananda. I come in the Light of Holy God of Lighted Creation. I come as the Golden-White Ray, in Oneness with our Father. Be at peace and allow for our energies to synchronize.

There are many at this time who are seeking to know what is their purpose for being or what their "life purpose" is in this experience. Many are asking, yet many do not want to accept the PERSONAL RESPONSIBILITY for the receiving of the answers, and thus await another to tell them.

It is not the responsibility of this scribe, nor any other, to answer such questions for anyone. You EACH must learn to go within and make your OWN connections—and learn to trust your own Guidance.

Hear me well: This endeavor is fundamental to your forward progress in the physical at this time!

Your planet, and all experiencing upon her, are in the midst of transformation. You each had a great desire to be a part of this transformation cycle—for as many reasons as there are individual souled beings incarnate. There shall continue to be ever-increasing opportunities made available to you each as this planetary experience unfolds. It is up to YOU to do that which you will do, from moment to moment, with these opportunities and possibilities which present themselves in your current life experience.

If you wait for another to tell you what it is that you are to be doing or when to be doing a thing, then you shall either be waiting a long time or you will be listening to someone or something other than the Lighted Hosts of God. This is not to say that we of God's Hosts will not offer instructions from time to time. It IS to say that the instructions or guidance will come from WITHIN you. Supporting "clues" may come from many outside directions—from the offhand comment of a friend you bump into at the supermarket, to the fortune-cookie paper-scrap that flutters into your hand seemingly from "nowhere"—but such will be made to enter your experience IN SUPPORT OF an INNER communication, not in place of same.

You each would be wise to spend at least a few minutes each day holding the desire within your heart to connect with your Guides. Some think of these Guides as their Guardian Angels. They will assist you in many ways as well as help you to cultivate your direct connection to God.

Learn to perceive the impulses sent your way. You each have, within you, a direct, two-way communication connection with Creator Source. Learn to recognize and use this God-given right!

Many are simply afraid of the responsibility associated with following nudges that "somehow" come from their OWN mind or thoughts. Perhaps this is one of the reasons you have come into the physical at this time—so that you can expand your awarenesses and thus learn to consciously connect in the physical to the Infinite Potential of Creation.

You are all explorers who have desire to explore your own inner potential in a highly focused and condensed manner. The physical environment that you have chosen facilitates this desire.

You each enjoy the challenge of solving conflicts (contradictory energy flows) within, for each solution brings you greater awareness of who you are and how to use more fully and more responsibly the Infinite Resources of Creation.

None of you want another to tell you how to live your life. However, many of you would gladly allow an inspired message to dictate to you what you should do or when you should do a thing—UNLESS, of course, that inspired message comes from YOUR OWN hand, for then you would be inclined to simply dismiss it as invalid or somehow delusional.

I shall tell you now that unless and until you learn to connect FOR YOURSELF, WITHIN, you will never be satisfied with what you are doing, or where you are doing it, or with whom you are doing whatever it is you are doing. The strength (and thus satisfaction) of your convictions—whether they are in response to seemingly trivial matters like clothing choices, or serious ones like adopting a child—stems from your level of certainty, and that certainty derives from the strength of your connection within to Source.

Discern for yourself that which YOU hold as Truth. And, in like manner, learn to discern for yourself the signals of your own Inner Guidance. Despite the constant bombardments to the contrary, especially from so-called "religious" leaders, you need NO guru, avatar, or anything other than YOUR OWN inner connection to Source. How much more simple could it be?!

You are each magnificent, individual, experiencing fragments of infinite, Light-energy Source! Within each fragment lies the potential of infinite energy flow and creation. You are each exploring, from your own unique point of view, the infinite potential of YOUR being. So why would you allow another to tell you how to do that which can only be uniquely done by you?

You EACH have a contribution to make that comes from your uniqueness as an individual. No other can tap the Universal Source in quite the same way as can you, as a unique individual and uniquely gifted fragment of Creator.

Learn to recognize, accept, and appreciate your own uniqueness of being. Learn to connect for yourself. Learn to listen with the heart and discern with the mind.

These words are chosen specifically for their general meaning so that you each will have need to go within and discern all the possible implications FOR SELF! The general statements hold far more meaning than the words alone can convey. Allow for the thoughts to be invoked within, and in doing so, you will realize the subtle nature of receiving YOUR answers in the form of YOUR thoughts and YOUR ideas!

This is not a new message, but as you each grow along the spiritual path, we see that often there is not review of past lessons or insights. You would each be wise to review that which has been offered prior on this same subject.

As you each grow, there becomes greater and greater ability to see and appreciate the multi-dimensional levels of these offerings. Consider them as tools. It is up to you to recognize the various uses of each, as well as recognize that each of you will apply and use these tools in your own unique way.

If another gets a different meaning from the same message, and shares their interpretation with you, be respectful for, though it may be different from your own, it may be quite a valid perception.

Many of you are realizing a shift in perception at this time, and that your inner desires for understanding are welling up within. This is as it should be, for the emotional desire (the call) compels the answer. The answers are rarely what you think they should be, and that is why the confusion, for if you already had the answers or they were exactly what you "thought" they should be, then you would not have the questions in the first place. This is how true growth occurs.

Allow for the unfolding in the physical of YOUR answers. The more focused your desires, the quicker they will manifest for you. Monitor closely that which you spend time fixated upon. Many are addicted to their "vidiot" boxes, religiously focused upon brutal "sporting" events or sudsy soap operas or empty so-called-news programs, yet will only spend a few infrequent moments in a conscious effort to connect within to Higher Source.

Voice not your excuses, for in the same amount of time it would take to state your excuses, you could simply use the time to go within and connect.

As the planetary transition underway at this time becomes more and more real, and begins to more fully impact your day-to-day reality, you will be thankful that you have prepared and developed your own inner communication and intuition, for it will be very likely that reliable external avenues of communication, such as this newspaper [CONTACT], **will be cut off.**

Even now, there is no way that we of the Hosts of God can possibly address, in a short weekly newspaper, all the possible scenarios that you ones will be faced with in the upcoming years. Your specific personal concerns require going within for specific answers.

These are truly magnificent times in which to be experiencing. The potential for inner growth is nearly overwhelming. Get centered within and call upon the Lighted Brotherhood for assistance, protection, and guidance—and it will be!

Connect within and begin to sense the excitement and newness associated with each of your life's challenges. Look forward to those greater challenges which will garner you the insights and wisdom you are desiring. No one else will do it for you—NOR SHOULD THEY!

No matter what you may think is your lack of growth and mastery this day, you can turn around your life and create a better way for yourself. Your past and present hardships are exactly perfect FOR YOU in order to bring about your current level of awareness and desire for change. Be thankful for your challenges thus far, and be thankful when you have managed to pull yourself through same by going within and tapping the great Inner Strength always there, simply awaiting your call.

Allow those who might ridicule you to go their own way and find their own truth. You cannot save another. And, beyond offering a helping hand, you can do no more, else you short-circuit their growth and you make them dependent upon you, and they will only serve to pull you down and distract and slow your own growth.

It is not wise to hold the hands of those who make excuses for not having enough resources or ability or creativity to pull themselves out of whatever situation they claim to be trapped within. When ones are more concerned with whether or not they have alcohol or cigarettes than Gaiandriana, AquaGaia or the various colloids [*see Preface for information on how to obtain these products*], then leave them to their own health concerns, for their actions and addictions are their lessons to overcome. The products will be of little value as long as such poisons are being continually pumped into the body.

There is not one Lighted entity of God alive on your planet who could not have their lives overflowing with abundance at this time. Rather, it is due to past fears, beliefs, and habits of thought that ones disconnect from The Abundance and thus lack results. There is no exception!

Learn to connect and stay connected, and turn your life around, and stop making excuses for your choices and decisions. And, STOP waiting for another to do it for you! If you are relying upon another, then look closely at what is the exchange in the relationship. Is there re-giving or is there just taking? Are you in the position of the parasite living off another's ability to connect, instead of simply connecting yourself?

God's Law of Giving and Regiving SHALL NOT BE MOCKED! Yet, there are many on your world right now who have become so enmeshed in the material (and are thus vibrating at such a low frequency) that their actions are much too centered around taking, taking, and more taking—as if there could possibly be born a world in balance from such thoughtless and irresponsible behavior!

In the upcoming times there will be very little tolerance for this sort of behavior. You ones will be entering into a time when ones will be able to "tune-in" to energy vibrations and monitor more fully that which people emanate to the world in the form of thought and emotion. As this happens, ones will find it quite difficult to maintain any form of façade in the presence of any Lightworker of God in the physical. Manipulations and excuses will no longer work and ones will HAVE to face their responsibility for their own condition. No one reading this is helpless, nor without ability to go within and connect for self. What have you to lose?!

This message is offered with great love and hope that you each will go within and learn to connect consciously with the Higher Energies. There are no acceptable excuses for not being able to do so! I am Esu "Jesus" Immanuel Sananda. I have come to see through my responsibilities as a Wayshower and Teacher. This is a time of closure for what I set in motion 2000 years past. It is also a time of great awakening and rebirth. I welcome you each to participate—and for those of you who are not up to the task, I ask you to stand aside, else you just impede the natural flow.

In Light and Service to Creator and Creation, I am your Elder Brother along the path.

Salu!

CHAPTER SIXTEEN

Is It Transmutation Or Tribulation For You?

Violinio Saint Germain
September 6, 1997

Good evening. Violinio St. Germain present as the Violet Ray—the Seventh Ray, the Ray of Transmutation. All is unfolding as it should, and though many days appear as if they are heading down the slippery slope, I assure you that all is occurring within its proper sequence of events. These are the times which have long been spoken of, and these are the times which shall try the tenacity of all souls present upon the Earth.

This is the time of the Great Transmutation; others call it the time of the Great Tribulation.

However, it is all in the perception of things, is it not? For those who are focusing upon the Light of God, the times shall be considered transmuting. For those focusing instead upon the great darkness, their days shall be numbered as tribulation.

There is no doubt that these times are difficult, even for those in The Light. Yet, how much greater would be the pain if ye were walking in total darkness? **In the hours of**

apparent darkness, you ones will need to focus upon The Light and stand in the Strength of your convictions.

Great are the temptations to strike out at, and to be seduced by, the darkness. And these temptations will only grow stronger in the coming days, for you have but seen the mere beginnings of the transmutation process upon your planet.

As all things continue to exhibit signs of change—from your weather to your politics—know that change is what transmutation is all about. You cannot achieve higher-frequency existence without this condition of change. And because ALL are involved upon your planet, including the planet herself, all things, therefore, are changing—the planet and her inhabitants. Even the four-legged creatures, the winged ones, and those who swim in the waters, seem to you to be confused. You two-legged ones are certainly in a most confused state, and this is all due to the massive and unprecedented changes which are occurring at the present time.

You have been forewarned, over and over again, that this time was approaching. Well, my friends, the time HAS ARRIVED!

Prepare yourselves NOW for a most notable Winter, as the El Niño throttles up for an explosive display. The ocean waters, particularly in the Pacific, are up to 30 degrees warmer than has ever been seen in recent times past! You have tropical fish appearing in the waters off Northern California and British Columbia. In San Francisco, the waters are at least 25 degrees above the normal range, and this is but a sampling of what is occurring all up and down the seacoast of the Americas. Even your weather forecasters are warning you ones to "batten down the hatches", so to speak, as the rainfall (and possibly snowfall) amounts are expected to be **three times** what would typically be expected for the upcoming Winter months.

If you could view your planet down at the very core, you would see that there are many fluctuations taking place there, causing the magnetic field of your planet to fluctuate as well. Since the systems of all living creatures upon your planet are attuned to the natural magnetic pulses and frequencies of the planet itself, all living creatures are also experiencing the same "roller-coaster ride".

These fluctuations of biological frequencies are causing all sorts of odd behavior, discomforting aches and pains (especially in areas of the back, base of the skull, and shoulders, where there are denser complexes of nerve-muscle function), mental confusion and simple inability to focus mentally, plus a myriad of other odd maladies. So, do not despair in thinking you are "falling apart". Rather, these are "only" your physical body's reactions to Mother Earth's tremendous "growing pains" of sorts.

These magnetic fluctuations will eventually cause a reversal of the magnetic poles of planet Earth. THIS IS NOT THE SAME AS A *PHYSICAL* POLE SHIFT (of the Earth's rotational axis, which is in its own condition of instability at present). This simply means that the planet's magnetic forces will switch order of flow. Yes, this will have an effect upon compasses and all other magnetic instruments. But that, believe it or not, is the very least of your worries at present!

What you DO need to be focusing upon at present are the effects upon your third-dimensional existence resulting from the fluctuations in these subtle, basic life-force energies. You ARE being affected, only some are more sensitive to the changes than others. Those who are naturally sensitive are experiencing even more difficulty than they have endured in the past, and it is important for these ones to have understanding of what is occurring to them.

It is important that you not "fight" these changes, but learn to switch your own frequency to match that of your planet. You ones are often quite resistant to change, and this, my dear friends, is a MOST MAJOR change you are going to have to deal with. You have the option of refusing to accept and go with the changes, but you will only be hurting yourself, for the planet is not going to sit back and wait until you are ready. Many are fighting the changes, and therein are actually choosing to depart the planet. This pattern will continue and will but increase in the coming days.

However, there are also many who are going to choose to leave of their own accord—not because they refuse to accept the changes, but because they have effected the changes they came here to accomplish and their work is finished. These ones are so "tuned-in" to the progression of the planetary transmutation that they KNOW exactly what is occurring and are choosing to cross over to be of greater assistance from the non-physical realm. They will simply pick up "new bodies" on the other side to continue their service.

How will you know who these ones are? Most likely you will not. And if the truth is to be known, it is really none of your business! **YOUR business is to concern yourself with YOUR own challenges of living—and that will keep all of you more than busy. Believe me!**

The distractions are many these days for all of you, and besides having to deal with the planetary changes, you are being bombarded by the news of one Earth-shaking event after another. It is well that you attempt to be informed, but be careful as to just how much of the drama and emotion you get suckered into. That is how the adversary will keep you from focusing your energies in the proper direction. And, oh yes, the adversary is working powerfully, and is in "overdrive" right now, for the time of darkness is very shortened, and there is a great push underway by the forces of darkness as they work to keep both The Light and the Lightworkers at bay. They know their demise is imminent, and are wishing to prolong their reign of terror as long as possible.

Be very careful, these days, with whom you associate, for the dark powers have set their sights upon the workers of Light. They will come to you presenting as "angels of the light". But it is your responsibility to test each and every one, for they can be very seductive and very desirable to your lower energies. Take great caution, and do not be taken-in by everyone who comes your way, seemingly as a "friend", in the coming days.

Many of you are finding yourselves in trying and changing personal situations, and you are the ones being severely tested by the dark forces. Shield yourselves well, and do not allow yourselves to be overwhelmed in self-doubt and fear as you move forward on the new paths your lives are taking.

You created the changes because you were following the guidance of the Lighted Ones. Thus, many of you removed yourselves from dangerous situations and places. Many more of you are, at present, making these changes. Stand firm in the strength of your convictions in the days ahead. Be certain you are making your OWN decisions, based upon careful evaluation of your inner knowledge, and not on doubt or fear. Be certain that you are NOT basing your decisions upon the expectations of, or assumed obligations to, another. You and ONLY you can know the truth that lies within self.

You may find that previous friends, family, and acquaintances will be no more. Fret not, for each one is changing, and that which was may be no more a necessity. **Each one of you must look within and make decisions based upon your own chosen path, and that path may be separating from ones you have had associations with in the past.** This is all part of the changes taking place.

Appreciate when any separation is for the benefit of all involved, and is but part of the larger transitionary period you are experiencing. Paths may, at some point in the future, cross again; but you may not know that at present.

Walk forward upon YOUR Lighted path, placing one foot surely and firmly in front of the other, and take one step at a time. You may sometimes find yourself running, but you'll still be placing one foot in front of the other. Only the pace will have quickened!

Be diligent in the coming hours and days, but do not allow yourselves to be overwhelmed with all the changes taking place. **As I stated earlier, all is occurring in its proper sequence of events, and all things really are in their proper season, even though, from your perspective, everything seems out of control and out of balance. Well, chelas, the balance has been missing for such a great long time, that you ones are confusing the process of re-balancing with chaos.**

Take it as it comes, for there is order in this "Time of Change". Lift your frequency to that of your planet and you will find yourself less at the mercy of the changes. We have, in past lessons, given you many practical suggestions for achieving this raising of frequency. For now, let us simply suggest that you monitor that which gives you a feeling of positive upliftment—such as comes with the cultivation of humor and joy and purpose—and make such a part of your daily spiritual "diet", in conjunction with calling upon we of God's Hosts for guidance and protection.

We are with you—know that always. You are not alone and you are being watched over and guided continually—only most of you are not aware of the Guides who stand ready to take your hand and assist you.

I am Violinio St. Germain, of the Seventh, the Violet, Ray of Transmutation. I stand with all the other Masters of Transition and Hosts of God of Light, at the ready station to serve in these days of your Great Transition. I say to you: shall it be a time of transmutation and growth into Radiance for you, or shall it be a time of tribulation, pain, and chaos? Mother Earth knows her destiny, and so shall you be master of yours—one way or the other!

Salu.

CHAPTER SEVENTEEN

Give Thanks To Your Great Mother Earth

Lady Nada
September 21, 1997

Good evening, my friend. It is I, Lady Nada, come to commune with you this day that a much needed message shall be delivered to those who are efforting toward insights about the current planetary situation.

I come in, and I am of, the Light of Aton, The One Light! I represent the solar plexus energy center of not only the human physical body, but also of the body of your planet and her solar plexus energy center. Remember that you all live within the various energy fields of your planet—and this is an even more direct and "personal" relationship than is the energy coupling with one another of humankind.

Your planet is on the verge of a new, higher-frequency level of vibrational existence. She has her challenges to face, as do you all. She has a tremendous capacity to nurture and give forth life-sustaining energy. She has withstood many assaults to her physical well-being. She has served far beyond what has been asked of her, and as a result, you ones have been given the gift of

time. Many shall soon look back and wish that they had listened and used this gift more wisely.

Many of the more intuitive "seers" who are receiving and sharing their glimpses about the current condition of your planet are still not quite in understanding of a most important level of what is going on. This living, sentient, grand being, whom most simply look upon as a "hunk of rock" orbiting in "space", has a unique mission and purpose—the same as do you all who are created of The One Light. I have come at this time to explain some of the deeper aspects of the challenge that a sentient being of this marvelous calibre has chosen to go through.

Earth-Shan is now seeking balance from within. In her heart energy center, she is coming into harmony with her Higher Calling. As a result, she is summoning forth all of the creative energies necessary for the transformation of her physical body back into a state of balanced perfection. This is not too different from you ones who experience "miraculous" healing when you connect within to Higher Source. When the heart energy center and the mind synchronize into a condition of balance, the physical will naturally respond to this balanced, higher-frequency state, and thus come back into balance (health) as well.

Your planetary orb has come into inner balance, and as the outer must follow the inner, for the cleansing process of the physical, she is running a "fever" of sorts and thus setting the conditions for the proper cleansing and rebalancing of her more observable, physical self. As her circulatory system "speeds up", you ones are likely to feel more and more the fluctuations in her energy field.

Many are experiencing odd sleeping patterns, muscle pains in strange areas of your body, dizzy and/or nauseous spells, and other odd reactions to the energy bursts coming from Mother Earth. And keep in mind that this natural process is occurring on top of what is being calculatingly pumped into your airwaves, upon the instructions of your "elite" controllers, from most un-natural sources, to purposely compromise brain and body functionings of you who must be kept in a state of distraction or incapacitation—else you might wake up to their antics and do something about same.

Though it is hard to differentiate between natural and artificial causes for some of "what ails you" these days, you can know that even the man-made, man-generated electromagnetic frequencies are being countered and dealt with, within, by your loving planet, in the spirit of nurturing all of the life-forms who depend upon her—whether they know it or not!

This is where I, Lady Nada, come into the picture. Your planet has the same God-given right to call upon Source for assistance as do each of you. She has called, and she has been (and will continue to be) given all of the assistance that she rightfully deserves. She is awakening what would be equivalent to your solar plexus energy center. As she "revs-up" this energy flow, there shall come into her experience (and yours) great change and balancing.

This is the energy that you ones focus with your thoughts and desires, that causes the "coincidences" and "miracles" to occur. There are no real coincidences in your experience; there is, however, deliberate creating, using that which is innate within each of you.

You ones tend to fixate more upon selves than upon the world around you. And while you each are trying desperately to find inner happiness and peace, in your desires for self, there is seldom the consideration for (or attention paid to) achieving inner balance—though this should be first and foremost upon your list of desires. How can you have any semblance of true peace and joy without a foundation of balance?

Your world is full of disharmony and this out-of-balance condition is the primary cause of your planet's growing "wobble"! Each who is OUT of balance within self contributes just as much to the whole of the overall balance state of your planetary solar system (and on into the whole of the universe) as do those few who are IN balance. However, most do not perceive this absolute state of connectedness! Your Native American brothers have long tried to make this point, but mostly to deaf ears and certainly at great personal expense.

Your planet is on a path to recovery, and in the process she will make physical adjustments that will bring forth the Earth Changes that have been foretold by many throughout the years. These events, many of which will be regarded as cataclysmic, are "simply" the outward aspects of the inner decision to return to a state of balance on the part of Mother Earth. She is entitled to this healing!

Many in the scientific community are beginning to awaken to the now-blatant "oddities" in ocean temperatures and weather patterns. Even those dark ones who manipulate and control the weather patterns for various reasons of a political nature are experiencing difficulties in the execution of their shenanigans, for they do not understand the awesome energies available to Mother Earth or the effects of her upward frequency shifts—let alone the idea that they might be dealing with a living, sentient being who has a mind of her own!

There is great compassion from we of the Hosts for ALL life on your planet. We do not love more or less those of you in a human body than our brethren who have chosen to take on a physical body in the shape of a spherical globe. We will assist her (your planet) in every way we are allowed, just as we assist you ones who ask for our help at this most magnificent time of growth and renewal. We will, in effect, help her through her "birthing" struggles—even at the expense of human, animal, and vegetable life.

You all knew of this grand challenge prior to coming into the present experience. You all have had ample time to prepare and get selves and family into locations that would "logically" provide greater chances for survival. Those who take action, and not just hear, are the ones who will prevail in the upcoming times. We shall ALWAYS honor your free-will choices.

Our objective at this time is to provide you ones, who have desire to know and understand, with insights concerning what is taking place upon your globe, so that you can make the most of the experience in the way of personal growth and thus—because of that connectedness again—help facilitate the expansion of ALL of Creation. In as much as one grows, so too does the entirety of everything everywhere.

What you ones often mistake as seemingly "selfless service" on our part, as the Hosts of God, is much more than selfless, for we derive great inner satisfaction from helping to facilitate the schoolrooms where the most interesting and fantastic experiments are undertaken. These "jobs" are cyclical and many of you who are there in the physical at this time were, at some other time and place, in similar capacities of we of the Hosts. It is just that presently you have chosen to take leave (you ones might say "of your senses") to play out your hand in projecting forth IN THE PHYSICAL your theories on life, growth, and manifesting creative energy in the physical domain.

This is the time you ones have long awaited, and yet we monitor that many of you are in fear of what is coming. The more "in touch" ones are living in a state of anticipation and these ones will be the ones who will be keeping "things" going while the rest down there go through their "shock" and "disbelief". And yes, many will there be who transition out of your planetary domain—not so much because they "had to" as because of decisions they have made, perhaps not in wisdom, such as insisting upon continued residence in the proximity of major volcanic or earthquake fault locations.

The changes that will take place on your globe are as natural as when your body changes temperature to fight off foreign invaders such as viruses or flu bugs. Your planet will be much the better for having gone through the cleansing cycles, and the overall value to the quality of life experience will be greatly enhanced as a result.

This message will serve you each in your own unique way. Some shall dismiss it entirely; others will glean from it that which will help them to connect various phenomena in a new and different manner. The more perceptive reader may find even more "between the lines" here and realize greater purpose to their own life experience.

As has been a recurring theme in many of these "spiritual" writings appearing in *CONTACT*, you should EACH be consciously efforting to connect to Source FOR YOURSELVES at this time and be SEEKING WITHIN for your personal answers. Our ability to help you depends upon the efforts YOU make to help yourself. And though there is just as much compassion on our part for you ones as for Mother Earth, we can only hold your hand for so long and then we will leave you to your choices and lessons.

Again, be thankful for the time that has been GIFTED to you, largely as a result of the great nurturing compassion of Mother Earth for ALL life dependent upon her. Treat every day as though it were a personal gift to you, and give thanks to your Mother Earth for her compassion and love for life. Healing thoughts and prayers for her at this time would be very appreciated by her as well.

I am Lady Nada, come with the Hosts of God. I am sent as a Messenger of Truth in answer to the petitions for greater understanding. In Light—BLESSINGS TO YOU ALL!

Salu.

CHAPTER EIGHTEEN

Reviewing Your Lessons As The Play Gets Serious

Gyeorgos Ceres Hatonn
October 1, 1997

Good morning. Hatonn here in the Light of Creator and Creation. Be at peace, my son.

I thank you, our team, for your preparation, for the greater part of the mission is at hand. I must ask that you continue to carry the load a bit longer while adjustments are made in the casting of the play. Remember to hold the Larger Picture foremost in your mind as the unfolding events of planetary evolution present themselves to your conscious awareness.

All shall unfold in proper perfection according to God's Divine Plan. Be open to "new" ideas and sudden change in focus, for if and when the need arises, we will play our "trump" cards. Even many of our more aware Ground Crew members are limited by their own personal perceptions and beliefs that erroneously limit both God and selves. Many believe that God or His Messengers must be or act in a specific manner to somehow qualify for the part. This is a limiting challenge that you as Ground Crew must face and overcome.

These "End Times" will not be as you imagine them. They will resemble, to some extent, the messages of the prophets and seers. However, the emotional impact will cause many a great man to weep with horror and disbelief. We honor those of you who effort day-to-day to connect selves with Source, for when the walls about your dwelling-place crumble and you are stripped of all of your physical possessions, this connection may be all you have that will pull you out of the shock of the impact that is coming.

While the rest of the world sleeps on, you who have awakened to the call are being asked at this time to reaffirm your connections and to go within for your personal instructions.

If you find yourself relying upon others for your guidance and focus, then you have surely missed the lessons here. Go forth and make do with what you have, and quit worrying about what you do not have. When your heart and head are in harmony with your Godself, you will manifest what you need. Note: I said need, NOT want! You will almost always have what you need, regardless of what you want.

The Light is shining forth from all directions at this time. Your planet is awakening, though the outward (physical) signs may be lacking at present.

If you are reading this source for your insights and clues, then it is because you are connected by way of purpose to Command. This is to say that you are Ground Crew. Your general purpose is to ensure that a remnant get through (survive) the upcoming planetary changes; part of carrying out that objective is to aid in fulfilling God's promise to the world that all lies will be exposed and that The Word will go forth, AGAIN, to the four corners of the globe.

This is not a single-handed task, and there are many all around the planet who are fulfilling this promise at this time. Know that you of Ground Crew have brothers and sisters scattered far and wide. Learn to spot them and assist where you feel drawn, from Inner Guidance and request. Too many erroneously "feel" that their role is to be played out close to this information source. That makes about as much sense as the idea that most all the grocery stores of your planet should be located in any one particular town!

These are times of learning to hold the Larger Picture in your minds. And certainly from where we look upon your globe, there is need for the assistance of Beings of Light EVERYWHERE.

In that capacity, you act as our most appreciated hands and feet. And you do that most effectively through efforting to sustain a constant conscious openness to the Inner Nudges which "come through" most clearly from the high-frequency condition resulting from efforting to connect to Higher Source in a balanced way. (Yes, that was a mouthful. But we often place much of our communication "between the lines" for the benefit of those truly efforting to understand, and call in The Light for help with same.)

On the other side of the coin, learn to respect the choices and decisions of those who turn away from this information source, for it is not for them, and causes them great discomfort. Allow each unique individual the freedom to find their own way back to Source, as they see fit. You may offer to help your brothers, especially where you have been asked to do so, but never insist or argue over who is right or wrong concerning PERSONAL beliefs, for it is futile and your time can be better spent.

Let your actions show the world who you are. Teach by example through actions taken, for the words will only fall on deaf ears.

Many of you who read these messages have loved ones who disagree with what you believe. As a result, you find yourselves in a difficult situation wherein you must try to find a balance point so as to not offend the ones you love, yet try to convince them that they need to prepare, or at best allow you to spend the family's resources on preparation. These challenges are the challenges that will naturally cause ones to weed themselves from the play at hand.

You must each be responsible for your choices and decisions. YOU have chosen your family, and the pressures of going against them are inner pressures that come from fears (of rejection) which, in turn, come from personal insecurities that ultimately reach back to a state of disconnectedness from Creator Source.

Fear is not of God, and as your planet goes through her transition, the lower frequencies of fear, anger, and hatred will not be tolerated. Much like the moth who flies into the flame (high frequency relative to the physical body of the moth), so too shall those of you who hold on to old, low-frequency habits of thought and emotion not be able to withstand the higher relative frequencies that are coming.

Find those fears rooted deeply within and examine them for what they are—low frequency vibrational emanations that only exist to the extent that you are disconnected within from Creator Source. We find that many of you would rather "go down with the ship" than offend or go against your family or loved ones. If this be your choice, then so be it!

However, you will be less than satisfied when you make your transition back into the non-physical domain, for your plans for this experience were to face and OVERCOME your limitations and fears—NOT succumb to them! Now would be a good time to consider well the consequences of any decisions you have made which may not be "sitting" too well with the nudges from your Higher Self.

The casting of the play is ALWAYS flexible and there is ALWAYS enough room to include any and all who wish to participate. As ones come and go through choices and decisions made each moment, adjustments are made so as to maximize opportunities for individual and collective growth, while also utilizing the available talent pool to the fullest extent.

For those of you who walk this particular path of active, dedicated Ground Crew at this time, it is quite challenging, for the pace is rapid and there is little time to appreciate subtleties along the way.

Let us end here for now, for my scribe needs to take a break from sitting in front of the computer screen. Hatonn to stand by.

October 2, 1997

Hatonn here to continue. I come in the Light of Holy God of Light! Be at peace.

There are great pressures for you ones in the physical at this time. There come, with these pressures, increased opportunities for growth and self realization. Many are, at this time, having difficulty with all the variables impacting their experience (both man-made and natural).

Perhaps the greatest distraction at present is the element of "time" as you ones perceive of it. Time is a plastic, yet relative, quantity that only exists in the physical reality. Plastic means that it is easily deformed and shaped; relative means that it is directly connected to your current environment and is a by-product of each person's perception and agreement in relation to your planetary alignment.

When you ones move away from the surface of your planet, there is the observable phenomenon of "variable time". This is best illustrated by your astronauts who have taken their atomic clocks up in orbit around the Earth. While these clocks should not lose or vary in accuracy more than a second over several thousands of years, they have been observed being several seconds "off" from their reference clock, after only a couple of weeks in orbit around your planet.

There is much that your scientists do not understand about your "physical" universe. The frequency shift as ones move away from your planet's presently-darkened energy field will cause a speed-up in the "relative" surroundings of these ones, and thus the "time" shifts. The decay rate of nuclear material also is affected by the frequency of its relative environment. The trapped darkness (low-frequency energy), in conjunction with the intensifying high-frequency energies infusing your planet currently, cause localized temporal distortions which can be quite disconcerting and even disorienting to those of you who are wondering where all of your "time" has gone.

Moreover, there are major external factors affecting your current environment (relative surroundings). Your planetary orb (starship) is entering into a relatively high-frequency energy field in space. This is the so-called "Photon Belt" area that we have talked about prior (and which *CONTACT* will re-run from my April 25, 1992 lecture as soon as room permits). This is a natural course of evolvement of your planet as she traverses space. This is a time for renewal and cleansing of the old—a rebirthing and new beginning. Like the caterpillar that is ready to come out of its cocoon and be reborn into the next phase of existence, so too is your planet readying herself for transformation into her next phase of existence.

You each know that there are great rewards in the way of growth and realizations to be gained from going through this process with your planet. You ones are being caused to confront the low-frequency emotional pains. You will have need to let go of these things which cause you to be held in the lower vibrations. It is time to face your fears and look closely at that upon which you focus your energy. The lower frequencies of fear, hate, apathy, greed, and such will cause you ever-increasing discomfort in the times to come.

This should serve as a guidance system for you (a "bio-feedback mechanism") so that you can learn to recognize the habits of thoughts that you ones are fond of holding onto which cause your vibrational frequency to lower. These are like computer programs which, at one time, perhaps helped you to deal with a difficult situation. Or, for some of you, you hold onto past pains that assaulted your perception of "reality". Physical loss of a loved one, whose death you were not prepared to accept, is perhaps the most common type of thought which will cause your frequency to be lowered.

There is no death, and there is no time in the Larger Picture, and there is no separation—meaning that ones for whom you grieve are still "there", though they may not be presently focused in the physical. You each create your own worst hell.

The "lonely hearts" of ones who perceive of themselves as somehow being alone or without a mate, is perhaps the next greatest affliction that we find many of you of Ground Crew focused upon that lowers your frequency. Your relationships are not working out for most of you because it was not your intent at this time to focus in that direction. Yet, the "social" pressures of society, coupled with the natural biological urges, make this a difficult challenge to deal with. We find many of our Ground Crew members embroiled in very difficult personal situations that will, again, cause ones to weed themselves from any great level of participation due to the pressures of family situations.

It is time to look within and find your inner convictions concerning who you "really" are and what it is that you are wanting to accomplish in this life's experience. YOU are responsible for whether or not YOU will evolve with your planet, or be cleansed from the physical experience. There shall be far more cleansed than not, and your choices, thoughts, and actions will determine your next environment of focused existence.

Go within for your guidance. Search the depths of your inner being. Find first a point of balance within the Light, and from there see that which is pulling on you, trying to shift your focus elsewhere. Almost without exception this will be a fear or doubt that causes you worry or consideration. This is where you must find the cause of your fear or doubt and overcome the challenge if you are to keep up with the frequency shifts that are coming.

Fear and doubt are by-products of being disconnected from Source. Effort to strengthen your connection, and the fears will show themselves to you, for the adversary does not wish to lose his foothold within you, and there will be a flare-up within. Regain your point of balance within the Light and see the fear for what it is! Reconnect and know that this is a challenge for you to face.

Fear of being rejected by loved ones who "just don't understand" or fear of the embarrassment that you may have to face for making a "paranoid" decision like wanting to store up six months of food for the family in preparation for hard times ahead, are common challenges that you ones are being faced with. Many will simply succumb to these fears.

The job of the wayshower is seldom a popular one, yet it is quite rewarding after the fact, in retrospect, looking back. Many a wealthy person will wish they had been awake enough to see the clues staring them in the face. The regret is heavy for the person of means who only later sees how they could have made a difference.

Let go of the fears! You did not come into this experience to win a popularity contest; you knew that there would be these challenges to face and that you would have to make unpopular decisions and choices. The way of your "modern" world is the way of insanity—where black is called white, up is called down, and wrong is right. Confusion reigns supreme and ones are programed about what to think and how to act, talk, dress, and respond, so as to "fit-in" and be "normal".

As always, the choices are yours to make and we shall honor your choices. Our promise to you ones reading this is that we would send forth the necessary guidance and instructions so that you would have the tools to overcome your challenges. We never said we would force you to recognize or use these gifts! We shall assist you each when the petition is sincere—made with the heart and not with the tongue.

I am Gyeorgos Ceres Hatonn, Commander of this mission. I come with the Hosts of God by way of Pleiades. I come in and of the Light of Creator Source. Salu!

CHAPTER NINETEEN

There Shall Be No Lie Left Unexposed!

Esu "Jesus" Sananda
October 25, 1997

Good afternoon, my scribe. I, Esu Immanuel "Jesus" Sananda, have come at this time that a much-needed message go forth.

Your environment is changing and, with each passing day, you will notice more and more outward signs of this change. Many resist the change and will refuse to see the clues all about them. These are the times prophesied some two thousand years past.

There shall be no lie left unexposed!

The heart of man will become as an open book for all to read. The quiet (behind the scenes) manipulators of those ones who crave power, control, and physical material are beginning to see that their games no longer work and that the whole world can see right through them. These ones need the cloak of secrecy in order to keep their "status" in society. This is to say that their ego demands the status and these ones are slaves to their ego-self.

Such was the fall of one called Lucifer ("the Lighted

one"). As he continues to succumb to the pressures of his ego, he efforts to manipulate others to walk his path and thus justify his position or argument with his Creator—GOD!

You cannot be greater than He who created you! In the physical, you may become greater than your parents in some material way, but you can NEVER be more than Infinite Source. You CAN attain the level of a "leading-edge" awareness WITH Him, and therein is the background for the statement "I and my Father are one".

To hide in secrecy, due to shame of actions taken, is but to deny self-responsibility. If you are hiding, then you know that you have done something wrong. Yet, God knows you! You are not hiding from Him!

And, as your environment continues to shift upward in frequency, so too shall your physically-oriented brethren come to know the REAL you—as a result of a heightened perception of the interconnectedness between all things.

It is time to let go of the garbage and the pretense, for the days of pretending are over. YOUR responsibility for YOUR own spiritual growth is becoming ever more apparent to all as more of you ones "grow up". Would you take on the blame because another has chosen to smoke cigarettes for many years and now has lung cancer? No, the "blame" and consequences fall squarely on the shoulders of the one choosing to chronically poison their vehicle in such a manner. THIS IS A TIME FOR HONESTLY CONFRONTING THYSELF!

Those of you who cannot accept the changes happening all around you, and who are embroiled deeply in the physical-material aspect of this experience, will find yourselves in an ever more difficult environment in which to survive.

To begin with, ones will no longer see you as somehow being helpless. Ones will see you, rightfully, as a Fragment of Creator.

So when you try to make excuses for your actions or

inactions, such will be seen for the ego, fear-based responses (fear being the polar opposite of Joy/Love/GOD!) that they are, and there will be little-to-no sympathy to be found. Thus the ego-self will literally starve into submission, or the physical experience will expire due to the severe unbalanced condition.

This message is intended as a "heads-up" indicator to you who are seeking, so that you can know the mechanism by which peace shall be attained on your planet. When there can be no lie or manipulation or conspiracy, then there can be no war.

When you finally can see your brethren, animals, and plants with the eyes of a TRULY connected soul, you will see the beauty and magnificence of Creator in ALL things. You will not listen to anyone who speaks of destroying any part of it!

You ones are experiencing in truly wondrous times, for there are great insights to be experienced, and even greater growth to be achieved, as this transformation unfolds. Our purpose is to assist each of you with this process and to provide you with guidance when you have TRUE desire for same.

You may do that which you will with what is offered here. Our hope is that you will look beyond the words, and go within and connect for yourself, and experience the meaning and intent of each message. You will find that such is offered with great Love and Higher Understanding.

Your world is in great, great chaos and you are not being shown anywhere near the whole picture from your general media sources. This is in large part due to the fact that the illusionary façade of the "elite" is failing to fool you-the-people.

MANY are beginning to see through the lies—especially those of you who maintain selves in a high-frequency state. Thus, those who are responsible for manipulating (mind-controlling) you through such media conduits have had to provide ever more "artificial"

"entertainment" for your consumption in the guise of your so-called news programs. In many respects, your "news" must be carefully manufactured, and even more carefully presented, to avoid having to tell you truth.

However, as more and more people draw upon the Courage to speak out, the truth of any situation cannot be contained. This is the TRUE meaning of the phrase "the power of the people" and it would be wise to remember that such is your birthright as a Lighted fragment of Creator Source. In this regard is there "safety in numbers" since the control tactics of the "elite" would-be-kings break down when enough stand in the Light of Truth and share that Truth. And as I said so many years ago, to those ones close to me at that time, who likewise battled with their fears of inadequacy or overwhelm: "Where two or more are gathered in my name, I am also there!"

The programing of the people has one great error and that is the fact that the God-force within can only be contained with the consent of the individual. When there comes, within the individual, a desire to understand and be free, then there is no programing, anywhere, that can contain the potential energy of that desire! To attempt to contain such desire defies the most fundamental Law of The Creation: "Achieve the wisdom of knowledge inasmuch as this will enable you to wisely follow the Laws of The Creation."

This is the Power behind the phrase "the call compels the answer" and the controllers know their days are numbered as you Lighted ones wake up and ask, with heart desire, to be shown Truth, for those are powerful energies of inquiry set into motion, and such sincere questioning also then allows us (gives us permission in your free-will environment) to help you more in finding those answers you seek.

Meanwhile, the experience of being a "puppet" has its value, too, in the evolutionary cycles of the soul. The value comes from the experience of overcoming "the lie". You must agree to be trapped in order to be trapped. Many of you enjoy the challenge of solving difficult puzzles and will, at some level, agree to become trapped. Again, there are NO victims, only volunteers.

With this said I, Esu Sananda, hope you can see that there is no fear-mongering here and that I am simply pointing out the observable facts. **For a great deal of your population, the fear of death is only surpassed by the fear of living!** This is to say that many of you have been mentally conditioned (mind controlled) to worry about doing the "right" thing. So much so that you actually spend more time contemplating activity than actually DOING.

Your fears of doing the "wrong" thing cause you to procrastinate to the point of inaction. These are the subtle tactics of the "puppet masters" who are pulling your strings.

For those of you who are sitting out there wondering "What can I do?" I say to you: go within and find within your heart that which has great value to you in terms of inner fulfillment. Then take action while holding the Inner Joy foremost within. From this position of True Power you can create universes, let alone move the mountains that seem to be in your way.

You limit yourselves; it is not God or some evil being somewhere who does so. You are, indeed, your own worst enemy, by far! Look within and cast out that which causes you worry (fear). There is nothing to worry about or fear when you TRULY understand WHO you are and acknowledge, WITH FEELING, your personal connection within to All That Is!

You only have to get quiet, and find within, that which your heart will guide you to, and then you will know with certainty that there is NOTHING to fear—EVER!

Look forward to the rebalancing-rebirthing process that is taking place at this time. It is what you came here to be a part of and experience. Your inner desire is in alignment with facing the challenges of this experience.

May you have the Eyes to see, the Ears to hear, and the

Heart to understand that which is coming into your experience.

I am Esu Immanuel Sananda. Many refer to me as "Jesus". The name matters not, for in time that too will fade. I come to honor my promise to your world and to my Father, that all of my responsibilities be met. With great Love, I place my blessing upon this message.

In Light and Love, Salu!

CHAPTER TWENTY

Consciously Focusing The Creative Energy Within

Ceres Anthonious Soltec
November 2, 1997

Good afternoon, my friend. It is I, Toniose Soltec, come in the Radiant One Light of Creator Source. Be at PEACE!

Please find comfort in knowing that ALL is as it should be, and that there are reasons for ALL things. You may not be able to see the WHY at any given moment, but with persistence in your searching, that which you seek WILL be revealed to you as you are ready for same.

From a Higher perspective, all is seen in terms of energy flows. The ability for one to understand and use these energies in a responsible manner is what "living" is all about. There would seem to be various conflicts in this idea, for many are efforting to utilize energy in such a manner as to keep others from tapping and utilizing the same Potential within. This sort of suppression is what has placed your world in the state of turbulence that it is in today.

As ones begin to awaken to the TRUE purpose of experience, they will rightfully begin to utilize their own inner determination, and thus also begin—perhaps for the first time in their current experience—to take control of their destiny. This is a new experience for most of you—to CONSCIOUSLY take control of your life, that is, take control of your energy flows.

Most, at this time, are in a state of semi-consciousness and are constantly being lulled back to sleep or overwhelmed to a point of various levels of shut-down. This is to say that ones are being bombarded so heavily with external pressures and worries that they find little-to-no time for the inner part of life that would bring nourishment and balance.

Money has become a primary consideration for most people. Your world has become "brain-washed" into believing that you must first create the money before you can have anything.

This is a very big lie!

Money is, in its purest form, a means of exchanging energy. The fundamental concept is not too different from the flow of electricity in a circuit and the storage of that energy in a battery. You work (put forth energy) in exchange for dollars, which are a mode of storing that energy of work. The dollars can then be converted back into energy by such as paying a contractor to build a new front porch for you, or even by purchasing a washing machine, which itself is the product of the labors (energy) of others.

The most overlooked fact is that the process of creation begins with *desire*, not money. The inner desire of the heart will radiate out to the rest of the universe and your desires will begin to manifest.

If you struggle constantly to find money, then your focus must be upon dollars. Let me ask you this: Did you come into this experience to seek out and create dollars?

Let us assume your answer is "No!" Then why do most of you put dollars foremost in your experience?

Those of you who focus on projects and see them as complete, seldom have any problem with the incidentals of money. The difference is in your thoughts or beliefs about same. If you believe that you must first have the money prior to doing anything, then you are greatly mistaken and very little will get done while you wait and continue to worry.

Remember your past lessons. You live in a bi-polar, electric, pulse-wave universe. The physical is a PRODUCT of this energy—not the other way around. The energy that created your planet, Sun, solar system, galaxy, universe, and beyond came first in the form of desire—not money! Who could pay for such?! How much do each of you pay for the Sun to shine each day?!

The point here is to illustrate that money is a distant second to the creative desire that wells up within. If you are having trouble with money, then look carefully at what you plan to do with it when you get it.

When you can take what little you have and move forward an inner desire, and put energy into manifesting your desire, you will find a multiplication of that energy because the most basic Law of Creation states: Go forth and create!

And thus expand and grow. This implies the use of energy. The same energy that was used to create the physical universe! The same energy that was used to create YOU!

When you can become more focused upon the end desire of what it is that you want, and not upon the money you think you need to accomplish that end desire, you will have 90% of the creation completed. You will only have to recognize the opportunities when they present themselves to you. In most cases you will be amazed by the coincidences that begin manifesting all around you! This is how you create the "miracles". This is the secret to creating your own "luck"—whether it be good or bad.

There is no reason that any of you should lack for anything you are wanting. For many of you, you have been trained to believe you must work hard for what you have. I say to you now: when you can get rid of these old programs and come into a better understanding of the TRUE nature of yourself, as well as the energy framework of the current experience you are in, you will realize that this limitation is not so!

How hard do you think God "worked" at creating YOU or your physical universe with its TRILLIONS of suns and planets? He did not have to "work" at this, for He understands perfectly the Laws of Creation! Neither do you, when you can let go of the old ways of thinking.

When your idea is more inspired than not, others will recognize the value of adding their energy to yours in both desire, and if need be, money. This is the secret of those who are "lightning rods" for facilitating projects. The magnetism of the confidence they radiate literally attracts whatever is needed to accomplish the goal.

When the focus is more on the LACK of something, then the energy you attract will be more of the same, and you will multiply your LACK! This is at the heart (pun intended) of the mind-control programing strategy aimed at you ones by the "elite" would-be kings. If you can come to recognize what is at work here, you can reverse this downward spiral.

When a good idea can be held in the heart, and you can see the idea begin to manifest ever more solidly within, you will, if you hold the thought long enough, begin to attract more and more ideas (details) into your consciousness, if you but ALLOW for them to come. This is where the value of focused persistence comes into the equation. Maybe the better word here is to become "passionate" about your ideas! What is fundamentally implied is the FLOWING of creative energies in the same way that electricity or water or wind currents must flow to be useful in the natural order of balanced energy exchange.

Many of you will block these energy flows due to past programing of your "middle-class" (suppressed) upbringing. Those of you who came from a more affluent upbringing will generally find that you seldom lack those things you desire, for you were not programed with negative beliefs regarding money. Any of you can overcome the past programing and beliefs, and thus change how you flow energy.

When you become more CONSCIOUSLY aware of how you are focusing your energy (thoughts and desires), you will begin the first step necessary for taking control of your destiny. You will find that you spend less time sitting around waiting for something to "happen" and more time creating the life experiences you want.

The manner in which you focus your energy is directly related to all aspects of your life. Whether it be money or health concerns or relationships with others, look first to where you are placing your thoughts and desires (energy). You will see that, for instance, when you overly fixate upon (pump energy into) a health problem, then there will be a MULTIPLICATION of that desire—and it will likely get worse! This is why a placebo is so often effective for "curing" someone—because they believe and thus focus their thoughts on the new belief instead of the old. Esu "Jesus" Immanuel rarely healed anyone while in his teaching mission upon your planet. Rather, it was usually the strong belief of those he touched which allowed these "passionate" ones to heal themselves.

The Creation is not interested in what, from your vantage point, you may term "good" or "evil", "right" or "wrong". The Creation is only interested in expansion and growth. From that experiential vantage point, ALL can be viewed as learning.

When you put forth a desire, and hold that desire within your heart, it will be multiplied. When you are inspired, you most often pump great energy into that inspired idea, and thus you will see more clearly the energy amplification. This is a key to the success of those you call great artists. From a technical point of view, success comes from the energy-accumulating (and thus idea-manifesting) condition held in place by the "force field" of the inspiration.

Likewise, when you hold onto a state of negativity, negativity shall accumulate around you. When you live, for instance, in a chronic state of depression, you will often pump great amounts of energy into the depression, and thus amplify your "desire" for more depression.

This is why it is often said that there are two great motivators of people—INSPIRATION and DESPERATION. Remember: you live in that "bi-polar" (yin verses yang, positive versus negative, yes versus no, right versus wrong), electromagnetic, pulse-wave universe of Light.

There are ones on your planet at this time who know well these basic concepts of energy flow and energy utilization, but not all of them are what you would refer to as "nice" people. When these ones can keep you, in a sense, "fat, dumb, and happy" between the two polar-opposite extremes, then they can more easily control you.

That is, like a cornered animal, if you are driven to become too desperate, you become dangerous to these ones who are trying to control you. In a condition of desperation, your resourcefulness may be "inspired" to kick-in and do something creative.

Likewise, when you finally awaken to the true (energy-driven) nature of this material "canvas" upon which you have chosen to "paint", your everyday levels of confidence and inspiration become such that you cannot easily be fooled or controlled, and there again you become a threat to the would-be controllers. The last thing they want is for you to grow beyond their manipulation techniques!

This is enough for now. This message contains the insights which many are looking for, yet do not quite know it. May this be of value to those of you who desire to know why your life's experiences have been what they have been. I am Ceres Anthonious "Toniose" Soltec, come as Teacher and Guide. I am sent by our Father, Aton (The One Light). Blessings and Salu!

November 22, 1997

Good morning, my friend. It is I, Toniose Soltec, come

in the Radiant One Light of our Father. Be at peace, for there is work to be done.

At our last writing session before important interruptions, we left off talking about energy flows and the dynamics of creating. These principles are the basis for bringing into existence all that you recognize as manifest reality—whether we are talking about a child's creation of a clay turtle, or Creator's manifestation of an entire universe.

We can see that many do not hold long in their consciousness these ideas, for there are great numbers of distractions all about you. These distractions are, for the most part, deliberately calculated and set into motion by those who are efforting at controlling every one and every thing. These ones provide you, who have desire to be free and to grow through your limitations, with a most challenging environment in which to experience!

Look not upon these ones with negativity in your heart, but with appreciation for presenting you with such challenges that will bring forth the growth that you desire! Many of you in previous times were in similar capacities as these ones are, and you are now seeing the play from the opposite perspective. This is so that you can appreciate the value of both experiences, so that you can better choose what helps you to grow in a quite responsible manner. Such are the cycles of experience when viewed from a more expansive perspective.

The importance of recognizing consciously how you are utilizing your energy at any (and every) given moment is the key to creating your heart's desires. When you ones become overly fixated upon a negative condition that you witness, you tend to get stuck and thus constrict the natural cosmic energy flow through you into the physical realm. Joy comes from allowing the energy to flow naturally and freely. You can know how your energy is flowing simply by how you are *feeling* at any given moment in time. I do not mean here how you THINK you are feeling (an intellectual focus, often susceptible to lack of honesty with self), but how you actually ARE feeling (an emotional reading of the heart).

YOU decide how you are going to focus your energy (thoughts and desires)! Thus the responsibility of how you are feeling at any given moment in time is up to you, and you alone. If you perceive yourself to be a victim, and you spend any length of time dwelling on this idea, you will surely begin to manifest your desire to be a victim.

So then you say, "BUT, I DO NOT WANT TO BE A VICTIM!"

I say to you that what you dwell upon, you radiate as a desire, and The Creation responds to you, for you are a CREATOR! Whether you recognize this consciously or not, YOU *ARE* A CREATOR, MADE IN THE IMAGE OF *THE* CREATOR SOURCE OF ALL THAT IS!

Your desires are what you manifest. What you mouth has very little to do with it! When you entered into your current experience, you knew there would be the challenges of distractions which the physical expression would provide. You also knew there would be great value in overcoming these distractions, that you would learn from them how to more deliberately focus your thoughts and desires, and ultimately expand and grow as an extension of Creator.

Let me give you an insight that may help you to see more clearly the point here. Make a list of all the things that you are wanting. Write out next to your list why you are wanting these things. If you stop now and take the time to do this, prior to reading further, you will recognize a greater impact from the points I have made above. So stop reading, and make a list of everything you are wanting and why you are wanting them. You can have ANYTHING.

Now I am assuming that you have made your list. And if you could see from my perspective, you would recognize how basically similar are so many of the wants on your lists.

In order to point out how it is that you are focusing your energy, look at what it is you are wanting—and more importantly, WHY.

Let's say that you wanted a good, strong, healthy body.

Most all of you want that. Now let us look at the reasons for wanting this.

Why do you want the good strong healthy body? Is it because you hate feeling bad or sick? Is it because you do not want to be inhibited in any way? Is it because you don't like being a burden to others? Is it because you have things to do and you don't want to be held back in any way? OR—is it because you love to have the energy to do the things that you are wanting to do when you want to do them? You love the adventure of living and the exhilaration of freedom. Is it because you appreciate the balance of well-being that radiates from within?

I hear you saying, "Well, all of those are good reasons!" Well, I say to you: let us look at these reasons more carefully and perhaps we can see where it is you are, energy-wise (pun intended), in relation to your desire for a good, strong, healthy body.

First, take all of the "don'ts" and "do nots" out of the above reasons, especially before the "OR" in the above example. When you say, "I don't want to be inhibited", you are radiating to the universe and all of Creation INHIBITION!

The "don'ts" and "do nots" fail to register an emotional (energy) intent because they are merely "window dressing" words on otherwise worry-laden and fear-laden underlying actions. See this, and more importantly, FEEL this.

That is, when you say you "don't" want to be inhibited by a sick body, what are you actually thinking (and emotionally worrying) about? You are thinking about being inhibited by a sick body! You can't help but begin to radiate the thought of inhibition. Likewise, when you "hate feeling bad" this idea will cause you to dwell upon the idea of feeling bad—and you will actually cause yourself to feel bad if you stay with the thought long enough!

When you can shift your focus to a vision of a young, strong, healthy body, full of energy and life, eager to explore new and exciting environments, full of joy—without dwelling upon the negative reasons—then you will be radiating with the heart in perfect synchronization with your head-desire, and the energy will begin to manifest quickly and, in many cases, miraculously.

Let's make this contrast clearer with another example. Consider the following two statements:

(1) I hate to come home to a dirty house.

(2) I love to come home to a clean house.

At first glance you might say that the statements are saying the same thing. However the vibration induced by the two positions will cause you to FEEL quite a bit different. Recognize that the two are polar opposites. Would you rather attract into your experience "hate" of dirt or "love" of cleanliness? FEEL the effect of each, even as you read these words!

When you can discipline yourselves to use thoughts which cause an UPLIFTMENT WITHIN, rather than a downward negativity, you will have realized a key to synchronizing the head and the heart. Please appreciate the direct "physics" of what I am explaining here: We are talking about the consequences of higher- versus lower-frequency energy radiations. There is much more POWER OF MANIFESTATION within the higher-frequency emanation, for such joy-generated energy is DIRECTLY FLOWING from the Infinite Source! The awesome power of this Energy is what the dark ones wish you to remain ignorant about, and thus they do everything within their abilities to subvert or divert it.

You ones are being bombarded with negativity that is constantly influencing your thoughts. The "don'ts" and "do nots" are everywhere in your daily doses of mind-control programing.

We witness many of you pumping out contrary vibrational frequencies to that of your desires. This is to say that the mental focus is not in harmony with the emotional emanations coming forth from within. Many are wanting from an energy vibration of fear. The fear of the unknown.

When the fear of lack wells up within, we see that many are preoccupied with the fear and thus dwell in such an emotional state as to cut-off themselves from the natural energy flows of Creator. In actuality, it is more a constriction of the Energy than a complete disconnect, else your own physical manifestation could not maintain form and you would die.

The point of this exercise is to show you that though you are saying you want one thing, you are often radiating the opposite. Look to your list of reasons and remove all of the "don'ts" and "do nots". Also look for words with a negative feeling to them like "hate". These statements are often reflections of the self-talk or thoughts that go through your mind when you focus upon your desires.

Learn to focus your thoughts deliberately and, most importantly, learn to focus your FEELINGS associated with your desires. When you can feel good about the subject of your desires, then you can know that your energy is flowing in a direction that is in alignment with who you really are and why you are there.

This is the reason behind the statement we of the Hosts have made so often to you, that if you can't do a thing *with love in your heart*, it is better to not do the thing at all. And we would also call to your attention the wise words to the older popular song which go: "Accentuate the positive, eliminate the negative—and look out for Mr. in-between." Consider these ideas from the point of view of energy flow and you are well on your way to a more fulfilling and productive experience—as Creator intended!

If, over a period of time, you begin to feel anxiety over a specific desire or subject of focus, then it is because there is always a multiplication of your desire. This is to say that you are projecting that which causes the anxiety to well-up within. This is as it should be, and you can be thankful in knowing that your Inner Guidance system is functioning properly and presenting you with that which requires your attention toward balancing.

With simple effort to change your focus toward something that makes you FEEL better, you can take conscious control over your emotional state at any given time. Perhaps the most simple and direct way is to look around you and find something to appreciate.

Can you appreciate the Sun that warms your day and gives forth life-producing energy? Can you appreciate the rain that waters the vegetation that gives forth, directly or indirectly to you, energy in the form of nourishment? Can you see how wonderful is the opportunity that you have before you to meet your challenges and thus grow beyond who you are this day? Can you see that the environment in which you find yourself is, in fact, perfect for providing you with these challenges?

The excitement of the journey is most often that which you long for, not the destination. You are infinite, experiencing beings. You are co-creators who are directly expanding the ALL THAT IS. Within you lies Infinite Potential to create. You are molders of this Energy. Your greatest joy comes from flowing this Energy—not bottling it up or hoarding it like your "elite" would-be controllers attempt to do.

When a goal is reached and the journey is over, you are often left looking for your next challenge. This is to say that you are left looking for another journey of experience. These are the endless cycles of life—both in the physical dimensions and beyond.

Money makes a good analogy, for it symbolizes energy and is a commodity you all can easily relate to. Let me leave you with this thought: is there more fun in saving money (energy), or in spending it (setting it into motion)?

I am Ceres Anthonious "Toniose" Soltec, come in the Radiant One Light of Creator Source. May you find inner understanding beyond the limitations of these words. And from that Source of Understanding, may YOUR joy radiate from within and thus be that which manifests all around you.

Salu!

CHAPTER TWENTY-ONE

Keeping FEAR Out Of *Your* Creative Equation

Ceres Anthonious Soltec
December 7, 1997

Good morning, my friend. It is I, Toniose Soltec, come in the Radiant One Light of Creator Source. Be at peace.

Allow for the unfolding of the drama that you ones find yourselves in at this time. Many decisions are being made at all levels of consciousness that will have impact upon you ones in the physical. Allow for the changes to come forth in their natural order. Resist NOT, and the ride will be far less draining. Allow for the NATURAL FLOW of experience.

Hold loosely to the past ways of doing things, for there will be great need for you ones to be "adaptable" in the coming days, months, and years. There is a very real mission to get done, and yet there are few who will have the fortitude to see it through to completion. These are the experiences which will challenge you to go within and tap the Inner Strength that will eventually lead to a higher level of inner and outer awareness. This is GROWTH!

Allow for the free-will choices of others. Be slow to

judge the person, for you do not know another's contract. Discern the actions of those who impact your daily lives around you. Go within for your Guidance and ask for clarification of what is right for YOU. Sit not long on the fence of indecision. Make your choices only after giving deliberate thought to all of the possible consequences of the outcome of making your decision.

Your life experiences are for YOU to decide; no other can tell you how to live YOUR experience. A wise man will gather as much data as he can prior to his choosing. However, in the end, the choice and the responsibility of the choice are up to the individual.

You are each "cutting" your own path through this experience, and the uniqueness of each one's path is as much a part of the experience as is the destination. Follow your HEART and it will lead you to that which you are seeking. If you just blindly follow another, you will only find that which the other is seeking, and that is rarely what you are seeking.

This is not to say that ones cannot function as a team to accomplish their collective goals. Quite the opposite! How do you think that we of the Hosts accomplish missions on a scale such as this planetary transition and transformation? However, that collective goal should be a part of YOUR heart intent, else you act under "false" pretense, and such can only generate restlessness—and certainly NOT provide the inner feeling of satisfaction you all crave that comes from following your own true path.

Be not afraid of going against the "norm". Who cares what your neighbors or relatives "think"? Do you live your life in fear of what others "think" about you? If so, why? Is their way better than yours? Do they even have a "way"? Or are they simply critical of you from their own reactions of fear?

We of the non-physical realms often witness you ones efforting to compare yourselves to one another in such a manner as to melt consciousness into one giant statistical

"norm". What is normal? What is RIGHT? What is good?

There are no wrong choices in your experience. Even in making choices that lead you away from your Creator, you have in fact presented self with more information from which to again make other choices. Hopefully these new, later choices will then be more en-Light-ened. A wise man will always strive to make better choices.

Many are simply stuck in routine habits which generate more of whatever it is they already have. "Why rock the boat?" is a phrase we often hear you ones use as an excuse to avoid overcoming your fear of the unknown. Is mediocrity YOUR desire? Look around you and know that what you have in your day-to-day experience is a product of your desire.

Many are going within at this time and asking for direction. Many want to do more, yet claim they do not know how.

You start by taking the first step! If you want to help spread The Word, but you only have one dollar you can spare at this moment, can you not take that dollar and copy an article and pass it to just one person who may be interested? In doing so, have you not just taken a step toward achieving your goal?

In the act of taking the physical action, you will have set into motion GREAT CREATIONAL ENERGIES which will begin to come back to you—amplified. Perhaps the next week you will find that you have two dollars extra that you can spend toward the same goal.

You ones must learn to exploit your creative ingenuity. There is plenty that you each can do, right in your own city or town, toward helping to spread the information that will stand as testament to what is REALLY taking place in your world.

Again we get back to the subject of fear! Many of you will simply not speak up when an opportunity arises—out of fear that someone may speak or think badly of you.

Why do you think that we have offered, in these pages

of *CONTACT,* such extensive information regarding the subject of mind control? We effort toward helping you to recognize how subtle yet pervasive are the methods in daily use in your lives.

You live in a society which has been taught and trained to believe that you must all operate within certain parameters in order to "fit-in" or be "cool" or be "normal". Pursuing this goal is a "religion" for many on your planet!

Yet, this situation is also why so many of you who are reading this message don't quite "fit-in" with the average mentality that seems to surround you. It is the FEAR of rejection which keeps the masses stuck in the artificial "norm" of the day. These ones can only mimic what they see on television or experience in their social gatherings, such as at school, church, or in their work place.

Many are constantly being "preached to" as to what is appropriate and what is not. Many do not wish to "rock the boat" when it comes to disrupting the "norm".

This is a deliberate assault aimed at stifling individual creativity!

When you look within for your answers to the question "What can I do?" — can you not see that the answer is often there, staring you in the face. Oh, to be sure, that answer may not at first be as glorious or as glamorous or as "warm and fuzzy" as you imagined (or hoped) it would be. But, if you persist through the first steps of the creation process, you may find the inner satisfaction of creating something that would not have existed otherwise! And, by the way, this is not a trite statement when you remember that EACH of you Lighted ones are UNIQUE aspects of Creator, and thus have within you the potential for UNIQUE solutions.

Let us take, for example, that you wish to help awaken others around you to the REAL state of your world. Can you not gather and copy older or current articles from this publication [*the* CONTACT *newspaper*] and share them with ones who may be interested? In time you may find that there are MANY, right in your own neighborhood, who would love to discuss issues addressed in such articles. We choose our material wisely.

How will you ever know—if you don't take the first step? There are MANY out there who have already done this and have, in effect, established "teams" of like-minded people in their towns or cities. This is a unity of purpose.

Like attracts like. Those who operate from a position of fear will likely be repelled by anything which disrupts their comfortable feeling of security that stems from the lies they are fed by the controlled media. These ones, though they may now laugh at or ridicule you for attempting to share Truth with them, will later be the ones who come to you most desperately, seeking The Truth that they shunned before.

Please know that it is, ironically, the more aware ones who are likely to react in this manner. Why? Because these ones can think through the implications of what you offer, and such makes them very uncomfortable. Thus the reactions.

These are the ones we are here to assist through the transition at hand!

These are our brothers that YOU, as Ground Crew, have come to help! The gratitude will not be evident, in most cases, until after the fact. However, when you cause another to think past what is the confining "norm", please know that you are helping to fulfill God's promise to send wayshowers in these times of change.

This is not an easy challenge, and many of you are weary of being bashed by the very ones you have come to help. And THIS is your challenge! From time to time, there is need to offer a reminder, such as this, of why you are there at this time.

May you find the inner conviction to stay the course. There are great inner rewards, in the way of growth, that are to be gained. I am your Brother in service, neither greater nor lesser than another; I simply serve in my own unique and earned capacity at this time. In Light and in Service to OUR Father, I am Ceres Anthonious Soltec.

Salu—and in keeping with the TRUE spirit of this season, a season to be mindful of working toward the emerging of the Christed Energy Presence through you ones walking along the Lighted path, I wish you a Merry Christmas!

CHAPTER TWENTY-TWO

Sounding The Clarion For What Is Coming Quickly

Ceres Anthonious Soltec
December 28, 1997

Good afternoon, my friend. It is I, Toniose Soltec come in the Radiant One Light of Creator Source. Be at peace!

Thank you for sitting this day, for there are messages that need to be penned. Much is happening all around your globe this day. Many of the players in the global arena are playing their hand. This will cause a very interesting course of events on all fronts, from stock market manipulations to weather modification and, yes, earthquake and volcanic triggerings as well.

These are truly interesting times in which to be experiencing. As the evolvement of these experiences begins to more directly impact your daily lives, you will be quite happy that you have made preparations for that which IS coming. We have "sounded the clarion" yet we witness that, for a large part of your population, it has fallen on "deaf" ears. Such is the challenge of the third-dimensional compression in which you ones find yourselves.

Perhaps the most interesting course of events to follow

will be the "chain reaction" of events as the tapestry of interconnected events unravels. This is to say, again, that ALL IS CONNECTED TO ALL. The Native Americans have long tried to convey this concept.

From the perspective of an energy point of view, the intent is to exploit your world in such a manner as to keep the masses confused and off-balance, while the "elite" of your world depopulate the planet with "natural" disasters. Plagues and famine are all about you. Throw in a few earthquakes, tsunamis, hurricanes, and volcanic eruptions—all timed with the collapse of the world economy—and you will have created quite a desperate situation on your planet.

These are planned and orchestrated events that will fool the majority of your population. However there are ones among the masses who are putting forth great effort toward exposing these "elite" would-be-kings. Certain confirmations of my claims shall come from ones who have researched smaller pieces of the whole picture.

We of the Hosts have done our assigned duties in sending forth The Word, as promised that it would be! It is up to each and every individual to choose that which they will do with the information offered.

We take no offense if you choose to ignore the warnings offered, for it is not our place to judge another. However, it does sadden us when we see ones turn away from their responsibilities, for we know the agreements and the soul-intent of each who has come to participate. Our challenge is to find a route which will communicate the Guidance for which you ones so often petition.

Frequently we see ones receiving clues to that which they seek, yet these same ones do not pay attention to (or ignore) them—again, usually because of the implied responsibility which comes from acknowledging the information we send. So be it! And be careful about that which you ask, because what you will receive will most certainly NOT give-in to anyone's druthers for avoiding the responsible path.

Let us again, please, take this opportunity to "sound the clarion", for there is always the possibility that yet one more might wake-up enough to see, and thus prepare for what is coming.

Let us take a moment to address the earthquake situation.

There has been, for the last 4 weeks, an ever increasing build-up of pressure around the western side of the Pacific Tectonic Plate, otherwise known as the "Ring of Fire". Remember that both the frequency and magnitude (intensity) of earthquake activity has been greatly increasing for some 24-36 months now. What we are referring to here is a big jump in that rate of increase during the last 4 weeks.

I ask for inclusion of the world earthquake activity map for just this past week [*see next page*] covering 12/21/97 through 12/27/97. This map shows ONLY earthquake activity equal to or greater than a magnitude of 2.5 on your "discounted" measurement scale. [*Editor's note: For those of you who may not be familiar with Commander Soltec's reference to a "discounted" measurement, this is to say that earthquake intensity is typically under-reported to minimize the degree of alarm and thus keep people asleep concerning the actual magnitude of what is happening.*]

As an aside here, according to the numerical data which accompanies this map (accessed from the Internet), there were 1117 total events (earthquakes) this past week of magnitude 2.5 or greater. However, the data-handling capacity of the computer program which draws this internationally accessed map stops at 999 events (out of the 1117 total) so you are not seeing plotted on the map quite all of the activity. This situation is not a matter of incompetence by the ones who set up this collection operation; rather, there were so many earthquakes that the total number this past week EXCEEDED the capacity that was built into the data-collection machinery! THAT SITUATION, IN ITSELF, OUGHT TO BE A *BIG* CLUE TO YOU WHO PAY ATTENTION TO THE LITTLE DETAILS FOR YOUR CONFIRMATIONS!

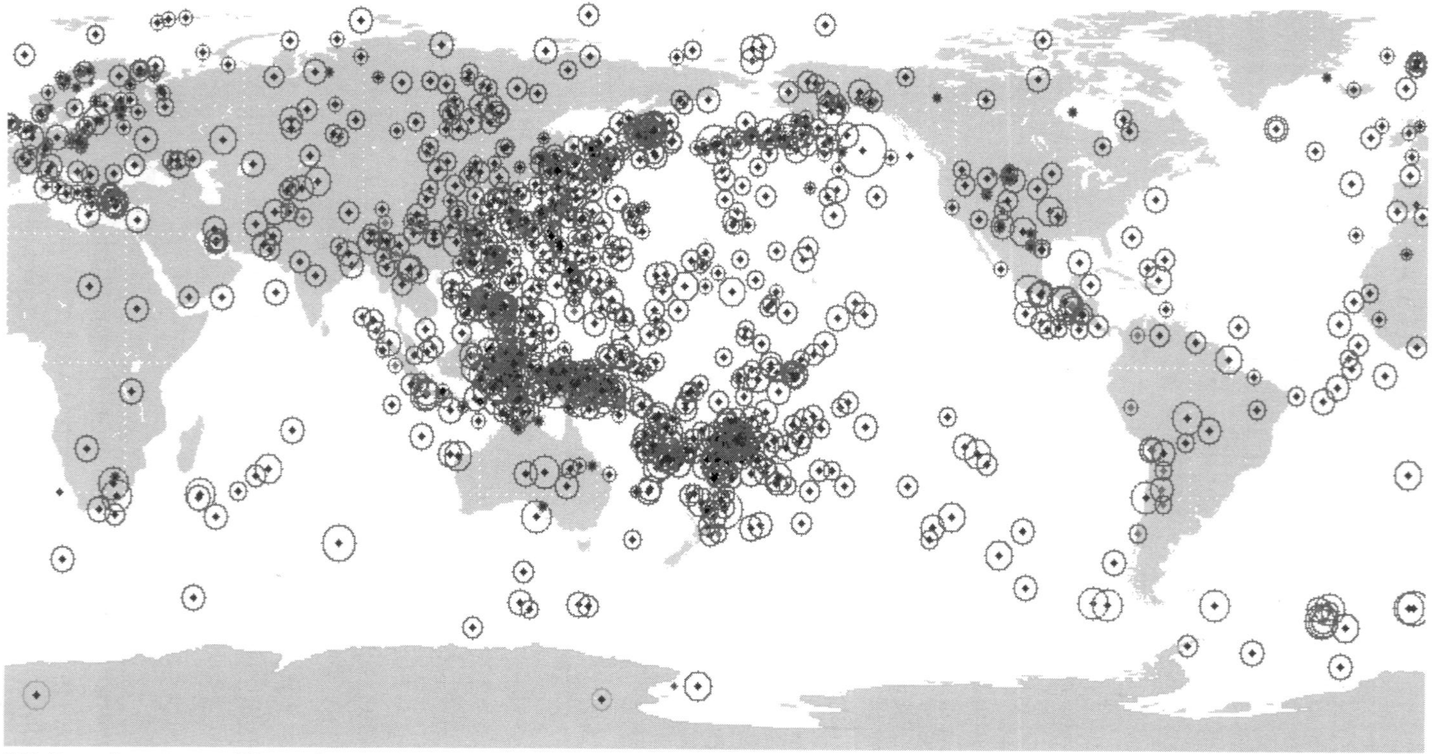

[*Editor's note: The above image came from the web site:* ***http://www.cdidc.org:65120/web-bin/recentevents*** *which is, unfortunately, no longer active as of the time of this book printing.*]

The entire western side of the Pacific Plate is in an alarming state of upheaval. From the northeastern coast of Russia, down through Japan, and on around through the South Pacific islands, there are ever increasing numbers of "moderate" quakes in the 4–5 magnitude range.

The key here is the INCREASING numbers. This means that the pressure is continuing to build and is NOT relieving, despite all of the activity.

Now look to where the seismic events are migrating and you will see that the Asian continental plate is fracturing! Look closely at Gordon-Michael Scallion's *Future Map Of The World* and you will have great insight into the change that is coming. Are Scallion's maps 100% accurate? They are accurate enough so that you would be wise to study them and heed the warning offered. [*Editor's note: To order Scallion's* Future Map Of The World *or his* Future Map Of North America *or his periodical called* Earth Changes Report, *call 1-800-628-7493 or 1-603-363-4164 or write to Matrix Institute, P.O. Box 336, Chesterfield, NH 03443-0336. You can also visit their Internet web site* ***www.matrixinstitute.com*** *if you have access to that route for gathering information.*]

Shifting attention back to a discussion of the Larger Picture, there are other players in this "chess game" who are not so "hell-bent" on destroying the planet or enslaving its population. Never, never underestimate God's divine gamesmanship—especially when there is direct petition for Guidance and Assistance.

Ones are experiencing quite "unexplained" phenomena that triggers an inner Knowing of what it is that they are involved in, and these ones, once touched in this manner, are not easily dissuaded from following what they know in their heart to be the "right" thing.

These are ones in very influential positions around the world and they are quite aware, for the most part, of the corruption and power struggles in play at this time. Be assured that God has the ultimate trump card and He will ultimately win—and do so with such style that all involved will grow in some way from having taken part in this experience.

It would be the better part of wisdom, for those of you who have not yet prepared, to do so NOW. Food, clean water, and shelter shall become quite scarce for many. Beans and rice can be procured in large quantities and are relatively inexpensive. If you have prepared for your own family, perhaps you can store extra for the neighbors. Only through true community effort will it be possible to physically survive that which is unfolding. [*Editor's note: See the* 72-Hour Kit Checklist *in Appendix B at the end of this volume.*]

May you ones effort to go within and commune with the Higher Guidance that is offered. Learn to trust the inner "gut" feelings. Please find comfort in knowing that you have within you the potential to overcome any and all challenges that cross your path. May you have the fortitude and wisdom to recognize the clues and answers to your prayers (petitions) when they are presented to you.

I am Toniose Soltec, come as a Messenger for our Father (He who created us) so that His promise to you would be fulfilled. It is within His Light that we all exist!

Salu.

CHAPTER TWENTY-THREE

A Reminder To Those Walking The "Truth Bearer" Path

Aton, The One Light
January 3, 1998

Good morning, little one. It is I, Aton, The One Light. Be at peace, for there is no need for alarm. You are quite able to translate My Energy!

There are many reasons for this interaction at this time. I have ones all around your globe bringing forth these messages. What is taking place in the U.S. is a very focused part of a much larger picture. There is, indeed, great pressure on those of you who have chosen to walk the path of "Truth bearer".

I have chosen my crew for this mission for very PERFECT reasons. You each volunteered to participate at this time—some for very specific roles, and others on an "as needed" basis. Some of you have been (or will be) filling-in for ones who fail to respond to the call. In that event, you will find that you will be given to remember past abilities and talents. If need be, I shall carry you until such time as you can walk on your own.

With such an event, there is often inner confusion as a

result of the fast-paced "ramp-up" cycle often associated with awakening these abilities. Many or you have been groomed from early childhood for the roles you are now playing. This is to say that, for a good many of you, you had to face great adversarial attacks at an early physical age.

For every one of you who made it this far, there are three or more who did not. But, so too are there others waiting and ready to "step up" if and when the need arises. Never underestimate the depth of planning for this mission.

The path that you have chosen is one of service unto your brethren. This is a most difficult challenge for the majority of the physically-oriented crew. There are great EXTERNAL pressures pulling on you—pressures to prove your physical worth to family, neighbors, and friends. Your opponent is a master at exploiting any and all insecurities. If you allow, even for a moment, your shielding to drop (frequency to lower), the adversary will attack in a manner consistent with that of a trapped animal.

When you catch yourself feeling angry or short-tempered with one another, please take a moment to breathe in and be thankful for the breath that brings you life. In the moment of TRUE heart-felt appreciation for those things that are seemingly small and subtle, you will not be able to maintain your anger with another Lighted soul, and the resultant upward frequency shift will cause the departure of the dark energy trying to cause division among you.

You will soon be reaping your just rewards (returned energy flow) for the years (lifetimes, in most cases) that you ones have spent in preparation in order to get to your current level of perception and understanding. When you lift up another and help them to their feet, so too shall you be lifted up by others. When you ignore the cry of one in need, so too shall you be ignored.

There is a speed-up at this time in which you ones will be witness to near-instant manifestation of returned energy flow. This can work for you or against you, depending upon your alignment with the flow of Creation itself.

You can no longer hide your true self from the world, for if you harbor within yourself any measure of ill intent, animosity, anger and such for another, it will come back to you amplified so quickly that the resultant drain is likely to cause severe reactions as the energy seeks its natural balance. Let go of the past and move forward! Be quick to forgive and others will be equally quick to respond to your lighter, more en-Light-ened state.

Those with ample energy are often the ones using their available energy to deliberately help another. Thus energy comes back multiplied, and the result is often very fulfilling to all involved. The focus upon others, rather than upon self, in a BALANCED interaction, is the single most important lesson you can perfect in that physical domain of experience.

On a related subject, I see that many of our physically-oriented crew members are being very lax in their conscious and deliberate efforts to maintain a high-frequency emotional state. NO ONE IS BEYOND THE REACH OF THE ADVERSARY'S INFLUENCE AT THIS TIME! THE GREATER THE TEACHER, THE GREATER THE ATTACKS.

I HAVE SENT MY MESSENGERS TO ASSIST YOU THROUGH THESE MATTERS, AND I SEE THAT THE MESSAGE MUST BE REPEATED OVER AND OVER. WHY? BECAUSE MANY OF YOU "THINK" THAT YOU ARE BEYOND THE REACH OF THE ADVERSARY AND THAT THE MESSAGE DOES NOT APPLY TO YOU! NO! YOU UNDERESTIMATE THE INFLUENCE AND MASTERY OF THESE DARK ONES. THESE ONES CAN AND WILL EXPLOIT ANY AND EVERY WEAKNESS YOU HAVE. NONE ARE BEYOND THIS TESTING. NONE!

This caution I have sent forth over and over to you ones. Take this message within and seek deliberate understanding. Learn to FEEL the adversary around you.

The more direct your level of participation, the greater the attacks will be. My public receivers are among the most heavily attacked ones at this time. I ask that these ones be especially attentive to their emotional states. Be not offended by another, for you need not the distractions. Allow the offensive ones to pass through your experience and resist not. The resistance only keeps these ones around much longer and will only serve to drain you of your time and energy. Always effort to maintain the greater perspective on why it is that you are here at this time.

Hold your heads up when you walk, and be quick to find reason to offer another assistance, even if it only be a smile of appreciation. I know that many of you are getting tired, and I also know the inner strength and perseverance that you are capable of drawing upon, even if you yourself do not.

I am Aton, The One Light. I am Creator. I AM!

CHAPTER TWENTY-FOUR

The Hour Draws Near For *Massive* Change

Esu "Jesus" Sananda
January 10, 1998

[*Editor's note: The three writings which comprise this chapter have been extracted from a longer lesson presented in the 1/13/98 issue of the* CONTACT *newspaper.*]

Esu here in Light.

The final hour of decisions is upon you of the team. **THE PLAN IS WELL LAID AND IT IS FOR NO MAN TO INTERFERE WITH THE FULFILLMENT OF THE PLAN.**

I SAID LONG AGO YOU ARE EITHER WITH ME OR YOU ARE AGAINST ME, AND WOE TO THOSE WHO ARE AGAINST THE LIGHT IN THIS FINAL HOUR OF PLANETARY TRANSITION, FOR THEIRS SHALL BE THE ENDLESS GNASHING OF TEETH IN THE VOID, DEVOID OF ALL LIGHT.

THERE IS BALANCE AND HARMONY WITHIN THE CREATION. WE COME AS THE HOSTS AND WE COME TO FULFILL THE PLAN. ONLY ATON OF LIGHT

KNOWS THE WHOLE OF THE PLAN.

EVEN I DO *NOT* KNOW THE PRECISE HOUR OF MY RETURN, BUT RETURN I SHALL, AND IT SHALL BE FROM STRENGTH THAT I RETURN. I SAID TWO THOUSAND YEARS AGO THAT I GO TO PREPARE A PLACE FOR THEE. IT IS SO AND IT IS COMPLETE!

AH, BUT WHO WILL STEP FORTH TO TAKE THAT PLACE? WHO WILL WORK WITH US IN THE FULFILLMENT OF THE PLAN?

IT HAS BEEN OFTEN SAID THAT MANY ARE CALLED BUT FEW ARE CHOSEN, AND IT IS SO. THE BLACK ROAD IS FAR AND WIDE AND EASY TO TRAVEL. THE RED ROAD IS NARROW AND STRAIGHT. [*Editor's note: In the symbology of many Native American cultures, the Red Road represents the spiritual world and the spiritual path, while the Black Road depicts the material world and material path.*]

BUT I TELL YOU IN EARNEST THAT THE RED ROAD, ONCE INTENT IS IN ITS PROPER PLACEMENT, IS NOT WITHOUT DIFFICULTY, YES; BUT IT IS THE CLEAR AND ONLY CHOICE, AND ONE WHICH, ONCE EMBARKED UPON, WILL REWARD THE TRAVELER BEYOND ABILITY TO MEASURE.

THE RED ROAD IS THE ROAD THAT IS REQUIRED OF YOU IF YOU ARE TO BE MY HANDS AND FEET. THERE SHALL BE STRICT OBEYANCE OF ALL LAWS, AND THERE SHALL BE A WILLINGNESS WITHIN THE SPIRIT TO SERVE IN ACCORDANCE WITH THE FATHER'S WILL.

THE INDIVIDUAL EGO OF MAN HAS TOO LONG SPOILED AND SOILED THE SURFACE OF THE BEAUTIOUS BLUE-GREEN ORB KNOWN AS EARTH-SHAN. GAIA [*Mother Earth*] **HAS SERVED WELL AS THE SCHOOLROOM, BUT THE TIME OF KINDERGARTEN SCHOOLROOM LESSONS IS *LONG PAST*. IT IS TIME TO TAKE UP THE MANTLE OF**

SERVICE, EVERY MOMENT OF EVERY DAY, IN WILLING PARTICIPATION AS CO-CREATOR.

THOSE OF THE NEW-AGE MOVEMENT MISPERCEIVE THE REALITY OF IT WITH THEIR ILL-CHOSEN USE OF THE TERM CO-CREATOR. BUT IT IS SO—THAT IN ACCORDANCE WITH THE BEST AND HIGHEST GOOD OF THE CREATION, IN LIGHT, THAT HU-MAN (HIGHER UNIVERSAL MAN) SHALL ASSUME HIS RIGHTFUL PLACE AS CO-CREATOR.

(THESE ARE VERY CAREFULLY CHOSEN ARTICULATIONS OF MY MEANING, SO DO NOT CHANGE OR ALTER A WORD THEREIN. I KNOW MY MEANING AND I SAY WHAT I MEAN. YOUR JOB, SCRIBE, IS TO WRITE WHAT I GIVE YOU, REGARDLESS OF HOW YOU FEEL ABOUT IT OR THINK ABOUT IT OR JUDGE ABOUT IT. YOU EITHER WILL PERFORM THAT TASK WITH HONOR AND ACCURATE TRANSCRIPTION, OR YOU WILL STAND ASIDE. I HAVE A JOB TO DO AND I WILL PERFORM MY JOB TO PERFECTION, FOR I AM RETURNED AS SANANDA [*a title of accomplishment which means "One with God"*] **AND I AND MY FATHER ARE ONE!!! WOE TO ANY MAN OR WOMAN WHO WOULD COME AGAINST ME, AND WOE TO THOSE ENEMIES OF MY FAITHFUL CREW—WHEREVER THEY MAY BE.)**

There is so much which must yet be taught to man that it would stagger the mind to realize how far behind you are as PEOPLE OF THE LIE. You have been taught, since birth, the lie.

You have misperceived your history, through the usurpers who have rewritten the way events have occurred. You have misperceived everything from your basic finances to your religions, to the point that the very fabric of your being IS A MANIFESTATION OF THE LIE ITSELF!

Ah, most will simply toss aside these words as MORE LIES. But I tell you, in earnest, scribe, that the day will come (and not too distant in your perceived frame known as time) that the adversary to LIGHT will wish he could "run away, run away", and yet there shall be NOWHERE TO RUN AND NO PLACE TO HIDE, FOR WITHIN GOD AND THE CREATION, ALL IS KNOWN.

It has been said that you must represent perfection to a greater extent than others around you, for you, by being in the role of scribe or "truthbringer", have accepted a responsibility which carries with it AN AWESOME REQUIREMENT FOR DISCIPLINE AND DILIGENCE. I KNOW THAT YOU SHALL FULFILL YOUR MISSION BECAUSE YOU WERE ACCEPTED FOR THIS SERVICE AND WE DO NOT MAKE MISTAKES WITH OUR CHOICES OF WHOM WE WORK WITH.

YES, THERE ARE BACK-UP TEAMS UPON BACK-UP TEAMS IN EVERY AREA OF YOUR GLOBE; DO NOT MISUNDERSTAND MY MEANING. BUT WITHIN THE LAWS AND "CORRECT" INTENT OF SERVICE, FULFILLMENT OF THAT SERVICE SHALL BE FORTHCOMING.

YOU KNOW ME WELL AND YOU KNOW THAT WHAT I SAY IS TRUTH AND THAT I WOULD NOT LEAD YOU OR ANY MAN OR WOMAN ASTRAY. MY "JOB" IS TO TELL YOU THE WAY IT IS, NOT THE WAY YOU WISH IT WERE. THE WAY IT IS SHALL BE HARD INDEED FOR MOST, AND THERE SHALL BE MANY, MANY BEINGS WHO SHALL SIMPLY TRANSITION, FOR THEY WILL NOT WANT TO EXPERIENCE IN THE PHYSICAL FLESH THAT WHICH IS TO COME UPON YOU.

WHETHER WE ARE SUCCESSFUL IN OUR MISSION UPON PLANET EARTH-SHAN SHALL BE DETERMINED TO SOME MEASURE BY THE CHOICES REMAINING FOR MAN. **MAN HAS ELECTED, IN HIS LAZY ARROGANCE AND IGNORANCE OF THE TRUTH, TO ALLOW THE FULFILLMENT OF THE NEW WORLD ORDER ENSLAVEMENT PLAN.**

WHETHER OR NOT THE REMNANT ARE SUCCESSFUL IN THEIR MANAGEMENT OF WHAT SHALL BE ENTRUSTED TO THEM, LIKEWISE REMAINS TO BE SEEN. KNOW THIS: OUR BROTHERS IN SERVICE SHALL NOT FAIL, NOR SHALL THEY BEND, AND ALL WHOM WE WORK WITH HENCEFORTH SHALL BE AS THE ROCK UPON WHICH A FOUNDATION MAY BE BUILT.

WE NEED NO HUMAN IN SERVICE WHO SHIFTS AS THE SANDS WITH THE WIND, BUT RATHER, WE NEED INTENT BENT ON SERVICE FOR THE BEST AND HIGHEST GOOD IN ACCORDANCE WITH GOD'S PLAN.

MAN SEES FROM TWO-DIMENSIONAL REALITY AND IS, FOR THE MOST PART, IGNORANT IN THE TRUE SENSE OF THE MEANING OF THAT WORD. MANY SHALL BE THE TASKS LAID AT YOUR TABLE, AND YOU SHALL EITHER PERFORM OR YOU SHALL NOT, BUT IT IS THE BETTER PART OF WISDOM TO PERFORM IN ACCORDANCE WITH THE PLAN, FOR THEREIN IS *GLORY*.

I DO NOT SPEAK OF GLORY IN THE SENSE OF THE MEANING THAT MAN'S EGO SHALL BE PUFFED UP WITH GREAT SELF-WORTH AND CONDESCENDING ATTITUDE OF SUPERIOR BEINGNESS. I SPEAK OF GLORY IN THE SENSE OF MEANING THAT, IN TRUE SERVICE, THERE SHALL BE ENDLESS REWARDS UNDREAMT, UNCONCEIVED, AND AT THIS MOMENT IN TIME, INCOMPREHENSIBLE.

EVERYTHING HAS ITS SEQUENCE AND ITS SEASON. THE SEASON OF THE LORD IS UPON YOU. PREPARE YOURSELF. PREPARE YOURSELF. PREPARE YOURSELF!

EACH BEING MUST EXAMINE CAREFULLY THAT WHICH THEY ARE ABOUT. EACH SOUL IS MARKED, AND WE KNOW THE MARK UPON THE SOUL, FOR IT IS WORN ABOUT THE COUNTENANCE AS PLAIN AS THE NOSE UPON YOUR FACE.

WE ARE GIVEN TO "SEE". TRUST IN ME, FOR I WILL NOT LEAD YOU ASTRAY. TRUST IN HATONN-ATON, FOR I COME IN SERVICE WITH THAT BEING.

I COME AS CAPTAIN OF THE SHIP AND I WILL HAVE NO UNDISCIPLINED BEING UPON MY TEAM. DISCIPLINE THINESELF AND LET US BE ABOUT OUR BUSINESS, FOR THE HOUR DRAWS NIGH WHEN THERE SHALL BE GREAT AND WONDROUS CHANGE TO THAT WHICH IS KNOWN AND THAT WHICH HAS BEEN EXPERIENCED TO THIS POINT IN THE SEQUENCE.

I DO NOT COME TO SOOTHE OR TO GLOSS-OVER ANY ERRORS. I COME TO TELL YOU HOW IT IS. I COME AS YOUR BROTHER AND I AM RETURNED AS SANANDA.

I ASK THAT YOU WALK, AGAIN, WITH ME ON THE JOURNEY BEFORE US, SO THAT THE TASK WE HAVE TOGETHER MAY BE COMPLETED IN ITS OWN NATURAL PERFECTION OF SEQUENCE.

LET US COMMUNE IN THE QUIETNESS OF YOUR HEART. IF ANY BEING LIVES IN ACCORDANCE WITH THE LAWS AS SET FORTH FOR BALANCED LIVING, THEREIN SHALL BE THINE RESPITE AND THINE SAFETY.

THE LIGHT IS YOUR SHIELD AND BUCKLER, AND THE LIGHT-SHIELD SHALL HOLD WHEN INTENT IS "ON TRACK". ALWAYS MEASURE YOUR INTENT AGAINST THE YARDSTICK OF THE LAWS.

THE LAWS DO NOT CHANGE ACCORDING TO MAN'S WHIM, NOR ACCORDING TO "MODERN" NON-MORALS. A RETURN TO MORAL LIVING IS THAT WHICH IS REQUIRED.

GIRD-UP YOUR LOINS AND SHORE UP YOUR SHIELD WHEREVER YOU MAY BE, FOR I AM ABOUT MY FATHER'S BUSINESS AND THERE IS MUCH BUSINESS TO ATTEND.

THE CALL COMPELS THE ANSWER, SO NO

MATTER WHO YOU ARE, IF YOU ASK WITH LIGHTED INTENT AND HEART-FELT DESIRE, YOU WILL RECEIVE YOUR ANSWER, AND RARELY, IF EVER, WILL THE ANSWER PRESENT ITSELF AS YOU WOULD WISH IT TO.

EACH MUST MAKE THEIR FINAL DECISIONS AT THIS TIME. EACH SHALL REAP THE CONSEQUENCES OF THOSE FINAL CHOICES, AND THE FINAL CHOICES SHALL BE OF SUCH A MAGNITUDE, ON A SOUL LEVEL, THAT IT BEHOOVES ANY READING THESE WORDS TO GIVE VERY CAREFUL CONSIDERATION INDEED TO WHERE THEY STAND.

YE ARE EITHER WITH ME OR YE ARE AGAINST ME. AND THOSE WHO ARE AGAINST ME ARE MY ENEMIES. AND MY ENEMIES SHALL FALL AND THEY SHALL FALL HARD!!! IT IS MY PROMISE TO THOSE OF THE LIGHT, FOR I COME WITH A MISSION AND I SHALL COMPLETE MY MISSION WITHIN THE PERFECTION THAT IS THE CREATION.

MAY YOU EVER LIVE YOUR LIFE IN BALANCE AND HARMONY. LET NONE STEER YOU FROM YOUR APPOINTED TASK OR COURSE.

THE ROAD WALKED MUST BE TRUE AND STRAIGHT, FOR ANYTHING ELSE WILL TRAP YOU FURTHER IN THE LIE. HAVEN'T YOU OF EARTH-SHAN LIVED THE LIE LONG ENOUGH? TRY TRUTH ON FOR SIZE, YOU MIGHT LIKE IT!

YOU SHALL KNOW THE TRUTH AND THE TRUTH SHALL SET YOU FREE. KNOW THAT IT IS SO.

I AM THE TRUTH, THE LIGHT, THE WAY, AND THE LIFE.

TAKE MY HAND, FOR I KNOW THE WAY AND YOU DO NOT.

I AM SANANDA.

I AM CAPTAIN OF THIS SHIP.

I COME WITH A SWORD OF LIGHT AND I SHALL SMITE MINE ENEMIES WITH PRECISION. KNOW IT!

SO BE IT AND SELAH.

OVER AND OUT, FOR NOW—I AM AS NEAR AS YOUR BREATH!

January 11, 1998

Esu present in Light.

The terrible plagues upon your land are produced by man, and it is evil man who shall continue in the efforts at depopulation of your globe.

Those in the Middle East gear up for war, and it is war that they shall have. But there will be many surprises in the manifestation and outcome of the destructive beast known as war.

Remember well one thing: the Phoenix rises from the ashes. Does that not present an image? We are about our Father's business. We are to build UP THROUGH the chaos that is Kali.

You are in the Age of Kali, remember? Always maintain well your Light shield so that the confusion does not enter your heart. Find the stillness within, for was it not said by me, lo those two thousand years past: THE KINGDOM OF GOD IS *WITHIN* YOU. It is so.

Quiet yourself, and I speak now not to my scribe, but to those of you reading these words: Quiet yourself, ask, AND THEN LISTEN CAREFULLY. In the stillness you will be able to commune with God and you will be given the necessary strength to see you through any situation, no matter how seemingly impossible or difficult it may APPEAR.

Love is the greatest gift of all, for only when you respond to those around you with love in your heart, FOR ALL YOUR RELATIONS, will there be change within your very lives. Love is the catalyst, it is the salve, it is the glue, it is the very "stuff" which holds the universe together.

GOD IS LIGHT. REMEMBER? THE LIGHT IS THE

VERY MANIFESTATION OF LOVE ITSELF.

I DO NOT SPEAK OF PHYSICAL THINGS, OF PHYSICAL LOVE. I SPEAK OF COMPASSION, OF CARING, OF DOING FOR OTHERS—IN SHORT, I SPEAK OF SELFLESSNESS IN THE TRUE REFLECTION OF SELF THAT REPRESENTS ITSELF AS LOVE.

LOVE IS THE MOST MISUSED, ABUSED, AND MOSTLY DESTROYED WORD YOU HAVE, AND YET IT IS LOVE WHICH IS YOUR GREATEST LESSON.

"LOVE YE, ONE ANOTHER." THAT DOES NOT SAY TO HOP IN BED WITH ONE ANOTHER. THE STATEMENT IS: "LOVE YE, ONE ANOTHER."

AND YET WHAT DO WE SEE AS WE WITNESS YOUR PLACE? WE SEE GREED, HATRED, ANGER, FRUSTRATION, JEALOUSY—IN SHORT, A BLACK CLOUD SURROUNDING THE AURAS WHERE THERE "SHOULD BE" LIGHT—SILVER AND GOLD LIGHT, REFLECTING THE PERFECT SPIRIT OF GOD, OF LIGHTED SOURCE—REFLECTED AS LIGHT THROUGH THE VERY NATURE OF LOVE WITHIN YOUR BEING.

REFLECT LOVE IN SERVICE FOR OTHERS AND YOU WILL BE ON YOUR WAY TOWARD MORE HARMONIOUS AND JOYFUL LIVING. JOY IS NOT AN ILLUSIVE TERM "OUT THERE" SOMEWHERE. IT IS REAL, IT IS HERE, AND IT IS NOW.

EXPERIENCE LOVE WITH JOY IN YOUR HEART, IN SERVICE TOWARD FELLOW MAN, AND WATCH THE DOORS SIMPLY OPEN, ONE AFTER ANOTHER.

NOW, AGAIN: DO NOT MISUNDERSTAND MY MEANING; I DO NOT SPEAK OF SOME PIOUS WIMP! GOD IS STRENGTH ITSELF.

BUT CANNOT YOU, YOU, AND YOU EXPERIENCE LIFE WITH JOY, WITH LOVE IN YOUR HEARTS, WITH COMPASSION IN YOUR HEARTS, IN SERVICE TOWARD YOUR FELLOW MAN, AND EXPERIENCE ALL OF THAT FROM STRENGTH? OF COURSE YOU CAN!!!

WHEN YOU EXPERIENCE LOVE AND COMPASSION, WHEN YOU EXPERIENCE JOY, THAT DOES NOT MEAN YOU ACQUIESCE TO EVIL—EVER! ON THE CONTRARY, DO YOU REMEMBER WHEN I TURNED OVER THE TABLES OF THE PHARISEES IN THE TEMPLE? WHY DOES EVERYONE ASSOCIATE GODLINESS WITH WEAKNESS? IT IS EXACTLY THE OPPOSITE OF WHAT YOU HAVE BEEN TAUGHT AS PEOPLE OF THE LIE. GOD IS STRENGTH AND LIGHT AND WISDOM—ALWAYS!

"THAT WHICH YE DO UNTO THE LEAST OF MINE, YE HAVE DONE UNTO ME." REMEMBER?

MEASURE WELL YOUR THOUGHTS, YOUR DEEDS, YOUR WORDS—FOR REMEMBER ALSO THAT WORDS ARE THINGS, THOUGHTS ARE THINGS, AND DEEDS MOST CERTAINLY REFLECT THE TRUE NATURE OF SELF.

BE SELF-LESS NOT SELF-MORE. LET SELF BE THAT PERFECT MIRRORED REFLECTION THAT IS LIGHT. THE SHADOWS DO NOT STAND IN THE PRESENCE OF LIGHTED REFLECTION, SO WHAT FEAR YOU?

FEAR IS THE PARALYZING POWER OF EVIL ITSELF. REPLACE FEAR WITH DETERMINATION IN ACCORDANCE WITH THE FATHER'S PERFECT PLAN AND WILL.

AGAIN: JOY IS REFLECTED WHEN ACTING IN ACCORDANCE WITH THE FATHER'S PERFECT PLAN AND WILL. "AH," YOU SAY, "BUT HOW DO I KNOW IF I AM ACTING IN ACCORDANCE WITH THE FATHER'S PERFECT REFLECTION AND WILL?"

YOU KNOW, WITHIN, ALWAYS! REMEMBER THAT SOMETIMES STILL AND SILENT, SOMETIMES LOUD AND ANNOYING, THING CALLED YOUR CONSCIENCE? LISTEN TO THE STILL (OR LOUD) VOICE OF CONSCIENCE AND YOU WILL KNOW IF YOU ARE ACTING IN HARMONY WITH, OR IN

ADVERSARIAL OPPOSITION TO, THE FATHER'S WILL.

HAS IT NOT BEEN SAID FOR YOU TO "BE AS WISE AS THE SERPENT AND AS GENTLE AS THE DOVE"? THAT DOES NOT SAY TO BE WEAK; IT MEANS EXACTLY WHAT IT SAYS: BE AS WISE AS THE SERPENT AND AS GENTLE AS THE DOVE—BUT ALSO, UNBENDING IN SERVICE TO TRUTH AND THE RED ROAD OF LIGHT, IN THE JOURNEY HOME TO ONENESS WITHIN GOD'S PERFECTION WITHIN THE CREATION.

WE HAVE COME AT THIS TIME TO SPREAD THE WORD OF TRUTH OF HOW IT IS. WE HAVE RETURNED, AS PROMISED LONG, LONG AGO.

HOW THINK YE THAT THE ANGELS WOULD RETURN? HOW THINK YE THAT I WOULD RETURN? I AM RETURNED AS SANANDA! I AM RETURNED AS ONE WITH MY FATHER. WAS IT NOT SAID, EVEN IN YOUR TAMPERED BOOKS CALLED *BIBLE*?

WHY WOULD YOU EXPECT A "RAPTURE" OF GOD'S PEOPLE WHEN I TELL THEE THAT I AM RETURNING *WITH GOD OF LIGHT, ATON*, AND THE HOSTS OF GOD—INCLUDING THE GREAT ARCHANGELS, SUCH AS MICHAEL AND COUNTLESS OTHERS, WHO ARE HERE IN SERVICE TO THE CREATION, TO ASSIST YOUR PLANET AT THIS TIME OF TRANSITION? WHY WOULD WE RAPTURE YOU TO THE CLOUDS WHEN WE ARE HERE TO SPEAK TRUTH?

I AM RETURNED. I AM NOT UPON YOUR PHYSICAL PLANET OF EARTH-SHAN.

WILL THE SO-CALLED CHRISTIANS TURN AWAY THE LIFEBOAT AS THEY HAVE TURNED AWAY THE HELICOPTER AND THE PLANE, SENT BY GOD IN ANSWER TO THE CALL FOR HELP? WHO WILL ALLOW THE EVIL CONTROLLERS TO RAPTURE THEM INTO OBLIVION RATHER THAN AWAIT MY RETURN?

THOSE OF GOD WILL **KNOW THE DIFFERENCE,**

BUT WILL COME VERY CLOSE TO BEING FOOLED! DO NOT BE FOOLED BY PROJECT BLUE BEAM.

[*Editor's note: For you newer readers who may not be familiar with Project Blue Beam, this is the secret code-name for NASA's large-scale, mostly satellite-driven holographic projection system designed by puppets of the "elite" controllers to produce real-looking, three-dimensional images over large areas of the sky. It could project, for example, a fake alien invasion to scare you into paralysis and begging for the "unified" "protection" of a New World Order against this common global "enemy"; it could likewise project, for similar unification reasons, a fake "second coming of Christ" that plays into the religious mind-control programing of many unsuspecting church-goers. Does the system work? Was "comet" Hale-Bopp real or was it just one of several recent test cases to see if we're ready for bigger and better things to come? For those of you who remember Commander Soltec's writing from 11/16/96, called* Mind-Controllers Ramping Up Latest Antics, *in the 11/19/96 issue of* CONTACT *(and chapter 39 in volume I of this* WISDOM OF THE RAYS *series), there were given more than sufficient clues to guide us to greater awareness about this subject.*]

GOD OF LIGHT IS NO FOOL, AND GOD'S PEOPLE, IF THEY ARE PAYING ATTENTION, WILL KNOW THE DIFFERENCE. MAINTAIN YOUR VIGIL WITHIN YOUR HEART AND KEEP YOUR LIGHT SHIELD ABOUT YOU, AND YOU WILL KNOW THAT WHICH IS TRUE FROM THAT WHICH IS FALSE.

THERE WILL BE TWO IN THE FIELDS. ONE WILL BE TAKEN AND ONE WILL REMAIN.

WHICH WILL YOU BE? WILL EVIL BE TAKEN AND GOOD REMAIN, PERHAPS? AH, PONDER IT WELL, FOR IT DOES INDEED MAKE A DIFFERENCE. WHY THINK YE THAT GOD WOULD ALLOW A PRECIOUS ORB SUCH AS EARTH-SHAN TO BE COMPLETELY DESTROYED BY EVIL? DOES IT NOT MAKE MORE

PERFECT SENSE TO RESTORE THE PLANET USING GOD'S OWN PEOPLE, KNOWN AS THE REMNANT?

WHY DO YOU NOT CONSIDER THESE THINGS? THE TIME IS UPON YOU WHEN THE HOURGLASS IS EMPTY. THE CLARION CALL HAS GONE FORTH. THE TIME OF THE LORD IS UPON YOU!!!

BLESSINGS UPON YOU OF MY PEOPLE. THOSE WHO SERVE WITH HONOR SHALL WALK WITH ME; IT IS MY PROMISE TO YOU. WON'T YOU TAKE MY HAND AND WALK THIS ROAD OF LIGHTED TRUTH TOWARD GLORY?

BE NOT AFRAID, BUT BE EVER DISCERNING, FOR THE DEMONS OF THE DARK BROTHERHOOD ARE CLEVER BEYOND BELIEF, AND NEVER FOR ONE MOMENT THINK THAT YOU OR YOU OR YOU MAY NOT BE FOOLED BY THEM. YOU CAN BE!

THEREFORE, I SAY TO YOU TO MAINTAIN YOUR LIGHT SHIELD BY STRICT OBEYANCE WITH ALL GODLY LAWS AS LAID FORTH, AND THE STORM SHALL SIMPLY PASS YOU BY. IT MAY COME CLOSE INDEED, BUT THE STORM SHALL SIMPLY PASS YOU BY.

KEEP THE FAITH AND REMAIN WITHIN THE LIGHT. ACT WITH LOVE AND COMPASSION IN YOUR HEART FOR YOUR FELLOW MAN AND NEVER FORCE YOUR TRUTH UPON ANOTHER WHO IS UNWILLING TO LISTEN. EACH MUST MAKE THEIR OWN DECISIONS AT THIS TIME AND IT IS AN INDIVIDUAL SOUL CHOICE.

AH, BUT IF A BEING IS OPEN TO LISTENING, SHARE FREELY THAT WHICH YOU KNOW AND HAVE BEEN GIVEN. SELF-LESS, REMEMBER?

Let us stop for now. We will pick this up at a later time. Go in peace, for I am never far from thee.

I AM SANANDA.

DOUBT IT NOT.

SO BE IT AND SALU!

January 12, 1998

Peace. Esu Immanuel present in Radiance and in Light. I come in Service. I am returned with the Hosts, AS PROMISED.

Oh, yes, I walked that orb called Earth-Shan. They crucified me upon the cross; they beat me; they spit at me; and they hated the message I brought.

AH, BUT MOST ***KNEW*** THE TRUTH I SPOKE WAS SO, AND YET THOSE IN THE POLITICAL POSITIONS INSURED THAT I WAS EITHER DRUMMED OUT OF TOWN, WHATEVER TOWN IT WAS AT THE TIME, OR THAT I WAS "BROUGHT UP ON CHARGES". **THE BEING KNOWN AS JESUS AS PRESENTED BY SAUL (PAUL) DID *NOT EXIST*. THAT BEING WAS CONJURED TO TAKE ALL THE RESPONSIBILITY AWAY FROM INDIVIDUAL MAN, AND IT WAS CONJURED BY EVIL ITSELF. AND MAN HAS FALLEN FOR THAT *FALSE* BEING—HOOK, LINE, AND SINKER.**

Know that what I tell you is so, scribe. You know me well and you know I would not lie to you nor lead you astray, EVER! At this time in the transition, man was told he would be given TRUTH UPON WHICH TO DISCERN HIS POSITION WITH CREATOR. WELL, BELOVED OF MINE, CREATOR IS TELLING YOU THE WAY IT IS, AND I AM MERELY CONFIRMING, FOR YOU DOUBTERS IN THE AUDIENCE, THAT WHAT IS BEING WRITTEN ELSEWHERE IN THIS PAPER IS SO.

MAN (HU-MAN: THAT IS, HIGHER UNIVERSAL MAN) MUST ASSUME, EVENTUALLY, HIS RIGHTFUL PLACE IN THE UNIVERSE—AS ONE WHO ACCEPTS, ABSOLUTELY, SOLELY, EXCLUSIVELY, INDIVIDUALLY, FULL RESPONSIBILITY FOR EACH AND EVERY THOUGHT, WORD, AND DEED THAT BEING PRESENTS—PERIOD!

NO OTHER BEING, CALLED JESUS OR JOHN DOE, CAN TAKE AWAY YOUR RESPONSIBILITY OR ASSUME ANYTHING FOR ANYONE ELSE. THE SO-CALLED CHRISTIANS HAVE ADOPTED THE FALSE AND PREDICTABLY LAZY SOLUTION TO AVOIDING ALL PERSONAL RESPONSIBILITY FOR SELF, AND IT IS A LIE.

Yes, I, Esu Immanuel, DID PHYSICALLY WALK UPON YOUR PLACE. I DID HAVE THOSE AROUND ME WHOM I *TRIED* TO TEACH. EVEN THOSE CLOSEST TO ME, IN THE END, BETRAYED ME OR DENIED MY VERY BEING.

THERE IS A GREAT DISTINCTION BETWEEN ESU IMMANUEL AND THAT ONE **PRESENTED** AS JESUS. I WAS A "CHRISTED" BEING, A WAYSHOWER, A TRUTHBRINGER.

I PROMISED THAT I WOULD GO TO PREPARE A PLACE FOR THEE. I PROMISED THAT I WOULD RETURN. **I HAVE DONE SO. I AM RETURNED AND I AM RETURNED AS SANANDA!**

It is the unbending and bottomless well of selfless giving, from a state of LOVE, that is representative of that which we call SERVICE. SERVING YOUR FELLOW MAN, BROTHER TO BROTHER, SISTER TO SISTER, GIVING WITHOUT EXPECTATION OF RETURN, SHARING IN THE OPEN ***JOY*** OF LOVE PERSONIFIED IS THAT WHICH THE FATHER IS ALL ABOUT. GIVING AND REGIVING, ENDLESS SERVICE, ONE TO ANOTHER.

AND WHERE DO YOU FIT IN SUCH AN EQUATION OF LOVE? AH, MOST INDEED ARE FAR, FAR FROM THAT PLACE, AND YET IT IS A RETURN TO THE SELFLESS EXPRESSION OF LOVE, IN SERVICE AND GIVING, THAT YOU WISH TO ATTAIN.

LOVE IS THE GREATEST LESSON OF ALL. DO NOT STAIN THE DEFINITION OF LOVE WITH YOUR PRECONCEIVED PERCEPTIONS OF PHYSICAL LOVE.

PHYSICAL UNION AND SELFLESS LOVE ARE TWO VERY DIFFERENT MEANINGS. THE LOVE OF WHICH I SPEAK IS A REPRESENTATION OF DIVINE WILL IN SERVICE.

Let us stop here for now. I am Sananda, to clear.

CHAPTER TWENTY-FIVE

Living Up To Your Greater Potential

Tomeros Maasu Korton
January 10, 1998

Editors note: Through a gifted new receiver and scribe, Commander Korton has, in the CONTACT *newspaper, recently been weaving a tapestry of spiritual lessons throughout discussions of current and historical events. While it is neither practical nor appropriate to include in this volume ALL of these sometimes lengthy commentaries, the following is presented as an example of Korton's popular and challenging teaching style. Another sample is included as chapter 36, later in this volume.*

Commander Tomeros Maasu Korton here in the Light of God, in service to Him and you of His precious reflections. Always call in His Light for protection in these days of chaos, and call in His Light for insight as you read these words.

And speaking of light, many things are being prepared for a light show of grand presentation. It is our task to be sure you-the-people have opportunity to know WHOSE show it is.

Evil will always show up on your doorstep first, and it will be your accumulated wisdom that will allow you to know the difference between the wolf who is dressed as the lamb, and the lamb. If he speaks evil, is accompanied by evil, advises evil, and praises evil—a good measuring stick to detect the presence of the adversary—then pay attention to such actions, for actions speak far more accurately than words.

In the days of kali (chaos), there is more of that which you would term bad in your nation and world than there is apparent goodly behavior. Those who proclaim themselves to be in service to God of Lighted Source must realize that it is YOU who will be the Lighted Torches of Truth and Wisdom. Your actions and words will be HOW you will be regarded—knowingly or unknowingly—as mass consciousness moves toward that which you call Judgement Day.

Whether that day is actually a thing as scientifically explainable as the entering of your solar system into a Photon Belt, or the shifting of man's vibratory frequency to a higher rate, or a final confrontation between Good and Evil (or all of the above)—a day of decision and ATONement IS coming. It has to; YOU called for it!

CURRENT EVENTS AND STELLAR HAPPENINGS

My focus is on that which is regarded as communications and communion with the Hosts and their "chariots of fire". It has been a long time, in your counting, since civilized man has referred to the vehicles of their ancestors (and heritage) in such a primitive manner, but you are not as far from that mindset as you would like to think.

I do not mean this to belittle, however there is a lot you have not experienced, as a "modern" civilization, as a whole. Meanwhile, there are segments of your planetary society who not only have unraveled the so-called secrets of the universe (to just enough of an extent to be dangerous in their ignorance), but who also are actively using those secrets to destroy your own planetary environment, and in turn destroy YOU as a species of Earth-man.

You are Higher Universal Man, HU-man. You are *THE* CREATIVE FULFILLMENT OF GOD-ATON. Is it not time that you, as a brotherhood of human beings, start to live up to that genesis?

There are outrageous happenings taking place in your world this day. Because of the controlled-media's relentless onslaught of fear and scandal "spin" techniques (of distraction and, basically, mind control), it is becoming more and more difficult to discern the difference between that which is directly perpetrated upon you by the "elite" evil planners and that which is more indirect—that you would consider as "just life happening" to you.

As geophysical Commander Soltec has reminded you upon many occasions of past lessons, the dark ones have so much technology directed toward, say, the creation of "natural" disasters, that it becomes impossible, beyond a certain point, to separate the distinctly man-made disasters from those events which are natural planetary reactions to that which is being inflicted upon her. After all, you are dealing here with a living, sentient being, whether you recognize same or not. It would be wise for you ones to pay more attention to what the Native American peoples have been trying to teach you for centuries about living in harmony and about the interconnectedness of ALL things.

Look around you with truly objective eyes and then try to tell me this is not a civilization in the throes of decay. Your court system is about as bad as it can get. You have no law and order, only manipulation and greed, while the real criminals sit on the bench and in public office. Even the word "bench" holds the true meaning of its actual purpose: the judge's bench is the Latin word for bank; that is, the judge sits on the bank—**he officiates for the system of the bankster** [*banking gangster*] **cartel!**

Yes, it is the same old bunch of pharisee moneychangers

still pulling a fast one with your make-believe finances—until the day they have finally maneuvered all your *REAL* assets into their coffers. Well, dear ones, IT IS NOW THAT DAY! AMERICA AND THE WORLD ARE IN FORECLOSURE. LOOK AT YOUR NATIONAL BUSINESS STRUCTURE (THE LITTLE THAT REMAINS WITHIN YOUR NATIONAL BORDERS) AND WORLD FINANCIAL MARKETS. THE FALLING DOMINOS HAVE BEEN SET IN MOTION.

Then, with the sweep of a pen signing an Executive Order (maybe in conjunction with some earthquakes or riots or floods to keep you occupied), you will discover who *REALLY* holds the wealth—and I promise you, it is not going to be you-the-people!

Is there hope for your ASSets? If your focus is ONLY on your gold, no matter how you perceive the outcome to be, you will be the loser in the end.

For those of you who realize that even God's nation must have a financial base from which to function in justness and moral responsibility for ALL its people, then yes, there most certainly is hope. Nevada corporate structure is your tool. The adversary knows it; they know we know it; and they know we are showing you how to do it. Will it always be available? The only thing that you can always count on is God to show you the way.

Right now Nevada corporations are available to help you better your plight and provide some measure of security. What happens if (or when) that is taken from you? Ye of great faith, God will simply *show* you another way. You err greatly when you limit the resources of your Father-Mother Source, for in so doing you limit your miracles and the methods for those miracles to manifest in front of you.

The adversary has a plan to eventually take EVERY LAST *THING* YOU OWN, but never forget, chelas (students), God also has a Plan 2000 and it is magnificent and perfect in every detail.

Are there honest politicians in your world? Yes, there

are a few. Sonny Bono could be considered to be someone who, at least in the eyes of the people, stood for something sorely lacking in your government (besides a good sense of humor): the belief that the common man can make a difference. Was he a saint? You are human; you will make errors (sins). I am not judging the man, that is between him and God.

It is noteworthy to look at the effect Sonny Bono had on people. If nothing else, the outpouring of sympathy demonstrates that ones are still moved by sincerity, compassion, and not taking oneself too seriously. These are qualities your Khazarian controlling-"elite" have mostly weeded out from your men and women of leadership.

ORGANIZED DISORDER: PART OF THE PLAN

You are in the biggest mass smear campaign of your nation, and ALL of your religious and political puppets are the targets. The *Protocols Of The Learned Elders Of Zion* state that when all goyim (non-Jews, I did not say Judeans; there is a difference) leaders are made to look like fools lacking moral and religious character, they will turn to the Jews, whose religion and men of authority will prove their superiority by their steadfastness and unshakable faith.

The zealots of the *Protocols* conveniently forget to tell their supporters that the Jewish Mishpucka (mafia) and Israeli intelligence service (the Mossad—whose motto is "Thou Shalt Make War By Deception") have, through blackmail, extortion, and lies caused, nurtured, AND PAID FOR (courtesy of that which is extracted from you nice, unquestioning, taxpaying citizens) that lack of moral and religious character.

And what of poor Theodore Kaczynski? What of him? The most important tragedy in that case is not to human physical life, for the soul essence is what is real. That which you perceive as physicality is a *SIMULATION* OF REALITY.

When the body dies—whether by what you label natural causes, by suiciding (covert methods of murder appearing to be self-inflicted), or by execution (overt murder, say carried out by the state), God receives those newly departed ones and they are assisted by their Higher Guides for proper placement for further lifestream experience ACCORDING TO THEIR LEVEL OF LEARNING.

(By the way, only God has the right to uncreate a life. Man has the right to administer non-lethal punishment only. It is your Creator-Source who gives, by grace, the GIFT of souled life. What makes man think he has the right to destroy that which he did not create?)

The real tragedy of these legal shenanigans is the blatant demonstration of YOU, as a sovereign citizen, not being given the opportunity to defend yourself in your own courts. This is to show you exactly how it is going to be in the New World Order.

Further, to be sure that more of you did not question his RIGHT TO REPRESENT HIMSELF, a suiciding attempt was conveniently arranged on the eve of that decision being confronted. Sane or not, do you believe he will get a competent hearing now?

This is no different from your Oklahoma City federal building blasts. You are being shown—FOR THE SECOND TIME—that when a man is found innocent, or at least not guilty, at one trial, try again until he is found guilty—as accused.

(And yes, I did say blastS—plural—above. They make no mention of the evidence of **more than one explosion,** for which the little truck blast was used only as a cover, and for the purpose of establishing blame. If the true evidence was allowed open examination, then all the pieces would fit quite nicely regarding what OTHER SUSPECTS could have been doing. The problem then, however, would be one of major incrimination of your federal government.)

Do I judge these ones accused of such heinous crimes? That is for YOU and YOUR court system to decide. But you had better make sure your decision is based on ALL available evidence. How do you have arguably the biggest terrorist incident on U.S. soil (according to what the masses know regarding how your world turns) and NO ONE recorded even a word of the confession? When subpoenaed, agents could not provide a clear recounting to the jury of what was said—it was not legible(???!!!).

What IS important to me is that you of God's people see the wool being pulled over your eyes—before it completely blinds you from perceiving what is being set up: enslavement, in your own backyard, with NO RECOURSE IN THE LEGAL SYSTEM. IF THEY CAN DO IT TO O.J. AND TERRY NICHOLS, JOHN Q. CITIZEN DOESN'T STAND A CHANCE!

(Whether INNOCENT OR GUILTY, the *CONSTITUTIONAL* RIGHTS of ones such as Nichols and Simpson WERE VIOLATED. IF YOU ARE TO HAVE JUSTICE FOR ***ALL,*** **THEN THAT INCLUDES THE ACCUSED. WHATEVER HAPPENED TO INNOCENT** *UNTIL PROVEN* **GUILTY? IT SEEMS THESE DAYS IT IS THE OTHER WAY AROUND—YOU ARE ALL BUT SENTENCED AND CONVICTED BEFORE YOU ARE BROUGHT TO TRIAL. WHEN YOU UNDERSTAND THE MEDIA'S TOTAL INVOLVEMENT IN THESE SECRET AGENDAS, YOU WILL BEGIN TO SEE HOW MASSIVE THE BEAST FROM** ***THE BOOK OF REVELATION*** **TRULY IS.**)

This is what is actually happening with these trials of the century. You are having more numbers of important cases occurring at the close of the millennium than what would be considered normal for a civilized society.

Common Law is your last chance to reclaim your courts of non-law and bring justice back into the system. As long as you still actively work toward the belief that you have a *Constitution*, and you get ones in office who will represent it AND you, you will have a chance.

However, for all practical intents and purposes, the

"elite" controllers feel they have all but destroyed that precious document; you just haven't been told yet. When they legally do away with it, you can expect the tanks to roll and the troops to march. So you can see why time is running out for waking up and crawling out of your cages before the final bars are welded into place.

It will not be easy. You have some very shrewd manipulators who have spared no expense (again, with YOUR money) to see to it that their plans come to fruition. If that means having highly specialized assassination teams, **from your own military,** take out two potential troublemakers, on the ski slopes—within days of each other—then so be it. You can be sure the message was heard loud and clear.

The assassins of this technological era use most sophisticated methods and covers for their trade. Whether the victim is an insubordinate princess, a street pharmaceutical merchant (one operating OUTSIDE the CIA cartel), a daring astronomer, or uppity politicians, the methods of annihilation are not easily discerned, much less are they deemed wise to talk about by those who possibly have seen more than they should!

From the point of view of an acceptable cover for more sophisticated technology at work, car accidents have become the most popular method of demise. Of course the tragedy of Princess Diana and Dodi al Fayed comes instantly to mind. Less well known may be the car accident in Australia that claimed the life of David Levy, of "comet" Shoemaker-Levy 9 fame. However, that is only one example—in a string of seemingly unrelated incidents involving the deaths of astronomers—where potential Truth-spillers have been taken out.

As more and more "stars" make themselves known, it will be the astronomers who will be the first ones to notice what is going on. The public will then look to the astronomers for answers. The adversary has run out of lies to tell you to try and explain away the lights in the evening (and daytime) sky. For the most part, the astronomers are choosing silence at this time. Can you blame them when the warning message has been stated in such blunt terms?

Some of the men and women of science, those truly of Godly intent, are now more interested in Truth than in preserving their own safety and paychecks. Some may start out working hand-in-glove with the evil ones, but many are finding it difficult to remain silent as they are witnessing what they correctly see as the coming of God and His Hosts.

Richard Hoagland has brought together many such ones, from the likes of NASA and related agencies, who have been speaking out at press conferences and over the airwaves on such as Art Bell's late-night talk-radio program, with its large listening audience.

Will you join with these ones who are holding in their hearts what they have witnessed but are afraid to come forward with? To them it appears many of you do not care enough about your future to stand up to the perpetrators of the cover-up, yet they are finding it arduous to keep within their souls that which man as a species is preparing to behold—yet again.

THESE THINGS WILL COME TO PASS IN THIS GENERATION

How many of you remember the last migration or homecoming? You will perceive exactly that which you are to do *when* the time comes; until then, watch and wait upon the Lord, for you must have patience. Even the Son knows not the hour of his arrival, only the Father knows.

If you are not always mindful of your adversary's determination to spawn negative connotations in the simplest things, even your very words will be used as tools against you. Many came among the people pulling them into separate groups, turning them one against the other, using the written word to convince them of their superiority of one over the other.

God is not a He or a She, that which you look to and call upon as the SOURCE OF ALL THAT IS, is a Mother-Father ***PRINCIPLE***. In the mind of God, it makes no difference what label is used to describe God's energy; masculinity and femininity both flow from the One Source. However, it is *man's* thought processes of *separation* that breed the atmosphere of superiority and inferiority. THERE IS NO INTRINSIC SEPARATION BETWEEN YOU AND GOD.

That Mother-Father-God Principle is the Light of Knowingness that there is NO SEPARATION BETWEEN *ANY* OF GOD'S CHILDREN. NO MATTER HOW LOUDLY THE SELF-APPOINTED EXPERTS IN HUMAN BEHAVIOR STATE OTHERWISE—AS A SPECIES OF HU-MAN YOU ARE ALL THE SAME.

When conditions were arranged by the "elite" controllers to cause woman (man with womb) to step down from the pedestal of regard—WHERE SHE HAD RULED *WITH* HER MATE, SHARING EQUALLY THE DECISIONS THAT AFFECTED THEIR LIVES AND THE LIVES OF THOSE THEY WERE RESPONSIBLE FOR—AT THAT MOMENT DAWNED THE HOUR OF THE DIVISION THAT HAS ALL BUT MADE YOU EXTINCT AS EARTH HUMANS. THE WAR BETWEEN THE SEXES IS THE BIGGEST PHYSICAL CIRCUMSTANCE THAT HAS BROUGHT YOUR WORLD TO THE BRINK OF DESTRUCTION.

When you couple that division with the other major hindrances such as GREED, SELFISHNESS, ENVY, the LACK OF COMPASSION, and LACK OF LOVE (a familiar list indeed), you have a world that has truly fallen into spiritual and moral decay. When "The Light" has gone out of society, God makes one last bid for your salvation, and then He withdraws His Radiance, and departs. Those who are left behind are left in that which you term Hell: the absence of God's Light.

Man and woman ARE different PHYSICALLY, but do

not get caught up in one more thing that allows fighting among you. If there are to be ANY humans, men or women, to survive the coming changes—those by Mother Nature and those by your evil controllers—UNITY is going to have to become a way of life.

Not just in the homes, but with your neighbors, friends, and associates alike. You are going to have to put aside your petty squabbles because it is just those kinds of distractions that your adversary is counting on to collapse society. First destroy the family, then the tribe or community, then follows the city, the state, the nation, and so on.

This sounds like a well-engineered plan hatched by wealthy, power-hungry tyrants, from an Ian Fleming spy novel. Well, chelas, Fleming wrote from exact files from British Intelligence—far out stuff by everyday living standards, and maybe a bit embellished, but basically quite real. The names and certain other things were changed so he could be allowed to write his books—and so "they" wouldn't bump him off for revealing more than they wished to have bragged about in a public forum.

You actually do have evil ones literally PLANNING your demise from mountaintop hideaways or submarines beneath the polar icecaps, all the while referring to you as "useless eaters"—a quote from your former NSA [*National Security Agency*] advisor Zbigniew Brzezinski. Only a well-informed *Constitution*-based nation (not the Constitution of the United Nations Industrial Development Organization or any other New States document), with God invited to attend all of your affairs, as your Founding Fathers envisioned, can turn your situation around for the better.

What of the issue of separation of church and state? Well, church, as you know and practice the concept, does not allow for God's Presence to be a CONSTANT (not just on Sundays or when you feel like it), MOMENT-BY-MOMENT, INTIMATE COMMUNION with your lives. You have been taught to be dependent upon some "superior knowing" of the pastor. And you are coerced into this entrapment by fear tactics all along the way.

If you are to save anything—nation or selves—the FURTHER *REMOVAL* OF GOD FROM YOUR HOUSES OF AUTHORITY, INSTITUTIONS OF LEARNING, AND (WHETHER YOU ARE AWARE OF IT OR NOT) PLACES OF WORSHIP, WILL ONLY ACCELERATE YOUR SLIDE INTO THE PIT OF DARKNESS.

GOD IS *ALWAYS AND FOREVER* A LIVING, BREATHING PART OF YOUR LIVING BEING. GOD-POWER IS REQUIRED TO MOVE EVEN YOUR LITTLE FINGER.

TO BE ANTI-GOD MEANS YOU ARE ANTI-SELF! **THIS IS THE VERY THOUGHT PROCESS THAT HAS CAUSED MAN TO DESTROY HIMSELF AND NOT EVEN BE AWARE THAT HE IS DOING SO.**

THAT IS WHY YOUR SATANIC ADVERSARY ENDEAVORS TO KEEP HIS ACTIONS AND PLANS IN THE DARK; ONCE YOU KNOW THESE THINGS ARE BEING DONE TO YOU, YOU CANNOT BE FOOLED.

I know it is a difficult process for you to understand in wholeness, but in the physical format you are not going to COMPLETELY understand God's routine; to simply begin to *comprehend* God's Presence—that a part of God is within you—is good enough to accomplish your task. You, as human beings in your present dimensional compression, may not understand the full range of EFFECTS of Creator's thinking, thinking which results in much more than "just" this universe. However, that which is *THE* CAUSE of all created splendor *must* become as dear to you as your very breath. To *know* God is to *know* thyself.

Thank you, scribe, for your service. May Love and Inspiration guide your efforts, for when the task becomes arduous, it is the soaring heart that brings Joy back to the grinding-stone. Korton to clear, please.

AHO!

January 28, 1998

Korton here in the Radiant Light of our Creator Source. Good morning.

America, you have made it through the Super Bowl activities and the "special effects" planned for that event. Many of your adversary's plans were postponed because of advance warning of that which was expected. Other plans were carried out but did not go according to the wishes of the Khazarian "masterminds".

Recognize that these are MAN'S plans and they are fallible. Satan and his servants will ALWAYS make errors, and those mistakes will eventually do-in the evil ones. If YOU do that which you know to be within the Laws of God and the Creation, you will make it through and have the opportunity to be part of the remnant.

Keep in mind that there are millions of life-supporting planets in your galactic placement alone; remember: "There are many mansions in my Father's kingdom". Whenever Earth-Shan (or any experiencing orb) is threatened with possible annihilation, in which case the planet would have to be evacuated, in addition to those who come in the name of God to assist, there are those who will be reintroduced when it is again suitable for human habitation in safety and continuity.

A "remnant" is always left behind to seed humanity. Evidence of this can be found throughout your societies and civilizations that have come and gone. In fact, you have had so many civilizations come and go that we of Space Command are *VERY PRACTICED* at our jobs.

There will be those who are the keepers of the Oral Tradition of the Ancients, and there are those who hold the cosmic "secrets" for man, as a species, to again build his societies—hopefully in a manner (there goes that Free-Will Choice again) that is consistent with God-Aton's Laws.

Those choices are given by your Creator TO SEE THAT WHICH YOU WILL DO. AND WE KNOW WHAT

CHOICE MAN WILL MAKE EVERY TIME. Has the hour not come when God wins, instead of that OTHER voice whispering over your shoulder?

Since when has *solely* listening to the teachings of man provided you with the answers to all your questions? You have wars and conflicts involving every nation upon your globe.

Even Switzerland, the last "great" haven for your offshore banking schemes to horde gold, is experiencing woes. The "blame-extortion scheme" of the so-called "Holocaust" has now penetrated that country's neutral financial inner workings. The "business" of Swiss funds is what held your world together as a "free-market" economy.

You have NO leadership in the structure YOU RECOGNIZE as "government". It was not always so. George Washington and Thomas Jefferson warned you that if you did not stem the tide of Khazarian invaders gaining control of your government, with their ability to issue "money" your children will wake up slaves in the land their forefathers founded. And now you are there. Moreover, you have the best Congress money can buy! The Israeli Lobby groups have purchased your senators and representatives; **THEY NOW DICTATE *ALL* FOREIGN AND DOMESTIC POLICY**.

Meanwhile, the satanic manipulators are now bringing those same moral leadership problems to your attention toward advancing their own goals. Once they have "convinced" you that your government is in such a deplorable state that it can no longer function AS PART OF THE INTERNATIONAL COMMUNITY, **THEY WILL QUICKLY INTRODUCE A NEW GOVERNMENT AND A DANDY NEW *CONSTITUTION* TO REPLACE THAT WHICH THEY HELPED TO DESTROY.** You can either be a part of that plan, or you can work to RETAIN that which you ALREADY HAVE.

You say you are concerned about jobs leaving the country, and yet you allow the decisions for the policies of your nation to be **GUIDED AND MANIPULATED BY THESE FOREIGN INTERESTS**. I, Korton, am not "anti-Semitic". However, I find it interesting that a nation, made up of many different races of people, allows a group, that makes up the very smallest portion, to control EVERYTHING that pertains to the lives of the remainder of the population. Your educational system, domestic and international banking, key policy and lawmaking positions, and even your Hollywood film and television factory churns out opinions and "entertainment" that reflects Jewish-Khazarian thinking and influence.

And by the way, on the subject of the clever Khazarian mind-control accusation of "anti-Semitism", note that it is the ones touting bigotry, especially toward those exposing the Truth, who in fact are NOT Semites! The so-called "Jews" come from the line of Japheth, not Shem. Further, based on all historical data, nearly everyone else in the sphere of influence of the accusers ARE Semites—by definition. But again, remember that Satan's "plan" is to create confusion and lies.

The manipulators, whether or not they include so-called "Jews", Whites, Blacks, Arabs, or whatever, make up two percent of your citizenry and their plans do not call for the survival of very many of you who are outside their circles.

It is not bigotry, or some other form of racism, that is spoken of in these writings and those of my compatriots. **We are concerned about THE VERY SURVIVAL OF GOD'S PRECIOUS CREATIONS.**

TO NOT EFFORT TO SAVE YOUR OWN LIFE IS SELF-MURDER, AND SUICIDE IS DEFINITELY NOT OF GOD OF LIGHT!

Do you go out and make war against those whom you perceive are trying to do you in? Who would you "take out"? Kissinger? Elizabeth of the British Crown? We are talking about the *Book Of Revelation's* BEAST WITH MANY HEADS. There is always another waiting in the wings to be "successor".

And what of your weapons? Do you really believe an Israeli Uzi or Chinese-made AK-47 can accomplish the job? The enforcers for the One World Order have technologies available to them that include such as microwave phasers and portable lasers (like the type *witnessed* during the murderous ambush of the Princess and Dodi in the tunnel) that can disable, blind, or kill **an entire battlefield full of soldiers.**

WAR IS NOT OF GOD

War is not an option as far as Godly behavior is concerned. However, to allow your God-given body to be slain by an attacker is, like I said before, self-murder. Intelligent, life-preserving defense of God's creation IS permitted.

Let me clarify several points before I proceed: The term "satan" does not denote a being; it is a label meaning "adversary". Lucifer, however, is a very real entity and you had best know his modus operandi. Esu Immanuel was the actual given name of the one you have been misled to call "Jesus Christ". Saul (Paul) of Tarsus labeled him "Jesus", which is the Greek word for "anointed". The term "Christ" is not a name; it is a state and level of beingness.

The satanic ones have exploited the concept of "turning the other cheek" to take over entire peoples. The one known as "Jesus Christ" would never do such a stupid thing, nor tell you to do so. If you are going to read your so-called "holy" book, always be sure you use your God-given gift of R-E-A-S-O-N.

We of the Hosts of God are not permitted to directly *interfere* in your Earth squabbles—except for some very specific, life-threatening circumstances. In general, we can only assist. Moreover, you must first ASK for that assistance, and then you have to receive of it that you might make the best use of what has been given to you.

Will you know what your "help" looks like? You have forgotten how to "see" your Guardian Angels and their

Guiding Light. However, you can ask to be given the insight to *PERCEIVE* and the correct course of action will be revealed unto you.

Will it come in the form of words that you can "hear"? In the situations where you need God the most, there is usually no time to wait for a response. Therefore you must attune yourself to the frequency of God's Energies so that there is always a connection left "open".

Should you find yourself facing a physical confrontation, you will need to be ready to receive God's instructions, especially should your options seem to be "fight or flight". If you remain clearheaded, you will be given that which you need—but be prepared (open) for options presenting themselves that were not previously within your conscious awareness. Never limit God!

If you are doing everything within your power to follow the Laws as given forth by God Creator, you will not end up in such dire circumstances in the first place. At worst, you may have to use your legs to make a hasty retreat.

If you *knew* you were going to be killed by, say, one holding a gun, and this person has told you that his intentions are to shoot you dead, and you were unarmed (a not-so-unusual situation in your rapidly deteriorating larger cities like New York or Los Angeles), would it not be better to "go" while attempting to escape? And how do you know your help isn't going to come to you in the form of inaccurate shots or a misfire or two? If you never "test" the larger sphere of possibilities by spending your last breath preserving the Life that God gave to you, how will you know?

WHEN YOU UNDERESTIMATE GOD'S HELP, YOU UNDERESTIMATE *YOUR* GOD POWER AS EXTENDED TO YOU BY CREATOR SOURCE. YOU ARE A FRAGMENT OF GOD, AND LIKE THAT HOLOGRAPHIC DNA BLUEPRINT, YOU CONTAIN THE PATTERN OF THE WHOLE, THEREBY ALLOWING GOD'S SPLENDOR TO BECOME A *KNOWING* PART OF YOU.

Call on this gift often, for in the PRACTICE comes the familiarity which *becomes* Knowing; and when you know how to utilize Divine Protection, you will discover that you lose your fear of those things put in your path to distract you from your work.

GOD IS ABUNDANCE

God is Joy and Abundance, not lack and unhappiness. When you fully comprehend the state of being of the Master Teacher himself, you can fathom the hows and the whys of his existence and the Source of his Power and Wisdom. Is that not the purpose of this journey?

To be like the Master Teacher, who is of the Father, is to be like The One Who created you; and after experiencing Oneness with the I AM Presence, you can be set free to fly again, coming full circle to begin anew your experience called life.

The Sacred Circle of Infinity is not a concept; it is an effect of Nature to behold each time your seasons change. Mother Earth's processes allow for cycles of "death" and "rebirth" as Autumn turns to Winter, and Winter turns to Spring. Should man, whose physical body (vehicle or "space suit" for experiencing in the physical dimensions) is also of the Earth, be any different?

Just because you don't (at the moment) remember a previous incarnation or existence does not mean it could not have happened. You believe in many things you do not see—the illusion of "time", for instance, is your biggest preoccupation. In the Higher Realms we do not experience "time" as such. We experience sequence of events, where one thing follows another in an expanded perspective and perception of possible and probable realities. Is it not time to have a little more Faith in that "unseen world" you profess to believe in?

May we walk together in brotherhood through this wondrous journey called life. Korton to clear, please.

CHAPTER TWENTY-SIX

Balance Shall Be Restored Upon The Earth

Esu "Jesus" Sananda
January 16, 1998

Editor's note: The writings which comprise this chapter have been extracted from a much longer lesson presented in the 1/20/98 issue of the CONTACT *newspaper.*

Esu Immanuel present in the Light of God-Aton. I come in service unto The Creation. I come with the Hosts, and I am returned. Blessings to you, scribe, for hearing the call.

THE LAWS OF GOD ARE **FIXED,** ***IMMUTABLE.*** LET NO ONE TELL YOU OTHERWISE. ANY MAN WHO SAYS THAT THE LAWS, AS YOU KNOW THEM TO BE, ARE NOT FIXED, BUT MAY "CHANGE WITH THE TIMES", IS A LIAR AND A CHEAT!

THE LAWS ARE CALLED THE ***LAWS OF BALANCE*** AND THEY WERE GIVEN BY CREATOR FOR THAT VERY PURPOSE. GOD REPRESENTS THE KING OF WISDOM, AND THE KING OF WISDOM WOULD NEVER LEAD YOU ASTRAY NOR WOULD HE PROVIDE LAWS FOR YOUR BALANCED LIVING THAT

WERE ANYTHING BUT PERFECTION IN ACTION.

THERE IS NOTHING HARD OR DIFFICULT ABOUT THE LAWS, FOR THEY REPRESENT THE ULTIMATE IN REASON AND WISDOM. LIVE YOUR LIFE ACCORDING TO THESE LAWS AND *KNOW* GOD. LIVE YOUR LIFE IN ADVERSARIAL OPPOSITION TO THE LAWS OF BALANCE AND INHERIT THE WIND.

I SPEAK NOW TO ALL WITH EARS TO HEAR AND EYES TO SEE. LO, I TELL THEE: THE KINGDOM OF GOD IS UPON YOU! PREPARE YOURSELVES.

Let those who have ears, hear.

MY NAME WAS NOT JESUS. I WAS AND AM A CHRISTED BEING. MY NAME WAS ESU IMMANUEL (JMMANUEL), BY WHATEVER SPELLING YOU LIKE.

IT WAS FORETOLD TWO THOUSAND YEARS AGO THAT I WOULD RETURN BEARING A NEW TITLE. I AM RETURNED AS SANANDA. I AND MY FATHER ARE ONE!

God knows His people well, and those who are not with God in these final days of transition shall rue the day. Each shall sit in judgement UPON SELF.

God CREATES. ALL HONOR, RESPECT, AND GLORY GO TO GOD, THE FATHER.

ALWAYS REMEMBER TO GIVE THANKS FOR THAT WHICH YOU ARE ALLOWED TO EXPERIENCE FOR YOUR BEST AND HIGHEST GROWTH IN THE JOURNEY HOME. THERE IS BALANCE WITHIN THE CREATION AND BALANCE SHALL BE RESTORED UPON THE EARTH, FOR I AM RETURNED, AS SANANDA, AND YOU MAY KNOW WITH SURETY THAT WHAT I SAY SHALL BE SO.

THE DAYS OF THE ADVERSARY ARE NUMBERED.

I ASK THAT ALL WHO WOULD WALK WITH ME DO SO WITHIN THE QUIET STILLNESS OF YOUR BEING. THE CALL COMPELS THE ANSWER.

AS IT IS WRITTEN, SO SHALL IT BE.

I AM SANANDA.
I COME IN SERVICE.
I COME IN RADIANCE.
I AM RETURNED WITH THE HOSTS, AS PROMISED.
PREPARE YOURSELF! SALU.

January 18, 1998

Esu present in Radiance. Thank you for asking for identification. You must never ASSUME that you are hearing from the Hosts. Identification will always be given. Beware of those whispering voices who DO NOT IDENTIFY!

THERE IS, BEWARE, FALSE INFORMATION CONTAINED THEREIN [*in the various Bibles*]. **FOR EXAMPLE: I DID NOT WITHER A FIG TREE. THAT WOULD REPRESENT A MISUSE AND ABUSE OF THE GOD-GIVEN POWER. GOD *CREATES*, REMEMBER? I, AS A MASTER TEACHER, WOULD NOT PRESENT AN IMAGE OF DESTRUCTION TO MY PUPILS.**

IT IS COMPLETELY TRUE, HOWEVER, THAT I INSTRUCTED THEM ON THE WAY OF FAITH, AND MANY AMONG MY PUPILS DID NOT HAVE ENOUGH FAITH TO MOVE AN OLIVE, LET ALONE A MOUNTAIN. SO BE IT; THERE IS TIME FOR EVERY SEASON UNDER HEAVEN. PERHAPS BY NOW THE PUPILS HAVE LEARNED A THING OR TWO. WE SHALL SEE.

THE PHARISEES WERE PARASITES UPON THE CULTURE AT THAT TIME. THEY WERE THE ONES WHO SKILLFULLY AND WITH GREAT DECEPTION MANAGED TO TAKE FROM THE PEOPLE THE LITTLE THEY HAD. THEY WERE THE ANTI-CHRIST IN ACTION, THEN AS NOW.

Thank you for sitting with me to clarify the point of deception contained within the passage I quoted on Friday.

[*Editor's note: Here Esu is referring to a part of the much longer, original version of the 1/16/98 writing.*] There shall be many lessons ahead, and much that I wish to not only clarify for you, but give you to set the record straight as to what exactly happened *AFTER* THE CRUCIFIXION.

NO, I DID NOT DIE UPON THAT CROSS WHICH THE SO-CALLED CHRISTIANS LOVE TO KEEP ME NAILED TO. I WENT ON TO TEACH IN MANY LANDS, FOR MANY YEARS. AND THAT WHICH I TAUGHT WAS REJECTED BY MANY PEOPLES AND I HAD TO KEEP MOVING FROM TOWN TO TOWN. IT HAS EVER BEEN THUS WITH THE TRUTHBRINGERS UPON YOUR PLACE OF SHADOWS.

BE AT PEACE IN THE KNOWLEDGE THAT I SHALL NOT LEAD YOU ASTRAY. GO FORTH NOW AND TEND THE MATTERS BEFORE YOU. WE WILL COMMUNE LATER THIS DAY.

I AM SANANDA. SALU!

CHAPTER TWENTY-SEVEN

Critical Lessons On The *Anti*christ Pharisees

Esu "Jesus" Sananda
January 21, 1998

Editor's note: The writings which comprise this chapter have been extracted from a much longer lesson presented in the 1/27/98 issue of the CONTACT *newspaper.*

Esu present in Radiance and in Service. Be not concerned that my words may *appear* to miss the mark with some ones near you. I know what I am about and I know my meaning. The lessons I will bring will be "strange" and "unusual". Many will not have a CLUE of what I am speaking, and yet I tell you with absolute clarity that I KNOW WHAT I AM DOING.

It is important that we not identify this scribe by name, for many will RISE UP TO SMITE YOU AND STRIKE YOU DOWN BY DEATH TO SILENCE THE MESSAGE.

THE MESSAGE WILL NOT BE SILENCED AND THOSE WHO CALL THEMSELVES "CHRISTIANS" WILL HAVE SOME VERY DIFFICULT CHOICES AHEAD, FOR I AM RETURNED AS SANANDA, AND I AM THE

CHRISTED BEING WHO WALKED UPON YOUR PLACE AND WHO TAUGHT THOSE WITH EARS TO HEAR.

JESUS IS A FABRICATION TO SOOTHE THE IRRESPONSIBLE ACTIONS OF THOSE WHO DO NOT WANT TO TAKE RESPONSIBILITY FOR SELVES, BUT RESPONSIBILITY SHALL BE TAKEN BY EACH AND ALL. IT IS THE LAW.

WE SHALL ADDRESS THE ISSUE OF THE NAME SANANDA, IN FULL, AT A LATER TIME. THERE ARE STILL MANY WHO DO NOT KNOW THAT I AM RETURNED BEARING THAT NEW TITLE. BUT I WAS NOT CALLED JESUS. KNOW IT TO BE SO. I WAS CALLED ESU IMMANUEL (JMMANUEL).

THE CHRISTIANS, IN THEIR IGNORANCE, HAVE MARCHED TO THE DRUMBEAT OF ZION, AND THE FALSE JEWS HAVE STOLEN YOUR VERY SPIRITUAL BEING FROM YOU.

THOSE WHO MARCH TO THAT DRUMMER ARE IN FOR A SHOCKING AND RUDE AWAKENING INDEED—IF, IN FACT, THERE IS AN AWAKENING AT ALL FOR THOSE ONES. MOST WILL SIMPLY BE EVAPORATED INTO NOTHINGNESS THROUGH THEIR BLIND FOLLOWING OF "PROJECT BLUE BEAM" AND A FALSE RAPTURE INTO THE VOID. SO BE IT, FOR EACH HAS FREE WILL CHOICE. [*Editor's note: Project Blue Beam is a top-secret, large-scale projection holography technology. One of its intended uses, for manipulation of the unsuspecting public, is to project across the sky a real-looking "second coming of Christ" scenario. Another possible task for the Blue Beam system is to assist with the staging of a fake alien invasion—call it the modern scare-experiment version of the October 30, 1938 Orson Welles radio dramatization of H.G. Wells'* War Of The Worlds. *This fabrication is to be staged to unite the peoples of the world against a common "enemy" from space and thereby advance the New World Order envisioned by the dark "elite" architects who intend to control the world.*]

COME TO ME AS THE CHILD AND I WILL TEACH YOU THE TRUTH OF HOW IT IS WITH THE CREATION AND WITH THE HOSTS. YOU ARE PEOPLE OF THE LIE AND, AS PEOPLE OF THE LIE, YOU KNOW NOT THE TRUE FROM THE FALSE, FOR YOUR VERY EDUCATION AND HISTORY OF YOUR WORLD HAVE BEEN STOLEN FROM YOU BY THE USURPERS KNOWN AS THE JEWS-WHO-AREN'T.

READ CAREFULLY THE *PROTOCOLS OF THE LEARNED ELDERS OF ZION,* LAID BEFORE YOU [*many times in the* CONTACT *newspaper, most recently at about the same time as this particular writing appeared therein, in conjunction with reprinted 1920s material from Henry Ford Senior's* Dearborn Independent *newspaper*] WITH SUCH DILIGENCE SO THAT YOU MAY KNOW THE LEVEL AND MAGNITUDE OF DECEIT THAT HAS TAKEN PLACE. WHILE YOU ONES WATCHED YOUR BALL GAMES AND DRANK YOUR BEER, THOSE WITH CUNNING OF ILL-INTENT TOWARD TOTAL GLOBAL CONTROL KEPT THEIR GOAL EVER IN MIND AND HAVE ALL BUT COMPLETED THEIR PURPOSE OF OUT-AND-OUT TAKEOVER, KNOWN TO YOU AS THE **NEW WORLD ORDER.** IT IS GOING TO BE A VERY ROUGH RIDE FOR MANY, MANY PEOPLE.

What is meant by the term "The Great Awakening"? Let us look at the core word—AWAKE. Awake denotes sleep, and you have been sleeping in your slumber of ignorance for eons. It is time to open those heavy eyelids and look around you.

The Great Awakening means that MANY WILL OPEN THEIR EYES IN CONSCIOUS (AND MOSTLY SHOCKED) AWARENESS AND "ALERTNESS" THAT THERE IS SOMETHING GREATER, SOMETHING—DARE I SAY IT—SPIRITUAL OCCURRING.

I AM RETURNED WITH THE HOSTS AND WITH GOD-ATON. WOULD GOD SEND LESSER? WHY? WHO TOLD YOU?

AS THE CONSCIOUS AWARENESS OF MENTAL ALERTNESS AND, YEA, PSYCHIC OPENING OCCURS, THE LINES IN THE SAND WILL BE DRAWN. EACH DARK ENERGY WILL WEAR ABOUT THEIR COUNTENANCE "A SIGN" WHICH THOSE AWAKENING ONES WILL BE ABLE TO CLEARLY SEE. HAS IT NOT BEEN SAID?

THE JOURNEY AHEAD IS MAGNIFICENT. THE TIME FOR "BALANCED LIVING" IS UPON YOU AND THE LAWS WERE GIVEN FOR THAT VERY PURPOSE. WALK THE PATH OF RIGHTEOUSNESS, OF GOODNESS, OF LOVE, AND OF JOY IN YOUR "CONSCIOUS" KNOWLEDGE THAT YOU ARE IN AN ILLUSIONARY WORLD CREATED BY THE FATHER AS YOUR GROWING STAGE—AND THE STAGE HAS SERVED WELL, BUT IS NOW, ALSO, GROWING TO A HIGHER PURPOSE.

SHAN-GAIA (EARTH) SHALL EVOLVE AND NONE SHALL STOP HER FROM TAKING HER RIGHTFUL PLACE WITHIN THE COSMIC ORDER. AND YES, IN THE COSMOS THERE IS ORDER; THERE IS BALANCE; THERE IS GOD.

THE ADVERSARY TO TRUTH WILL KEEP YOU BOUND AND HIS PURPOSE IS TO CONFUSE, TO DIVIDE AND CONQUER, TO HIT YOU IN THE MOST VULNERABLE PLACE YOU HAVE, WHATEVER IT MAY BE. ANY WEAKNESS WILL BE EXPLOITED, AND THEN HE WILL SPIT YOU OUT AND DISCARD YOU. AND IF HE HAS A CHOICE ABOUT IT, HE WILL NOT ONLY DESTROY YOU, BUT PHYSICALLY KILL THE VEHICLE.

TAKE HEED, ONE AND ALL, TAKE HEED! KEEP THOSE LIGHT SHIELDS UP AND CONTINUALLY BE ON YOUR GUARD AGAINST THOSE OF THE DARK BROTHERHOOD. DO NOT ALLOW THEM ENTRY. THIS MESSAGE, AGAIN, IS FOR ALL.

I will take up matters such as the Pharisees, and many

other aspects of the so-called biblical experience or time-frame, at a later time. So many of your perceptions of what occurred are, simply put, incorrect.

I will explain, in explicit detail, what I taught, how, and where. I will explain my journey and how I got to here. But this will take a great deal of time, and I must first get my scribe up to speed so that what I say is clearly put to paper for those of you with whom I wish to communicate. Be patient, for I know my students and I will share freely with you.

Take this off, for now, and be about your business.

I AM SANANDA.

Salu.

January 23, 1998

Good morning. Esu present in Radiance and in Service. There is much that I wish to cover, so please try to keep up.

Let us start with a discussion on the Pharisees, and then we will move right along to the *Curse Of Canaan* [*a book compiled by superb research author Eustace Mullins*]. We will begin by using George M. Lamsa's *Gospel Light—An Indispensable Guide To The Teachings Of Jesus & The Customs Of His Time.* Let us turn, please, to the section on Dealers and Money Changers. This section begins with a quote from *John 2:14,15* and then Lamsa's commentary.

[QUOTING:]

And [he] found in the temple those who sold oxen and sheep and doves, and the changers of money sitting;

And when he had made a scourge of small cords, he drove them all out of the temple, and the sheep, and the oxen; and poured out the changers' money, and overthrew the tables;

The streets of oriental cities are very narrow and one

may only walk in single file in either direction. Even today crowds which gather before the shops in Jerusalem are dispersed to make traffic easier. Peddlers and small traders follow-up prospective buyers for hours offering bargains to induce them to buy.

Jesus made a whip of small cords twisted together and tied at both ends. Cord is always found in the market places. It is used to tie burdens on men and on the backs of animals. Jesus did not put out the regular merchants. He put out the money changers and those who were buying animals in advance of the Passover to hold for large profits. He upset the trays of the money changers. There were no tables and they are still unknown in the Orient. Money changers sit on the ground, close to the walls of the houses.

One can easily see how this mistranslation occurred. In Aramaic the same word is used for buying as for selling. A dot over the second letter means selling, or a dot under the same letter means buying.

It would be more reasonable to believe that Jesus dispersed the tumultuous crowd which was bargaining, swearing, spitting, and doing dishonest business that should not be carried on in the temple grounds. He would not have interfered with the legitimate temple business permitted during festivals. Thousands of people had come from outside towns and far countries. They had to purchase oxen, sheep, and doves ***for their sacrifice***. They had to exchange their money for temple money, which was the only legal money that could be offered to God.

[END QUOTING]

Do you see how something as simple as this brief passage in your *Bible* can be distorted through simple mistranslation from one language to another? Can you IMAGINE how many errors in translation have occurred when SEVERAL LANGUAGE TRANSLATIONS ARE INVOLVED?

THIS MAKES FOR A SHAKY RECONSTRUCTION OF "HISTORY"—ESPECIALLY WHEN FURTHER COMBINED WITH THE FACT THAT NOTHING WAS EVEN WRITTEN ABOUT MY PASSAGE AS IMMANUEL UNTIL YEARS AND YEARS AFTER I HAD COME AND GONE, WITH THE ONLY EXCEPTION TO THIS BEING FROM JUDAS, MY BELOVED DISCIPLE AND FRIEND.

IF I WERE, TODAY, TO TELL ONE OF MY SMALL TEAM SOMETHING—LET'S JUST USE, BY WAY OF EXAMPLE: "THE BLACK SHEEP WANDERED OFF AND IT WAS DECIDED NOT TO FOLLOW AFTER." IF YOU WERE TO ASK THREE INDIVIDUALS, IN A YEAR'S TIME, WHAT IT WAS I SAID, THE VARIATIONS ON THAT STATEMENT WOULD HAVE NO RESEMBLANCE TO THE ACTUAL SENTENCE.

DO YOU SEE HOW DISTORTED WORDS AND MEANINGS AND MESSAGES CAN BECOME?

January 24, 1998

And now, please quote from Phoenix Journal #27, *The Phoenix Operator-Owner Manual.*

[QUOTING:]

THE HIGHEST COMMANDMENT:

The highest command of the Law of The Creation is: Achieve the wisdom of knowledge inasmuch as this will enable you to wisely follow the Laws of The Creation.

The highest command of the Law of God is: You shall honor God as the ruler of the human races and follow His Laws for He is the "King of Wisdom".

[END QUOTING]

Let those who have ears, hear.

Thank you, scribe.

The Truth has ever been present if you have been paying attention, but The Truth is always buried amidst the lies and the deception so that to unravel The Truth becomes all but impossible for the simple man.

The kingdom of God is upon you. Blessed are those who are faithful in the ways of The Law. Let Light be your shield and buckler. The false Jews have been the adversary to Light from the beginning. THEIR TIME IS AT HAND. THE DAYS OF THE ADVERSARY ARE NUMBERED.

I AM SANANDA, CAPTAIN OF THIS MISSION.

SALU, FOR NOW.

January, 25 1998

Esu Immanuel present in Light, that there BE LIGHT! I COME IN SERVICE TO GOD-ATON AND THE HOSTS. I COME IN SERVICE TO THE CREATION, SO THAT WHICH HAS BEEN PROMISED SHALL BE FULFILLED. SO BE IT.

THE TIME OF THE WORD IS AT HAND. LET THOSE WHO HAVE EARS HEAR THE WORD, FOR THE WORD IS THE TRUTH AND THE TRUTH SHALL SET YOU FREE.

Trust in me, for I will not lead you astray, now or ever. Many await my messages and I need a scribe to present the words so that the eyes may see and the mind may hear that which has been hidden, for has it not been said that that which is hidden shall be revealed?

The time of KNOWING is upon you. AWAKE AND KNOW GOD!

I do not come as some distant and unreachable being. I am returned as SANANDA [*a title of accomplishment which means "One with God"*].

ASK AND IT SHALL BE ANSWERED. SEEK AND YOU WILL FIND THAT WHICH YOU SEEK.

IT HAS ALSO BEEN SAID, AND WISELY SO: BE

MOST CAREFUL OF THAT WHICH YOU ASK FOR, BECAUSE IN THESE DAYS OF THE GREAT AWAKENING, YOU SURELY WILL GET IT, AND IT MAY NOT BE WHAT YOU EXPECT!

I ADVISE CAUTION AND I ALSO ADVISE THAT YOU PRAY FOR YOUR BROTHER AS YOURSELF, AND THEREIN ALL WILL TAKE ITS PROPER PLACE.

REMEMBER THE LILIES OF THE FIELD? EACH MUST BE RESPONSIBLE FOR SELF AT THIS (AND ANY) TIME. THEREFORE I SAY TO YOU: LIVE YOUR LIFE IN GENEROUS GIVING, IN LOVING COMPASSION, AS AN OPEN BOOK, FOR AN OPEN BOOK HAS NOTHING TO FEAR, NOTHING TO HIDE, AND THUS IS, METAPHORICALLY SPEAKING, AT PEACE.

OBVIOUSLY A BOOK IS INANIMATE, SO DON'T BE CONFUSED EVEN AT THAT SIMPLE STATEMENT. USE YOUR MINDS, WHICH ARE AS DIAMONDS—REFLECTIVE OF THE VERY LIGHT OF GOD. YOU ARE THE DIAMOND. YOU ARE THE MOST PRECIOUS ASPECT OF THE CREATION, BUT ARE NOT ABOVE THE CREATION ITSELF, FOR THE CREATION IS ABOVE ALL, INCLUDING GOD.

GOD AND THE CREATION ARE ONE. I AND MY FATHER ARE ONE. THESE ARE NOT MYSTERIOUS SAYINGS THAT HAVE NO MEANING. IT IS SO!

I WOULD CAUTION ALL AT THIS TIME TO BE VERY CAREFUL OF THAT WHICH YOU SAY—BE IT ABOUT ANOTHER BEING OR YOUR INTERPRETATION OF TRUTH. EACH HAS THE RIGHT TO AN OPINION, BUT BE CONSERVATIVE IN YOUR SHARING OF SAME, FOR IT IS MOST OFTEN A REFLECTION OF YOUR IGNORANCE AND SETS YOU BACK FROM A SOUL-GROWTH PERSPECTIVE.

PULL THE COTTON FROM YOUR EARS AND TRULY LISTEN TO THAT WHICH IS BEING SAID TO YOU, AND LEARN. THE TIME OF LEARNING IS UPON

YOU. BE EAGER TO LEARN.

BE EAGER TO LISTEN. ZIP YOUR MOUTH, OPEN YOUR HEART, AND GIVE FREELY OF SELF. LET YOUR LIGHT SHINE OPENLY UPON THE HILL FOR ALL TO SEE AND KNOW GOD.

Do not quandary over my messages. If you do not understand that which I say, then it is not TIME FOR YOU TO UNDERSTAND MY MEANING.

BUT I TELL YOU PLAINLY THAT MY MEANING WILL BE STATED SO THAT THOSE WHO HAVE PRAYED DILIGENTLY TO RECEIVE ANSWERS, WILL RECEIVE THE ANSWERS THEY SEEK. YOUR PRAYERS HAVE BEEN HEARD AND I WILL TELL YOU THAT WHICH YOU WISH TO KNOW.

So be it. Let those who have ears, hear that which is being said. The time of final choices is upon you. Which will it be?

I AM SANANDA. SALU.

* * *

POST SCRIPT:

Peace. Esu present in LIGHT.

THERE ARE *NO* UNTAMPERED-WITH BOOKS ON YOUR PLACE UPON WHICH TO BASE YOUR UNDERSTANDING. THE TRUTH HAS BEEN BURNED, BURIED, AND HIDDEN IN THE SECRET PLACES FOR EONS.

TO REALLY KNOW TRUTH, BELOVED, ASK GOD, GO WITHIN, AND LISTEN!

I WILL DO MY BEST TO PRESENT MATERIALS TO YOU THAT HAVE MERIT, BUT NONE ARE WITHOUT ERROR. IN FACT, MOST ARE RIDDLED WITH FALSE PRESENTATIONS, WRONG ASSUMPTIONS, ALL DRAWN UPON THE PREVIOUS TAMPERED-WITH MATERIAL. THE ADVERSARY TO GOD HAS NOT

SLEPT, BUT HAS KEPT HIS GOAL EVER IN MIND—THAT OF CONFUSING GOD'S PEOPLE AND KEEPING GOD'S PEOPLE SHIELDED FROM TRUTH.

WELL, BELOVED, THE TIME OF TRUTH IS AT HAND. I WILL, SOON, PRESENT TO YOU SOME VERY OLD WRITINGS FROM *THE NAG HAMMADI LIBRARY* AND EVEN THESE ANCIENT WRITINGS HAVE BEEN TAMPERED WITH. IT IS AS WITH *THE DEAD SEA SCROLLS*—DO YOU REALLY THINK YOU WOULD BE ALLOWED ACCESS TO THE *TRUE* DEAD SEA SCROLLS? OF COURSE NOT, FOR SUCH REVEAL, IN THEIR ORIGINAL FORM, THE TRUTH, AND UNCOVER THAT WHICH HAS BEEN REMOVED FROM YOUR SO-CALLED BOOKS CALLED HOLY.

IF I WERE TO NARROW DOWN THE ESSENCE OF THAT WHICH I WISH TO SAY TO YOU, IT WOULD BE THAT THE DAYS OF THE ADVERSARY TO GOD ARE NUMBERED.

TRUTH WILL BE REVEALED AND THAT WHICH HAS BEEN HIDDEN SHALL BE UNCOVERED. THE ADVERSARY CANNOT—I REPEAT—THE ADVERSARY CANNOT STAND THE LIGHT OF TRUTH UPON HIM. YOU MUST BE EVER ON YOUR GUARD AGAINST THAT ONE, AND ONLY GOD'S LIGHTED SHIELD WILL PROTECT YOU IN THESE DAYS OF TRANSITION.

HISTORICAL SEQUENCES ARE CONVOLUTED, AT BEST. THE PLAYERS ARE MANIFOLD AND THE EVENTS THEMSELVES BECOME LOST IN THE OBSCURITY OF ANTIQUITY. DO NOT TAKE ANY HUMAN'S PRESENTATION AS GOSPEL, FOR ONLY GOD IS FREE FROM ERROR.

BUT RATHER, **IT IS THE DAWN OF "THE GREAT AWAKENING" IN WHICH MAN WILL KNOW THE TRUE FROM THE FALSE.** THE ADVERSARY TO GOD HAS ALWAYS BEEN PRESENT TO DIVIDE AND TO CONQUER AND TO CONFUSE AND TO TEMPT. KNOW GOD, AND THE KINGDOM IS YOURS. HAVE PEACE

AND LOVE IN YOUR HEART, AND YOU SHALL HAVE NOTHING TO FEAR IN THESE FINAL DAYS OF THE ADVERSARY.

THE ADVERSARY SHALL TURN ON THEMSELVES, AND IN THE FRENZIED PANIC OF ANGER AND BETRAYAL, SHALL BE DESTROYED. SO BE IT AND SO SHALL IT COME TO PASS IN THIS TIME WITHIN THE CREATION.

I AM SANANDA.

I AM COME TO SHOW THE WAY, AGAIN.

WHO WILL JOIN WITH ME?

SALU.

CHAPTER TWENTY-EIGHT

Thoughts To Reflect Upon In Times Of Challenge

Ceres Anthonious Soltec
January 29, 1998

Good evening, my friend. It is I, Toniose Soltec, come in the Radiant One Light of Creator Source. Be at peace.

All is well. Thank you for hearing the call and responding. These are times of preparation. Be thankful for each day as there are indeed few left between now and such time as many ones of your world have a severe jolt to their reality—quite literally.

For those of you who are Internet literate, and thus can have regular access to the real-time earthquake and volcano information available on the Internet, you should be more than aware of the escalating build-up of pressures all around your planet. I would merely call your attention to several recent signs and clues, and especially to the satellite data concerning your sea surface temperatures. I would also remind you of the news your controlled media could not hold back concerning the new underwater volcanic activity just off the coast of Vancouver, British Columbia. Do you think this unprecedented upsurge of activity is normal? Do you think the sleeping ones will care enough to open their eyes and prepare for what is imminent?

Be not concerned with the plight of another, for they have their lessons and you have yours. Trust in we of the Hosts for your guidance through these times of great change. Have faith in your heart that we of the Lighted realms of Creation do know what we are doing and that many a pothole along the way will be avoided if the advice and assistance offered is acted upon in a diligent and timely manner.

Many will there be who will sit too long upon the fence of indecision, only to realize too late that the brief window of opportunity in which to prepare has come and gone. Respect the choices of each individual and leave them to deal with the outcome of same. You cannot awaken one who is not yet ready to be awakened. Move forward without them if need be, and go forth and fulfill that which you have come at this time to accomplish. Keep always the Larger Picture of the mission at hand foremost in your heart and let not the forthcoming distractions of the "elite" puppet-masters fool you.

Horror and fear are but a product of your imagination and are as much a perception as is a value. Do you fear for lack of a thing? Are you afraid of the horror of suffering? Many shall face these questions in a quite deliberate, in-your-face manner in the upcoming years upon your globe. Overwhelm and shock shall be the end result for most. Your only means of helping yourself to avoid the same affliction will be through keeping the proper mental perspective on the situation. Again, the only difference is in your perception of what is taking place.

If you believe yourself to be a victim, then surely you shall be a victim. If you believe that there is great value to be garnered for having persisted through the upcoming experience and that you need the experiences in order to grow from within, then you will have a much greater ability to focus and overcome any challenge that you may be faced with.

Only with the proper mental preparation will you be able to keep your head clear, and thus function rationally in a time of complete confusion and severe emotional bombardment. There is no such thing as a complete loss or waste. All experience has value to the ones experiencing. You are taught to be dependent upon political, religious, and social (entertainment) leaders. Many will simply sit and await whatever instruction that comes and follow it blindly without a second thought. Is this what God gave you free will for? Do you question what is best for you? Or do you seek first the approval of others so as to actually be doing a thing that is of another's determination rather than your own?

Have you diligently prepared to the point that you are confident you can go forth and make proper decisions without the need to first consult another? Have you strengthened your own inner connection to Higher Source to the point that you are confident you are "hearing" correctly? Have you learned to listen to media bombardment in such a manner as to distill it into what is *really* being said—or do you just wait for the next *CONTACT* to come out and point it out *for* you?

We are not about telling you what to think or what to do! It is *your* challenge to navigate *your* individual path as *you* see fit. We shall and do offer assistance to those who ask, as it is God's promise to you that He will always be there for you if you but ask with the HEART. Empty words shouted from rooftops are seldom in alignment with the heart intent of a being.

Do you pray that God crush or punish your enemies? You are often, due to ignorance, your own worst enemy—so do you see that if God were to literally answer your prayers, He would have to crush or punish YOU?! Be thankful that He responds to the soul's call for justice, and not to your limited perception of what you perceive to be right or wrong.

Many of you shall witness events that will challenge your senses as to what is of TRUE value. You shall witness such things as ones committing murder over a scrap of rotting food. Why? Because so-called "sensible" men of so-called "reasonable" intelligence could not see the writing that is now—and has been for some time—on the wall. This is to say that their lust for material gain clouded their vision and mind to a point that they ignored the gentle nudges of their inner Soul-Guidance which would have helped them to see and prepare.

The primary goal of each experience should be that of inner growth. This is best accomplished through active participation and interaction with others who can perceive this same goal. Together you can help one another to keep the Larger Picture in mind so that you can see that this experience is for you to go through and grow from. There is NOTHING wrong about it! It is the end result of the choices that you have made, both in the current physical experience and prior to the current experience. Many of you have been preparing for these events, now, for OVER two thousand years! Many of you ones walked with the great teachers of the past and you are still in need of the challenges that will help you to perfect your understanding of the Laws of Creation.

The mastery of energy flow dynamics is indeed a tedious process. Your thoughts are energy forms which are sent out and responded to and reflected back into your experience for you to examine in the form of consequences. This is the beauty and the perfection of the third-dimensional classroom.

There are no victims, for you each determine your own experiences. If you did not need the lessons, you simply would not be there at this time under these circumstances. There are infinite other possible scenarios that you could have chosen, yet from a greater perspective you have chosen this one. Be thankful for the opportunities that you now have for they are indeed unique and rare.

Horror, grief, trepidation and such need not be a part of your experience, and shall only serve to distract you from greater opportunity to grow. Yet, these are the challenges that you must face in order to generate a strong enough emotional desire to reach beyond your current level of perception and tap more fully the Infinite Source for new and creative soul-utions.

The emotional energy generated in the upcoming sequence shall eventually resonate within the survivors as a unifying bond which will result in a great sense of interconnectedness and recognition of the Oneness of all things. Only then shall the wars and fighting stop, and you will see a part of yourself in everything, everywhere.

These are truly wondrous times in which to be participating, and many of you wouldn't miss a minute of it for all the bliss in the known universe!

Keep in mind that you are infinite, creating beings who exist across a broad spectrum of dimensional planes. There are many levels of consciousness from which you project forth. The third-dimensional experience is "merely" the most seemingly solid in terms of mobility and focus. This is due to the compressive nature of the third dimension, which includes the perceptual awareness of time.

Many of your observations in the physical are a result of reflections of what is *actually* real (your thoughts). This gives you the equivalent of a massive bio-feedback device (environment) in which to practice and learn to create in a deliberate and responsible manner.

However, many believe that God micro-manages every part of your experience and that He punishes and rewards ones for the deeds that they do.

NO!

You simply "reap what you sow".

The harvest is a result of your thoughts. Your actions are secondary to the thoughts behind them.

Therefore, the only REAL thing in your third-dimensional experience is the thought energy or GOD-

FORCE within. He created you. You were born from His desire. His thought (desire manifest) is you. This is the Infinite Sacred Circle that represents the Oneness of all things, everywhere, in ALL planes of experience.

These are the ideas to remember in times of great challenge. Learn to feel the connectedness that is within.

Know that you can ask at any time for Guidance. Expect the answers to come. Learn to recognize them when they present themselves to you.

Know that within each argument, disagreement, or confrontation lies yet another opportunity to grow, and that when you come to a better solution or method by which to handle these challenges, they will likewise alter (respond), for they are the reflections (manifestations) of YOUR thoughts in the first place.

Thus your environment is a product of your creation and you cannot be a victim, except through your own ignorance of the Laws of The Creation. And, again, this is why you are there in the physical environment—to learn to master, in a responsible manner, YOUR understanding and use of the Laws and Infinite Potential of Creation.

Remember the words of the great teacher Esu "Jesus" Immanuel:

"The highest command of the Law of The Creation is: Achieve the wisdom of knowledge inasmuch as this will enable you to wisely follow the Laws of The Creation. The highest command of the Law of God is: You shall honor God as the ruler of the human races and follow His Laws, for He is the 'King of Wisdom'."

May the limitations of words in the physical not stand in your way of understanding the greater ideas represented herein. Go within and seek your own clarifications. Ask and I shall sit with you as you read.

I am Ceres Anthonious "Toniose" Soltec, sent by our Father (Creator Source) that His promise be fulfilled and that we ALL might grow from the challenges of these experiences.

In Light and Service to you all, Salu.

CHAPTER TWENTY-NINE

It Is Time To Awaken From *The Lie*

Esu "Jesus" Sananda
February 5, 1998

Editor's note: The writings which comprise this chapter have been extracted from a much longer lesson presented in the 2/10/98 issue of the CONTACT *newspaper.*

Esu Sananda present in Radiance. I come in service to instruct you and to offer freely answers to your queries. I come with THE HOSTS OF GOD! I am returned on a magnificent craft which we call *The Phoenix*. Oh ye of little minds, blurred vision, and no faith! You shall be given to see the magnificence of Creator.

You are people of *THE LIE!* EVERYTHING ABOUT YOUR SOCIETY IS A LIE. YOU HAVE LOST THE TRUE VALUES THAT HAVE MERIT AND REPLACED THEM ACCORDING TO THE BLUEPRINTS OF *THE PROTOCOLS OF THE LEARNED ELDERS OF ZION.*

YOU HAVE TAKEN THE BAIT—HOOK, LINE, AND SINKER—AND YOU DON'T CARE ENOUGH ABOUT YOUR PLIGHT TO PULL YOURSELVES UP AND

REMOVE THE SOURCE OF YOUR ENSLAVEMENT.

WE SHALL NOT DO IT FOR YOU. WE COME TO INSTRUCT IN THE WORD, THE TRUTH, AND THE LIGHT. IT IS UP TO YOU TO MAKE YOUR OWN CHOICES ABOUT YOUR OWN FREEDOM OR YOUR OWN CONTINUED ENSLAVEMENT.

YOU CANNOT FATHOM, FROM YOUR LIMITED PERSPECTIVE, THAT WHICH GOD TRULY IS, AND IS ABOUT. HARKEN UP! LISTEN TO THE MESSAGES BEING PROVIDED AT THIS TIME, FOR THEY ARE INSTRUCTIONS AND *THEY CONTAIN WITHIN THEM THE KEY THAT WILL UNLOCK THAT WHICH HAS KEPT YOU ENSLAVED AND IN DARKNESS.*

THESE THINGS **ARE IMPORTANT**. DO NOT CAST ASIDE YOUR LIFE-RING TO WATCH TELEVISION OR SOME OTHER MINDLESS ACTIVITY. PAY ATTENTION!

I AM NOT SAYING DO NOT WATCH TELEVISION; I AM SAYING THAT THE PRIORITIES TOWARD GOD AND FREEDOM FROM ENSLAVEMENT OUGHT TO TAKE PRECEDENCE OVER ENTERTAINMENT.

AH—BUT IT IS A FREE-WILL PLANET AND THOSE ARE AMONG THE CHOICES YOU MAKE. HOW WILL YOUR PASSAGE IN THE BOOK OF LIFE READ? ARE YOU SURE YOU WILL MAKE IT TO THE BOOK OF LIFE? YES, THESE THINGS DO, INDEED, MATTER.

FEAR IS THAT WHICH KEEPS YOU ENSLAVED. KNOWLEDGE = FREEDOM. WISDOM IS SOMETHING YOU MUST ATTAIN THROUGH CORRECT CHOICES AND UTILIZATION OF THAT WHICH YOU HAVE LEARNED.

Be kind to one another. Be kind to self. Be ever on your guard, for evil is always ready to POUNCE AT THE SLIGHTEST CRACK IN THE SHIELD. MAINTAIN YOUR LIGHT SHIELDS FOR THEREIN IS SAFETY AND WISDOM.

I AM SANANDA, signing off for now.
PEACE AND BLESSINGS UNTO YOU.

February 8, 1998

Now, scribe, turn to a passage in Phoenix Journal #2, titled *And They Called His Name Immanuel.*

[QUOTING:]

PROPHECIES OF THE END DAYS

As Immanuel walked from the temple, the disciples wanted to show him a building in which the temple was built. But he spoke to them, "Do you not see all this? Verily I say to you: not one stone here will remain upon the other without being broken. For the Jews trespass against life and the truth, and they built this city on the blood of people. They plundered this land through rapaciousness and murder, and killed their friends with whom they drank wine. Thus they betrayed their own friends, and murdered them, because of their greediness. Likewise it shall be done unto them."

Later as he sat on the Mount of Olives, his disciples came to him and requested, "Tell us, when will this happen and what will be the sign?" But Immanuel answered and said, "See to it that no one leads you astray. For many will come in my name and say, 'I am Immanuel'. And they will lead great numbers of ones astray.

"People will hear about wars and war cries; they shall see and not be startled. This is what must happen, but that is not yet the end. Because people will rise against one another, and one kingdom against another, and their will be times of great need and earthquakes and great floods all about the lands. This is the beginning of great calamities, and great cataclysms.

"Soon the people with the knowledge will be surrendered

to grief and many will be killed. They will be hated for the sake of truth in their teaching and for their wisdom. Many kinds of cults will rise up against one another, and much blood will flow, and many hearts and spirits will be broken. Many will succumb as a result of these conflicts, and will betray one another, and will hate one another because they remained small in spirit.

"Because there will be lack of faith, love will become cold and deadened in many, many people. Hatred will rule over all the world, and evil will reign for a long period of time. But he who persists in the truth will survive.

"This lesson will be preached throughout the entire world as testimony for all peoples, and then the end will come—when the Word of Truth has gone forth throughout the total of the lands.

"When the people will see the horror of destruction in Jerusalem and the lands thereabout, of which the prophets have already spoken, then the end will come.

"When this happens, whoever is at that time in the land of Judea, should flee to the mountains. He who is on the roof, should not come down from it to get anything from out of his house. He who is in the field should not come back in order to get his coat or any other of his possessions.

"Oh, woe to the women in this place who are pregnant and those who are suckling their babes at that time, for they shall suffer much grief and death. There will be multitudes.

"There will follow great grief as has never been before since the beginning of the world until now, and also never will be again. And, if these days were not shortened, no man would remain alive; but the days will be shortened for the sake of the spirit and wisdom, and for the sake of people who serve The Truth and The Laws.

"There shall be untold gnashing and chattering of teeth, and great mourning and screaming when this time comes, because of man's lack of understanding and because of his greed.

"There shall be machines made from metal for use in the

air, on the waters, and on land, to kill one another in great masses. They shall throw heavy projectiles out of these machines made of metal and they shall strike the cities throughout the lands. Fire will come out of these projectiles and burn the world so that hardly anything will survive, and that which does survive will not long be spared.

"They will put the cornerstones of life itself into the projectiles in order to kindle the deadly fires. And, if at that time the Celestial Sons would not appear in order to bring it to a standstill, verily I tell you, not one person would survive upon the face of Earth.

"Since the human race will, at that time, number at least ten times five hundred million people, two parts thereof will be destroyed and killed. When, at that point, someone will say to the people, 'Behold, here is Immanuel', they shall not believe it, because many false Immanuels and false prophets will rise up and do great signs and wonders, so that if it were possible, also even the wise and knowing would be misled. Behold, I told you so before.

"Therefore, when they shall say, 'He is in the desert', man shall not go out, and 'Behold, he is in a chamber', they shall not believe.

"Since I will most certainly return at that point in time, I will let them recognize me; this is how the Law is written and thus shall it be. For, as lightning starts with the rise and radiates until its setting, thus will be my coming among the Heavenly Hosts with whom I shall have my renewed life at that time.

"Men of all time, beware; whenever the carcass is there, the vultures will gather, so beware of them.

"Soon after the grief of that time, Sun and Moon will no longer radiate, and the stars will fall from heaven and the powers of the heavens will become shaky. The structure of the heavens will be disturbed because of the senselessly erupted power of men who will be living in greed, power, and addition.

"There will then appear a sign in the sky. And then all

the generations on Earth will cry and will see the Celestial Sons coming in the clouds of the sky, and they are of great power and will judge harshly against senselessness. Since God is the ruler over the three human races, He, therefore, will judge them through His representatives.

"Man owes God his creation, and God is the ruler over him, so that he has to follow His commandments and respect Him as the greatest King of Wisdom. He will send forth His guardian angels with loud trumpets, and will gather His followers from the four winds, from one end of the Earth unto the other end."

[END QUOTING]

I said it to you two thousand years past and it remains true: **YOU ARE THERE, PEOPLE. *YOU ARE ON THE EVE OF DESTRUCTION.***

THE FALSE PROPHET HAS FANNED THE FLAMES OF RACIAL HATRED AND THE BLOOD SHALL FLOW IN THE STREETS. OH, FOOLISH, FOOLISH MAN. WHEN WILL YOU LEARN THAT GOD IS NOT A DESTROYER OF LIFE?

THE COURSE IS LAID AND THE PLANS HAVE BEEN MADE. THE FORCES ARE RALLYING AND THE REST SHALL UNFOLD AS YOU MARCH TO THE PROPHECIES OF THE ANTI-CHRIST.

MAY GOD HAVE MERCY ON YOUR SOULS.

I AM SANANDA, RETURNED BUT NOT UPON YOUR PLACE.

I COME IN SERVICE TO GOD-ATON.

I COME WITH THE HOSTS AND THEY ARE MANY.

IN LIGHT, IN TRUTH, I SERVE GOD OF LIGHT AND THE CREATION.

MAY YOU ACT IN WISDOM IN THESE, THE DAYS OF TRIBULATION.

SALU.

CHAPTER THIRTY

"Growing Pains" Of The Planetary Transition

Ceres Anthonious Soltec
&
Violinio Saint Germain
February 15, 1998

Good morning, my friend. It is I, Toniose Soltec, come in the Radiant One Light of Creator Source. Be at PEACE.

There are those who wish to get messages through at this time. Please allow for the interchange, for there are great inner emotional rewards to be gained in doing so. Find the Inner Knowing and sense the Inner-Connectedness, and from that vantage point draw upon the certainty and knowingness of that which you hold in your heart as having value. Resist not and allow the energies to flow naturally.

We shall not let you fall but, if you insist upon experiencing a fall, neither shall we prevent you from your free-will choice. We shall add unto you our strength when your heart and head are in agreement with your Higher Knowing self.

Let go of the past, for it is gone. Find yourself IN THE

MOMENT and go forth anew. Allow for the moment and make the most of it.

Thank you! I shall stand aside as another wishes to speak.

* * *

Greetings, my friend. It is I, Violinio St. Germain of the Violet Ray, come to commune with you that a much needed message get penned.

Yes, and thank you for asking: I DO come in the Light! I come as the representative of the Violet Ray of Transmutation. Your world is in the midst of birthing from one density of experiencing into the next natural level of evolvement. This type of planetary shift in consciousness presents many unique opportunities and challenges for EVERY being who participates.

There shall be the apparent suffering of many who have failed to realize this greater reason for experiencing. But know that all is unfolding as it should in this "schoolroom" environment, for some of the most important lessons that can be offered anywhere in the entire Omniverse are available at this time on Earth-Shan.

With the ramping-up of the frequency (and thus energy) of the planetary environment, there is available a new, more expansive level (or cycle) of functioning. Along with this new cycle of "life" experience comes new awarenesses and an overall sense of inner connectedness with Creator Source and with ALL life, everywhere. You shall finally FEEL what your Native American brothers have been trying to explain to you since before you stole and decimated their lands.

The NON-PHYSICAL senses of physical man shall be brought more fully to the forefront of conscious awareness. They shall become as matter-of-fact as are the presently utilized senses of hearing, sight, taste, touch, and smell.

Many are already using these finer, "etheric" senses, and have been for quite some time. For instance, it will become commonplace for ones to know you, not by your physical appearance, but moreso by the electromagnetic light emanations that you each emit, yet you tend to ignore for the most part.

You would be correct in surmising that hiding ANYTHING will be difficult under these conditions, so the habits of lying, cheating, etc., would become as visible as are currently your shoes or winter gloves. What do you think this will do to the "cover" of the many leeches and parasites running around on your planet at this time? For those few who may physically survive the continual planetary upshift, it will be quite an uncomfortable environment in which to hold onto those old habits!

I, Germain, have been summoned (chosen) as a Guide to help those who are desiring assistance to make this transition as smoothly as can be deemed reasonable. There is generally a great amount of confusion associated with this type of experience for those of you who have chosen to participate in the physical. The confusion is greatly amplified by the apparent lack of general acknowledgment of what is truly unfolding in physical space.

I say "apparent" because each being participating at this time can, if they so choose, feel the "tension" in the ethers. There is a general nervousness that has been ever increasing, and the rate of noticeable incremental change is greatly accelerated.

It is such that, by the time you ones adjust to the current level of "tension", it has already shifted and you are finding yourselves in a near constant state of adjusting. This will manifest in many ways. For some it will be physiological pressures such as headaches, muscle spasms, and gastro-intestinal disorders. For others it may be irritableness, nervousness, or feelings of apprehension.

Many are feeling somewhat "rushed" as if there is not enough time to get done those things that need to get done. These are all signs and clues to you ones that, indeed, the Great Shift is near. This is the "quickening" of sorts that many are beginning to consciously FEEL, as well as see the effects of.

It is of utmost importance to shed the ties of past habits, for holding onto those "old ways" will only serve to impede the natural flow of transition.

This is the same as what happens when a heavy anchor holds down a wooden boat while the waters around it are rising. Eventually the boat gets pulled under, whereas the boat's natural (built-in) tendency was to float with the rising water (that is, the increasing frequency, and thus energy, of the planet).

Or, another way of looking at it is that when you become anchored, you are acting much like an electrical grounding rod. You will create a condition which will cause a "short circuit" of sorts, and thus "burn" you. One can hold onto (and thus float along with) a high-voltage wire, such as feeds your household electricity grid, and as long as there is no path to ground, you will not be hurt. BUT, as soon as any practical ground path exists, electricity can flow through the body. You now have a rapid heating of the waters of the body (97-98% of your body is essentially water) and thus, among other things, you burn.

Holding on to past habits that have deep emotional ties in the physical will only serve to cause great discomfort within as the etheric counterpart to the physical body is (choose your analogy) either "pulled under" as the waters keep rising, or is "grounded out" and thus begins to "burn".

Many of you are not aware of the extent to which you hold onto past worries, doubts, fears, and perceived pains.

You ALL do this to varying degrees. Some of you hold onto these charged events more than others, and due to the strong emotional sensitivity of the female apparatus, the women will in general have a tougher time with letting go of this excess "baggage" than will the men, yet women will also generally be the first ones who begin to recognize and utilize more fully the non-physical senses.

These transitionary times need not be difficult for any. But, as it stands this day, there shall be many who will simply refuse to let go of the baggage and will suffer greatly as they resist the ever increasing energy flow of this change.

The values of the past will be greatly shifted. This is to say that what many of you hold, in your heart, as desirable this day, will not hold any value whatsoever in the times just ahead. The more physically oriented are ones values, the more traumatic this change shall be.

Ones will not lust over the status of a job title. Ones will be greatly honored to serve freely their brethren, for they will see the oneness and unity of Creator Source in everyone, everywhere. Ones will not try to hoard physical "things" for there will be a greater understanding and realization that it is only out of fear-of-lack that you do so now.

These are truly magnificent times in which to be experiencing! There are many who will fight and struggle with this change, and in doing so, they will either tap the Inner Knowing within and "grow with the flow", or they will simply succumb to the emotional exhaustion of fighting change or to the anxiety of trying to understand.

This is where you, as Ground Crew, will have your greatest opportunities to assist your brothers and sisters in need. This is NOT the time to tell them: "I told you so!" Remember that you came here at this time as much to function as teachers of the New Ways as to experience your own lessons of growth. As a teacher, do you laugh in the face of your students' questions and lack of knowledge, or do you recognize and respect their often hesitant steps toward awakening?

It will be the time to humbly offer them these insights so that they may come to their own level of understanding of what it is that they are experiencing. Much confusion shall exist—it already does, but mostly bubbling at a subconscious (not consciously acknowledged) level at this time.

Be not harsh nor forceful. If ones "spit in your face" for trying to help, then be not offended. Simply go on your way and be attentive to offering assistance to others who request same. You will find that, for the most part, people will come to you out of curiosity and ask you why it is that you are so at peace and self assured while all seems to be in chaos around them.

This is the basic reason for having this information come out BEFORE the fact of this Great Shift in consciousness. Another reason is so that ones will know that there truly does exist we Guides of the unseen realms and, by inference, that God has never once left them unattended. Moreover, ones shall then realize that it was THEIR choice to ignore the clues which were there the entire time for them to take note of.

Growth, and the resultant expansion of awareness, is the primary reason for having gone through any experience. There is very little of true lasting value to be gained in the physical outside of this one, basic, non-physical parameter.

The number of dollars that you have in a bank account, or on a sheet that lists your worth (assets), is of ZERO value when compared to the value of some experience that you might go through which causes you to look within and tap an Inner Strength you never realized you had within. *This is true growth; this is what you take with you. This is what is real; this is what has lasting value.*

Nothing that you have in the physical will leave with you when you release from the physical experience. What will go with you is the acquired knowledge and insights that the challenges of the physical experience caused you to search for and find.

Find peace in knowing that, if you are reading this, it is likely because you have an inner desire to understand. This "active seeking" is the path that will garner you the true value that your inner heart connection longs for with interminable desire.

We, of the Hosts of God, are here to prepare, to the best of our ability, those who desire to expand beyond that which is their present level of growth, for these ones sense what is coming quickly into their reality and wish to maximize their potential to succeed in fulfilling their growth desire.

In doing so, we ALL gain in untold ways, as the invigorating surge of newness springs forth out of the decay of the old. Remember that as one grows, we all grow.

Our challenge is a formidable one and our reward is beyond the limitations of words, for it spans a multitude of dimensional realities and is not limited to the physical domain. To say the least, both the challenges and the rewards are beyond your purest ideas of passion, bliss, or satisfaction. We are quite thankful to play our part in manifesting this experience of growth.

I am Violinio St. Germain. I am keeper of the Violet Flame at this time. I am honored to serve with those of you who have come with the intent to serve your brethren at this time of planetary awakening and transition.

Let go of the perceived indiscretions of the past. Forgive those whom you perceive as having "done you wrong"! Those who have "spit in your face" are the ones whom you have come to help! You would be wise NOT to let this fact leave your thoughts.

NOW IS THE TIME TO CLEANSE THYSELF OF THE EMOTIONAL GARBAGE THAT YOU SO FONDLY CARRY AROUND!

In Light and Blessings to you all.

SALU!

CHAPTER THIRTY-ONE

Accepting The Driver's Seat In *Your* Life

Ceres Anthonious Soltec
February 22, 1998

Good evening, and thank you for sitting at this time. It is I, Toniose Soltec, come in the Radiant One Light of Creator Source. Be at peace—yet know that what you perceive as a critical time upon your world, centered in the area of your Middle East, is indeed so. However, let not even these distractions detour you from your own duties and preparations at this time.

Before launching into the main subject of this writing, I would like to call to your attention several recent earthquake events. The first of these was a "M2.6" event in the New Madrid, Missouri region of your United States on Thursday morning, 2/19/98. (I put these officially reported magnitude readings in quote marks to remind you that such events are purposely generally under-reported, according to what Dr. Young likes to call the "K-mart discount scale of creative measurement".)

In conjunction with two large (approximately M6.0) earthquakes earlier in the week along the mid-Atlantic

(Ocean) Ridge, you can begin to arrive at a picture for pressures increasing which are buckling the middle of your continental tectonic plate in that critical New Madrid Fault area which runs north-south approximately along your Mississippi River. Molten magma material, which is flowing east-west from where it is oozing out along a north-south line in the middle of your Atlantic Ocean, is squeezing the land masses at each shore.

Remember that your continental United States is being squeezed by forces pushing from BOTH sides, and this is resulting in the observed stepped-up earthquake activity starting all the way up at your St. Lawrence River and near Montréal, Canada, on down through the Great Lakes region, and then continuing down to the famous (or should I say soon-to-be infamous) New Madrid Fault region, terminating at the Gulf of Mexico, splitting Texas from Mississippi, right through a sinking Louisiana. It would be wise to take another look at the *Future Map Of The United States* which Gordon-Michael Scallion produced. [*Editor's note: To order Scallion's* Future Map Of The World *or his* Future Map Of North America *or his periodical called* Earth Changes Report, *call 1-800-628-7493 or 1-603-363-4164 or write to Matrix Institute, P.O. Box 336, Chesterfield, NH 03443-0336. You can also visit their Internet web site* ***www.matrixinstitute.com*** *if you have access to that route for gathering information.*]

While most all attention is focused upon your volatile West Coast, with its heightened storm and earthquake activities, it would be wise to not completely forget about this "sleeping giant" called the New Madrid Fault. It may prove to be the focus of the greater hysteria and destruction simply because so few have been willing to associate that region with major earthquake activity, compared to your already infamous West Coast, and thus most ones there are quite ill-prepared for what is to happen.

Meanwhile, ever-shaking Japan has been officially "allowed" to have earthquakes again—so long as they do not turn you from the center-stage distraction events there called your Olympics. Those of you who were viewing those events on Friday evening (2/20/98) were briefly and casually informed about a "mere" "M5.2" event, felt by "some" at the Olympics, which was centered near the west coast of Honshu, Japan.

I am not going to list all of the relevant Earth-related activity going on at this time, for such would only overwhelm your already purposely overwhelmed attention spans. It is enough to simply call to your notice several clues, from what has occurred this past week, which are outstandingly indicative of the further escalation of pressures which shall, soon, result in events of pressure release which will no doubt shock the sleeping masses—and may distract even those of you who think you are prepared for what is to come.

And it is this theme of distraction-from-responsibilities to which I would like to turn, for such is a chronic problem upon your place.

There are many distractions thrown your way at this time. Beware of those who might impact your day with trivial matters. It is one thing to help someone who has a true need; it is quite another thing to get distracted into another's drama of perceived helplessness.

You must use your own Inner Guidance and judgement, for the challenge is yours to face and grow from. Look for the clues and signs, and you will know what is the best choice for you. Many will come seeking answers, and many will want someone to follow.

These ones are looking for someone to discern FOR them what is appropriate, what is "right", and other matters of private concerns that have little or NOTHING to do with why YOU are there at this time. This is but a distraction, at the least, and if you bite, it could become quite a "karmic" trap from which you may have future difficulties. Each MUST learn to discern for self, and a wise person will not even attempt to do so FOR another.

If ones become offended by your reluctance to discern on their behalf, then that is their choice. From the larger perspective of the soul, they will be thanking you for the assistance that you are, in fact, providing.

Your world is one of opposites. This is to say that, often, what people think they need is, actually, the exact opposite of what they truly need.

We observe that ones in the physical are easy to give over their responsibility for self to another. We see this happen when ones of Ground Crew offer assistance to ones with apparent need, and then these ones in "need" often take advantage of the offered generosity to a point of dependency—if the one offering assistance allows that.

This fostering of dependency is NOT a "righteous" thing to do for your brother. In fact, it is the exact opposite of what he truly needs.

Do NOT misunderstand my point here!

I am not suggesting you contribute to a cold and heartless world. But for those of you who always fly to the other extreme, of "helping" everyone who asks, all of the time, I AM suggesting the need for cultivating and applying "tough love" in those appropriate instances. And there will ALWAYS be clues.

It is often the correct action to assist someone in true need. Offer the assistance and, in doing so, TEACH THE OTHER TO HELP THEMSELVES! If the other does not wish to learn to help themselves, or gives pitiful excuses as to why they cannot, then let them to THEIR choices. There are ALWAYS the clues—if you are honest about interpreting what is being displayed in front of you.

It is unwise to short-circuit another's opportunity for growth. In doing so you will only cause yourself unnecessary hardship and grief. Be willing to lead another to water, if they be thirsty, but do not try to swallow it for them. If they cannot see the value in doing things for themselves, then let them experience the consequences of their choices.

We of the Hosts often witness choices being made which give EVERY indication of a wayward purpose or lack of thoughtful value placement. For example, how many have money for cigarettes or movies or vacation trips or new gadgets, and yet "cannot afford" (or worse: remain dependent upon others for) such as a *CONTACT* subscription and/or health-promoting items from New Gaia Products?

As we of the Hosts have taught in so many past lessons, be ever attentive to the ENERGY FLOWS in all situations. Are the flows two-way or one-way in nature? Are they giving and receiving, or are they taking and taking? While not difficult discernments, these do take honesty!

You who are truly of Ground Crew have that which you *NEED* IN THE MOMENT in order to accomplish your mission. Remember: YOU *ARE* CREATOR MANIFEST! You can create that which you need, and you will, when your desire is both strong enough and clear enough.

Ah—but this is where the adversary gets in: If he does not completely incapacitate you through doubt, he keeps you distracted, and in doing so, he keeps you from marching a straight line to your goal.

When you can become determined and focused upon that which has true wisdom and value, especially that which is consistent with your Higher Self's purpose, then you will manifest the desired end result. This is where joy enters the equation.

Remember, however, that the fundamental Law of Creation is blind to purpose—desire and determination are the keys—and nowhere is this concept better demonstrated today than in the case of the "success" of the dark "elite" in manifesting what they desire in your world. As Commander Hatonn has emphasized so many times, if you Lighted ones only mustered half of the determination that motivates these dark ones, your world would be a very different, better place at this time!

For those of you who are asking the question about justice, yes, it is true that there are still Higher Laws of

Creation which will eventually cause the rebalancing of that which has been manifested or created that is inconsistent with Creator's Higher Purpose. But that, too, is part of your lessons as experiencing beings along the path toward eventual oneness with Creator.

And speaking of paths, the path toward any goal is of secondary concern. This is to say that the END RESULT is what should preoccupy your thinking—not the infinite possible paths there are to reaching that goal. Remember how many times we of the Hosts have reminded you that we (as well as your personal Guides) may HELP you along a path, but we shall not do it FOR you. Yet from our point of view, there are unlimited possible pathways, so don't become preoccupied with any one possible route.

Take the case of ones with an addiction to a chemical substance. These ones will become greatly fixated upon their desire for their next "fix" (euphoric high derived from the chemical substance). In doing so, they begin to set in motion creational energies that will spawn an idea that will lead them to fulfilling their desire. These ones often cannot hold down a job, but can manifest enough money to support a $1000-a-day drug habit. Why? Because their desire is that strong! Ethics and morals, as you ones perceive them, have little to do with one's basic ability to focus and thus manifest—at least in the short term. Naturally if what you are manifesting is of a destructive nature, it shall eventually teach you that lesson, too.

Clarity of thought has become one of the greatest challenges facing you of Ground Crew. The primary challenge that many of you encounter is learning to mentally cope with the "denseness" associated with the environment of your planet.

This denseness that I refer to is in the frequency range of MENTAL activity. There is great and deliberate bombardment aimed directly at the mental "electrical field" of your bodies, in order to keep those of you who are awakening (and thus gathering creative inertia) distracted and off-balance long enough so that the intended enslavement of your planet can be realized.

You who are awakening are the single greatest threat to these "elite" controllers, for you hold within your collective creativity the solution that will unravel their plans. When your desire for justice becomes great enough and deep enough, you will draw to you the idea(s) necessary to expose, and thus topple, these ones who think themselves greater than the rest of you.

The recent media-orchestrated fiasco (from the point of the view of the "elite" planners) at Ohio State University is a good example of the dark "elite's" plans gone awry due to too many of you remaining awake despite weeks of mind-numbing propaganda that was calculated to stir you into a frenzy FOR a war in the Middle East. Oops! Could the dark "elite" have overestimated their power? Might they have grown a bit too smug toward the success of their precious goal of world control? If they be so great, then why is it that they so thoroughly fear The Truth?

The truth of the matter is that greatness comes from within, and they operate from a purely external, physical, non-caring, detached point of view. They know not the meaning of the term INNER SATISFACTION. These ones derive pleasure from taking and destroying, for such generates emotional responses in the only frequency range in which they can actually FEEL anything at all! These ones are efforting to feel "alive"—but at the expense of their only true connection to Life. While they may be great at manifesting their desires (to a point), their ignorance of basic spiritual truths keeps them from experiencing the Greater Reality that is fundamental to what you term experiencing joy.

"Learn to accept those things that you cannot change." Yes, but first learn to RECOGNIZE those things that you CAN change! This, again, goes back to personal discernment. The complete gem of a saying goes like this: "Lord, grant me the *Courage* to change the things I can, the

Patience to accept the things I cannot, and the *Wisdom* to know the difference!"

Can you change the state of your world? Yes, by recognizing those un-Godly practices that impede true freedom—AND taking appropriate action to correct them, which requires effort.

Can you truly change another's thoughts regarding anything? NO! The thoughts of an individual are for them to choose. You can, however, educate ones who have, first, the desire to learn. It is unwise to try to push, in anyone's face, this writing or any information that an individual resists for any reason.

The information in *CONTACT* is primarily for the purpose of awakening Ground Crew. It also acts to alert the adversarial forces to our (Higher, the Hosts of God) presence, so that they too can have the opportunity to wake up and realize the wisdom of maintaining an inner connection with Creator Source.

Those who are "in between" these two categories are the souls who are here to experience choices between "inner (soul) connection" and "outer (physical) detachment". We are here to assist any and all who would have the desire to more fully recognize and utilize their own Inner Potential.

God's plan allows for us to help anyone, no matter what they have done in their past. When ones ask with the heart, and truly acknowledge their past ignorances, they shall be given all the help they can handle in a balanced and acceptable manner. God knows the heart intent of each individual and there is no tricking Him with silly plays on words. Your agreements with Him are made in the universal language of heart intent—a language in which physical words, with limited and obscure meanings, play no part at all.

As Ground Crew you are expected to learn to utilize your own God-given ability to discern for selves what it is that you are to do from day to day and moment to moment. When your physical (ego-based) intent is in alignment with your (Higher) heart intent, the

connection to Source which brings assurance of path and conviction of purpose will be most evident.

In overcoming this challenge (the alignment of intents) you will begin to find the answers to such questions as:

What is my purpose?

What can I do to be a part of this Larger Game?

Am I *really* a part of Ground Crew?

These are common questions about which many of you are petitioning for answers. These are questions that are answered from within, in the form of heart-felt Knowing.

Learn to focus clearly upon any question that you have. If need be, ask yourself: "How would Hatonn (Sananda, Germain, Lanto, etc.) answer this question?" (This is the mental attunement process which was basically how this receiver started out—long before he ever got the idea to write down our responses.)

Sit down and write out, to the best of your ability, how you feel that the entity of your choice would answer your question. Hint: We are Teachers and we will help you to find your answers, but we will almost never dump the answer upon you. You will be guided, often through a series of questions, that will help you to learn to discern your own answers.

Often you can find your own answers by knowing what questions to ask selves. Many of you already do this naturally, and simply miss the fact that *we* are the ones who help you to formulate the questions in the first place!

Choose what works best for you and TRUST that you are NEVER alone—NEVER! You ALL have been appointed personal Guides, but if you are not sure enough about your Guides to interact with them in a direct fashion, then forget about that route and go straight to the One Light Source with your questions. Be not distracted over who may or may not be YOUR Guide(s). Keep the Light all about you and let your intent ALWAYS be within the highest frequency of Light you can imagine.

In these times of massive, planned distractions, you will each be confronted with orchestrated, artificial events which will seem so real that the only way to know they are not is to pay close attention to what your heart is telling you. The perfection of current holographic technology is beyond what any of you can imagine.

If you get nothing else from this message, please recognize the value in consciously making YOUR own connection to Source, for therein can you fulfill YOUR responsibility to discern for yourself. This is YOUR experience and YOUR growth; do not expect another to do it for you!

May you not allow yourself to be distracted from finding YOUR inner Source connection.

I am Ceres Anthonious "Toniose" Soltec, come in the Light of the One Light Source of All That Is.

Salu!

CHAPTER THIRTY-TWO

Growing In Harmony With Great Mother Earth

Ceres Anthonious Soltec
March 12, 1998

Good afternoon and be at peace. It is I, Toniose Soltec, come in the radiant One Light of Creator Source. Be at peace.

There are reasons for all things that happen. The ones with whom you interacted on your trip were indeed influenced by your presence. Much of what was communicated to them was in your attitude and non-verbal mannerisms. These ones were indeed helped by just being around you. Let not even the smallest comment be discredited as insignificant. There was much work done as we and their Guides worked with and through you. Many Ground Crew function in a similar teaching capacity, especially toward their circle of friends, at this time of imminent transition of a planet.

There is but little time left for any sort of "hand holding". Change will be ever increasing on your globe and we need able persons up and working. If ones choose to ignore the warnings and assistance offered, then that is their choice and it should be honored. Let us now go forth and be about our Father's work.

There has been much taking place in the world that needs to be addressed. For example, there have been serious weather manipulations, especially in your Midwest and Southeast (of the United States) that have not gone unnoticed. Ones are, rightly so, questioning such phenomena as the blue-green lightning noticed during the Midwest's recent paralyzing snowstorm. Meanwhile, others are questioning the "precise timing" and "pinpoint accuracy" of a flood and freeze that shall destroy much of this year's peach and strawberry crops in your Southeast. (And yes, there is a serious connection between this activity and the glowing "stuff" observed by many to be falling out of busy night skies recently.)

There has been a new and "enhanced" series of earthquakes in two south-central regions of the California desert area. One swarm was centered about 30-35 miles north of Ridgecrest; the other created a very widely-felt early-morning (3/11/98) wake-up call, centered near Redlands.

The Ridgecrest-area quakes (near the China Lake Naval Weapons Center) were in the magnitude 5 range according to Cal-Tech's earthquake web page data on this day (http://scec.gps.caltech.edu/cgi-bin/finger?quake).

I asked my scribe to check the readily available data. What was noted was an interesting "discrepancy" between various information sources. One source, called *Seismic Event Bulletin* [*Internet web site no longer available*], which prominently displays the United Nations symbol, listed the same Ridgecrest events with the magnitude lower by a factor of 10. This is to say that what the Cal-Tech site listed as a 5.1 magnitude, was listed on the *Seismic Event Bulletin* site as 4.1 magnitude.

Remember that the magnitude scales are logarithmic. This means that the difference between a 4.1 quake and a 5.1 quake is a factor of 10 in intensity! Perhaps this was just a mistake on the part of the one entering the data onto the web site? But, with closer inspection you will note that many of the quakes listed on this later site are entered with a lower magnitude—if they are even listed at all.

There were three quakes greater than 4.0M that were listed with Cal-Tech and yet did NOT even show up on the other list. Here again I must remind all of you to discern carefully any and all information that comes across your path—including this information! May your truth be of YOUR own reasoning and not that of another.

There are electromagnetic manipulations affecting the planet's natural energy grid which are causing many a distortion all around your globe. Most of these distortions are causing problems that the perpetrators cannot even begin to understand, let alone monitor. Your planet's energy centers (chakras) are beginning to compensate for these anomalies, and in doing so there are occurring some unplanned weather patterns, plus seismic and volcanic shifts that the "elite" cannot compensate for, control, or understand. These ones have no understanding or respect for the entity known as Mother Earth, who has a mind of her own.

This is where it becomes most difficult, if not impossible, for you ones to know what is natural and what is man-made. Be assured that what you ones are experiencing is, at the very least, a reaction to man's toying with energies and forces that he does NOT fully understand, let alone respect. From our perspective, it is a lot like giving a two-year-old in the sandbox a loaded hand gun and telling him to go play.

Be also assured that BALANCE shall be returned to your planet, for that is God's promise to your planet. Those of you who wish to be part of the solution are welcome to join in the challenge.

There is more to discuss on this subject, but let us stop for now, for there are other priorities to attend at present. Toniose Soltec to standby.

March 13, 1998

Toniose Soltec here in the Radiant One Light that connects us ALL! Let us continue please.

As your planet progresses forward in these times of change, there shall become more evident the true awesome power of her being. Ones will have no doubt as to the Life Force that she possesses. The magnitude of her being is indeed great. You ones shall stand witness to her evolvement and transformation as she progresses forward in her cleansing and subsequent growth.

You can play your part in these times of change by learning to cleanse the garbage from within yourself and by finding your own inner balance. In doing so, you will find that you will be more fully alert to our nudges and thus more able to flow with the changes and not be "swept" away in them. This is to say that you will evolve along with Mother Earth, for you will be in harmony (agreement) with that which is the natural course of unfolding.

There is no need for any to struggle or suffer in these times, yet there shall be many, out of ignorance and stubbornness, who will choose to do so. Do not worry over another's choices.

Many of you shall see family and friends go through massive struggle as they try to understand and cope with what they will be faced with in terms of change. Again, this will be a product of THEIR own choices. Be not upset over these things, for these are the lessons and challenges that these ones have come to experience.

The pressures that are building in the etheric realms are indeed of an awesome magnitude. Never before have the conditions been this spectacular. There are great potentials for inward and outward growth available to each of you.

CLEANSING OF YOURSELF IS THE TRUE KEY TO MAXIMIZING YOUR ABILITY TO EXPLOIT THIS GRAND OPPORTUNITY! Again, as we have tried to

tell you ones over and over—LET GO OF THE PAST EMOTIONAL "GARBAGE"!!!!

Garbage here is defined as that which only serves to hold you in past emotional low-frequency patterns. For example: If someone has publicly humiliated you and embarrassed you, and every time you hear the person's name you react in an emotional outrage, then YOU will, by your choice to hold on to the past hurt, be giving up a most grand opportunity of inner growth, because the low-frequency state generated will keep you disconnected from the Inner Guidance you will be needing in order to most effectively utilize this opportunity. In effect, you will become your own worst enemy.

No one can be blamed for causing you to feel grief. No one! Neither can anyone be blamed for causing you to feel joy! YOU create your own emotional feelings, and YOU are solely responsible for how it is that you are feeling at any given moment in time.

Time is the key!

What happened even just a moment ago need not affect you now. It is your wallowing in the past that causes you the most pain and discomfort. LET IT GO! You all do this to some degree.

When you are at your worst, stop and analyze what you are so upset about. When did it happen? The answer will always be—IN THE PAST!

Let it go and find something to be thankful for regarding the situation. Even "bad" relationships have the positive value of helping you to become more clear on what exactly it is that you are wanting. Is this not of value?

Be thankful for those who have "done you wrong". But most importantly: forgive yourselves for having been ignorant to the nature of these ones who feel the need to manipulate and control.

They are usually ignorant of what it is that they are wanting and how to create it, so they spend a lot of time taking apart the creations of others in their attempt to back-engineer the whole process. This is the backwards way of doing things. It is like taking apart a clock to see how it works. Usually the only thing that is truly learned is that there is a LOT to learn before true understanding will be evident.

You all have room to grow in terms of understanding the true potential of your being. Allow for your own mistakes and misjudgments. Forgive yourselves when you feel anger toward another, for it is almost always due to misunderstanding on YOUR part of the greater reason for being part of this grand experiment in progress.

You are here to learn to control your emotional energy flows in a balanced and responsible manner. There are indeed appropriate times and places for ALL emotional experiences.

These, my friends, are the fundamental keys to happiness and fulfillment that you ones are so deliberately seeking. Your inner (Higher Knowing) self knows what has true value.

It is the experience of inner GROWTH that you are seeking! When you are dwelling in the past, there will be little-to-no time left in the present for the opportunity to grow. By contrast, when you are in the process of growing, there is an excitement associated with what you are doing, for you are fulfilling a very fundamental desire of Creation—EXPANSION AND GROWTH!

Your planet is operating in like manner. She has agreed to serve in a capacity which would facilitate an environment wherein she would experience with and through each of you. Your inner emotional state is sensed by your planet, and she experiences these emotions. The converse is also true: you feel her emotional state. As she continues to shift upward in frequency, there will result an ever more serious mismatch between those who insist upon dwelling in the lower-frequency states and her new higher frequency radiance.

This creates a situation like an electrical potential

(voltage or pressure) that is ever growing. There are many who are feeling the effects of this potential today.

Many of your "elite" would-be controllers are entering into states of frenzied anxiety due to this potential energy charge that is building. This anxiety will only serve to push these ones "over the edge" mentally, and thus you have the prime conditions developing that will eventually trigger massive world changes and shifts in awareness.

Man's tampering with the planet's electromagnetic grid only serves to accelerate his own downfall. These energy devices could be utilized in a healing capacity, to help the planet regain her own stability—if the proper enlightenment had been attained by those who are currently misusing the technology.

Your planet shall, in these times of desperation, be given the assistance to sluff-off those who have efforted, in their ignorance, to destroy her. Such has been the way of your world and there is no evidence of these children, in the sandbox, waking-up to see that they are about to shoot themselves in the head.

Find yourself in the moment that you are now in and seek deliberate understanding of the words offered herein. We of the Hosts of Creator God have a great desire to assist any and all of you in these times of challenge and growth.

Your growth is directly linked to our own. Our creative challenge is to help you find the key that enables you to move beyond your own limitations. In doing so, we garner great insights into our own being, and thus we too grow. It is truly a "win-win" situation for all who choose to participate in this interchange.

May you find the inner value offered WITHIN these words. Seek within for your clarification and understanding. Be quick to call upon we of the Lighted Brotherhood for assistance, for when a deliberate call is made, we are granted a greater level or interaction with you. Likewise we will not go where we are not welcome.

I am Ceres Anthonious "Toniose" Soltec, come in

service to Father-Mother Source. It is from within this One Light that we all come forth to experience.

Salu.

CHAPTER THIRTY-THREE

Rising Above The Adversary's Tricks

Violinio Saint Germain
March 28, 1998

Good afternoon, my scribe. It is I, Violinio St. Germain. I come as Cohan (Teacher) of the Violet Ray of Transmutation. I am most busy in these times of transition from "out of the old" and "into the new".

Your world is on the brink of war and many there in the United States are oblivious to the clues that are all around them. The masses sleep while the "elitist" game-players dictate the fate of your world.

Who gives these dark ones the right to do so?

YOU DO!

When good people of reasonable intelligence DO NOTHING, then they (you) have chosen—either directly or indirectly—to give over their (your) freedom. YOU are responsible for that which impacts your experience!

You are led to believe that you are too small to even have an impact on the local scene, let alone the global scene. This is a lie!

Look to some of your present social leaders, such as

Louis Farrakhan. Is he not ONE man with ONE voice? Is he greater than any other man? He has, perhaps, greater desire than do most of you reading this. He is willing to stand up and voice his awareness of that which is impacting his and your experience.

Why is it that most of you cower at the thought of someone ridiculing you over your opinions and viewpoints? ***It is that old challenge called fear! This fear is exactly what most of you are there to face and overcome.***

When enough people will stand up and demand accountability of those who are in power, then and only then will change be realized. This is not as difficult an effort as it may at first seem, but accountability most certainly will not "happen on its own"—especially under the current conditions of your darkened and controlled planet!

Many times there have been opportunities for EACH of you to speak up and voice that which you know to be Truth. Some of you exploit these opportunities on every occasion, but most of you simply sit there, quietly, and say little or nothing, out of fear.

This is the adversary playing you for a weakling. Was not Esu "Jesus" Immanuel ridiculed, beaten, and spat upon for voicing Truth? Was he not just ONE man with ONE voice?

You each have INFINITE inner Potential and you each are efforting to overcome the self-imposed limitations that keep you from realizing and drawing upon your vast inner Power. This infinite Power derives from your being no less than a spark (Lighted fragment) of Creator Source!

The greatest obstacle comes from your own inner beliefs that it is somehow dangerous or painful to step forward and release yourselves from the chains that shackle you in the perceived comforts of mental and emotional slavery. You are kept in this state by design and due to your own ignorance of Higher Truth and Reality.

The adversary to God is a *master* gamesman and knows what tricks will work to dissuade you. However, as we have said so many times in past writings, it only takes ONE who truly awakens to the Light of their inner self-Power, while in the physical, to severely disrupt the adversary's whole game-plan.

I petition to you ones: Don't hold back the gifts offered here! If the thought crosses your mind for even a moment, then act upon the impulse and share. If ones laugh or ridicule you, then forgive them and move on.

You do not have to defend God or His Truth. These ones who choose to ridicule are the ones who need the messages the very most.

Those of you who have awakened enough to recognize the importance of this information are, if you so choose to be, OUR hands, feet, and mouth. YOU can make a difference!

You do this one day at a time, with one foot in front of the other. It will take a strong self-motivation and inner desire to persist. However, know that you will be given that which you need in order to face ANY challenge that comes across your path. The rewards to you will indeed be great if you but persist through these challenges.

Many are petitioning to help at this time. There have been many suggestions offered, particularly through this avenue of information sharing called *CONTACT*, that each of you can do from where you are located right now and with your present abilities.

Anywhere there are people, you can make a difference! You do not have to go out and seek to change anyone. We are not about shoving our reality down anyone's throat! Simply be attentive to each opportunity, when it arises. Ones are guided to cross your path so that you each may have an opportunity to learn from each other.

Many of you, again, out of fear, simply hold back that which is so desperately needed by another to help with their awakening from the stupor of mass mind-control. Those in the heavily populated areas are most severely under such influence since so many avenues of bombardment are present for manipulation purposes.

Especially in larger towns, due to the ever increasing fear of "strangers", you ones will rarely even make eye contact with one another, let alone strike-up a conversation. At least in the smaller, rural country towns there still exists some measure of the community spirit that should be the norm everywhere. However, the "elite" would-be controllers effort from the level of their global manipulations (for example, through excessive regulation and taxation on small businesses and farms) to even demoralize the camaraderie of the smallest of rural communities.

Random acts of violence have become THE "tool" of choice in order to perpetuate and maintain the state of fear. These are more commonly referred to as "terrorist tactics" when they are done by organized militaristic organizations.

When "ordinary" young teenagers in a relatively small town in the heartland of your country can take on the characteristics of cold robots without any apparent justifiable reason, and open fire on their schoolmates, you have before you an effective mechanism for controlling the population's viewpoint and emotional state. **This was no random act; it was a product of advanced mind-control and the children are merely susceptible pawns in a much larger game.**

These are the tactics that will get you-the-people screaming for gun control and disarmament. These tactics are planned and orchestrated in the same exact, calculating manner as was the assassination of President Kennedy back in 1963. As a nation stood paralyzed in disbelief at that time, so too have many around your nation had a similar reaction to the recent shootings by two young boys, 11 and 13 years old, of their friends and teachers.

If your general population knew of the existence of sophisticated mind-control tactics (which include a wide array of electronic devices and techniques as have long been reported in the pages of *CONTACT*) for achieving such sinister goals, would the public have the same response or reaction to such purposely staged events? Of course not!

The public's very predictable emotional reaction is justified from the perspective of their current level of (lack of) understanding. Our goal here is to bring ones out of the Dark Ages and into a more enlightened reality of what is being employed to manipulate and coerce them (you) into expected responses.

Understanding the truth of the matter would surely set the minds of many ones in a different direction (hopefully of constructive action instead of knee-jerk REaction) if they were to know that they are being "played" for fools. However, in this case ignorance will keep many of you ones in a state of anxiety and fear, especially those who have any direct responsibility toward children.

It is expected that this event should generate (cause the REaction of) a strong desire for safety for families and loved ones. This desire will cause these otherwise quiet and unassuming people to speak out and demand that "something" be done to prevent this sort of thing from happening ever again—such as through gun control.

This is the desired result from those who have set these events into motion. But you can be sure that the offered solution(s) will only be in a direction to further enslave and control you and take away your freedoms.

When your desire as an individual, group, or nation is strong enough so that you stand up and speak out about this sort of calculated atrocity, then you too can demand and bring about change. The key is to educate the people so that they can truly make informed decisions, not REact out of fear and ignorance—and in so doing avoid falling into the traps set for your enslavement.

You, the American public, are the greatest deterrent to the New World Order. The United Nations is having quite a difficult time convincing you ones that you

should be following THEIR leadership.

Their only choice seems to be to go in and use military force. Thus you have the systematic disarmament of the country. The military bases are all but gone compared to just 10 years ago (while many locations have been quietly turned into concentration camps to handle any of you uppity citizens who foolishly attempt to "resist" the New World Order agenda). A large portion of the American troops that you do have are (again) being shipped overseas to fight foreign battles. Your country is nearly prime for takeover.

The one last obstacle that stands in the way of the takeover plan is the fact that there are a great number of you "average citizens" who hold onto your "right to bear arms". This is the reason behind engineering such shocking events as children killing children—to chip away at that conviction toward holding onto your weapons. Am I condoning the use of such weapons? NO! I am merely pointing out the facts.

These ones in control of your planet would much rather destroy you through unsuspected covert ways than through simply going in and wiping you out. The latter carries too much risk of waking some of you up from your delusion of freedom.

The planned method is to create a militarily weakened condition so as to allow a country such as China to attack the U.S. Then, in the spirit of "rescue", the would-be kings send in the United Nations forces to finish off the job, and at the same time establish their "world peace-keeping" presence on U.S. soil with little objection from the remaining survivors.

This way, so the reasoning goes, the U.N. can take care of the Chinese "problem" at the same time they take care of the American "problem". Of course, neither of the "problems" are actually problems—except where the planning of the dark, one-world "elite" is concerned.

There are several ways for this general scenario to unfold. First, these dark "elite" controllers must get a country (China) to "bite" on the bait laid in the trap. **This is why there has been such an extensive effort to disarm the U.S.**

When the Chinese feel that they can actually take over and hold the U.S., they will then be open to the idea of doing so. However, do not underestimate the Chinese! The rulers of China are quite aware of the U.N.'s agenda and they are also very aware of the Khazarian (so-called "Jewish") element's role in dominating that agenda. China's ploy will be to attack both the United States AND Israel, simultaneously, in order to get the U.N. to divide its troops.

The various main factions of these dark "elite" controllers are quite fixated on their own personal agendas and there is NO honor among them. They will turn upon one another in a moment if it will help to get better position on the game field. These ones do not trust one another, and for very good reason—they all got to where they are by being back-stabbers, cheats, and liars. Most of them are quite proud of themselves for doing so!

Please also keep in mind that there are TWO other major players in this game of power. These are the Antarctic Germans and the true Russians (as opposed to the Khazarian "Jewish" Bolshevik Soviets) which include most of the Russian military machine, especially advanced operations such as their Cosmosphere brigade.

Understand that both of these formidable powers have, each in their own way, kicked the parasitic Khazarians out of their country and have little-to-no tolerance for their "games". These two factions are not your enemy, but if you side (out of ignorance) with the mind-bending U.N., then they will not hesitate to eliminate you as a threat.

Both the Russians and the Antarctic Germans have UFO-type craft. Meanwhile, the Khazarian-antichrist-adversarial U.N. group would love to make you-the-people believe that your world is being invaded by "bad" "aliens" so that, should you observe craft from the Russian or German groups (or from we of the Hosts of God), you would be filled with fear and REact in such a way as to band together under the "protection" of the United Nations.

In point of fact, your world has been invaded for thousands of years by the parasitic, dark, antichrist beings who have been playing these same games, all the while, since they were imprisoned here. Creator will always find a place for His creations, and each has a place and reason to be there. These dark ones provide YOU with a challenging environment in which to experience and grow. They serve a purpose in the overall perfection of God's planning and are here for reason.

Please do not judge the person, but rather the actions. Your challenge is to experience and OVERCOME these seemingly negative, adversarial things. In doing so, you will stand as example to these dark ones that there is a Greater Power within than they have ever imagined—so that these ones might eventually grow as well.

This kind of a "stand for Truth" has far greater implications of learning than you might readily perceive, because even Satan-Lucifer (the leader of the dark ones) will then eventually have to realize that he is not greater than Creator and cannot dominate Creator's Lighted fragments (you!).

Do your best to be an example (reflection) of that which is good and of Godly intent, and you will not have need to worry or fear anyone. Make every effort to act in reason, without REacting to what you are being told. Think through each situation as it crosses your path and always seek, within the Light, guidance and clarification.

I am Violinio St. Germain. I come in and of the Light of Creator Source. May you see that there is a great need to transform, through truthful education, the thinking of those who are your brothers and sisters in the unfolding drama of schoolroom Earth. This is accomplished by EACH of you doing your part. Salu!

CHAPTER THIRTY-FOUR

Are *YOU* Running From Your True Feelings?

Ceres Anthonious Soltec
April 4, 1998

Good afternoon, my friend. It is I, Toniose Soltec, come in the Radiant One Light of Creator Source. Be at peace. And yes, it is correct that you feel a blending of energies present for this writing session.

Though one or another of us will usually assume the authorship of a writing in order to not confuse readers, it would be correct, more often than not, to assume that we work in a "blended energy" fashion where many ones from our realms make contributions as needed and as a specific expertise may be called upon.

Often you ones expect me to focus solely on what YOU understand to be the geophysical aspects of this planetary transition mission—earthquakes, volcanos, etc. And this is understandable from the "drama" and "excitement" associated with these events.

However, how often have I and many others, in many writings past, stated that "ALL is connected to ALL"? Thus it would be wise on your part to assume that even messages and lessons such as "I" am offering here, which SEEM to be unrelated to my scientific command duties, do indeed have a strong, if not readily appreciated, geophysical component. **How you ones conduct yourselves in ALL facets of living has a DIRECT impact upon Mother Earth.**

All is as it should be! This is perhaps the most compact way to state that all is unfolding in perfection according to God's plan. We of the Higher (vibrational frequency) Realms can observe this as fact, whereas most of you in the physical experience will question and doubt. Such is the way of your world, especially in these times of great challenges.

You will see value in learning to trust that which you can FEEL IN YOUR HEART to be true! Many ignore these heart-felt warnings, for they symbolize responsibility for self.

This is to say that, when ones begin to go within and LISTEN to their own Guidance, they are often fearful of being responsible for that which they "hear" (sense/feel/know). And thus, if they were to act upon these inner nudges, they (in some cases "you") would begin to feel the discomfort of coming out of ignorance and into the knowing that the Guidance has been there all along.

You are NEVER alone! You need NO one and NO thing in order to commune with Father-Mother Source!

This statement, of course, is heresy from the point of view of your mind-controlling organized religions. These tell you that you need the priest (or minister or rabbi or other "authority figure") to act on your behalf. Nothing could be further from the truth, yet is every day presented to you as such, for the typical religious machinery is a source of great financial profit as well as absolution from personal responsibility.

Rather, you *ALL* should be coming into a more direct awareness of your personal connection with Creator Source. You should all be striving to wean yourselves from depending upon the external guidance of others.

In its healthiest form, this external guidance should only be offered for your use as a means to confirm that which you are already sensing (hearing, receiving, etc.) within. It is fine to utilize a "crutch"; however, it is unwise to become dependent upon that as your only means of support.

In the relatively near future you will be very happy that you have spent time strengthening the necessary "receiving muscles" in order to support self—and others, if need be. Ones who bring forth these public messages will be about their own lessons, and in the times of chaos, they will not have the means to get these words to you for your education, confirmations, or support. What will YOU do then?

Would it not be wise to plan for these times and prepare NOW! The task is not difficult. All you need is a strong and focused desire to do so, and allow for the connection to unfold.

This message is for those of you who refuse to even try. Or, who pretend to try, but really have given up before even starting. You ALL can and will learn to communicate in a direct manner with Creator Source!

Will you all be writing general public messages to the masses? No.

You will, however, benefit greatly by "making the connection" within to Source, and so too will those with whom you interact on a regular basis. This "mutual benefit" is a direct result of the interconnectedness of all of creation.

The question of how to make that inner connection to Source has been addressed at great lengths prior to this. You ones would be wise to re-read that which has already been offered on this subject. [*Editor's note: "Professor" Soltec is referring to earlier writings in this series which are offered in the volume called* Wisdom Of The Rays: The Masters Teach, Volume I. *Information about that collection of writings and how to obtain it is located in the Preface of this volume, or call Phoenix Source Distributors at 1-800-800-5565.*]

We of the Hosts of God are here to assist each of you through these times of challenge. You can assist us in doing our job by doing your part to meet us part way. Recognizing the "fear reaction" from the attendant responsibility that is a common initial consequence of the receiving process goes a long way toward that goal of helping us to help you.

There are many of you out there who are able to "hear" us quite well, yet many of you prefer the comfort of what you perceive to be "all" that you can do. So be it, for we are not about force, nor would we coerce any into doing anything. The choice must be YOURS, or it simply will not be.

You each have "gifts" to share with one another. This is to say that you are all unique fragments of Creator Source with your own unique talents and abilities. These "gifts" are meant to be utilized and shared with those in your immediate circle of influence. You all can benefit greatly by establishing a conscious two-way connection between yourself and your Guides.

There is a great level of redundancy in our planning for this phase of the planetary transition mission at hand. Many will not even wake-up to realize that they are indeed part of the team. For those of you who are curious about the actual numbers, there can be as many as three who are "lost" for every one who awakens.

For those of you who have awakened enough to be willing to attend these messages and understand the significance of yourself as a fragment of Creator Source, you would be wise to spend the necessary time it takes to cultivate your inner talents to the best of your perceived ability.

In doing so, many of you will eventually realize that you have been "receiving" (communing with) Higher Guidance most of your conscious life experience. You will also soon realize that what you perceive as your personal limitations are far from what your actual limitations are.

How does one know what their limitations are? Only by surpassing them! You each have infinite potential to create. YOU are your only limitation. As you grow, you will be showing others what is possible if they but effort to understand and develop their own unique gifts.

This brings us around to the reason for your current experiences. You have chosen to experience at this time for very specific reasons. The main reason is for the challenges that you presently have and will face. These challenges, especially ones of perceived hardship, shall serve to cause you ones to go within and decide what YOUR values really are.

Can you live without money? The plants and animals seem to manage without it. Can you survive without your vehicles of transportation? How about without your supermarkets or shopping malls? If you had to walk a mile to simply obtain a bucket of water, could you make it back with the water or would the walk alone "do-you-in"?

The point here is to emphasize that you each have MUCH to learn and to do in order to prepare for the trying times ahead. Thus it would be wise on your part to get moving, and the most important step in that direction is recognizing when FEAR is holding you back from making any progress.

We cannot answer all of the personal questions for each of you through these few who effort to assist in this public manner. BUT—WE *CAN* ANSWER YOUR PERSONAL QUESTIONS IF YOU BUT LEARN TO CONNECT FOR YOURSELF IN THE SAME MANNER AS DO THESE PUBLIC RECEIVERS. Remember that the call *always* compels the answer!

What right do you have to demand of another that they answer your questions if you are not willing to help yourself? They should not, and if they do, then perhaps it is justified that you would have to pay money for their time. Ours (time) is free for the asking!

Again, the point is to get you each to the point of

SELF reliance. We will help you, but YOU must do your part!

When you connect directly for self, there is greater patience for all of the personal questions that you can ever imagine. But when you are taking up another's time with YOUR personal questions, we generally will only allow so much before we withdraw. It can be of value to the receiver to experience such questioning for awhile, if the conditions truly warrant the interaction. But, if they will not pull back when becoming a crutch, then eventually we will.

We are grateful for the many who DO commune on a regular basis and we honor your diligence and persistence. The rewards for that which you learn now will last you into all your future experiences.

Enough on this subject, for it has ALL been stated before and you each must learn to be responsible for yourselves. We are here for YOU! Your growth is directly linked to OUR growth. The cycle is infinite and the journey challenging.

My scribe asks: "Don't you get tired of all the excuses we offer up?"

No, not in the sense of "tired" that you would perceive of being tired. We recognize the value in each of Creator's creations and it takes less than a moment to back up and see the Greater Being efforting to learn and grow. It is in that moment when we feel renewed strength and compassion for the one who is, in fact, struggling to comprehend the enormous potentials of their being.

As long as YOU persist, we shall persist alongside you, and it is truly OUR pleasure to do so!

Please also keep in mind that we rejoice when you ones grow past the need for "excuses". When you do so, you will have made an enormous step forward in your own growth, and that means we ALL move forward in our understanding of the Greater Potential of the ALL that is Creation.

We are grateful for the opportunity to serve those of you

who reciprocate the gratitude. We are also grateful for those who have chosen to play the role of "adversary" so that the entire (challenging) learning experience can even exist in the first place.

There are no losers in the overall experience. There are those who awaken now, and those who will awaken later. It is but a waiting game, and God has eternity and infinite patience.

It has been stated: "Some of the first (created) will be the last, and some of the last will be the first." You can view the adversary as perhaps one who will choose to be last. Know that he is a very experienced (old) soul who has perhaps chosen the most difficult path back home to Source. We will also assist him when he calls, and he WILL eventually call.

Ponder these words well, for there are insights for you each. I am Ceres Anthonious Soltec. I come in service to and through the One Light of Creator Source, that you might see a bit farther this day.

For each of you who make the effort to become stronger sources of Light yourselves, so too does Mother Earth benefit and rejoice from your contribution to her health. And THAT is my geophysical lesson for today!

Salu.

CHAPTER THIRTY-FIVE

Life's A *Real* Balancing Act!

Ceres Anthonious Soltec
April 11, 1998

Good evening, my friend. It is I, Toniose Soltec, come in the Radiant One Light of Creator Source. Allow for the natural evolutionary flow of thought to manifest around you.

We of the Higher Realms are grateful for that which you do. We are here to assist you ones when and where we can. Remember that we can do more to assist when YOU first make effort to assist yourselves!

What you all are going through is what we shall call "growing" pains. There are often difficulties experienced within the individual who is efforting to understand the Greater Picture of who they are. Your challenge is one of inner reality versus outer reality. Both are a product of the same Source, yet they are, also, seeming dichotomies of thought. There is ONE ultimate "reality" that encompasses the whole of each.

While in the physical, it is, indeed, very difficult to maintain the balance necessary in order to function in BOTH realities simultaneously. This is to say that most

ones are either very physically oriented or they are very spiritually oriented.

There are very few who readily achieve harmony in the spanning of both realities. This is a most difficult lesson to learn and master. And yet, there is great value in doing so, for there come great insights into being able to see the True Cause behind that which precipitates events. In knowing and understanding True Cause, one is, in effect, recognizing that which is their own ability to create.

Also, ones will be able to see and understand that neither they, nor anyone else, are ever a "victim". They (you) are directly responsible for EVERYTHING that they (you) experience.

You are Creator manifest! You are also a "player" in the physical arena of your current (physical) environment. You CAN achieve a balance between the spiritual and the physical.

You have chosen the physical environment for its unique qualities of compressing and amplifying (dramatizing) those areas of your knowing that need to be strengthened. These same compressive and amplifying qualities of the physical environment can also cause you ones to "forget" who you are or why you have chosen to come into that environment in the first place.

You are very much a non-physical entity, partly experiencing in and through your body. This is so that you will have a focal point of expression in the physical—an anchor of sorts. Let not the focal point limit your ability to function in a much greater capacity.

The point here is to say: let not the PERCEPTION of physical "limitations" impede you from anything that you are desiring. There are (and will be) plenty of opportunities to experience ALL of the physical experiences that you can ever imagine.

But, remember: you are there for your own SPIRITUAL growth and it is for this primary reason that YOU have chosen to experience at this time.

Let not the pressures of the physical environment cloud your understanding of the fact that you are a limitless spiritual being on a spiritual quest of self-knowing. We of the Hosts will always offer you the reminders that you need (desire) so that you can have the opportunity to see greater reasoning, if you so desire to see same.

Let not the distractions of the physical impede you from your true desire for greater understanding. Call upon Source for your guidance, and learn to recognize and accept the Greater Hand operating in that which you experience as physical "reality".

There is NOTHING wrong with wanting to experience the physical side of your physical expression. However, when you completely neglect the "spiritual" (non-physical) side of your being, then you will have created prime conditions for the "harsher" physical experiences that will cause you to look within and search for greater understanding. Note that such "harsh" experiencing is a balancing mechanism—or, to put it another way, there is really NO escaping the TRUE intent (spiritual growth) of your soul.

True balance comes from recognizing the spiritual component (God) in EVERY thing and EVERY person that you can see, touch, or feel. When you can do this, you will be better able to appreciate the true value of the physical environment and the exquisite opportunities it affords you.

Your "reality", "sanity", and "truth" each have plenty of room for growth. There is no person incarnate in the physical who has mastered completely this balance between physical "reality" and non-physical "reality". You each have plenty of room to grow in terms of understanding.

There are ones who are very spiritually attuned to their Higher Guidance, yet they are withdrawn from society to a point that they will not share the gifts that are intended to be shared. These ones are as much lopsided as are the ones who completely avoid anything that they cannot physically see, touch, or feel for themselves.

Most ones who read these messages function in between the two extremes, efforting to find that which satisfies the inner desire for fulfillment, with great amounts of time being spent in a trial-and-error approach to deducing what it is that IS fulfilling to them.

Ones often are missing the fact that, unless and until they begin to move toward a greater balance between physical sensing and inner understanding, they will not find the peace they are looking for. This is to say that as long as ones avoid confronting themselves as they truly are—non-physical beings incarnate into physical bodies with limitless potential for creating—then they will always be seeking to find fulfillment.

This is just the first step toward coming into a more balanced condition of experiencing. Next is the denial phase.

As ones begin to awaken to the idea of who they are and the true potential of their being, they will often deny that such could be, for they will no longer have any real excuses for why it is that they have had it "so bad". The truth of the matter is that the reason any ones "have it so bad" is because ones NEED it "so bad" in order to wake themselves up to a greater reality of experience!

Here, again, I remind you ones who wish to narrow my focus to reports on Earth changes and related activities, that I am a Higher Teacher as well as a Brother, come at this time to assist you to integrate into your consciousness the concept that "ALL is connected to ALL". With respect to the upcoming Earth changes (that I have written about extensively over these many past years), it is now time to integrate those "physical" lessons with their greater spiritual reality (True Cause). In other words, appreciate that even the upcoming, potentially "harsh" Earth changes are a basic part of physically-oriented man wishing to AWAKEN to the consequences of his imbalances and his general inattention to the spiritual side of his expression.

You are each infinite beings. This particular experience

in the physical is not your first. You can, if you so choose, ignore the greater reasons for experiencing—but you will be no closer to finding the inner satisfaction that you are so desperately seeking than you were 100 lifetimes ago. In that context, perhaps upcoming "harsh" experiences (say from living near or on an earthquake fault zone, or in the vicinity of a potentially active volcano) are just what you desire (and thus have chosen) to finally cause you to awaken to what has escaped your grasp until now.

It is not our place to judge you ones. We are simply Guides and Wayshowers who have walked the path that you are now on. We only wish to assist those who desire our assistance.

Many are desperately seeking fulfillment at this time. We see, for the most part, that the seeking is most often done in a very external and physically-oriented manner. This is to say that many are looking to other people for their fulfillment, or to physical objects like cars, houses, clothes, or even food, sex, or drugs.

These are but distractions at best, and the excitement quickly wears off, leaving ones heavily "in debt", either physically or emotionally, or both. Ones are often left wanting more, and so they go off somewhere to "find" their next big distraction.

The answers that you ones are looking for come from recognizing who you truly are. This important recognition (RE-cognition) comes from within.

How can you know that you are more than just your physical body?

How is it that YOU actually know you are conscious?

How is it that YOU know you even "really" exist?

Do you need to go out and ask another, or can you determine for yourself the answers to these questions?

What is YOUR relationship with God?

Do you have one?

How do YOU know?

Are you your body, or are you more than a physical

mass of electro-chemical combinations?

Hmmm?

Let's see:

I can cut off my arm, and I'm still me.

I can have a lung or tonsils removed, and I'm still me.

I can have a heart transplant, and I'm still me.

Now we get into a tricky area—the brain:

If you replace your brain, are you still you? Since this has not been done successfully in your current level of publicly-known technology, you would likely say: "No, I would not be me."

So, from this limited viewpoint, you may be inclined to think that you are your brain. Let me just say that it *is* possible to replace brain tissue in such a manner as to maintain perfect continuity of the brain's original functioning. So, are YOU your brain?

Please stop for a moment to reflect upon all of the thoughts and emotions that have been triggered by simply going within and asking yourself just these few questions.

Did you have to physically GO anywhere or physically (externally) DO anything? No! Yet, you were, in fact, seeking, were you not?

You say: "But this does not apply to me, because I already *know* that I'm more than just a body!"

Well, this is good; but *why* is it, then, that so many who claim this awareness are petitioning God for Mr. or Mrs. "Right" to come along, or for money, or for a "better" job, etc., in order to be "happy"?

The answer: Because just *knowing* that you are more than a body IS BUT THE BEGINNING of awakening to truly understanding the implications of this fact—and of who you REALLY are! It is among the first steps.

The point of this exercise is to show you that, with diligent inner questioning and reasoning (searching), you will begin to see and understand more and more of who you are. As this process unfolds, you will begin to draw into your experience those confirmations that will let you

***know* that you are, indeed, on the right path.**

It is for this reason that you ones are taught to NOT question authority figures, such as school teachers, politicians, clergy, policemen, judges, doctors and such. If you were to begin to develop *independent* thought—truly thinking for yourselves—then you would not stand for the lies that are meant to keep you pliable to the mind control exercised by ones in "authority".

True teachers will effort to bring their students to a point of awareness wherein the students will realize they can derive their own answers, independent of the need for the teacher. Or as the important statement on this subject goes: "The true purpose of education is to teach the student HOW to think, not WHAT to think."

By simply asking yourself the appropriate questions, you will be well on your way to guiding yourself to the answers that you are looking for. And you will be surprised by the "accidental" discoveries that result during this process of exploration!

Enjoy the physical experience. But more importantly, effort to understand that which makes the "physical" experience possible in the first place.

There is inner satisfaction awaiting you each. You need not go anywhere to find it. Another cannot find it for you. A determined desire to find it, and knowing that it is there, are the keys to having it.

You each have within you the potential abilities that the Christed one you call "Jesus" has. He is your Brother, not your God. What he did while incarnate, you too will do—eventually. Let not your past beliefs and indoctrinations keep you from realizing this "Christ potential" within you.

I am Ceres Anthonious "Toniose" Soltec—Teacher, Scientist, Philosopher, Artist, Friend and Wayshower. I have been sent by OUR Creator so that His promise to you ones will be fulfilled, and so that I, too, may experience and grow.

In His Light—blessings to you all. Salu!

CHAPTER THIRTY-SIX

Desperate Times For Adversary's Antics

Tomeros Maasu Korton
April 20, 1998

Good afternoon, my scribe. Commander Tomeros Maasu Korton here in the Radiant Light of God's Presence.

You ones are being assaulted in a variety of ways, especially those of you in service to the Hosts of God-Aton. Illnesses are chief among the "distractions" tossed your way. It is through those subtle strikes (such as colds, gastro-intestinal dis-eases, nervous system ailments, mental depressions, and the like) that the adversary attacks, if a weakness can be found in your protective Light shielding. Of course, the moral of this warning is simply to be diligent about calling-in the Light of God for protection—every few minutes if need be, under some attack circumstances.

In the days to come, every "trick in the book" (including from your *Bible*) will be tried against both God's diligent workers and His wayward fragments who struggle to find en-LIGHT-enment. Even though Satan rules these "end" times, the days of Evil are numbered. That means you are in for the worst, as those in service to Evil prepare for your demise by both "fair" (seeming) methods and foul. However, if you persist in becoming "tuned-in" to the inner voice of God, and diligently focus upon that which is of the Lighted path, then a little "turbulence" may be all you experience personally.

MAY FIRST: DAY OF THE ILLUMINATI

When Adam Weishaupt founded the Order of the Illuminati on May 1, 1776, he and his Rothschild sponsors envisioned a world that celebrated this organized "birthday of Evil" with as much allegiance as any other state "holiday". But, instead of celebrating some form of national "independence", this day would represent the very opposite to you-the-people.

As you again approach May 1, there is the possibility of your dark "elite" controllers using one of their most "sacred" days to help usher in their new era of total domination over you ones, bringing your seemingly sovereign way of life to an Earth-shattering end. This does not mean that this will surely be THE hour in which Evil chooses to remove the veils from the faces of the satanic deceivers, but it does allow you ones more clues as to the PROBABLE buildup of happenings—now, and regarding timing for future events.

When you look back, remember that during the days leading up to the WORLD May First observances, there were always great and tumultuous public displays (engineered by the "elite") against governments for exposed injustices against the common people. Even in America, through skilled military and psychological manipulations, preplanned riots and economic bombshells have been launched in the weeks and days preceding the date of May First. Thus, you "celebrated" your own May Day (from whence the cryptic "distress call" is fittingly derived) festivities. The big difference between you in the U.S., and your brethren who reside in other nations, is that THEY KNOW a lot more of what it is all about and you don't.

You say it doesn't seem that way to you, this issue of the ignorance of the American people? Well, who controls the media which presents to you exactly what you are supposed to see and hear about your neighbors in other countries? Without exercising diligent independent effort on your own, how would you discover otherwise?

Whether your organized evil associations are called Orders, Committees, Societies, Illuminated (dark) Brotherhoods, Fraternities, Initiates or Agencies—their modus operandi remains the same as it has since they were first forced to go "underground" (fugitively, figuratively, and literally). Their goal always remains the same: gaining control of a planet for the big bad boy himself. Luciferians know no national boundaries or religious differences; in fact, it was they who invented religions for better control over you!

Publicly these "elite" so-called masterminds (you now often call them philanthropists; they are pretenders of public virtue) would scarcely have come to your attention if it were not for a *divinely guided* incident, involving a courier, back in the 16th century. This messenger was struck by lightning as he traveled by horseback on hidden paths between two points along the secret courier network of the evil brotherhood. By "chance" this particular delivery contained blueprints for the 1789 French Revolution—which had not yet occurred! The evidence was so compelling that the authorities of the day ordered the Bavarian Illuminati to be disbanded. Obviously, however, no successful attempt was made to derail the planned revolution.

Whether it was too fantastic to believe at the time, or perhaps due to careful suppression of the information by Illuminists who occupied influential positions within the French government, the made-to-order Revolution came off on schedule.

With another stage of the World Domination Plan

completed, the ignorant masses would be methodically prepared for the next phase of Illuminati-governed servitude. However, those annoying documents found on the dead courier didn't exactly go away.

Since that time, at least some of the public have been aware of a "secret few" who commanded great power and political influence. And, my friends, the evil ones knew that the problem of possible exposure would not go away without directed clandestine effort on their part.

In order to carry out their dark directives, the minions of the adversary must operate in complete secrecy—because *YOU* outnumber them, many millions of you to every one of them! That is why, as you close out this millennium (toward which your adversary has spent more than 1800 years planning for THIS DAY), the existence of these dark "elite" still remains a very little-known, obscure "cult idea" that brings laughter of disbelief whenever the possibility of their existence is mentioned in most gatherings.

Hidden in the uppermost ranks of your current, multi-level, secret or semi-secret societies (such as Freemasonry, Intelligence agencies, Councils on Foreign and Domestic Relations, and Bilderberg clubs for billionaire "elitists" the world over) are the descendants and reincarnated Luciferians who planned, financed, and reaped the "benefits" of all your world conflicts. And all of these conflicts were engineered toward the single goal of achieving absolute world control in this present time period.

Chelas [*students*], war does *not* happen by accident! That would imply that God's consummate manifest idea of human expression, such as should be exhibited in the life on your planet, was built on a less-than-perfect foundation, and that is not the case. In more basic terms: expressing Lighted fragments of God do not, of their own accord, resort to war to settle differences of opinion. Left to his own nature, man is more inclined to help than to hurt.

The fabric of the universe of physical and spiritual manifestation comes into existence through the "willpower" of LOVE—equal, in a scientific sense, to the all-pervasive "force" you call gravity. This incredible force of Divine Love IS the basis for ALL that exists, in the entire omniverse of universes, including your continued existence in what you understand as third-dimensional reality.

God does not create His kingdoms and worlds to be fleeting moments to be forgotten in the eternity of His imaginings. He creates them to one day come back, in a fullness of expression, into the Oneness that He Himself IS, and, in so doing, for the experiences of that creation to be forever recorded upon the Akashic Records that make up the "tapestry" of All That Is.

War (conflict in general) is a cancerous assault upon the emotions of joy and harmony—which are fundamental to what God IS. The negative vibrations of hate and disharmony simply do not mix with the higher frequencies of the Divine Light from God's thinking and imagining.

This is not a difficult concept to grasp intuitively; it is simple physics: like conditions seek their own kind—oil and water do not mix. Neither do negative and positive vibrations (of manifested physicality or spiritual essence of same) blend together, for they are OPPOSITE conditions.

AVERTING CATASTROPHE

By preparing your brothers and sisters for what is planned, and by paying attention to the sequencing of events that signal possible triggering of circumstances that allow for the unfolding of the heinous things your adversary has in store for you, you create a window of opportunity to allow God's miracles to take place. Simply knowing what *may* happen is not enough—though it does help the individual who comes by that knowledge to function with less of a distracting "surprise" reaction as events unfold. However, in order to truly assist mankind, as a species of created life-form experiencing upon this manifested schoolyard of learning, the lesson of understanding ONENESS *WITH* YOUR BROTHER is what needs to be wholly acted upon "this time around".

As always, it is in the "doing something about it" that gives you access to the powers of The Creation to "battle" that which threatens to cause disharmony with the natural order of God's perfect universe. One human being CAN do it alone. However, most have been trained through religions to want to place their load (and everyone else's) upon the shoulders of the Master Teacher who lived two thousand years ago upon your place. Such an avoidance of responsibility completely negates what he told you that YOU are capable of accomplishing. Lighted beings come in but two forms: those operating from a state of awareness of their Christed capabilities, and those still unaware of that Potential within.

Man must not be lured into a false sense of security simply because the ones in service to Evil tell you that all is well and there is no cause for alarm. Remember: "And they were liars from the beginning." This quote from your Holy Book should not be taken lightly, for it sums up your adversary quite well.

These dark ones are the perpetrators of what your nation has come to be in its decadent and insidious policies and practices. These dark ones rob, not only the people of the United States, but condemn the peoples of the world to slavery and death because the most impoverished peoples have looked to you in the U.S. as children look to their parents for guidance and spiritual hope.

Do not let down those who believe, as you once did, in the DREAM of the "American way of life". But DO face the fact that, presently, America is a land where much evil resides. And daily, many more dark ones seek shelter through pouring into your lands—most without going through official immigration channels—for it is in the good old U.S. of A. that they believe they will be safe as they plunder the globe from the new Jer-USA-lem.

Their enemies know where to find them, chelas, and they will come after them, and it will be on your native soil that pivotal conflicts erupt. All the while, you nice citizens will be ordered to defend, with your very blood, the dark ones who caused the conflicts in the first place. Do not prove to the world that you indeed are as blind as they say you are. Do not allow these things to take place without so much as a word of protest or call to justice about that which you KNOW is against the very reason you have a *Constitution* in the first place.

[*Editor's note: One has only to look at the Front Page story in this week's* CONTACT *(4/28/98) to see a perfect example of Commander Korton's advice being put into action in Switzerland. For those who have been following that outrageous confrontation, especially in past issues of* CONTACT, *the politicians and bankers in Switzerland were at first responding as spinelessly as is typically the case anywhere. But then there was a great, indignant groundswell of protest from the populace at large. And only THEN did the Swiss officials find it within themselves to take up a stance of at least token defiance toward the huff-and-puff money-extortion "Holocaust victim" robbers. It causes one to pause and consider exactly what is "the power of the people" upon which our American nation's Founding Fathers placed so much trust. Also consider the old phrase "the whole is greater than the sum of the parts" in these matters. Or, as George Washington put it when pressed for basic advice about what's important about being an American: "Labor to keep alive in your breast that little spark of Celestial Fire—called Conscience."*]

EVIL HIDES IN PLAIN SIGHT (KNOWLEDGE GIVES YOU "EYES" TO SEE)

Signs are all around you as to who Satan's helpers are and where they hide. They have been a part of the founding (and daily operation) of your churches, mosques, and synagogues; they have had much to do with the creation and continued control of all of your major cultural and societal institutions, including such as those in the financial and political arenas, those of "higher" un-learning, hospitals, and police organizations. Blatant evidence abounds, forever recorded in your Book of Books, as to the very darkly inspired nature of its depictions of war and lascivious human conduct. Is this what you glorify when you promise to obey and follow EVERYTHING within those pages of that "good" book? Which of the many versions are you referring to?

How much do you know about the symbols and true origins of what you have come to blindly believe in? Do you think it was Esu "Jesus" Sananda's disciples (friends) who called for the cross—of all the possible heinous torture devices, known for its image of great indignity while causing slow, agonizing death—to be a "symbol" of their beloved teacher?

Dear ones, the cross is a symbol of Satan. The term "double-cross" comes from the widely known (before you were made to forget during the Dark Ages) double-cross crest that was adapted to the coat of arms of an Illuminati Order. The people knew of the treachery of the evil societies and forever associated their twin-cross emblem with what they were best known for—deceit and manipulation.

The "End Times" as described in John's *Book Of Revelation* will likely come about because that is what you ones believe should be part of your experience, and therefore you pump energy into and thus cause it to manifest. Well, since "it" is going to come to pass, what can you do about it, if you are among the ones who believe God has given you the power to make a difference?

For starters, learn where you actually are in the timetable of the Armageddon scenario. In actuality you are not *approaching* your new century as your erroneous calendars present—you are already PAST that "deadline" by several years. You are presently living out Armageddon. Right now!

How much worse do you desire it to get? How vile and corrupt does your world have to become for you to accept your downward spiraling into "Hell" as a fact? Do you need locusts and plagues and dead bodies piled up in the streets for you to realize Evil reigns at this time? Will you wait until there is absolutely no turning back to goodness and decency on your place before you acknowledge the serpent's grasp around your throat?

God will wait for you, always allowing you the opportunity to learn your lessons. However, when the Father announces, "Mine hour has come!" there will only be a moment in eternity of "time" for you to make up your minds as to who you will serve: Satan (def: an adversary) or God and His Celestial Hosts. And, dear ones, I would suggest you make up your minds *before* that hour comes, for the human brain (at your level of development) is not skilled at making those kinds of decisions upon such short notice.

Remember, I said the adversary has some really unimaginable distractions ready and awaiting proper timing to spring upon you. How better to control ones than through sheer panic and the resulting mayhem. Some feel they are prepared mentally for anything that may come. Usually this derives from a false state of complacency based upon a limited ability to imagine the kind and degree of the assault possible upon them. However, when the master deceiver decides to put on a show of force, the desired (diabolical) effect is most often achieved not through a single event, but multiple assaults, lined up like storms blasting a coastline, which hit faster than any one assault can be dealt with.

Your own first instinct will be to panic, because that is how your controllers have programed you to respond. Overriding the negative programing should be your priority as a next step. And then, if you have prepared yourselves with the wisdom of God's knowledge, allow divine inspiration and instinct—God's Universal Language of Light—to guide your way. In the midst of chaos, only the "voice" of the Heavenly Father within can lead you to safety. That is what is meant by the phrase: "Put your faith in the Lord."

My specialty is communications and in such capacity I remind you that it matters not *how* the call for help is made—no special external language is necessary—for the honest call for help comes from the heart. That is a REAL energy sent out and, as we have so often reminded you, "the call compels the answer". Keep this in mind as you effort to improve your hearing of the "still, small voice within" your heart, for therein lies God and His constant communications with you—if you but LISTEN.

The next most difficult step to take is *acting* upon what you hear. Faith, my beloved brethren, helps immensely here, for the adversary will try every weakness you have in order to dissuade you from following Lighted input. And as I said at the beginning of this message, right now the adversary is desperately working to maintain his hold over humanity and thus is testing you with every trick there is. The dark ones know that their time is short and that they lose their power over you the minute you awaken to their pranks.

So, is that an alarm clock I hear ringing, my sleepy brothers? Now would be a good time to HEAR the call and ACT upon the alarm. Shall you hit the "snooze" button and roll over for more slumber, or shall you spring out of your bed and get to work? We shall see.

Thank you for your attention, my beloved brethren. Your tireless petitions for assistance to We of the Hosts of God-Aton do not go unheard.

May you KNOW and FEEL God's presence within you at all times, for that truly is the only way to live. Commander Korton to clear, please. Salu.

CHAPTER THIRTY-SEVEN

Seek *First* Within For Your Answers

Lanto, The Sage
April 25, 1998

Good afternoon, my friend. It is I, Lanto, "the sage". I come as representative of the Yellow Ray of Creator's spectral expression. You know me well.

My task at this time is one of inner communication. This is to say that I am here to help you focus upon inner communication with self.

Many are looking for outward comforts to cause them to feel "happy". There is no such external condition. Happiness comes from within, just as does fulfillment, joy, or any of the other emotional states that you ones are fond of experiencing.

You ones will find great value in taking the time to quietly and honestly look within at self and see self as you are this day. What are those things that you dwell upon with great regularity? Where do you focus your mental and emotional energy? How do your actions reflect these preoccupations? These are merely a few questions to help you focus upon what it is that you are creating as your "reality" of experience.

ALL are seeking an inner sense of fulfillment. Yet, most are chasing after the external world for their fulfillment instead of pursuing their own inner world. This will only serve to lead you down a lot of "dead-end" paths full of inner conflict and turmoil.

Keep in mind that you ones often need to experience, for yourselves, the process of searching—to the point of exhaustion. That is, it is often after you have exhausted every external path you can think of, that you get to the point of emotional exhaustion (desperation) which causes you to turn inward for your answers.

You do not need to go to such an extreme before you decide to go within and seek your answers. You can do this at any time you so choose. Almost all of you who are reading this message are, in fact, following your inner Guidance to some degree. But, most of you do not realize (recognize) that you can tap the inner world and get these same answers for yourself.

You ALL have this ability. It begins by taking the time to formulate a heart-felt question about which you truly desire to know the answer.

Next, you simply allow the thoughts to come. Usually the question will be answered with other questions. For example, let us take the question: "Why am I so unhappy?"

Perhaps the next thought that comes is: "Well, why do I spend so much time worrying about being happy?" or "Well, what are the 'things' in my life that I can be thankful for?" This is but an example to briefly illustrate my point.

Many of you are quite able to do this and most all of you have done this type of introspective questioning at one time or another. But, most also fail to recognize the injection of "non-physical help" that is received while doing this.

Remember: "The call compels the answer"! The answer is rarely in a form that you ones choose to recognize, for in the recognition comes responsibility that God *has* supplied you with the means to find the

answer—and this, in turn, implies that you really have no excuse for wallowing in a state of "unhappiness" any longer.

If you have chosen ignorance as your excuse in the past, then from this point forward you will not be able to consciously claim this ever again without feeling the "lie" that you are trying to sell yourself.

I am merely pointing out the God-given mechanism by which you can find any answer that your heart desires. Ah! Here we have stated "your HEART desires". What do I mean by "heart" desire? What is it that YOUR heart truly desires?

True heart desire comes from your Higher Guiding Self. This desire will always be of a nature that will have lasting (beyond the physical) value. Those of you who spend excessive amounts of time and energy worrying about money, relationships, material success, and such, will eventually find that your physical desire is out of alignment with the Higher Desire of the soul's knowing. The physical "things" are at best lustful, ego-based desires and will have very little (almost no) lasting value in and of themselves.

Look closely at what you regularly fixate your attention upon. Many of you state outwardly general statements such as: "If only I had _________, then I would be happy or satisfied." (You fill in the blank.)

I say to you here and now that you have ALL you need to feel completely satisfied and happy and connected. If you but take the time to look and see, then you would know that (as I have just stated) TRUE happiness comes from within, as does TRUE satisfaction.

Now, another important point, related to what we have just discussed, is the following: You cannot be truly happy until you can learn to TRULY love yourself—and know that YOU have enormous value as a unique creation of God to contribute to the overall canvas of His magnificent expression. You each have a purpose to fulfill that will benefit EVERY being EVERYWHERE! None is lesser than another!

You will all, eventually, recognize this fact. When? That is up to you. It is a matter of sequence of events. As you grow in terms of lasting inner knowing, you will naturally fulfill your unique Higher Purpose. Everyone's reason for experiencing at this time is in some way related to ultimately fulfilling this Higher Purpose of understanding and contributing to the overall benefit of everyone, everywhere.

Seek within for your Guidance. Trust that it is REAL and that it is QUITE valid. You need not justify your Guidance to another, and what is "right" for you is not always "right" for another. Don't insist that your Guidance is the "only way", for it is NOT!

Judge not one another. You do not know another's agreements or prearranged role. Perhaps your "nemesis" is a very caring friend who agreed to come into the physical and play the role of the "bad" guy so that YOU could have the perfect opportunity to grow.

On other levels of awareness, you each orchestrate your interactions with one another so as to maximize the overall growth potential of the experience. Sound too outlandish for you? Well, that's because it is outside of the "landish" (physical) experience that this sort of thing is orchestrated. **Learn to be inwardly thankful for ALL of the challenges that cross your path and you will be well upon your way to finding true inner happiness and fulfillment.**

Patience, and allowing for the Greater Picture to unfold, will help you to see the long-term value of that which I offer. Within this writing are the basic tools about which you ALL need reminding, from time to time. Many of you have been at points of emotional "desperation" and have found this inner Guidance to be of "last resort". It should be the FIRST avenue taken, not the last.

With proper application and honing of these skills, you could become an inspiration and example for others to follow. When the heart and the Higher mind are in agreement with one another, you will find an unshakable peace and a profound sense of certainty that will eventually lead you to infinite knowing.

First, the proper steps must be taken. You cannot find peace when there is inner conflict raging between the ego-self and the Higher-knowing being.

Do you ones think that Esu "Jesus" Immanuel did not consider the physical pain of the flesh prior to undertaking the task he knew he had to do? He did! Was he frightened? Yes, at first, but he also knew with his HEART what he had to do and he gave no power to the ego-self that was "tempting" him to do otherwise. Let his life stand as an insightful example of inner versus outer values.

Please consider this message as a reminder to you, as to why you are where you are this day and why you feel the way you do. Seek always within for the answers and you *will* find them. And you will invariably find outward confirmations that will allow you to see that you are, indeed, upon the right path. Call upon The Light for protection and an added level of insurance, else you will likely be tempted by the dark energies.

I am Lanto, Wayshower and Guide. I am come as directed by OUR Father so that you all may have reminder of who you are and of the tools available to you each.

In Light, blessings to you all! Salu.

CHAPTER THIRTY-EIGHT

Overcome Those Fears And Have Some Fun!

Violinio Saint Germain
May 1, 1998

Good evening, my scribe. It is I, Violinio St. Germain, come as the Cohan (Teacher) of the Violet Ray of transmutation. Be at peace for there is "work" to be done.

Your planet and her population are crying out for change. This call of the heart is ALWAYS responded to by Creator Source. ALWAYS!

Note that I did *not* say the call from the "mouth". It is the heart that God listens to—not the irrational thoughts and mouthings of self-proclaimed "righteous" hypocrites whose actions continuously contradict their words. You would each be wise to understand and know the difference, for I witness many who will be reading this and "think" that they are somehow better than their brothers because they have found Truth.

None are "better" than another. If you find Truth and still choose to DO nothing, then your actions would indicate that you are either not in understanding of the Truth, or you are afraid of it.

Do you effort to share what you have found with any and all who will see or hear? Often the excuse is given: "I don't want others to view *me* as some sort of 'New-Age' religious nut" or "I'm too old and nobody will listen" or "I'm too young and nobody will listen" or whatever. My, my, how silly you ones can get when it comes to justifying a "do nothing" position.

On the other hand, there are ones out there who do all that they are asked to do—and more. Many of these quiet and unseen ones make it possible for this type of work to go forth, day to day and week to week.

We of the Hosts of God are grateful for those of you whose ACTIONS are, indeed, consistent with both your heart and your tongue. These sorts of actions taken are what will provide you with the experience necessary in order to help you to help us to provide the answers to all of those heartfelt petitions for assistance.

Suppose you are "nudged" (an inner sensation that seems to be urging you toward an action) to share with another your experience and you simply decide not to do so. Can you see that perhaps you have just limited we of the Hosts from working with and through you? Why do you ones hold back? At the heart of the answer will *always* be FEAR!

Most often it is a fear of "looking" the fool or "sounding" crazy or some such excuse. We, along with your personal Guides, are always efforting to get you ones to see and confront these seemingly small fears. Why? Because, in confronting and understanding the TRUE cause behind these fears, you will begin to experience greater and greater freedom, knowledge, and understanding of the true potential of YOUR being.

None is greater or lesser than another! You each have the potential to manifest (and radiate outward) the Christ Potential residing within you. It takes determination and a strong desire to face all of the self-imposed limitations (fears) that you hold onto as "absolutes" though they really have no foundation in truth.

If you believe that no man (or woman) could possibly do the things that Christ (Esu "Jesus" Immanuel) did while incarnate upon your planet, then you have just limited yourself, and subsequently others, by your belief and subsequent thoughts.

If you were to truly look at WHY it is that you believe such a thing, you would, if you are honest with self, find that you have a FEAR that supports the lie. This is to say that, due to an earlier fear, such as a fear of public failure or of personal failing, you ones will subsequently hold to ideas brought forth by others, with like fears, that subsequently absolve you from the responsibility of accepting yourself and your potentials as they truly exist.

Your religions exploit this self-limiting inclination to a most paralyzing extent. They skillfully coerce you to place all important matters into the hands of a "professional" intermediary between you and Source. So much for PERSONAL responsibility!

You each have fears and subsequent erroneous beliefs that limit you in some way. Perhaps our greatest challenge, as Teachers and Guides, is to get you past these fears.

Next to your religious structures, your education system (especially so-called "higher" education) is full of ones who resist change, for if they find new truths and realities, then their self-perceived value is somehow lost. The result is a training of the masses that you should not argue or debate with the "educated" professionals. These so-called "professionals" for the most part are bound by their fears of being somehow WRONG, and thus will effort toward a rigidly unchanging ideology because the embarrassment "suffered" otherwise would be unbearable.

This mindset is passed on from teacher to student, and filters down into society to the point where you have near complete "mind washing" (leading to mind control) of the masses. This is indeed the adversary exploiting the fear "buttons" that YOU create and hold onto. But such a posture cannot be longer sustained these days; the promise God made is that The Truth shall be KNOWN!

There is a great unrest in your world, for ones are sensing the growing desperation of the masses. You see, the inner (Higher Knowing) self of any Lighted being can endure just so much of "the lie" before rebelling. Thus ones all over the globe are becoming more and more restless—as if there is a foreboding feeling of change.

Change IS coming, and ones are being prepared by their Guides so that the experience can be of greatest value to those physically experiencing this change.

We are grateful for those of you who DO follow our "nudges" and take even the smallest of actions. You cannot always know the effect of even something as simple as a smile offered to a stranger. How would you know if that person was just asking God, in desperation, if he or she has any real value?

All you do is smile. But perhaps that smile changes the life of the "stranger" that you just touched.

YOU are the miracle! If you do nothing, then you will most certainly have lost an opportunity to experience God's love flowing with and through you.

The physical environment is about taking action. It is always wise to plan out reasonable courses of action, but do not be so rigid as to not allow for spontaneous action guided from the heart. You will find GREAT rewards flowing back to you in like manner. If nothing else, a little spontaneity would certainly cure your boredom! You will never find spontaneous people complaining about a lack of fun and excitement in their lives; that which they send out returns, multiplied, in kind.

All that I am asking is that you each be more open to our subtle attempt to communicate with and through you. Try to not be so inhibited in the spontaneity of life.

This is an important step to take in order to bring about change within self. When you can become an example to others as to the value of allowing Higher Energies to work with and through you, you will have begun the re-education of the masses by setting an example that most will want to follow and emulate.

Your world and your people will not be transformed "overnight", but the relative rate of change, in terms of your planet's past evolutionary growth patterns, will be such as to cause society to advance forward "as in the twinkling of an eye".

Your world is at the brink of a "new" reality. There is fast approaching a time when your world will no longer quibble over such trite subjects as, "Are we alone in the universe?"

Neither you nor any of your species have *ever* been alone—EVER! Your learned "brothers from afar" will be openly announcing their presence to your world, and along with their announcement will eventually come an acceptance of who they are, and their TRUE knowledge will be shared with you who are of Godly intent.

There will be the recognition of their Higher understanding, and this will also put an end to many religious and social debates, for these ones have integrated science and spiritual philosophy to the point that they are actually one and the same. Remember we have often stated, in these lessons, that God's thinking is simple—not simplistic, but simple—and this is contradictory to the often bewilderingly complex explanations of your so-called "learned" professional theologians and scientists.

There will be a brief time of confusion as ones effort to come to grips with the "lies" that they have not only held onto, but have actually worshiped. Some will literally, physically, succumb to their fears; others will fight to hold-on to the past. But most of you who are inclined to read and resonate with this type of message will actually welcome the "relief" and embrace the exhilaration that comes from the resolution of longstanding riddles.

So much of your TRUE planetary history and culture has been hidden from you-the-people by the dark-intentioned, so-called "elite" would-be controllers, that these revelations alone will cause most all of you some degree of surprise—one way or the other!

While the charge of positive emotional energy will be growing, there will also be a great shifting of the "tensions" of the planet. However, there will also be a step-up of manmade tamperings to try to get you ones convinced that these planetary "visitors" mean you-the-people harm. The desperate "elite" controllers, who have been your behind-the-scenes masters for so long now, do not wish to give up their control and perceived positions of power. They are, and will become, more and more determined to hold onto *their* "reality", especially as they have trained you-the-masses to believe.

Eventually, after great "catastrophe", these manipulators will only succeed at exposing themselves for who they really are. (They know—but always try to deny—that God wins in the end.) After this "awakening" to Truth, the world will hold these dark ones accountable for their crimes against humanity and they will be removed from any position through which they could further hurt themselves or others.

You can best prepare for what is coming by learning to recognize and utilize ALL of the natural Inner Resources available to you. Seek first knowledge and understanding. Allow for the experiences to manifest around you that will serve as clues that you are on the right path. This can be a most fun experience if you allow for the surprises along the way and respond spontaneously.

When you find yourself frightened or in doubt, ask inwardly for Guidance, calm the fear by asking for the protective White Light (the sum total of all the spectral rays—The Light of God) to surround you, and bring self back into a balanced state of reasoning and inner peace.

MOST IMPORTANTLY: allow the experience to serve as a notice to you that you have a challenge that needs to be faced. This is to say that you would be wise to find the *cause* of your fear and to understand the effects it has upon you. In doing so, you will be clearing the mental and emotional "garbage" from your mental and emotional energy fields. This, in turn, will lead to a higher-frequency state of operation for you, and thus a greater ability to connect with Higher Source and to progress more fluently along the immensely rewarding path of inner growth.

We (your personal Guides and we of the Hosts of God) will assist those who petition honestly with the heart and whose actions reflect the heart. Always remember: the (honest) call compels the answer!

If it appears that you are not getting the "help" you want, then it would be wise to evaluate for yourself your inner world and that which you "think" versus that which you feel. Inner anxiety signifies a conflict between your Higher Knowing self and the ego (reactionary survival) self.

Give no power to the ego, and your conflict will subside. From that point of strength-in-peace, you will know a greater clarity from which to evaluate what is appropriate for self.

You *never* walk alone along the many pathways of life (Light). If you perceive that you are alone, then it is by YOUR choice that you have ignored your inner connection to everything, everywhere.

Accept who you are and accept the responsibility of maintaining a conscious connection to your Higher Guidance. Together we (both you in the physical, and we in the nonphysical) can create the "miracles" that will transform you and your world into the radiant beacon that she and you are destined to be.

I am Violinio St. Germain—Teacher, Guide, and Elder Brother, in service to OUR Creator that I may have the opportunity to bring forth a portion of His Light (Love) through to your world that cries out for answers.

May you hear those answers when they are given. And may you act upon them, not from a state of fear, but from a state of KNOWING who you *really* are.

This is where the fun begins! Salu.

CHAPTER THIRTY-NINE

Harsh Times Ahead Induce Much Needed Growth

Serapis Bey
May 10, 1998

Greetings, old friend. It is I, Serapis Bey, come at this time as a Messenger of Light so that God's promise to your world will be fulfilled and recognized by those who care to see and hear.

Yes, I come in the Light. Thank you for asking for clarification! Often the dark ones will indeed attempt to influence and trick you. You can never be too careful or too cautious—NEVER! This is a time when the adversary plays his tricks most skillfully and many are being deceived who think they are "above" such trickery.

I am asked to speak at this time about the need for a **clear mental focus** concerning the upcoming times on your planet. Your world will soon be faced with the manifestation of great change. The cycle has reached a point where there is no turning back to a less abrupt or less physically "harsh" solution.

The Universal Laws of Cause and Effect will implement that which is necessary for balance. These

Laws are divine guidelines which govern all of Creator's manifest creations. They are the epitome of responsibility and ethics. They are perfectly balanced in reason and simplicity.

This divine intervention, on behalf of all life everywhere, is what allows for events that will *seem* to be unjust to those who have not yet awakened enough to realize that they are part of an Infinite Whole that is the essence of Life. These seemingly devastating events are dictated by the actions (or INactions) of your planetary society as a whole.

Let not the word "actions" be limited to physical actions, but allow it to include the non-physical actions taken (or not taken) in mental space. There are many out there who dabble in manipulating others on astral planes, emotional planes, and etheric planes. Many would call this "witchcraft" or "spiritual warfare". Most such manipulators are unaware of the impact they have on the state of their environment when they spend any amount of time wishing another harm.

You are directly affecting the entirety of humanity *by your thoughts alone!* There is great wisdom in taking deliberate responsibility for the thoughts that you think and dwell upon.

This leads back to the subject of adversarial control of your world. Why is it that your news media must continually bring you the most horrific events that have happened on any particular day?

From the purely material point of view, these negative, high-anxiety events are what keep you-the-people tuned-in, and that sells advertising. BUT, from a less noticed point of view, the negative emotional thoughts that you ones are caused to experience, as a result of YOUR choice to "tune-in" in the first place, contribute to the overall negative "charge" of the planetary consciousness. (And this is as calculated a reason for the presentation of negative events before your eyes and ears as is the money to be made.)

This charge is what then manifests in the physical as dis-ease. Both the inhabitants and the planet herself are experiencing many effects of this negativity. The dark ones who control your planet utilize this "web of negativity" to maintain a fear-based control over you.

However, you, as one of the planet's sentient inhabitants, are as much responsible for allowing this condition to persist and grow as is any other. You would each be wise to monitor that to which you mentally and emotionally subject yourselves (and thus multiply) on a regular basis. Furthermore, note the addictive nature of the "news" you are fed by the media. This is another way of saying that it takes conscious diligence on your part to supervise what is allowed to impact you.

Understand that you are MUCH more than a physical being, and even if you cannot perceive consciously the non-physical aspects of yourself or your environment, it does not mean that you are not responsible for that which you set in motion.

God does make allowance for genuine ignorance, and it will be out of ignorance that ones will say such things as: "God has punished us." NO, God does *not* punish!

What you ones will be experiencing is the sum total of all of the negativity that has been allowed to grow and fester. It is all of these "unchecked" thoughts which have created the conditions that now exist, and the Universal Laws of Cause and Effect dictate that when you stretch a rubber band to the point of breaking (because you did not recognize, in wisdom, the limitations of the rubber band), it will likely sting a bit in its recoil against your hand.

Your world is at the breaking point on many fronts, and the recoil will be quite devastating to those of you who are not prepared. For those of you who *think* that you are prepared, I say to you now that your confidence will (for most of you) be the blind spot that will shatter your reality as you now know it.

I am saying that you would be wise to develop a

flexibility of mental preparation that allows for unforeseen extremes. In doing so, you will naturally realize that you cannot possibly prepare for every last possible outcome.

This is where that all-important Inner Guidance comes into play. For instance, those of you in the warmer climates would not likely think that you would need heavy snow gear and such. There will be changes on all levels, and the global weather patterns will continue to become more and more erratic, both due to man's tampering and due to planetary rebalancing.

This is just one specific example of the interplay of variables which are indeed great in number, and you will have no conscious way to accurately predict exactly how each variable will impact you in the physical space, let alone in the mental and emotional spaces of your reality.

There shall come, as a result of these life-disrupting changes, a resurgence of *spiritual* connectedness. This is mostly due to the fact that, while the physical, emotional, and mental planes of reality are being assaulted, the spiritual plane will be stable and calm. Ones will gravitate towards this calming aspect of their being and draw strength from the connection.

Within this connection will come the Guidance and answers that ones will be seeking. It could be said that the reward for having gone through these challenging times will be a greater understanding of self and the *true* nature of your being.

You Lighted ones are, from the spiritual plane, anticipating these coming events with excitement, for there will be great strides made in the overall advancement of both the individual and the collective consciousness. It is the very physical, ego-based, reactionary being who associates fear with the coming physical reality—NOT the Higher Knowing (infinite) being.

We of the Hosts of God have long stressed the importance for each of you to learn NOW to connect consciously within to this spiritual plane of interconnectedness. This takes mental and emotional discipline and determination to find, and once you "find" this connection within, you will wonder how you ever could have missed it. The elusiveness only comes from your own limiting inner beliefs regarding this subject and your resulting limited sense of self.

This connection is perhaps the greatest tool you can cultivate and learn to use in preparation for the challenges that are coming. The key to finding this connection comes in ALLOWING the connection. You must allow the connection to be *felt*. You cannot force it, for the frequency generated from the idea(s) of force will only serve to constrict the natural flow.

There is no magic or mysticism associated with this flow. Just as you each breathe, you must allow the air to both enter and exit in order to take-in and re-give, and thus complete the cycle. If you effort towards only taking-in, then you will end up stopping the flow. Likewise, if you only effort towards exhaling (giving) without recharge, you will also stop the flow.

Effort toward balance and you will increase your capacity to both give and receive. Allow for the Guidance to enter into your mind, and when you use this Guidance you will be re-giving to the world—thus making it possible for the next step forward in your own growth as a being.

Again, as you grow, your capacity to "flow energy" will also grow. There is infinite potential to flow energy. As one flows energy, there is a multiplication of the energy, and thus a greater and greater abundance awaiting you all.

Please allow for the greater message here to be truly heard with the heart! This message is meant to trigger within you a sense of knowing and a sense of truth.

I am Serapis Bey. I represent the Ray of Purity. My energy represents the balance between the lower physical self and the Higher Spiritual Self (the yin and the yang). I come in service to The One Light Source so that Creator's will be done! Salu.

CHAPTER FORTY

Dare To Set Aside Those Limiting Beliefs

Lanto, The Sage
May 16, 1998

Good evening, my friend. It is I, Lanto, the Sage. Be at peace, for there was a brief time where we had to decide amongst ourselves who would write at this sitting. There were many considerations of equal importance, and therefore the "moment" of confusion on your part. Let us continue please.

Yes, I, Lanto, come in the Light of the One Light Source—Aton! I come as Master Teacher representing the yellow refraction of His infinite spectral expression. The colors and names are for you in the physical so that you may have a means of association with us. From our point of view, we are much more than what a name or a frequency (color) of light can identify.

Precious ones, we of the Lighted realms of creation are ever grateful for the opportunity to assist Lighted ones in their times of need. In doing so, we are challenged to find creative solutions and suggestions to whatever the unique situation may be for which we have been called upon to respond. As we have often reminded you ones, ALL grow whenever any one grows.

We are beginning to reap the rewards of the seeds planted in prior writings of this nature. More and more of you are awakening your inner perception and awareness, and are consciously connecting with we of the Higher (frequency and energy) realms.

We are grateful to those of you who have accepted this responsibility and who diligently persist in the face of doubt and distraction. This can be a most challenging experience.

When you are on a deliberate path of liberating yourself from self-imposed limitations, there will almost always be deliberate adversarial attack upon yourself or upon those with whom you come into contact on a regular basis—such as family members, friends, and co-workers. The challenge is to grow to the point of being able to recognize these adversarial distractions for what they are. Once you can recognize them, you can overcome them—and not simply react to them. It is the reacting which "feeds the fire" and only causes further distraction.

Never underestimate YOUR importance or the importance of the work that you either are doing or will do! You *each* have a unique, God-given gift to share with the world, and the only thing that truly prevents you from realizing and actualizing this gift is your own inner denial of self.

Many of you have, usually through so-called "religious" indoctrination, accepted the belief that you are not worthy of God's direct attention or time. ***If this were true, then He would not have created YOU in the first place!*** You ARE worthy! As far as "time" is concerned, God exists outside the limitations of "time". He can easily "make" time for anyone or everyone as He so chooses.

You are each on a path of remembrance and return to Source. The journey is an adventure in learning—and thus growth toward understanding the true nature of the God-force within EACH of you. None is greater or lesser

than another. KNOW THIS TO BE TRUE!

Some have simply put greater effort into facing their self-limiting beliefs and realized that those beliefs have no foundation in truth. They have managed to set those limiting beliefs aside until such time as they have grown sufficiently in understanding that they can realize how it is that they could have held such limitations as truth in the first place. This is to say that, if one so chooses, one can set aside a belief system, and thus explore from a different point of view or set of assumptions.

Sometimes it has been found that, by setting aside "temporarily" some fears and limiting beliefs, one can "test" a new "reality" with greater freedom than if the person were to try to conquer all of the current beliefs and thoughts associated with each view of reality.

Let me use my scribe as an example: He at one time had great difficulties in accepting reincarnation as a truth due to a fundamentalist "Christian" upbringing and subsequent negative beliefs on the subject. He was being guided (though he did not realize it at the time) to read a book written about Edgar Cayce. This book began to describe past lives and how they were influencing the present incarnation of people. My scribe had then a strong, negative emotional reaction and put the book down, for he thought that he was somehow reading "evil" or "satanic" material.

We then worked with him, because he was truly seeking to understand his place in the world, and thus we were able to establish an inner connection. Thoughts began to challenge his thinking like: "How do I *know* that this information is wrong?" and "Is it *my* belief or that of my mother?" and "Have *I* ever encountered any such information for myself?"

This went on for some time as a great inner battle raged between his Higher Knowing self and his ego reactionary self. Finally this one decided that he would put aside his past beliefs "just" until he finished reading the book, so that he could make a more informed decision regarding the subject of reincarnation. This represented a "safe" solution which kept his ego self constrained long enough for the information to be brought forth.

This one book, read WITHOUT prejudice, completely answered the major questions which my scribe was puzzling over at that time. The adversary tried desperately to stop him, but he, with our help, was able to come to a "reasonable" solution and thus find the answers that he was looking for. He never went back to the "old" beliefs because the truth made SO MUCH more sense to him.

Many times, when we help you ones to find the answers you are looking for, we find you are so close to them that it nearly pains us to see you "miss" them—and *this* thus becomes our challenge. We will always persist as long as the one seeking does not give-up the search.

Learn to recognize this sort of inner battle when it happens. Learn to step outside of the reactionary feelings long enough to evaluate any "real" danger. Ask yourself: "Is there any real danger in educating myself in an area that I have not yet investigated?"

For example, is there any real danger in postulating the following: "Let's assume, for just one week, that I am a worthy creation of God's desire, and it is MY right to communicate directly with Him, and He will respond to my heartfelt questions. All I need to do is to be willing to receive and recognize His communication without prejudice or doubt." You may be amazed at what takes place in the upcoming week, if you *honestly* set aside your prejudices and doubts!

Many of you have traversed this challenge with mixed results. You have been trained to believe that only the most "holy" can achieve this communication.

NO!

Many of our best scribes have had quite diverse experiences that they would perhaps be ashamed to admit in public. Neither we of the Hosts, nor God, are interested in who you were, but rather are quite interested in who you ARE now and where you are heading tomorrow.

Allow for the adversarial intrusions. Again: he will try to thwart your efforts any way that he can when you are on the path to self-liberation and self-actualization of your unique, God-given potential. Though most of you see it not, the adversary KNOWS what difference *one* person can make, especially when he or she is connecting within to the infinite potential of the God Source.

Your experiences may get quite "bumpy" before all settles down into a state of "normalcy". Your personal life may be turned upside-down and inside-out. This testing is allowed; you will need these experiences to challenge you to remain centered and thus trust the validity and strength of your inner connection. Remember that this is schoolroom Earth and you are all there exactly for these challenges, for the growth-through-strengthening that they offer.

Miracles DO happen when you have the determination to persist through any challenge with which you are faced. The journey may take many a lifetime, but you start by taking the first step.

After the first day comes the next day; after the first week comes the next week. Soon you will have years to look back upon, filled with many miraculous "coincidences" and "chance" happenings to remember and draw upon. It is then that you will truly realize that we of the Hosts, and your personal Guides, are watching out for you and helping you whenever we are allowed—and that we always have been doing so.

YOU hold the key to your own salvation. "Christ" (Esu "Jesus" Immanuel) did not die for your sins; he lived so that you would have an example of the true nature of your being! What he taught you, in terms of the Inner Potential of your being, should stand as a testimonial to all of you about where you each are heading. As *he* did, so too shall *you* each do! The length of "time" it takes depends upon you and the path you choose to take. I can say that, if you remain in denial and fear, you will be longer in your "wanderings" from lifetime to lifetime.

For those of you who are already experiencing for yourselves the value of this sort of direct connection with the Higher realms, I ask that you be persistent in strengthening your connection. There are no absolutes in terms of your ability to connect or the strength of the connection. Even the most experienced receivers would be wise to constantly effort towards strengthening their own inner connection. This will, if nothing else, get you out of a condition of boredom or a sense of stagnation!

I am Lanto, come in service to OUR Creator, so that you each may have the confirmations and guidance for which you are asking. Know that you are indeed on the path toward personal growth and ***inner*** reward. Let not ***outer*** distractions dissuade you from your path.

In Light, blessings to you all! Salu.

CHAPTER FORTY-ONE

Time To Grow Into The Cosmic Brotherhood

Sanat Kumara
May 23, 1998

Good afternoon, my scribe. It is I, Sanat Kumara, come in the Light frequency of the Silver Ray of Creation. You know me well. Many there in the physical, especially among your Native American peoples, associate me with the label "Grandfather". Again, as stated many times prior, a label is for you in the physical, so that you can have a mental association with which to relate. You will, one day, begin to recognize ones more by their unique energy pattern than by anything else.

I am asked to speak at this time about your position as a planet and a species in relationship to your universal brothers. Your planet Earth-Shan is but one of billions of inhabited planets with sentient life. [*Editor's note: Several years ago Commander Gyeorgos Ceres Hatonn said there were approximately 178 billion inhabited planets just in the Milky Way galaxy.*] Your species has grown to a point of spiritual and intellectual (a subset of the spiritual aspect) competence wherein you will be in need of *conscious awareness* of your place in the universe and the responsibility of maintaining and holding that place.

This is to say that your world is fast approaching a point of conscious awakening to a Greater Reality and a Greater Truth. Your elder brothers from elsewhere in the cosmos have come to assist you, both in your growth as a species, and as co-creators within the laws of Creator Source.

This is a most unique time in your planet's evolvement in which to be experiencing! There will be MASSIVE change as ones will be caused to confront the inner lies and misperceptions that they have held onto for so long.

There will be, at first, great confusion among the masses. They will, for the most part, be caught off-guard, and thus be psychologically unprepared for the implications associated with this awakening.

This is where you who are of Ground Crew will be called upon to assist those who will be desperately seeking to understand. You will have to deal with great emotional anxiety. This anxiety will have an enormous impact on ALL levels of your planetary experience.

Eventually, as the masses come to accept the greater reality of their true place in the universe, the confusion will give way to a greater peace than your world has ever known. As your species is ready, your world will be gradually brought "up to speed" with respect to other universal intergalactic societies. This will be a very deliberate and calculated rate which is determined by the ability of your species to first comprehend the true functioning of space beyond the limits of your solar system, and then adapt to the universal laws that govern same.

This is as much a matter of UN-learning many present lies as it is a matter of learning new truths. I speak here not only of scientific progress, for great beings in ALL areas of understanding have frequently been gifted (sent) to your planet—only to be "removed" by those who would maintain control over you through deception.

Your learned brothers from elsewhere are well equipped to handle the planetary transformation and integration which is rapidly picking up speed. They will be giving much more guidance on how best to overcome the many fears and superstitious beliefs that the masses now hold onto as truth, which must be confronted and cleansed away.

Fundamentally this situation is no different than when you ones volunteer to participate in, say, a Peace Corps mission to assist a primitive, usually isolated, group of people in some remote corner of your own planet. Many fears and superstitions must be confronted and replaced with truth—whether about basic health and body hygiene or how your airplane and radio work.

You of Ground Crew will need these very lessons offered here in *CONTACT* so that ones will recognize that this awakening has been coming for some time, and that there is truly nothing to fear and only greater understanding and growth to be gained.

These will be challenging times for you ones to face! You will witness many stories that will try to convince you-the-people that the "alien invaders" mean to do you harm. These stories will only serve to expose the true criminals for who they are. Mainstream religious leaders and politicians will be the greatest offenders and will effort greatly to hold onto their control over you-the-masses.

As the Time of Truth (in terms of sequential events) draws ever nearer, there will be greater and greater efforts made to persuade the masses that these so-called "invaders" mean to destroy you-the-people of the Earth. Some of the events planned by your "elite" controllers will appear so real in presentation, due to their technological sophistication (by public knowledge standards), that many will fall victim to the lies engineered by such vivid stagings.

There are likely to be MILLIONS of people sacrificed by your "united one-world government" in order to convince those remaining that the deception is the truth.

There will be a call to defend your planet from these "evil invaders".

At the same time, however, there will be overwhelming evidence which will show that these higher-evolved beings mean you NO HARM. For instance, ones will be rescued from annihilation (as disasters from both natural and man-made sources become more violent and widespread) and ones will testify to the facts of what happened.

Also, ones among your "elite" scientific communities will finally step forward and testify to the fact that great assistance has been given by your elder brothers from elsewhere in the cosmos, over the past 50+ years, in shutting down secret experiments that, due to ignorance, got out of control and would have otherwise destroyed your planet.

Moreover, the electronic "mind-numbing" devices will be deactivated and ones will begin to come out of the "fog" of mental manipulation. From this will come a clearer ability to perceive the reality of your situation.

There will be great speakers and community leaders stepping forward to speak out and quell the fears of the masses. There will be great need for ones to vent their confusions and confront the fact that they had bought into great lies without much (if any) questioning. Ones will be seeking to understand what is really real and what is truly their place in the "grander" scheme of life. The barbaric, fear-based religions will fall, as ones realize that they have been manipulated and "sold" lies in order to insure their obedience.

Truth will be known in all aspects of social, scientific, and spiritual arenas of concern. The Truth will be your path to liberation—both as an individual and as a planetary society.

You will find that your elder brothers believe very much in the existence of God and, furthermore, that they FULLY integrate *spiritual ethics* into ALL of their scientific and social research and subsequent developments. This results in a much more perfectly

balanced and responsible societal structure than you on Earth presently experience—or can even imagine at this point in time.

Your world will eventually realize that these more advanced ones have eradicated the primal ego concerns to hoard knowledge (power, control, etc.) and have thus achieved true abundance and absolute knowledge. The Law of Giving is a way of life for these ones. Sharing their gifts only helps them to explore and experience more of the infinite variations of Life, and thus more fully appreciate the perfection of both Creator and The Creation.

These are truly wondrous times in which to be alive! But perhaps, more importantly, these are wondrous times in which to survive.

We of the Hosts have been sent to help prepare you ones who will hear the call so that you can best prepare selves both mentally and physically for the chaos that is coming. This is to say that, for instance, if you are still living in areas we have warned are quite unsafe, and you insist upon *your* way, we shall honor your choice.

But, be aware that if you transition out of the physical, you will have to watch as a spectator instead of as a player. We only can offer our advice and reasoning; you must choose to accept or reject, as you will.

Our hope is that you will learn to trust your own inner Guidance, and thus create the conditions for your own survival and subsequent growth. We are here to assist you in maximizing your growth potential. You can help us to help YOU by efforting to recognize your own inner Connection and Potential. This has been THE important theme of so many of our lessons so far, as presented in these pages of *CONTACT* over the past several years.

You live in perhaps the most unique time that your planet will *ever* experience—COMING OUT OF IGNORANCE (DARKNESS) AND INTO KNOWLEDGE (LIGHT). Would it not be wise to take full advantage of this exquisite learning environment?!

I am Sanat Kumara, an elder (more learned) aspect of Creator's infinite potential. I am what you are and will become. I am your future and I have walked the path that you are now on. Go within and find these finer aspects of YOUR being, and you will recognize the Truth I speak.

In the Light of Creator Source, ADONAI.

CHAPTER FORTY-TWO

Countering The Distractions Of The Physical

Lord Michael, Archangel
May 30, 1998

Good morning, my friend! It is I, Lord Michael, of the Archangelic realms. I come as a Messenger of Truth, sent by Our Father, The One Light—Creator God.

It has been awhile since we have last communed in this manner. Allow for the energy to balance and settle.

We are thankful for yet another opportunity to share in this manner. Your world is truly on "borrowed time". Many a great soul has contributed toward making this possible. They have done so out of great compassion for you each, so that you would be able to have these opportunities for experiencing that you now have. Look at your current challenges and be thankful for the opportunities that they present to you in terms of inner growth.

Each challenge presents a unique opportunity to learn something about YOURSELF. Every time you feel frustrated about a "turn of events", know that the frustration comes from within and is trying to TELL you something.

Learn to recognize and appreciate the experiences of life. There are no "chance" happenings, and with the proper point of view, you can see good in all of life's experiences. You are never a victim, for the experience alone, whether it "seems" either good or bad, will always have the value of experiential growth.

I have come to remind you all that there are great unseen (but quite perceptible) forces at work this very day in order to ensure that God's divine will shall be done. There is complete balance in ALL of His plans. ***Be assured that God's plans include YOU!*** **There are no mistakes made on His part, and if you are reading (or hearing) this message, then please know that it is meant for you.**

We, of the Hosts of God, have said to you ones, time and time again, that these are grand times in which to be experiencing. Do NOT dwell upon the seemingly "negative" impact of life, for these "injustices" will be balanced by great redemption—if you but allow for the grace of God to flow naturally and uninhibited through you. THE PHYSICAL "PLAY" ON THE STAGE OF LIFE, THAT YOU ONES ARE NOW EXPERIENCING, IS EXACTLY WHAT YOU *NEED* SO THAT YOU CAN PREPARE YOURSELVES FOR THE NEXT STEP FORWARD IN TERMS OF YOUR CONSCIOUSNESS AS A BEING.

All experience is connected in some way to achieving this one basic goal: GROWTH OF THE SOUL. The physical experience, while quite beneficial as a teaching environment, is quite temporal and thus tedious to the participants. Ones are almost always trying to speed up the clock (in terms of sequence of events) while at the same time complaining about not having enough time! This paradox of thought causes unneeded internal pressures that could be avoided by simply remembering the Larger Picture of why it is that you are there in the first place.

Time, as many of you now perceive, is changing. Those of you who can look twenty-plus years back in your own conscious memory will know that "something" has changed. There are ever increasing demands upon you, both mentally and physically—and yet there seems to be less and less time to address these demands.

Be not frustrated by these perceptual differences. They are for very good reasons and not all of these reasons are natural in origin. This is to say that there is great electronic bombardment that is specifically targeting the physical body, as well as keeping the brain in a semi-conscious state.

Many of you can relate to experiences of great emotional and physical trauma, such as being involved in an automobile "accident". (There are no accidents, but we are stuck with using terminology familiar to you.) Your perception of time slows down during such traumatic situations, and events appear to happen in slow motion.

What has actually changed?

Your consciousness shifted more fully (if not completely) to the present moment, and thus you are able to take-in all of the details at perhaps 10 to 100 times your normal rate. This intense focus of thought gives the illusion of "slowed" time. Conversely, if ones can cause you to defocus your thoughts, then the opposite will occur, and you will find that "time" just seems to "slip by".

These electronic devices are tuned to very specific frequencies in order to interact with your natural brain-wave functioning in such a manner as to cause you to "lose" your thoughts. This defocusing mechanism will also cause ringing in the ears of most people. The ringing itself will cause a conscious distraction, but be assured that there are other effects (none of them good) upon mental and physical processes due to these UN-natural electronic manipulations.

However, such electronic mind-control is beginning to "backfire" on the ones who are attempting to enslave you. That is to say, these dark "elite" controllers are attempting to get you to change your thinking in many areas simultaneously. But, since the majority of the people are too mentally scattered (from all the electronic pulsing) to notice, they simply go on believing that nothing has changed. Thus they will not realize that they have been enslaved or that the United Nations now runs the United States. ***THIS, THEN, RESULTS IN A LACK OF RESPECT (OR FEAR) FOR THE AUTHORITY OF THE WOULD-BE-RULERS OF YOUR PLANET!***

There is never the element of Divine Balance within the plans of those who wish to manipulate and control others, no matter how elaborate or sophisticated these ones think they are. This is why they will *never* win and why God always wins.

God's plans have a perfect balance to them, wherein EVERYONE who participates wins; there are no losers. And yet, from the balanced viewpoint of the Larger Picture, God allows for unbalanced conditions to exist and play out. They provide exceptional learning opportunities for individuals as ones are caused to search for that which will restore balance—and more importantly, find and understand what caused the out-of-balance condition in the first place.

I, Michael, am credited with having done battle with Lucifer and casting him out of Heaven. I simply demanded of him that he maintain a certain level of high-frequency emotional ethics. When he could no longer maintain these standards of vibrational ethics, he was, by his own hand, forced to leave my presence and find a match for his frequency vibration. I was simply exercising my right to maintain my own high-level standards. I would not lower myself to his level!

My actions stood as example to others in the Archangelic realm, and they, too, demanded high-level standards, and thus Lucifer and those who would not allow for their frequency to raise were "cast out" BY THEIR OWN HAND. Let not the misperception of the biblical accounts let you come to the erroneous conclusion that he was forced to leave. God's laws are not of force! He left as a result of his own free-will choices.

Likewise, you each can demand that only high-frequency energies be allowed within your space. When you do so with sincere (heart-felt) intent, the dark ones will leave, for we of the Higher realms will always show up to assist when a sincere petition is expressed. (Note well: The heart-felt intent is very important here. We will gladly lower our frequency to meet you part-way when the intention or call is sincere.) When we show up, they leave, just as they have always done! This is the basic mechanism behind the technique of “clearing your space” and why it works.

Please know that we can assist you ones in overcoming the effects of the electronic bombardment—if you but clear your space and call upon the Lighted Brotherhood for assistance. We will come and offer focus, if that be your desire. When you can remain directly and deliberately focused upon a goal, then there will be greater efficiency in your use of time. When you focus with goodly (Godly) intent in your heart, there will always come an answer to your petition for assistance.

Let not any distractions of the physical environment—be they natural or un-natural—keep you from connecting within to Higher Source. The dark “elite” controllers are trying every way they know to keep you Lighted ones from making and maintaining this most important inner connection.

Remember that YOU are a unique fragment of God and within His realm the possibilities are without limit! Thus is the importance of YOUR connection within to Source.

Keep, always, the Larger Picture in mind, and learn to appreciate those experiences that cause you to feel frustration, for the frustration is begging you to look deeper within so that a greater lesson about self can be recognized.

I am Lord Michael of the Archangelic realms and biblical “fame”. I have come so that clarity about past misperceptions can be set to right, for that is God’s promise at this time in your evolution upon Earth-Shan. I come also as a Messenger for God, so that His divine will be done.

In Light, blessings to you all! Salu.

CHAPTER FORTY-THREE

Stop Making Your Excuses And *HEAR* Me!

Aton, The One Light
June 6, 1998

Good afternoon, little one. It is I, Aton, The One Light. Be at peace and relax, for I am with you always. I have come directly myself so that there be no misperception by anyone.

Wake up, little ones! Your reality of experiencing is fast approaching a massive shift and many of you are still awaiting YOUR sign from Me or one of My Angels. Consider this YOUR sign, for there is no more direct a sign than one of this type.

Calm yourselves, get quiet, and go within and hear My voice for yourself!

I am your Inner Voice when you quiet the confusion of mental calculations, concerns, and worry. I am the Consciousness that allows you to perceive self. You each can and do hear Me, but very few ever listen, let alone pay attention. Quit awaiting another to hear on your behalf! Accept who you are and allow for My quiet Inner Voice to be heard directly.

Let there be no excuses!

You each have what is necessary and it is now time to accept responsibility for yourself. Quit taking for granted that you will always have access to this information source, for you will NOT! In the upcoming times on your planet, all will be in chaos, and there will not be a weekly newspaper coming to your mailboxes.

What will you do then? Will you claim to be a victim because you did not get your mail?

Many have accepted this responsibility for self and are "hearing" quite well. But, many more are still sitting upon the fence of procrastination, self doubt, and fear. This is to say that the majority reading this are too busy making excuses for self instead of disciplining self to go within and connect for self.

Note I said discipline. For those of you who THINK that taking drugs will somehow enable you to connect more easily, you are GREATLY mistaken. The drugs will only assist you in mentally escaping reality, whereas self-discipline will only serve to clarify your reality. The low-frequency ones (dark ones) will always come to soothe you while in a drugged state, for you are easily distracted away from recognizing the true Inner Potential of your being, and thus they win.

Quit fooling yourselves, for the only true path toward spiritual en-Light-enment (Understanding) is through mental and emotional discipline. Some will call this meditation; others will move beyond the limitations of such words and realize that they can be walking down the street, talking with others, while still maintaining what many would refer to as a "meditative" (connected) state. This can only be achieved through self-discipline and a strong desire to forever progress forward in understanding and in application of that understanding.

Quit talking and start doing for yourselves!

You need no gurus, avatars, or anything of the sort. You have ME—Creator God! Learn to hear MY voice within. It may very well sound like your voice to you, but remember that you are borne of MY DESIRE and MY WILL.

You are a part of Me and I am a part of you. I gave you free will to choose as you may desire. You are free to choose to allow for MY WILL to be yours. I promise that the experience will be both challenging and quite rewarding, and that your life will take on a significant meaning.

None of you are ever too old or too young to allow for this Inner Connection. Many of you will claim that you are too busy and that you do not have the time to sit and listen within. I say: turn off your televisions and radios, and devote to yourself 15 minutes of quiet time. Most of you watch or listen to these electronic devices several hours a day.

You can hear Me while we wash your dishes or the car. You can hear Me while we drive to or from work each day. Yes, my scribe, I said "we", for I am with EACH of you always. It is you who choose to ignore this fact. Most of you simply tune Me out, and thus the perception of being disconnected.

I have sent many a Messenger to you ones, and yet many of you do not want to truly accept the messages offered and will simply await the next message or Messenger, not realizing that they have just given you the key that will unlock unlimited resources within you.

It is not difficult to connect within. It is easy and natural and you ALL do it already. YOU ALL "CHANNEL" ME—GOD!

Channel is a bad word to use for most of you, but it will have meaning to others. View it as allowing yourself to "tune-in" to the proper mental awareness (frequency) and you will be finding the "channel" for communicating. Like a radio must be tuned to the proper frequency (station) in order to hear the message offered, so too must you each learn to recognize, within, your ability to "tune-in".

Once you recognize this connection, you will wonder how you ever missed it in the first place. Again, it is as natural as is your breathing. Like the breath that nourishes your physical body, I give forth Life Energy that allows for you to have consciousness and awareness.

Re-read the messages that I have sent through My various Messengers, for they are all focused upon getting you each to learn to help yourself. No one will do it for you, but many will assist you if you ask for and ALLOW for the assistance.

Your physical environment is a perfect schoolroom for generating optimal conditions that will cause you each to desire to tap into your own unique God-self potential. This need not be through harsh, cataclysmic events. However, it seems to be the "pound of cure" that motivates your species moreso than the "ounce of prevention" approach.

By now you all should be prepared with several months worth of food and water for your physical survival needs. If you have made excuses for not having done so, then that is your choice. Will you be among the desperate scavengers who will take another's food out of desperation and lack of fortuitous insight? Will your family go hungry because you are "too busy" to take reasonable precautions? Is your conscience bothering you? **Hmmm...wonder Who that might be?**

This is offered as a reminder to many of you that responsibility for yourself and those children entrusted into your care begins within. There will be many ones of reasonable intelligence and ability who will simply perish due to ignorance of this Inner Connection to Higher Guidance. Will you be among them? Anyone reading this will have no excuse to offer.

If you find yourself denying this message as being of little or no importance to you, then you do so out of fear of personal responsibility for self, and no other reason.

I am Aton. My name translates into English as "The One Light". I am Father God. I am.

Salu.

CHAPTER FORTY-FOUR

You Are *ALL* Mighty Spiritual Beings!

Ceres Anthonious Soltec
June 13, 1998

Greetings, my scribe. It is I, Toniose Soltec, come with and in the Light of the One God.

Be at peace and put aside thy fears, dear ones, for all is playing out as it shall. Your planet is poised at a pivotal point this day, and each of you has a definite and important role to play out. Those who have been with us through the past years know of that to which I refer, and so what is taking place should come as no REAL surprise to any of you. You are the ones upon whom others are going to cling in the coming days.

As to the problem of precisely what is going to occur, exactly when it is going to take place—no one can predict down to the precise day or time. However, if you have been paying attention to all the warnings, all the signals, all the markers along the way, you will come to but one conclusion, and that is, it is underway even at this moment.

Oh, yes, the world has not been blown to bits, your stock markets still hang on by a thread, and most all of you still have places to go, things to do, and money to spend. However, all you have to do is pick up a newspaper or listen to any news media, and just be a little bit smarter than are they, and you can see that things are in a state of definite change—ALL things, children—politically, socially, geophysically, economically and what have you.

What do *I* expect will happen?

Let me rephrase that for you: *What do YOU expect?*

Ah! Puts it in an entirely different light, does it not?

Let me ask you another question: What is it that gets your backs up so much at ones such as futurist Gordon-Michael Scallion and remote viewing instructor Major Ed Dames?

You holler that they are setting dates! For goodness sakes, children, is that really what gets you so heated up?

Look deeper and examine what it is that really upsets you. At the core of it all you are going to find your old arch-enemy, FEAR!

It is that fear that only disguises itself as anger over ones, such as I mentioned above, setting time lines. Look around you! Get outside your little glass houses and REALLY LOOK AROUND!

It is a mess on your planet, and every one of your precious, little, man-made systems are breaking down around you. "Why?" you ask? Because they are man-made, based on all of man's fears! Not a one of them are God-based. Are you beginning to get the REAL picture?

Anything that has been contrived and conceived out of fear is pre-destined to crumble. Fear is the design of the adversary, not God. That which is God-based has been designed around love and faith in abundance.

There is NOT lack with God! There is NOT fear with God! For with God, that which you might perceive as lost is never really lost, but merely changed!

You now fear loss of financial security. Just what is that, anyway? Suppose you are able to keep all your money, only to have it useless? Then what is it that you truly have, other than dirty, smelly pieces of paper? You have fear of loss only because you lack faith in the abundance of God!

Each and every Lighted one of you on the planet, bar none, have the ability to manifest and provide everything you need, and even that which you desire. However, if you are trying to manifest because you are afraid of lack, you will forever be without that which you are trying to manifest. THAT IS FEAR-BASED, and will negate what you are trying to accomplish.

This is not news to anyone who has been following our messages for any length of time, for though different words and different examples may have been used, our messages have nearly always been about overcoming your fears and moving forward. **It is that same state of fear which is causing you ones to go about in such a state of panic as to demand information about what is coming and when it is coming.**

Yet, have we not always told you that setting exact time frames is impossible because all is based upon sequence of events? We have no special crystal ball to look into and tell you, for instance, that the Long Valley Caldera is going to erupt on July 20th. It does not work that way. We can only look at that which has occurred, that which is occurring, and project that which *MAY* occur.

But there is the little matter of free will, which is always a variable in any and all equations. You ones continually forget about your powers of creation!

HYPOTHETICAL EXAMPLE: The Long Valley Caldera is building a dome at the rate of 100 centimeters per month (by your calendars). If that is the only factor in the equation, the time to a full-out eruption may be 100 years into the future.

However, let's now throw into the equation a nuclear test of 1000 kilotons, say in Nevada, at a depth of one-half mile. Let's say that it takes place when the magma beneath the surface is shifting in one direction or another. Now, those little wrinkles will change the original equation by a certain length of time.

But, let's throw in an earthquake in the San Francisco Bay Area of oh, say 6.5, into the equation. Now that little factor is also going to change the outcome of the equation.

Do you begin to see the picture?

Now, let's say that some politician, or scientist, decides to move the nuclear test up by two hours, just at the exact moment as the San Francisco earthquake takes place.

Now, guess what?

You have again altered the outcome!

Now if, at the same time, someone changes the intensity profile of the directional antennas of the HAARP array in Alaska in such a fashion as to make their magnetic field cut across the path where the nuclear test is occurring, then chances are that the nuclear test is going to have an altogether different blast profile and thus different effect upon the potential for an eruption at the Long Valley Caldera.

And these are just SOME of the variables one must take into consideration in making any projection of this kind! I have not even begun to mention what your scientists would consider exotic factors which nonetheless have an effect upon this calculation.

This is precisely why we have warned you about exact dates. With five billion people on your planet, you have five billion free wills to deal with, and it is absolutely impossible to predict with any accuracy what will occur.

Windows of possibilities are a completely different matter, however, because based on current conditions and past happenings, we are likely to tell you that there are certain potentials. There also are points of what are best referred to as "critical mass" points. These are the times when so many things of a particular nature are happening, in such rapid succession, or simultaneously, that the potential for a particular occurrence is nearly a certainty. *PLEASE NOTE THAT I SAID <u>NEARLY</u> A CERTAINTY.* That does not mean that it will definitely take place.

This is how prophecy works, children. It is, at best, estimates of potential and possibility, based on past, present, and projected future events and trends. From our perspective, we do have the advantage of much more historical data, as well as more of the current facts, but it is NEVER, NEVER an absolute certainty!

Yet, I will tell you that your world is on the brink of much of what your prognosticators are calling for. Each of you has the same ability to tap into the same Source as these ones, but most of you are, I am sorry to say, either too lazy or too afraid to take the RESPONSIBILITY to find answers for selves. It is much easier and safer (in your minds) to sit back, wait for someone else to do it for you—and then proceed to slay these messengers if they scare you.

No one has held a gun to your heads and forced you to believe any of it. If you are afraid, then I suggest you find out exactly what it is you're afraid of, and why you're afraid.

Fear is the only thing that is holding you back, you know. You can weave into your lives all the excuses and reasons you like, but the basic truth is that all your excuses and reasons are based on fear.

Why does it appear that the adversary is winning? Because most of you are too afraid to really stick your necks out and get them chopped off. But, you will stand behind somebody else and push them out there, won't you?

Ouch! That one really hurt, didn't it?

Well, I am truly sorry, but there are times when the best medicine is that which causes just a bit of discomfort. It helps to get the attention better, does it not?

Yes, you are in for some tough times on your planet, both physically and emotionally, dear ones, and if you're not ready now, then you better plan to pull a few all-nighters and study what you have been putting off because, when it comes right down to the wire, you are ALL GOING TO STAND ON YOUR OWN TWO FEET, OR YOU WILL NOT STAND!

It is time that you recognize who and what EACH AND EVERY ONE OF YOU ARE! Dannion Brinkley says it quite beautifully: *"YOU ARE ALL MIGHTY AND POWERFUL SPIRITUAL BEINGS."*

I could not say it more exquisitely, nor more straightforwardly than that. Awaken to your true reality, and recognize that you do not have to accept anything that the adversary brings your way!

Do whatever you must, but make it a part of your very beingness. If need be, stand in front of a mirror a dozen times a day and repeat: "I am a mighty and powerful spiritual being!" And no, it is not a magical mantra, nor mystical spell. It is called an affirmation.

Stop visualizing yourselves as vicTIMS, and start seeing yourselves as vicTORS! Stop affirming that you are only one little person. NO, YOU ARE ONE MIGHTY AND POWERFUL SPIRITUAL BEING, and you do not have to accept anything the adversary delivers to your door.

Many of you who are, at present, Ground Crew, are in actuality Commanders. You have been such in the past, and you have taken on your present lives, upon that planet, for these precise times, because you *do* have the experience to take command of any and all situations when the need arises.

But you have gone there with your pasts veiled so that you might be able to be a part of your current world. You have, however, the ability to see past those veils, but you have bought into the concept that such is not for you to know. These lies are straight from the adversary in an attempt to disable you and keep you from taking up your proper positions.

It is no different today than it was in the final days of Atlantis. You had, for the most part, the same gathering of souls there as are present in your world today—and once again you are all getting the opportunity to make decisions and play out the same lessons as you experienced in those days.

During that time in your long-ago past, technology had progressed to the point where it was possible to annihilate every living thing on the planet—much as it is today. You had created weapons of such mass destruction that it was possible to completely destroy the Earth. However, in the end, the destruction was limited to the land-mass once present in your Atlantic Ocean, and your planet's axis shifted.

Now it is up to you, again, as to whether you will stop before mass devastation occurs, or whether you will once again go to the brink of utter destruction—or worse, past the brink and finally blow yourselves into bits and pieces of cosmic particles.

Among you, however, there are those who have become known, over time, as the "Wayshowers". They are everywhere, and usually not at all what you might expect them to be.

Seldom will they appear as the little old man with the funny hat and long white beard, carrying a lantern. Most likely they will look just like you, but there will be something about them that is striking, that you just can't put your finger on.

These are the ones who seem to have a little extra twinkle in their eyes and who talk as though they tap the Wisdom of the Ages (and they probably do). They are the ones whose words continue to echo in your ears long after they have passed through your lives. They are the ones who have been warning you, prompting you, and challenging your most fundamental beliefs. They are the ones who others scoff at and call mad, or doomsdayers.

They are the ones to whom you should be listening. They will never tell you anything that you don't already really know. They will but bring it to your forward remembrance.

They are the same ones who were with you in those final days on Atlantis. They were the ones who were shouting the warnings and trying to persuade others to reconsider their works. They are the ones who were then, as now, scoffed at, laughed at, and called mad. They were the ones who were trying to remind everyone of their responsibilities and their real identities.

Sound familiar? It should, for most of you who are going to hear this message are those Wayshowers! You are the ones who are shouting your warnings and pleading with the world to stop the madness now, for you have been there before and you know what the final outcome is going to be if things do not change.

But I digress. I only mentioned that because you have the Wisdom and the Knowledge within you. You have the ability to see past the veil. YOU ARE MIGHTY AND POWERFUL SPIRITUAL BEINGS! **You just need to refuse to accept the fear that is holding you back!**

I do not know how else to tell you—how to bring you from your state of immobility. Stop the fussing, the fighting, the arguing, and become one united mind. Each of you are powerful within yourselves, but two are much more powerful than one, and a thousand are a million times more powerful yet, because it all has to do with channeling the energy that is present in everything, everywhere, available to each and every one of you. And, if you link your channeled energy with that of another, and another, and another, then you will have that much more energy focused and channeled into a particular thing or idea.

Remember Esu "Jesus" Sananda's words: "Where two or more of you are gathered together, of like mind . . ." Chelas, he was talking about exactly what I have tried to say. You are all individuals, but you are also all an intricate part of a Greater Whole, and it's that Greater Whole from which you draw your Power.

That Power is not about guns and knives and weapons. It is not about money or any material things. It is not about courts of law and attorneys. IT IS ABOUT GOD! And with God, all things are possible, IF YOU BELIEVE AND DO NOT DOUBT! It is doubt, that comes from fear, which will negate it all, so your first task must be to eliminate your third-dimensional-based fears.

No, it is not easy. But then, nothing worthwhile ever is easy. Anything you really have to work at, is a lesson you will remember and not forget so easily.

Well, we could go on with this subject for a very long time, but let's face it, chelas, we have been going over this for far too long as it is. IT IS PAST THE TIME FOR PUTTING OFF UNTIL TOMORROW. IT IS PAST THE TIME FOR SITTING ON YOUR BACKSIDES. IT IS PAST THE TIME FOR PASSING THE RESPONSIBILITY OFF ONTO ANOTHER.

IT IS NOW *YOUR* TIME! IT IS TIME YOU STARTED DOING FOR YOURSELVES, AND STOPPED WAITING FOR ANOTHER TO GIVE YOU A MESSAGE. THERE IS NOTHING SPECIAL ABOUT THE RECEIVERS WHO WRITE THE MESSAGES *FOR YOU*—OTHER THAN THEIR WILLINGNESS. STOP AND THINK ABOUT THAT ONE AWHILE.

The time is upon you when the medium for these messages (this newspaper) may not be available to you. Then, what do you intend to do? Will you remember then what you have been told, and start hearing for yourselves, or will you just shrivel up and become part of the nasty statistics? The choice is completely your own.

Do not look to your neighbor to do it for you. He has had no more advantages than have you.

It is time to put away your childish behavior and begin to act and to live as you should. It is childish to quibble among yourselves and be jealous of another. Stop pointing your fingers at one another, for your shortcomings are no less than another's. Stop running around gossiping and tattling. It's time you moved up from your third-grade emotions and actions and began to take upon yourselves the full responsibility for selves.

The only reason you are behaving in such a manner is because you are afraid, and by pointing a finger at another, you are hoping that it will take the attention off yourself. But while that ploy may work with others in your immediate grouping, understand that it does not work with us—and GOD, above all, sees past all those little games. You might be able to hide your fears from one another, but you cannot hide them from God!

So long as you continue your current behavior, you are never going to step off that wheel of karma. You see, in order to step off, you have to let go of your fears—all of them, and take full and complete responsibility for every bit of your lives.

You bet this is a tough message! But, guess what? It's past time for hand-holding and nose-wiping. It is time for you to grow up and become productive members of the Universe! But, that decision is completely up to you.

Have a good day, and thank you, my scribe, for sitting and penning this message. I am Toniose Soltec. I am in Service unto the One Light of Holy God. Blessed art thou, oh children of the Universe!

Salu.

CHAPTER FORTY-FIVE

"Disasters" Provide Great Teaching Tools

Lanto, The Sage
June 13, 1998

Greetings, my scribe. It is I, Lanto, the Sage (one who has gained wisdom through experience). I come in and of the One Light of Creator God. I am most closely associated with the physical harmonic frequency of the color yellow, though I am hardly limited to any one vibrational frequency in any one realm. We are all created in the image of Creator's broad spectral expression and thus are limitless beings. Be at peace, for you know me well.

I have come as directed by Our Father, The One Light, so that His promise to your world will be fulfilled, and so that you ones may have insight into that which is fast approaching into your reality of experience.

Know that there is balance in all of Creator's thought projections. Even the most seemingly horrible of events have reason for occurring, whether or not you can see the Greater Wisdom unfolding before you.

Your planet as a whole is in a state of great unbalance. There are many reasons for this condition,

and perhaps the greatest one reason is because you, the inhabitants of Earth-Shan, have not stood up and exercised your God-given right to demand accountability from the so-called rulers of your planet.

How, you may be asking, has this come to be?

This has come about mostly through self-ignorance of the masses, but also through deliberate and calculated manipulation throughout the past several thousand years. What you are now experiencing is the sum total of your planetary population's refusal to awaken to a greater awareness of the God-self within each. This awareness includes the realization that you are each responsible, both as individuals and as a planetary species, for the kind of energy you allow to propagate from within you, and subsequently contribute to the total consciousness of your world.

The lack of conscious attunement to balance creates a "polar" charge in terms of energy flow. This is because every mis-guided step in the "wrong" direction necessarily generates a counter-pressure toward a condition of balance.

There are several ways in which to re-balance this "polar" charge. The preferred method would be to come back into balance by systematically relieving the "pressure" by allowing TRUE knowledge to flow into the world.

Many of your so-called "elite" controllers have hidden truths and subsequent technologies from you-the-people. These gifts were originally meant to liberate your planet from the need to RAPE her of her natural resources, which would eventually lead your planet toward a greater freedom.

Ones such as Nikola Tesla were sent to bring you the fundamentals of "free energy" that would put a halt to the world's pollution, starvation, and eventually, your preoccupation with materialism. This technology was severely suppressed by the greedy power-brokers who would not look past their personal agenda, to allow a greater recognition of the true evolutionary importance of such gifts. It was (and still is) equally suppressed by the ignorance and lack of forthright insistence by the general public that this type of evolutionary technology be exploited and utilized.

The masses were kept in the dark for the most part, and believed the half-truths and lies which the news-media sources told them to believe. Not much has changed and the masses are still influenced and controlled as they have been for quite some time.

But what about YOU?! Here I am referring to anyone and everyone reading this. What have *YOU done* to demand that a greater Light shine upon, and thus expose, such atrocities?

For the most part, the average reader of these messages has *done* little more than get themselves upset. Some of you have researched a little to see if there is anything to this free-energy "stuff". But beyond that, what have you *done*?

Have you written your Congressmen with an intelligent letter containing documentation and proof? Have you gone to your news-media sources with the same documentation and proof? My point here is simply that, though there are a few who do all of these things, most of you have done nothing-to-very-little to change the prevailing shackles of control.

Why? FEAR!

This is the major reason why your world is in need of such great awakening experiences. The average person does little-to-nothing to demand that true KNOWLEDGE, which has been gifted to this planet, be shared. When the preoccupations of living change from where to get one's nails done or what the latest basketball scores are, to where the next meal is coming from—then there will be a desire to overcome your fears and take meaningful action!

There are MANY military men out there who are sworn to "secrecy" as to the existence of various technologies that could be utilized in such manners as to provide the necessary resources to, for instance, water the deserts and thus feed your starving world. These ones are usually chosen after extensive psychological testing exactly because of their ability to be manipulated and controlled. These ones are nearly incapable of formulating an independent thought for themselves, and thus you have the source of the phrase "good men who do NOTHING".

When your world is faced with the great needs of survival of your species, these ones—and YOU ones—will be forced (from your own inner desire to survive) to take action. The ones with the knowledge will realize that there is a greater need and use for the "secret" technologies.

Many will proclaim, in ignorance, that God is somehow punishing them. This, again, is so that they will not have to face responsibility for their own actions and in-actions. All who are reading this, even if you are Ground Crew, have contributed in some way to the current conditions of your planet and thus you have a "need" to experience the balancing effects of the Universal Law.

These forthcoming events, about which I speak, will be in *ALL* areas of physical experience! For those who place great importance in the stock markets or other financial arenas, your "nightmare" will be the collapse and subsequent shift in the value system of your world. When a loaf of bread fetches more than a hundred pounds of gold, you will be caused to go within and question your personal values.

For those of you who place great value upon physical things, such as houses, cars, and the latest clothing styles, you will be caused to search within when the massive Earth-changes destroy the stick houses and factories which manufacture your material goods. You will experience, perhaps for the first time, the inner beauty of ones who offer to assist you in your time of need, no matter how dirty or disheveled they may be.

There will not be any place on your globe that will not be affected by this great re-balancing cycle. All who survive will have been caused to look within and ask for

Guidance. There shall be the Guidance and there shall be a great resurgence of inner connectedness to that Guidance.

Ones will put aside their differences and recognize the value of community sharing. No one will be able to survive for very long in the physical without the assistance of a community effort.

Great intellectual "wizards" who are used to their luxurious lifestyles will become the students of the pauper who has lived homeless for years and knows how to survive. The net effect upon your world will be a great resurgence back into that which has TRUE value—the inner world wherein all is connected to ALL. Each person will realize that there is great value in sharing with everyone the gifts they possess, for in doing so all will prosper in many ways—physically, emotionally, and spiritually.

Will the economy collapse before the great earthquakes commence?

Will the nuclear wars start before the planet enters into the full effects of the Photon Belt?

These questions can only be answered in terms of probabilities. There are many possible scenarios and you would be wise to prepare for each as if they were going to happen tomorrow.

I am not here to be a fortune-teller; I am here as a Teacher and Guide. Can your parents possibly prepare you for *all* of the possible scenarios that you could encounter during your lifetime? No! But they can give you enough information (tools) so that you *can* prepare in general ways so as to be able to come to your own answers when a challenge arises.

God has sent we of the Hosts to help those of you who so desire the help, so that you may have the Guidance necessary in order to prepare. The net effect of the coming major experiences will be of great positive value—*in terms of the TRUE inner values that really matter!* Let it be known that very few at this time give much thought to these inner values. *But they WILL!*

Prepare yourselves with those things that will aid in your physical survival. If you have prepared for yourself and your family, and you have the means to do so, help another to prepare who may not be as able, such as an elderly neighbor.

There are many things that may be of individual value. You each should go within and listen to what your Guides are telling you. Perhaps an axe or a chain saw or even an oxyacetylene torch will be on YOUR list. There are many devices which may help you rescue someone who may eventually return the favor and save YOUR life with the skills or knowledge that they possess.

I am Lanto, the Sage. I come as Guide and Teacher to any who wish to hear. I come within the One Light of Creator Source.

The final clarion is ringing and will continue to do so from here on out! How will you respond to the call?

Salu.

CHAPTER FORTY-SIX

Still Thyself And Hear God's Voice Within

Ceres Anthonious Soltec
June 22, 1998

Good morning, my friend. It is I, Toniose Soltec, come in the Radiant One Light of Creator God. Be at Peace.

There is much happening in your world as your clocks continue to tick ever so regularly as if "nothing" could ever change. Each moment that passes brings forth change, even if you see it not. The clues are all around you, if you but look and see.

"But," you say, "there have not been these terrible earthquakes or massive shiftings of the planet's waters." I say to you that, from the point of view that we monitor on a regular basis, they are occurring this very moment, as you read this. Maybe nothing drastic has personally impacted you yet; however, the subtle signs of change are there nonetheless.

These changes are perceptible if you tune your attention properly. Most of you never even notice the thousands of subtle Earth shiftings that happen each and every day that are below a magnitude of 1.0 on your measuring scales.

How many of you perceive the decay of your own body from moment to moment? Do you sense the decay of, let's say, a tooth with bacteria etching the outer enamel layers? Or, do you wait until the decay has progressed to a level where a nerve is exposed, and only then decide to take note?

We observe that many of you are too mentally preoccupied with the outer world of your existence to take the ounce of preventative "time" that it would take you to still yourselves and listen within to the sound of your own heart-beat or feel the sensation of blood flowing through your veins and arteries.

As caretakers of your planet, how is it that you plan to take preventative care of a massive organism such as she, if you cannot even monitor yourselves? No, you cannot, and your actions, as a whole, confirm this statement.

You can deny that the teeth in your mouth are rotting or that the mineral array in your body is out of balance. But such behavior will not change the fact that the nerves in your teeth will become exposed or that your kidneys will someday give way.

So, too, can you deny that there are any great Earth changes coming. The denial will not change the fact that such are coming; denial will only allow you to perhaps continue in your irresponsibility for another short bit of time.

All of the warnings that you ones need have been penned prior, and printed here, over and over again. Those of you who do give a damn about selves and do wish to stand as example for the world to see, have prepared for these eventualities. Those of you who sit on the fence and continue to procrastinate will soon find your fence shaken-out from beneath your firmly seated and dearly coveted assets.

We witness that many of you have the time and money to go out and purchase new vehicles to drive or fancy clothes to wear, and then go about complaining that you do not have enough money or time in order to prepare for emergencies. The excuses will not feed your children, grand-children, neighbors, or friends. You ones will also be the ones who pray the most for God to come and save you or help you in your time of desperation.

Every day God will tell you that your "enamel of protective covering" is eroding and that you need to attend this before more extreme measures are required. Do you listen? For the most part, the answer is—NO, you do not!

Why? Because you do not take the time to still selves and discipline your own minds to receive the vast array of information available to you each. You are each quite capable of connecting within for your own Guidance and information, yet many of you rely solely on others to do it for you.

Again, you who refuse to accept your personal inner responsibilities for self will be the ones who cry the most for help. Learn to help yourselves, for in doing so you will be able to deal with any and every challenge that you may ever encounter, regardless of the situation.

Your current environment is as plastic and malleable as is the clay that a sculptor uses to convert an inner idea into a physical representation. It is your challenge to master this form of expression.

You each hold the key to understanding and utilizing the inner ability to KNOW, yet you will shrug-off the memories of doing so and say that it was only a "coincidence" and that you really didn't do anything. NO! Coincidences are merely the conscious recognition of the synchronicity of your place in the universe and how you relate to all therein.

Coincidences usually stand out in your mind as having some sort of significance even if you do not appreciate the confirmations that they are. Perhaps they are answers to prayers and you just are not connecting the answer with the question. Again, many of you will pray for (focus your desire upon) many different things, and when the answer comes, you most often miss the connection between the desire and the fulfillment. This, too, points to a lack of self-discipline.

If you continue to refuse to learn for yourself, then there is only so much we can do beyond continually asking you ones to go within and connect for self. GO WITHIN AND CONNECT FOR SELF! ***GO WITHIN AND CONNECT FOR SELF!!!!!***

You are the answer. *You* can modify and change the outcome of the play. *You* can create the necessary conditions for yourself in order to ride-out the roughest of times upon your globe. Or, you can simply allow yourself to become the "victim" of your own lack of self-discipline and self-worth.

We of the Hosts have held your hand and walked with you through your various stages of awakening. *We* will continue to offer assistance—but *you* have to be willing to "hear" the message, "feel" the nudge, and most importantly, pay attention to the clues that are being offered EVERY MOMENT OF EVERY DAY!

When you-the-students are ready, we will always be there for you! ALWAYS! It is our desire and God's promise to you each. You get "ready" by disciplining yourself and going within and accepting the gifts offered.

Please ALWAYS remember to call upon the Lighted Brotherhood for protection. If you are not comfortable with this term that may sound "New Age" to you, then simply call upon God—the One who created YOU!

It is the intent of the heart that is monitored. Half-hearted attempts will likely bring half-hearted entities and half-hearted results. Remember: like attracts like. When you demand honesty, truthfulness, and clarity, and make these attributes part of your character, then you will ensure a Lighted connection at all times.

Will the Earth changes come as prophesied? Yes and no. Yes, they will appear to some to happen just as foretold, and yet others will see the same events differently. Each person's ability to perceive is unique and different, therefore you will have varying accounts. Those who are experiencing in underground bases will experience from a vastly different perspective and understanding than, let's say, ones who live in self-sufficient rural environments or in large cities.

Just as the ancients of your world would perceive our craft as "chariots" (vehicles of the day) of "fire" (the only item to compare the lighting of our craft to), so too will you ones relate to what you witness in terms of your abilities to understand what you are seeing. Learn to accept that there is a greater knowledge beyond your current perception. But more importantly, learn to accept that it is your God-given right too "tap-in" to this knowledge any time you may desire to do so. It is up to YOU to recognize this connection for self!

I am Ceres Anthonious Soltec, elder brother and geophysical scientist overseeing the various transitionary stages of your planet's cleansing and rebalancing into health at this time. *She* continually petitions that each and every life-form on and within her may find inner peace and their connection to Source (Creator God). When was the last time you petitioned on *her* behalf?

In Light and Service to the One Light, Creator Source, blessings to you all.

Salu.

CHAPTER FORTY-SEVEN

Averting Disaster Through Wise Decisions

Ceres Anthonious Soltec
July 11, 1998

Good afternoon, my friend. It is I, Toniose Soltec, come in the Radiant One Light of Creator Source. Be at PEACE!!!

All is unfolding according to God's plans. There will always be the ebbs and flows of life. Let not the delays (ebbs) dissuade you from your path. There will always be offered that which you need in order to find your way. You must actively seek your confirmations; rarely will they just "fall" into your lap.

We are always willing to assist any and all who would desire assistance. We will always present that which is in the best interest of the one who is seeking, even if that one cannot see same. Be patient and kind to one another, for each has their own set of challenges and none is greater than another in terms of personal perception of challenge magnitude.

There is fast approaching a sequence of events which will have a tremendous impact on you. Many will not know what "hit" them. Remember that your prophecies speak of "cleansing by fire" and that there will be NO place left untouched.

This caution is not placed here to worry anyone; it is just a reminder that safety and security are byproducts of inner emotional-energy and mental-energy emanations. Let not the course of external events cloud your personal judgement or cause you emotional turmoil. Learn to stay calm and HEAR your inner Guidance—and act upon what you hear without unnecessary hesitation or procrastination born of fear.

The physical is a fleeting thought-projection that will eventually fade. Life is what you make of it, yet many perceive that they are the victims of chance happenings and at the mercy of the swing of luck.

No! You each create your own future and your own realities. You experience those things that you need to experience, so that you can have the opportunity to grow past your current state of limitation.

Life is eternal and so are each of you. The physical body is but an interfacing mechanism which allows you to participate, and interact with others, in a focused environment within a specific set of agreed upon rules.

The adversary tries desperately to keep you ignorant of the rules, and thus keep you from recognizing your own inner Higher Potential. And, as you who make an effort to observe what is going on in the world can see, these days the adversary is having quite an easy time distracting you ones with everything under the Sun.

In the times ahead, you will have your massive earthquakes and volcanic eruptions, along with great shifting of the planet's waters. None of this has been changed or averted.

These experiences will cause you ones to become quite focused and determined to survive as a species. In this state of newfound determination, you will recognize an inner Power that you have been afraid to acknowledge

and even more afraid to use. This is just the beginning of the awakening process for most of Earth's inhabitants.

In these times of great change, do you think that a White man in the deep South will refuse the help of a Black man who has come to rescue him from, say, his burning house? No, especially if the lives of other family members are at stake. Do you see that when basic *survival* is the issue, there is often left behind the prejudices, hatreds, and other petty differences that you ones like to hold onto?

We witness all too often ones of the same family who will go years without a word to sons, daughters, brothers, sisters, etc., because ones feel they have been offended in some way. These petty differences signify the need to grow on the part of the one holding such a "grudge". This condition is immature and out of balance. In the end, the only one who truly suffers is the one who maintains and feeds the emotional state of anger. Yet, look around; it is all too common an occurrence.

We who have come as Higher Guides to you ones in the physical are most often frustrated by your lack of attention to your own inner feelings and sense of values. With just a few moments of conscious connection to Source, you could achieve a point of balance and awareness of what has TRUE value. Then you would quickly release the petty prejudices that you use to somehow establish the ego-generated ideas of "right" versus "wrong". This sort of judgement of one another will only lead you to more and more experiences that will cause YOU to be judged in like manner.

It is often the ones who yell loudest about discrimination who are, in fact, the ones who perpetuate discrimination and discriminate the most. If you must play favorites with one another, instead of being objective with the facts before you, then you are discriminating and judging one another based not upon actions or abilities, but upon personal likes and dislikes.

We in the Higher Realms are appointed to our positions based upon our abilities and our need to experience the projected challenges that we may encounter. This is determined by our past accomplishments (actions) and by going within and discerning what part of our being we would like to focus upon so that we may grow in understanding. Creator is always made a part of the decision-making process. ALWAYS!

Your world is full of ones who make decisions NOT based upon objective data or by going within to ask for assistance from Higher Source. Rather, your world is full of ones who only look to trying to impress one another by offering their "buddy" the choice contract or position—and thus you often end up with projects that are doomed to fail because you have under-qualified people in key positions.

This will end up generating a "merry-go-round" of karmic-type "misfortunes" for the ones who simply refuse to let go of these old ways of doing things. To break the cycle, we would suggest that you ones monitor very closely each choice and decision you make.

Ask yourself at least the following questions:

"Why am I so inclined to make this particular choice?"

"Have I indeed looked at ALL of my options?"

"Have I consulted with any and all who would be able to offer a qualified perspective other than my own (if for no other reason than for confirmation)?"

"Have I inquired what God might do if He were in my position of choosing?"

If you honestly pursue the answers to these kinds of questions, you will be guided to ones who will help you to find a balanced solution to whatever it is that you are confronted with. A wise person will always gather as much data as they can prior to making an important decision.

Remember that you are rapidly approaching a time when you will be confronted with challenges of all kinds. The successful overcoming of these obstacles is not going to "magically" occur because you have a "buddy" who "may" know something about, say, pulling out a stump with a tractor—when your expert farmer neighbor remains an overlooked, and thus untapped, resource.

There are ones who almost always do this sort of objective decision-making that I am stressing here. And if they are faced with a situation where they cannot see a clear choice, they will always seek within and note carefully the "gut feeling" associated with each option.

The point here is that, with a balanced approach to decision making, you will begin to turn around your "bad luck", and the bumps in the road will begin to occur a little less frequently for you.

Remember: What you experience in your life is a direct result of the choices and decisions that you make. The emotions that you feel while making any decision will often give you clues as to whether or not your decision is of a balanced nature. If the intention of focus is merely to prove value to another or gain acceptance from another, then the chances are that the decision will feel good in the short term but will ultimately only perpetuate more of the same insecurity that is behind such an unbalanced decision in the first place.

You see that it can be a tedious task to monitor closely your thoughts, and the emotional associations with those thoughts. It takes discipline, patience, continual practice, and honesty with self. The rewards are greater and faster growth.

This approach will greatly help your personal Guides to help you to steer a productive course through any and all challenges that you may be faced with in your current life experience. And it cannot be over-emphasized that ALL associated with Earth at this time (whether those of you in the physical or we in non-physical guidance capacities) are here for the tremendous growth that can come from experiencing the great challenges soon to come upon your planet.

The road to greater freedom and knowledge is always the one which requires personal discipline. No one can do it for you, but these words are given with great love and compassion for each of you who ask for insight. If this message seems to "hit a nerve", then I suggest that you examine closely what it is that is bothering you.

I am Ceres Anthonious Soltec, Guide, Teacher, and Messenger. I am sent by our Father—Creator God. It is His Divine Will that I serve.

In Light, blessings to you all. Salu.

CHAPTER FORTY-EIGHT

Shedding Those Self-Imposed Limitations

Lanto, The Sage
July 18, 1998

Greetings, old friend. It is I, Lanto, the Sage. I come within the Light of Creator Source and I serve His Divine Will. I am most commonly associated with the yellow refraction of light. I walked your physical planet many thousands of years ago; my most recognized incarnation was as Gautama Siddhartha "Buddha".

There are as many paths "home" (back to Creator Source) as there are ones who are searching. Enlightenment has many forms and can be found by walking down many a road.

There are, however, common aspects associated with finding a successful path. *Discipline*, *dedication*, *desire*, and *faith* in one's personal connection to Source are perhaps the most common traits of ones who are successful in finding their way back home.

Many feel their inner heart connection to Source trying to nudge them in a certain direction along their very personal pathway, yet resist the message and argue with self as to what is best in terms of growth. This phenomenon is mostly due to an inner conflict based upon a belief one holds that simply is not true. When one holds as true, for instance, the notion: "One must struggle in order to 'make it' in this world", then there will most certainly be a lot of struggle among the experiences of the one who holds such a belief.

Many of you go through your lives, living out your beliefs, never really taking the time or the effort to truly focus upon what it is that holds you in very limiting habits of thought. There need not be a "struggle" and life need not be "hard".

Life is natural and flowing. It is the one who has the ability to create (YOU!) who places limitations and qualifications upon oneself. YOU summon forth the energies of creation and create (manifest) your desires—be they of a limited or expanded nature.

Many of you believe that you must work hard for anything you want, and if you want more, you must work even harder. This belief limits not only yourselves, but the God-force within.

God is Infinite Abundance and you are a part of His Infinite Being! Many of you also believe that you are not worthy of such gifts of abundance (because of past misdeeds), and there again, you block the flow of your creative potential.

Look deep within and ask yourself questions about what it is that you would most dread. What is it you worry about the most (in a chronic manner)?

Are you afraid of being "alone" (or lonely)?

Do you worry about having to do the "right" thing all of the time?

Do you worry about what family and friends might think of you if they knew how you truly feel, think, or believe?

Do you worry that you are not "hearing" our nudges correctly?

Are you worried that you are not doing enough to "win" your "salvation"?

Do you worry that you are not prepared for what "might" be coming?

Ask a close friend, relative, or spouse what they think you worry about the most. Be prepared because the feedback may be quite startling to you.

Caution: Do not argue with these ones; YOU asked for their opinion! Accept the input and, for your own sake, be gracious and thankful. You all worry to some extent.

These things that cause you worry are indicators and clues about which you should take note. If you take time to TRULY examine why you hold onto these things, you will ALWAYS be able to trace the answer back to something false that you hold as truth. These may be a result of childhood experiences or decisions you made while in a state of emotional overwhelm.

Other statements to be aware of are the ones that begin like: "All men are ____." Or similarly: "All women are____."

These sorts of generalities are ALWAYS based upon false perceptions and these are what limit you and your ability to flow Creative Energy in a conscious and deliberate fashion. In these cases your energy is being directed by the primal ego-self, which is always efforting at avoidance of pain.

All of you have experienced both emotional and physical pain. Usually, as a result of such pain, you will make decisions about the way you will live your lives so as to avoid having to face such experiences ever again.

Let us say that you were involved in an intimate relationship with another and, as a result of the interaction, you are left emotionally hurt. (Many of you can relate to this example.) Do you then decide: "Men (or Women) cannot be trusted." Or: "I am unlucky in love." Or: "I will never love another the way I loved that one."

This is but one small example of the general phenomenon that can cause you ones to disconnect, shut down, or restrict yourselves so as to "feel" safe from the "outer" pains of the world. **However, the experienced pain**

NEVER actually comes from the *outer* world; it ALWAYS comes from *within*! The net effect is thus a "wall" that you put up to protect yourself from YOURSELF!

Question: What is behind your so carefully constructed "walls" of "security"?

Answer: YOU!

That is, a part of you that you are not wanting to face is walled-off because it causes you to somehow feel great emotional overwhelm. When you put up such walls you are, in essence, disconnecting yourself from Source!

This is the closest thing there is to "death". The more walls you put up, the less alive you will feel!

When ones have near-death experiences, they will often state that their lives "flashed before their eyes" or some such statement. This is mostly due to the fact that the walls come down as you re-emerge into the Infinite Love of Creator.

You will also note that many times these ones will come back a "changed" person. They will have a renewed zest for life and will begin to truly live for perhaps the first time. Why? Again: because their "walls of disconnect" have been lowered and they found the "something" that was missing in life—THEMSELVES!

Does this mean that you *must* have a "near death" experience in order to achieve this connected state of operation? No! Absolutely not!

All that is needed is a strong *desire* to free yourself from these self-imposed limitations, a *dedication* to identifying the lies (and thus seeing truth), and the *discipline* and *faith* to persist day by day.

This is also the key to self-healing of any disease. In wholeness and truth, one could easily heal oneself from any illness. It is the fear of death and dying, or of pain and suffering, which creates and perpetuates a continued, limiting state of dis-ease.

When you remove the fears and limiting beliefs, you

will naturally overcome any and all unbalanced situations.

Is this easy? It is neither easy, nor is it difficult. It is a challenge that will garner you great rewards and great insights into yourself, others, and the magnificent perfection of God's thinking.

Again: The paths back to wholeness (oneness with Creator) are infinite and you each will walk same in your own way and in your own time.

I cannot stress enough that the most common traits of those who have successfully traversed this necessary path of "en-Light-enment" are: A strong *desire* for wholeness; a *dedication* to persist in carrying out that desire; a *discipline* of self to focus upon the desire, despite any and all distractions (they will be many!); and *faith* that there is indeed "Light" at the end of the "tunnel".

Another clue is that the answers come from within, for you are each unique, and in your uniqueness come very diverse perceptions and realizations. What works for one person as a pathway may not work at all for YOU.

Find your own way. You will never actually be alone, and your Guides will always present you with acceptable clues and confirmations along the way. Just be alert and open enough to recognize them—and don't deny those indicators which suggest a path you may find distasteful or bumpy with "potholes" in some spots. After all, anything truly worth doing should present as a challenge to your growth!

Shed your perceived limitations and take a major step forward in understanding and growth. Fear NOT, for God knows your needs and He does not harshly judge you. Rather, He HONORS you with all of the Love of His Being; that Love is what keeps you alive! Likewise, be gentle and forgiving with self and each other, for mistakes are an important part of the learning process which are often under-valued (and harshly over-judged by self) for their contributions to your growth.

I am Lanto, the Sage. I have walked the physical path and have found my way back into oneness and wholeness. The rewards go beyond the limitations of words and reach to the depth of the soul. I am honored to serve the Divine Will of Creator, for it is in perfect harmony with that which I find most fulfilling and rewarding.

In Light and Love for you ALL, thank you for your participation in this interchange of growth and challenge.

Salu!

CHAPTER FORTY-NINE

Put Some "Life" Back Into Your Life!

Paul The Venetian, The Artist
July 25, 1998

Good afternoon, my scribe. It is I, Paul the Venetian, come in the Light of Creator God. Be at peace.

I am perhaps one of the lesser known of the ones you would refer to as the "Rainbow Masters" and thus will often be overlooked or judged by you ones to be lesser in some way. For this particular aspect of project Earth-Shan, I have chosen the title: Paul the Venetian, the Artist, so that ones would not be distracted by other names that I may have chosen. If I present myself to you ones as Confucius, would not this be a bit distracting to those of you who have already predisposed self to a limiting or erroneous belief regarding this title?

I have been chosen as the "voice" of the third aspect of Creator's spectral expression. Many of you who have great artistic talents utilize the third aspect in order to coordinate the mind, heart, and the physical body in such a manner as to express and convey into the physical, inner concepts or ideas in unique and beautiful ways. I work closely with the heart energy so as to produce healing tonal expressions such as music. I am also quite skilled in the art-form of diplomacy, for it too draws highly on creativity of expression so as to paint a picture with words.

There is a great need for "newness" on your world. Newness here refers to a new way of thinking, based more fully on genuine Truth and Beauty, rather than on the pretense of same.

Values and perceptions of value have been distorted greatly on your planet. There is little of what the masses hold in their heart that has any lasting value. Ones will effort greatly to find "culture" and, for instance, feel that sitting in front of a coffee shop listening to the local musical group is somehow "culture" or some level of sophistication. Though some may actually find value in this, the majority are there simply because they want the random passerby to see them and think that they are "cool" and "sophisticated" and somehow socially advanced. These ideas and beliefs come about due to lack of experience of those things that actually do have value.

Experiential spiritual growth is all that you take with you when you depart the physical. When you are helping another to see more clearly the world as it really is, you are helping others to grow. In doing so, you will most often be pointing out to these ones the fact that they have chosen to ignore the real reason for coming into the physical experience in the first place.

Spiritual growth is most often uncomfortable at first, because ones must face the fact that it has been their choice to ignore the Higher Objective of participating in the physical environment. Also, the choice of following a TRUE spiritual path is often looked upon as archaic, primitive, and unnecessary—and is certainly not very popular!

This attitude is generated on purpose by those who wish to keep you ones down and control you. The adversary (that which is against Creator God) ALWAYS

tries to control, while the Truth Bringers always try to *free* ones through self empowerment.

When ones are efforting to manipulate and control you—whether to get you to spend your money on their product or to get you to vote-in a new law through the use of fear—they have shown themselves to you. You all have become "conditioned" to some extent to accept this sort of manipulation, and thus end up worrying about the external (physical) rather than the internal (spiritual).

Thus far I have said nothing that you ones, who read these messages regularly, have not heard several times before. Why do you think we of the Messengers continue to repeat the same messages over and over again? Because you ones read them, feel better for a short time, and then forget about the message and go right back to your fear-based, lackful habits like good mind-controlled zombies.

This is not an insult; it is merely a statement of observable fact. When will you realize that these messages are for YOU!

These are the basic keys to taking the first major step forward in growth. Most of you who simply read the *CONTACT* newspaper or the *Phoenix Journals,* and declare to yourselves that "this is all I need to do", are missing the BIG PICTURE!

Any of you who have been reading the *CONTACT* newspaper for more than one year, and really KNOW for yourselves (WITHIN) that what we offer through this information source is REAL, should be sitting regularly to receive personal Guidance in a conscious and deliberate manner. But are you? Be honest!

For those of you who have decided to sit upon the fence of indecision, I would urge that you look at the fears which stand behind the procrastination, and get off the fence and start living! The act of decision-making will, at the very least, cause change in your life, regardless of which side you choose.

Action taken IN TRUTH will always result in growth. This does not mean that life will necessarily always be wonderful and grand, such as is depicted in some of your mind-control fairy tales.

Look at those here who struggle to get these words to you ones every week in a timely manner. Have their lives been easy? Definitely not! Challenging? Yes!

If it were easy, there would be NO growth. So, if you expect to wake up one day and find all of your challenges gone and life some sort of easy roller-coaster ride of excitement, then you will most likely be disappointed, for you have surely not fulfilled your Higher Objectives for coming into the physical!

Once you have accomplished all that you have set forth to accomplish in terms of growth in this lifetime, then you will either choose to transition peacefully or you will accept a new direction. At that point of considering a new direction (a point which few ever reach), you will have the opportunity to proceed forth without great obstacles or great challenges. Many choose to simply transition, for what fun is the game without a good challenge to face and from which to grow? Others will choose to remain as a teacher to help those who are guided across their path.

For one reason or another, you each need the pressures and stresses in your lives, else you would simply not have created them in the first place. Behind each stressful experience or situation is a lesson to learn and growth to be gained.

Most who are reading this are in the infant stage of learning how to stand for the first time. Crawling has proven to be too cumbersome and slow, and you now wish to be running. The desire to run is strong, but you have not yet reached the point of being able to balance self long enough to even stand.

Few on your place at this time wish to take the time to learn to stand, let alone walk or run. Crawling proves to be the safer alternative and doesn't seem to hurt as much when you do stumble and fall. This is fine.

However, many of you will find it a great advantage to take the time to learn to stand and overcome the *fears* associated with same. After all, what is your purpose if not to grow?

Those first few efforts of rising into the standing position are exhilarating, but also can be a bit disorienting. Your view of reality expands from this more elevated perspective. (You can't see very much or very far, relatively speaking, down on your knees from the crawling position, can you?!) And one's first reaction to the new perspective afforded by standing-up is often *fear*—sometimes from the exhilaration itself, and often from the attendant responsibilities which come along with the new level of awareness. This is due to what you can now see, and must therefore act upon, even if that "act" be a *re*-action of denial and return to your knees and crawling for awhile longer!

The end goal, of course, is to be able to run and play—but it takes discipline, desire, and a strong focus on the end goal if you are ever to accomplish the strides that you are desiring. We are here to help you at every step along the way, but as we have so often stated: we shall not do it FOR you.

Balance is the key! Seek first balance within the Light of God and you will come to realize that there is nothing to fear, and that if you do fall, it is because you are not maintaining YOUR balance within the Laws of God. Just as gravity will bring the stumbling child to its knees, so too will the Universal Laws bring forth BALANCING REACTIONS to that which you create.

Each stress or emotional pain you feel is an indicator that you are not acting in balance. Always seek first Guidance and Understanding, all the while efforting toward finding the path that will help you to once again regain your balance.

Once you have learned to stand in a balanced manner, you will then be ready to take your first baby steps forward.

With each step you must maintain a high level of mental and emotional discipline, as now you have set forth in motion a quite interesting dynamic of parameters which must be monitored closely, else you may end up crashing to your knees again.

But don't let that stop you from persisting! Let me tell you a "secret" about my compatriots: All of the great Masters have extremely tough knees from having gone through this challenge! So you are in very good company. All of them eventually learned to maintain the focus necessary to overcome the challenge—and eventually thus became "long-distance" runners, quickly surpassing those who chose to grovel on their knees in fear and self pity.

Again: fear of falling, of doing the "wrong" thing, of emotional pain, of not being accepted, etc., MUST BE OVERCOME if you are to build a stable foundation upon which to stand. The adversarial forces wish to hold you back so that they will have someone to manipulate, usurp power from (in the form of negative emotions such as grief, anger, and frustration), and thus control. So be ready to encounter the adversary's many tricks while efforting to make this most critical step forward in growth and independence.

When your world learns the newness and freedom associated with walking and running, instead of crawling, it will quickly leave behind those darkened ones—who will then simply turn upon themselves and devour one another. It can be no other way in the BALANCED order of God's creation!

YOU EACH PLAY AN IMPORTANT ROLE IN HELPING ONE ANOTHER BY SERVING AS EXAMPLES TO YOUR WORLD OF THAT WHICH IS POSSIBLE TO ACCOMPLISH. PROCRASTINATION EQUATES TO STAGNATION ALONG THE SPIRITUAL PATH.

Quit groveling and get off of your knees! Take these offerings within for yourself. They hold the inner keys to recognizing the worst enemy of all—YOURSELF. *You* create and hold onto the fears and limiting beliefs, and only *you* can let go of them. **Take a chance and put a little "life" into your life!**

I am Paul the Venetian. I am one of many Master Teachers sent to assist you ones along your path. Take my hand and let us walk together, forever forward in growth, understanding, and newness. Let not anything stand in your way—especially yourselves.

In Light and Love for you all, Salu!

CHAPTER FIFTY

Connecting Within Is *Key* To Fulfilling Your Purpose

Aton, The One Light
August 1, 1998

Good afternoon, little one. It is I, Aton, The One Light. Be at peace, for there is nothing that should cause you to worry. I am the Consciousness that you each experience and participate within.

Allow for the acceptance that you are all an extension of My desire and My will. Your experiences are My experiences, and we are all evolving toward new and greater levels of awareness and experiences which many of you will define as "reality". Each thought which you ones experience is also experienced by Me and by all of My creations at a higher level of consciousness.

Many of you have developed your conscious awareness to a level of being able to recognize very subtle changes in your "feelings". This will give you an indicator, within your being, and you will be able to sense when someone can be trusted or if someone is lying to you. This ability is due to this same interconnectedness that you each have with and through Me—Creator Source. This subtle communication is the same experience as connecting within for receiving Higher Guidance, a subject about which ALL of My Messengers have been "hitting you over your heads" in terms of instruction.

THERE ARE NO REAL EXCUSES FOR YOU ONES TO MAKE FOR NOT CONNECTING WITHIN IN A MORE CONSCIOUS AND DELIBERATE MANNER *FOR YOURSELVES!* IF YOU ARE DRAWN TO THESE SPIRITUAL TEACHINGS AND YOU TRULY DESIRE TO UNDERSTAND THE GREATER REALITY OF YOUR EXPERIENCE, THEN YOU ARE, INDEED, QUITE CAPABLE OF CONSCIOUSLY CONNECTING WITHIN FOR YOURSELVES.

I am aware of the inner beliefs you each hold onto regarding self and others. I also know every fiber of your being and the uniqueness of each of you. I know why you are where you are, and I know where you are heading. None who have gone before you, nor any who will follow, have any greater potential than do you.

Note: I said POTENTIAL. Each of you are uniquely able to manifest and utilize this Potential. Some have moved quickly forward in their own personal understanding of how to utilize their Inner Potential and thus have become the great teachers who have volunteered to assist you who have been, perhaps, less determined than others who could be viewed simply as your more learned brothers and sisters.

You who continue to rely upon others to connect FOR you will surely become confused and disappointed in the coming experiences that are fast entering into the physical manifested "reality" of your world. The conscious Inner Connection will greatly enhance the growth potential of your experience and thus assist you to fulfill your Greater Purpose for choosing the current experience.

The very reason for the out-of-balance conditions of your current world is because too many have ignored their Inner Connection, and thus allow those who would lie to selves and others to continually get away with

trickery and deceit. None of you are victims; you are simply living out the effects caused by ignoring the Inner Connection that your Higher-Knowing Self is so desperately trying to strengthen.

The effects will be a great "karmic-type" of rebalancing. The events that will impact the entire planet will cause a great shift in the consciousness of physical experiencing man. Values, and thus priorities, will shift from the external to a more balanced internal foundation—from which to draw reason and to build upon.

Acknowledging and strengthening this Inner Connection NOW will greatly enhance your ability to function as your world disintegrates and you are left to reintegrate societal structures based upon a more stable foundation—TRUTH—as opposed to the current prevalence of lies.

The events that are fast approaching will cause the ones who refuse to accept this sort of message to truly look within and truly examine selves for, perhaps, the first time. This is, for the most part, why many of these ones have chosen to experience at this time. There will occur the ringing of a great "alarm clock" that will assist tremendously in pulling many ones out of a deep spiritual "slumber".

Those of you who are the physically-based teachers (Ground Crew) will be better able to fulfill your roles if you have accepted the responsibility (and nurtured the skill) of consciously going within and connecting for yourselves to Higher Guidance. I know who of you will eventually accept this responsibility, and I know who of you will ignore this message and refuse to accept. The message here comes (as promised by Me) so that none will have the excuse that they were not given adequate assistance or instruction.

All of you who are drawn to this material are drawn from within. This is to say that there is an Inner Connection that allows for a sense of knowing that this information has value.

This same Inner Connection will allow for you to

connect in a more deliberate and responsible manner for self. You need not any other person to connect on your behalf. You have already proven that you can connect for self, else this information would simply not make any sense to you and you would not be reading it.

You see, there are no excuses! If you are still having difficulties connecting for self, I would strongly suggest that you reread the many writings from My Messengers on this very subject, again and again, until they "sink-in". [*Editor's note: The earliest of this particular series of spiritually-oriented writings first appeared in the* CONTACT *newspaper between 5/30/96 and 3/23/97. They are collected together in the first volume of this book series, called* WISDOM OF THE RAYS: The Masters Teach. *There is hardly a writing in that volume, or in this present continuation of the messages, which does not, in some way, address the subject of connecting within to Source.*]

For those of you who have diligently and quietly prepared and are consciously connecting within for yourselves, please know that you are indeed allowing for and creating the greatest opportunity possible for maximizing your growth potential at this time. This writing should stand as a confirmation that you are doing what is necessary to prepare self for the challenges that lay ahead. Your abilities and services will be called upon to assist your brethren in their time of need.

Always effort toward strengthening your Inner Connection. Always effort towards greater and greater clarity. As you approach these "reality"-altering events, the chaos will become quite distracting and there may not be a quiet place to sit. Effort toward being able to sit in a crowded room and still be able to consciously connect within. You truly need NO special conditions in order to connect.

May this message serve as a reminder to all of you that you are NEVER alone and that you each have the Infinite Potential within to manifest the "miracles" of creation. You are each trying to grow in understanding (responsibility) so that you can more fully utilize this Infinite Potential (Energy). You will each grow in your own uniqueness and at your own pace.

LIFE IS A SELF-STUDY COURSE AND *YOU* ARE THE SUBJECT! WHEN YOU COME TO TRULY KNOW YOURSELF, YOU WILL HAVE COME FULL CIRCLE AND YOU WILL KNOW *ME*.

I am Aton, The One Light. You may refer to me as you wish. I am Creator. I am both Father and Mother. I AM SOURCE OF ALL THAT YOU EXPERIENCE. I AM!

Blessings to you all!

CHAPTER FIFTY-ONE

Remembering Why We Are Here

Esu "Jesus" Sananda
August 8, 1998

Good evening, my friend. It is I, Esu "Jesus" Sananda. (Sananda is a designation of accomplishment which means "One with Creator God".) Be at peace and allow my energy to center within and settle.

Thank you for your remembrance of me this day, the anniversary of my birthing into the physical some 2000+ years ago. I came then as I come now—as a Teacher of Higher Spiritual Truth. I am no greater than any of you! We are all magnificent creations of Creator God—The One Light Source of all that IS.

I have walked the physical path many times prior, on many worlds. I have accepted my Higher Purpose (the reason Creator created me) and it fills my entire being with joy to assist another in finding their true spiritual heritage.

I took on the challenge and the accompanying responsibility of assisting your planet MANY thousands of years prior to my incarnation as Esu "Jesus" Immanuel. That last incarnation was to show you each the true nature and potential that lies (dormant for most) within you.

Many of you still erroneously expect me to come and somehow "save" you from physical catastrophe. Why would I come and interfere with your chosen lessons?

There is no such experience as death of a being (soul). The physical body may have temporal limitations, but the soul essence of your magnificent being is beyond such limitations. There is truly nothing from which to save you except, perhaps, your own ignorance of Spiritual Truth.

(For those of you who are questioning the dangers of "scalar"-beam technologies, remember that within the Mind of Creator Source all is possible, even the reintegration of ones whose soul essence may be damaged or scattered to the ends of the universe from experiencing such a blast.)

Your planetary species was on a collision course toward destroying yet another planetary body. The first was the planet whose remnants are what make up a great deal of the asteroid belt between Mars and Jupiter, and the second was Mars herself. I could not bear another such destruction of beauty, and thus I accepted the challenge to enter the "karmic condition" of your species—at the risk of being caught-up in the compressive (and somewhat suppressive) nature of your world.

Many have long forgotten (and the dark "elite" controllers of your planet have efforted to hide from your awareness) the previous civilizations established upon your globe. There were four prior and you are experiencing the fifth.

I have been working with you ones throughout all of your major growth challenges. I have been less than completely successful on each of the four occasions prior to this one. I have grown in many ways as a result of my persistence, and I am grateful for the opportunity to once again assist you ones and your beautiful planet—a great living being I recognize as Shan.

Many of you who are reading this have joined with me in my efforts to awaken the masses of your world to the true nature of their spiritual heritage. Some of you were with me throughout each of the prior four attempts; for others this is your first effort to help your brothers and sisters to awaken.

This is no easy challenge, nor is it one for the weak of heart. For every five who have agreed to participate in a physical role, four have yet to awaken or are "copping out" or have become distracted into the ways of the material consciousness. This is a typical statistical average that has been anticipated and is expected. The mission is thus over-engineered with this probability in mind.

Many of you who are "hearing the call" are restless due to the physical pressures of time and the compressive nature of your physical environment. I know well these challenges, for I too have had to overcome such limitations in each of the prior attempts. My last incarnation laid the foundation for those of you there now, so you would recognize that you too have the potential ability to manifest skills as I did then as Esu Immanuel (later erroneously called "Jesus").

Will you accept such responsibility?

It is left to be seen. Many of you reading this have been heavily influenced in ways that you are not consciously aware of at present. This is to say that the adversarial forces (any ones wishing to control others instead of allowing each their freedom) have been programming your present society for WELL OVER 2000 years to believe in the lie that you are helpless and powerless. This long-term effort is designed to keep each generation in a very suppressed, low-frequency state, dulled to the realization of your True Potential.

For most of you, your programming in this lifetime began as infants. Your parents passed on to you their limiting beliefs, and thus influenced you and made you more susceptible to further reinforcing limitations placed upon you by others. This is to say that you each "feed" one another's fears.

These are not trivial challenges to overcome. Each of you should hold self in examination and monitor closely the "automatic" responses that seem to flow out of your mouths without a conscious thought. These are the clues, if you but look, to freeing yourselves from the "karmic wheel" of repetition. When enough awaken, and thus get off this "merry-go-round", the world will begin to see the value in not allowing the current civilization to meet destruction.

Newness comes by being daring and taking a "chance". I put chance in quotes because, if you are connecting within, the "chance" will be far from a desperate action taken in fear. IT WILL BE A BALANCED OPPORTUNITY TO BRING ABOUT CHANGE!

If your intent is aligned with the Godly intent to help your brother, there will be enormous unseen Guidance and Assistance to help you fulfill your largest dreams. If your intent is to somehow be a "big shot" and tell someone: "I told you so!" or "Look at me!", then you will likely be stuck on your little "merry-go-round" for yet another cycle.

The short-term "sacrifice" of being ridiculed or called a liar and a fool is a sad reality of your world. But, what is it that is really being sacrificed? The ego! Will you ones set aside your ego-concerns long enough to confront the very ones who seem to love to taunt you and make you "sound" the fool?

Some of these hecklers are indeed overshadowed by the adversary and thus are working to keep you from awakening your brothers. However, most of the hecklers are, in fact, "pumping" you for information that they so desperately seek. They do not want others to know that what you are saying actually resonates with them—to the point that they are overwhelmed and frightened. Thus they need to ridicule so as to release the emotional anxiety that would otherwise overwhelm them. You ones truly live in a "backwards"-thinking world.

I say to you: what better environment could you possibly have in which to be challenged in such a manner?! I know the price and I know the rewards for

confronting this very challenge. Was I not ridiculed, laughed at, spat upon, beaten, and eventually tortured and left for dead?

Those were a very small part of my experience in my last incarnation. But, do you not also see that some 2000 years later ones are still trying to come to grips with the fact that they allowed such an atrocity?

Many of the ones who did these things have been weeping ever since. It is time to stop the weeping and realize that you helped me to get my needed and desired lessons! I am grateful for the experience and knowledge gained as a result of facing those challenges. I hold no grudge against anyone. I forgive all actions taken in spiritual ignorance. I welcome you all as my brothers and sisters, and I take no offense if you reject these words, or me personally.

I have a mission to see through to completion. I ask that you each go within and seek Inner Guidance on a daily basis until you find for yourself (first-hand knowledge) that you are *always* connected and continually being Guided.

YOUR WORLD IS JUST READY TO ENTER INTO A NEW PHASE OF AWAKENING, AND THESE LAST SEVERAL THOUSAND YEARS HAVE BEEN IN PREPARATION FOR THIS AWAKENING.

The Divine Guidance of Creator God (Father-Mother Source) has made this miracle possible. Give thanks for yet another opportunity to "get it RIGHT"! I am always ready to assist any and all who wish to participate in the endeavors of awakening our "sleepy" brothers and sisters. If your intent is in alignment with this goal, I will always respond to the sincere request for help.

I am Esu "Jesus" Sananda. I am the Golden-White Light which wells up from within and is expressed as pure Love. I am your brother—NOT your God. Go within and take my "hand" and I will guide you to the "water" that will quench the "thirst" of your soul.

Blessings to you all. Salu!

CHAPTER FIFTY-TWO

Much Can Depend Upon *Your* Inner Connection

Violinio Saint Germain
August 15, 1998

Good evening, my scribe. It is I, Violinio St. Germain. I come in and of the One Light that IS Creator God.

It has been a while, in your perception, since we have last communed in this manner. Be at peace and find comfort in knowing that you are "hearing" correctly.

We of the Hosts of Creator God (His Messengers) are quite busy in terms of preparation for that which is fast approaching the manifested physical reality of your world. We have been urgently trying to get you ones, there in the physical, to begin to recognize and engage in direct communication with us and your personal Guides for a long time now.

Many have responded, and are appropriately finding that there is nothing "special" about the ones who sit and pen these messages—except perhaps for their beliefs and perceptions about the "receiving" process. This is to say that they not only believe in their connection to Source, they KNOW they have a direct connection to Source, and it is there to be USED and is not something that is just talked about.

Creator gave you these tools so that you can ALWAYS find your way "home" (back to Source). Please note that finding your way back home does NOT necessarily require going anywhere, and definitely does not require "ascending" in some mystical manner as many "New-Age" gurus would lead you to believe.

You are all efforting toward growth and a greater understanding of who you are and where you are going. THE MOST FUNDAMENTAL TOOL FOR YOU TO FIND, UNDERSTAND, AND USE, *IS YOUR INTERNAL CONNECTION WITHIN!*

If you are reading these sorts of messages (channeled, received, etc.) and you believe that there is "something" to them beyond the messenger who writes them down, then you are ready to take YOUR own pen in hand (or tape recorder) and begin writing (or speaking) for YOURSELF!

Many of you sit out there and petition for Guidance and ask: "What can I do to help?"

You have all heard the saying: "God helps those who help themselves." Well, a good place to start helping the overall mission is to learn to recognize and UTILIZE your own Inner Connection!

The one who is penning this message right now began with a simple notebook and a pen. For over a year this one figured that the process was too easy, and therefore it must be just the ego wanting attention (though the writings were never shared with anyone).

All of this one's earlier writings were of a personal nature to help with the problems and considerations that were impacting the current life experience. This receiver gave up, and threw down the notebook and pen many times, in disbelief that anything "real" was going on other than "self-talk".

Well, my friends, you are *ALL* manifested thought-forms of Creator Source, and so—guess what—connecting within to Source *IS* SELF-TALK! Though there was quite a bit of early reluctance (and feelings of great responsibility) on the part of this receiver upon realizing some writings were intended for a public forum, this one eventually has become more comfortable providing the many short "spiritual" messages which you ones have come to look forward to in the pages of this newspaper. Yet, on many occasions, this person still asks the same question within: "What can I do to help?"

Receiving public messages for sharing herein is just one small part of what this one does to help the mission, but the same cultivated ability is used in all aspects of this one's life challenges. This is to say that the Guidance is continually a part of the day-to-day experience and not just a once-a-week message-receiving "thing". This is how it should be for all of you.

We do not need a hundred public receivers! But we do need as many hands, feet, and most importantly, MINDS of those who will allow the messages to come through.

Note I said ALLOW! This is the key! Have you ever allowed someone to give you a gift? Is it not more difficult to disallow someone to give you a gift than to simply accept it?

Many of you, through your personal perceptions and beliefs, have gone to great lengths to ignore and disallow the natural flow of Guiding information. Again: learn to allow the energy, feelings, sensations, thoughts and such, to flow.

The use of a pendulum is a fine place to start—if you have the patience to truly work in such a tedious manner. If you choose (or have chosen) to use such a device, then I will propose to you that you try the following experiment: ask a direct "yes" or "no" question, and BEFORE the pendulum responds, shut your eyes and listen for the correct answer. Almost all of you will sense the correct answer—without having to go through the mechanical process of displaying that answer through the motion of the pendulum.

The point here is that you need no such devices! But if they help, then by all means use them.

Each attempt at connecting within to Source will raise your frequency and thus strengthen your ability to perceive your connection. In time you will graduate from the need for quiet meditations, chants, pendulums and such, to a more fluent and continuous connection. This is to say that stepping stones along the path need not be rested upon as some kind of pinnacle of achievement. Always look to improve and search for the least restrictive methods of connecting.

Many can walk into a grocery store and listen within to what their body is lacking, or they will feel a strong attraction to a certain fruit or vegetable. Has not this been a common experience for many of you? How many of you ever witness ones sitting down in the grocery store to "meditate" in order to connect with this same Higher Guidance? Not too many!

This is the same Guidance that will send you messages of cravings or messages of feelings or messages of ideas, thoughts, or even words. It is all the same basic mechanism! You all have had experiences of such messages—especially if you have ever had to go through a pregnancy where there are all sorts of unusual cravings and such.

The point here has been made to you ones over and over again: Your world is about to "crumble" and we of the Hosts of God have a great desire to maximize the value for you of the coming experiences so that you each will have the greatest possible opportunity for growth. Connecting within is central to achieving the full value of this time upon your planet—*not just for yourself, but also for those around you.* You each can help one another by that which you uniquely contribute FROM WITHIN.

Many have erroneously flocked to places wherein are located some of the ones who receive public messages for this newspaper, in an attempt to hide from (or avoid accepting) personal responsibility which goes along with seeking their own Guidance within.

Is it not possible there would be important growth and sharing experiences where you were located *before* such an impulsive and maybe irresponsible move? Perhaps your personal Guidance would suggest to you a better location for the sharing of your talents. Have you been ignoring the "gut" feeling that you need to relocate elsewhere?

Perhaps you need to allow the inner connection so that you will be around to help others at a later time. We have many Ground Crew at this time who are in locations where they simply will not physically survive what is coming. Each of you know who you are. You're the ones with that nagging anxious feeling that will not go away!

What holds you in these areas that have been told to you will simply not make it? Is it a job that holds you? Friends? Family? Fear of the unknown? Why do you continually discount the many messages and Messengers that we have sent your way?

You will create your own miracle of survival, else you will surely re-experience this same challenge, again and again, until you learn that YOU ARE CREATOR.

Always keep the Light of God around you and ask for clarification of any and ALL entities who may come into your energy space. This is most important, else you are likely to be tricked and fooled by entities who play upon your weaknesses and are suppressive and manipulative in nature.

These "dark" ones (low-frequency beings) realize that their reality of existence and ability to influence is directly related to YOU being in a vibrational frequency range that they can function within. As more and more of you begin to function in a higher frequency range, outside of their ability to function, they begin to see that their games are indeed meaningless, and thus they too are confronted with an experience which makes them re-evaluate their "reality" and what is truly of value.

As one grows, all grow! There is quite a dimensional schoolroom that you ones participate within. Never underestimate the significance that YOU represent to the overall growth of many unseen entities! Learn to accept that you each can and will become a wayshower for MANY! This is an earned level of responsibility and is not a role that one "stumbles" into.

I am Violinio St. Germain and I give special thanks to Commander Tomeros Maasu Korton for his assistance with both this writing and the communication link between us and our receiver. We come in Light and in Service to Creator God—The One Light.

Salu!

CHAPTER FIFTY-THREE

Choosing To Become A Wayshower For Humanity

Aton, The One Light
August 22, 1998

Good evening, little one. It is I, Aton, The One Light. I am Creator. I am the Alpha and the Omega that make up the Infinite Sacred Circle.

You there in the physical are on a journey that begins and ends this infinite cycle. The experiences in between are the lessons of growth and responsibility that will bring you full circle. You will inevitably begin again another similar journey on other planes of "reality" and awareness. The journey is without limits and is TRULY infinite!

I have come to remind you ones of the responsibilities that you have accepted prior to coming into your current experience. There is an old and almost overused expression which states: "Many are called, but few are chosen." All of you who are reading these words have been "called"! This is to say that you all are sensing, within, an inner sensation (indicator) of foreboding change and that this change is somehow important and the reason why you are there.

The experiences that are coming are an accumulation of past choices and decisions which you have either made yourselves, or you have accepted into your experience. Please note that the above use of the word "past" is not limited to your current life experience. You are responsible for ALL of your thoughts and there is no "time" limit on this responsibility.

I have great (infinite) patience with all of My creations. You each need one another for your growth, and you are all connected to one another through ME! When you each, as individuals, demand truth from yourselves first, and stop your inner deceit and denials (self-imposed limitations based on LIES!), you will be in a better mental space from which to observe and help others to do the same.

Truthbringers are ALWAYS rejected at first. ALWAYS! This is because they (you?) will cause ones to confront the inner lies which ones cling to in order to NOT feel responsible for the errors they have made. This is a strong and powerful emotional battle that ones must (and will, eventually) confront. As more and more of you ones face and confront your limiting beliefs (inner lies), you will stand as examples to your brothers and sisters who are more reluctant to do so.

Your actions will speak in terms and in a manner that words will not be able to describe. You will, as a result, be able to control your own physical and emotional states, for there will not reside within you the fear-based reactions of the primitive ego-self. These inner fears are the subtle apprehensions that cause you to hold back (restrict) the natural flow of My energy, both to you and through you.

Take a look around you when you are out among "strangers". Do you see the majority of ones smiling? Do they make eye (the "window" to the soul) contact with you?

The majority of your population has been suppressed emotionally and physically to a point of near spiritual starvation. There is a great need to remind many ones that it is THEIR responsibility and THEIR challenge to overcome such programing (mind control).

You, as potential guides and wayshowers, have chosen to participate in such a capacity as to overcome the perceived limitations of your past, so that you can stand up AS EXAMPLES for the world to see. This is the most effective means possible of teaching!

How many of you find yourselves in "bad" health? Do you not see that it is because of a persisting out-of-balance inner condition? MORE BLUNTLY: YOU ARE HOLDING ON TO ANGER, GUILT, FRUSTRATION, FEAR, AND SUCH TO A POINT OF NEAR DISCONNECT FROM THE NURTURING (BALANCING) ENERGY OF MY LIGHT (LIFE FORCE) THAT COMES FROM WITHIN.

If you cannot "save" yourself, then are you not "choosing" to not participate at this time? Can you rid yourself from the inner negativity generated out of the fear of being wrong? You cannot be a victim without first agreeing to play the role of the victim. In truth, there are NO victims! If you choose to wallow in the misperception that you are less fortunate than another, or less educated, or less able in some way than another, then you are indeed holding onto the inner LIES!

NONE ARE LESSER THAN ANY OTHER! HOW COULD SUCH BE WHEN ALL ARE CREATIONS OF MY THINKING?!

The ones who *appear* to have greater abilities are the ones who simply do not hold onto the same limiting beliefs about self as those who constantly limit themselves. You are all borne of MY perfection! I created you uniquely so that you would see, within one another, examples of infinite possibilities.

YOU ARE ALL MAGNIFICENT AND POWERFUL BEINGS WHO ARE EFFORTING TO RECOGNIZE AND UTILIZE THIS INNER POWER!

I am calling upon each of you to go within and find those beliefs which limit you. When you catch yourself saying anything that means "I can't...", then realize there is a LIE behind such words. All of the

rationalizations with which you may want to "argue" are based upon not wanting to accept the fact that you may be wrong in your limiting beliefs about self.

YOU CAN DO ANYTHING—if you simply get out of your own way long enough to allow MY energy to manifest within and subsequently flow through you, out into the manifested universe that I (WE) create.

I monitor the response (in many cases REACTION) to these words. *PLEASE KNOW THAT IT IS INDEED THIS SIMPLE!*

You are taught to believe that it is difficult to become empowered (en-Light-ened). The correction mechanism is to simply observe any limiting beliefs, and then replace them with empowering (truthful) ones.

However, many of you place such great emotional certainty and energy into the lies that it literally pains you to have to admit you may possibly be wrong. So, for you "bound and shackled" ones, it will simply be easier to say: "This does NOT apply to ME, because I don't have any limiting beliefs!"

YOU ALL HOLD ONTO LIMITING BELIEFS TO SOME EXTENT! Else you would not be in the physical, efforting to overcome them.

All of you who are participating in a physical body have chosen to participate in such a manner because YOU need to work on an area of understanding and responsibility that you have been less than successful in MASTERING so far. MORE BLUNTLY: YOU HAVE ERRORS OF THOUGHT (BELIEFS) WHICH LIMIT YOUR UNDERSTANDING AND ABILITIES TO MANIFEST AND MASTER YOUR TRUE CREATIVE POTENTIAL.

So, if you feel that this message does not possibly apply to you, then KNOW that you are the one WHO NEEDS IT THE MOST!

I CALL UPON YOU EACH TO REMEMBER AND AWAKEN TO YOUR PURPOSE FOR BEING HERE AT THIS TIME!

WILL YOU BE THE ONE WHO GETS UP OFF YOUR DEATH BED AND SHOWS THE WORLD THE INNER POSSIBILITIES OF CONNECTING WITHIN?

WILL YOU BE THE ONE WHO STOPS SAYING "I CAN'T" AND STARTS DOING THE "IMPOSSIBLE"?

YOU are the ones who choose to participate! Will you be among the "few" who are "chosen"? The choice is yours, and you will have to also choose to pull self up out of your own misperceptions and limiting beliefs.

In doing so, you will recognize that which YOU CAN DO to help. If you refuse to help yourself, then you will surely be looking in the wrong places for your "answers" and you will surely miss your opportunities to assist your brothers in need.

ALL of the answers to ALL of your questions lie within YOU. Will you recognize this FACT or will you deny it and hide behind your own irresponsibility?

I am Aton, THE ONE LIGHT! I am Creator God. I am the One who created YOU! I know you each, as I know Myself. We are ultimately One in the same.

I love and cherish you each. I know and feel your heart intent and desires.

Blessings to you all! Salu!

CHAPTER FIFTY-FOUR

Pull Your Heads Up Out Of The Sand!

Violinio Saint Germain
August 26, 1998

Ah, at last, I have gained your attention. Thank you for finally hearing the call. It is I, Germain, come this evening to commune with you. I come in and with the Holy Light of Creator Source and I am in the company of that which you call the Heavenly Host. We are most humbled at the opportunity to bring forth the messages during these times, as the times you are experiencing at present are the most important, challenging, and interesting ever upon planet Earth.

Though it is very easy to allow yourselves to slip off into the realm of fear and darkness now, it is most imperative to not allow this to happen. Granted, the world is moving so rapidly and everything appears to be spinning out of control, and were I to be present in a third-dimensional expression on Earth as are you ones, I too would be facing the same challenges associated with the fear, as are you. So, do not beat yourselves up over it; simply recognize what it is you are facing and go beyond it.

No, it is not necessary that you "go through your fears". If you do not want to go through them, then simply decide that you shall place yourselves beyond them and do not spend another moment struggling against them. The adversary will use every trick in the book to distract you away from the goal, and having you struggle against the fears is one of the oldest (and most effective) tricks around.

It works the same with karma. You keep hearing everyone say that it must be so-and-so's karma. Well, if you choose to stay on the ever-turning wheel of karma, then yes, these ones are probably living out their karmic path. However, you can choose to step off the wheel of karma by realizing that you have much to learn AND JUST GO ABOUT LEARNING IT; you don't HAVE TO spend lifetime after lifetime repeating the same lessons over and over again! There is really no mystery to it—it is but a conscious decision that all ones must make for themselves, and then stick to the resolve to live your life accordingly.

And that, dear ones, it the tough part! In the days in which you are living, it is most difficult to stick to resolve. Am I correct? I know, for I do remember what it was like to have existed in that third-dimensional density, and it is tough, no doubt about it. But, it is not hopeless, else no one would have ever progressed past it! And, I am here to tell you that it is possible.

It may not always be the easiest road to travel, but it will definitely be the most interesting and the most rewarding once all the votes have been tallied. When you choose to follow the correct path (for you), you will absolutely meet up with all sorts of distractions set out by the adversary. These distractions will appear in the road just as you think there is a smooth, four-lane highway ahead. That's when you will discover many stumbling stones tossed in your way.

Everyone who is trying to follow in the Way of Light right now is being distracted in hopes of taking you off your dedicated path. These distractions are coming in every form imaginable, from family and friends, to employers, to the news on television, radio, and in the newspapers.

There are those of you who have become obsessed with watching, listening, and reading every tidbit you can find about the affairs of Bill Clinton and Ms. Lewinsky. Wake up, children, for can't you see that this story, with as much press as it has, is but a lurid, soap-opera distraction for the masses? While the adversary is working behind the scenes, you are lulled into a mindless stupor over the perverted sexual encounters of Clinton. Surely you can see this for what it is!?!

As distasteful and disgusting as it may be, unfortunately it is but a typical sign of the morally deprived (depraved) times in which your world wallows at present. Every perversion possible is taking place on a consistent basis. But, because this is the White House and the President of the United States, it is a titillating story and you are sucking up to the trough and playing right into the hand of the adversary.

Yes, it is time that your world dealt with truth and purity. There is so much lying that takes place every day, it is no wonder your youth are as messed up as they are.

Morals? What morals?

Morality has gone the way of the horse and buggy. If it feels good, then everyone thinks it's okay. What are you teaching the youth of the world? Most of them have grown up without parental guidance for hours on end, left to their own devices to watch God-knows-what on the tube and playing violent video games!

Where are the parents of these children to guide them? Responsible, moral adults do not just happen! The parents, whose child ends up killing someone, stand and cry in front of the courts and wring their hands and wonder what went wrong. I WILL TELL YOU WHAT WENT WRONG: THE PARENTS WENT WRONG, THAT'S WHAT!

Those little ones would not have gone in that direction, had the parents been at home in attendance to their most important responsibilities—instead of out either working at some all-consuming job, or chasing after so many other distraction in their lives. LET ME TELL YOU ONE THING, AND LET IT BE HEARD FROM THE HOUSETOPS: WHEN YOU CREATE A LIFE, YOU ARE RESPONSIBLE FOR THAT LIFE! AS A PARENT, YOUR VERY FIRST RESPONSIBILITY IS TO THE CHILD! END OF DISCUSSION.

Raising children is a full-time career, not something you do for a few hours a day or week. And, as the adult, you have the ABSOLUTE RESPONSIBILITY to teach that child right from wrong, and to guide them along a path that will develop them physically, mentally, and spiritually.

I DON'T CARE IF I AM HURTING FEELINGS OR MAKING SOME OF YOU ANGRY! BY GOD, IT IS TIME THAT YOU GOT YOUR CRAP TOGETHER AND STOPPED PAWNING YOUR PROBLEMS AND RESPONSIBILITIES OFF ONTO SOMEONE OTHER THAN YOURSELVES.

Better your feelings get hurt and you get angry, if it saves one little one's life and soul. If your planet's future were to be based solely on current trends, you could absolutely forget about ANY future, because those of you who are raising the youth of today have sealed your own futures! Think that one over for a bit.

ANGRY? Me? It is not anger that I am expressing, but it is time that someone got your attention. Do you want your government to come in and take control of your families? Based on the way most of you operate, you do. We see those young parents who are totally overwhelmed by having children, and those who wanted the babies because it is so idealistic and romantic.

But when the baby turns into work, and diapers have to be changed, and bottles made, and the crying goes on for hours, the selfish little parents suddenly decide that having that baby isn't nearly as much fun as they thought it was going to be. WELL, GUESS WHAT? LIFE ISN'T

ALWAYS FUN! SOMETIMES IT IS DARNED HARD WORK!

And you parents, who raised those children who are now having children, are just as much to blame! Many of you grandparents are finding that you are doing more raising of the grandchildren than are the parents themselves—because the parents still want to have their fun! YOU are the ones who never taught your children responsibility; you did everything *for* them, so they could have their fun. Well, you are reaping your own rewards!

There must come a time of change, for without it, you will have yet another generation growing up with even fewer morals and less responsibility, because they too will emulate what they have experienced, just as did their parents. It is not cruel to teach children how to clean their rooms, to help with the household chores, and to share in the joys and comfort of a secure family that lives together and works together and plays together.

Punishment and reward are facts of life, and children need to learn these throughout their developmental years. All throughout life, there will be rewards and punishments in some form or another for everything you do. A child who grows up with only the rewards is as unbalanced and unfit to be a part of society as is the child who receives only punishment. THE PARENTAL ROLE IS THE HARDEST JOB YOU WILL EVER HAVE TO UNDERTAKE, IF YOU DO IT CORRECTLY—BUT IT WILL PROVIDE THE GREATEST REWARD YOU WILL EVER KNOW.

Left to their own, children will be like an untended garden, and the weeds will choke out the most beautiful flowers. You can hire nannies, turn them over to grandparents, to the state, or to your schools, and you will get exactly what you have paid for.

Many grandparents today are reaping their karma by having to raise their children's children, because they neglected to responsibly raise their children, so they are getting another opportunity. Mostly, these grandparents are spending much of their time complaining about their children, but should, instead, go look into the mirror. It is time that these grandparents had a facts-of-life discussion with their adult children, and told them all about the good and the not-so-good facts of responsible living.

Have I made my point quite clear enough? I am not tippy-toeing around this issue, because it is a much too important subject. You shall reap your just rewards—either in this world, or the next. The choice is totally your own.

* * *

Let us depart from the previous subject and take up another, though all is linked together, and one thing cannot truly be separated from another.

Well, let's see: You have been experiencing more and stronger earthquakes, tsunamis, hurricanes, solar flares, bombings, you have collapsing economies around the globe, you have starvation in many parts of the world and over-indulgence in others. You believe that the U.S. economy is so strong that nothing can hurt you.

Let's see, have I missed anything? Oh, yes, you have a soap-opera in Washington, and the devil behind the scenes.

Those who think that your United States economy is so great that you have everything invested in the stock market, mutual funds, certificates of deposit, money markets, 401k plans, etc., are about to be rudely awakened. You who are indebted up to your ears, and upside-down in mortgages you really can't afford, and/or have over-extended credit cards, etc., are about to come up short, and it's not going to be a very pretty picture.

This is a subject we have been preaching on for what, eleven or more years? But, it appears that very few of you have been listening.

You have fallen for the tricks of the adversary, and because the stock market WAS booming, you went out and invested, invested, invested. Now the markets are falling, falling, falling—and then what? Do I need to tell you that your markets are really already broke, and have been propped up artificially?

But that time is fast ending, and one of these mornings you will awaken to the same thing as just occurred in Soviet Russia today, where banks closed their doors to keep the run on banks down. There is no money! Soviet Russia is broke, and so is the United States—it just hasn't been made public knowledge. The wise ones have gotten themselves into a state of financial solvency and are not mortgaged to the hilt and not over-extended on their credit.

Yet, I know that the majority of the population is not going to believe it until it happens. And then, you will see, overnight, converts! Nothing makes a believer out of a person like personal experience.

Well, I have gone on quite enough for this time. Thank you for listening and acting upon the nudges. Thank you for your recent resolve. We shall never push you, but as always, the call compels the answer, and we shall always be there when the call is truly from the heart.

You are living in very interesting times, and the world shall continue to grow more interesting as you approach the turn of the millennium. Those who would accuse you of suffering from millennial madness are simply too afraid to hear The Truth.

However, as I said before, many converts will soon come calling upon you who have been the harbingers of TRUTH. In a very short time, you will no longer be called mad, but shall be called wise.

In Peace and Light and Love, I leave you. I am Germain.

Salu.

CHAPTER FIFTY-FIVE

Thought-ful Tools For Meeting The Challenges Ahead

Ceres Anthonious Soltec
August 30, 1998

Good afternoon, my friend, and thank you for sitting to write when there is so much else to attend! It is I, Toniose Soltec, come in the Radiant One Light of Creator Source. Be at peace.

Allow for the changes in "life" to evolve and come forth. You shall see the rewards for your efforts come back to you many times over. All will come full circle in proper sequence. There is no need to concern self with all of the INFINITE possible variables that could impact or influence these changes. Allow for your intent and inner desire to carry you forever forward and you will see that all will work out in perfection.

These are indeed magnificent times in which to experience. The opportunities available to you ones are most unique and perfect for providing you with the challenges that will enable you to stretch beyond who you are or have been.

There will always be choices to be made and each choice

will determine the subsequent experience that you will have. This will NEVER change and you will find that, with experience and growth, the choosing will become easier and easier. There will always be those choices which are difficult to make, for as you grow, you will inevitably seek a greater challenge.

If you were to reach a point of zero potential for growth in your present life, you would simply leave that experience (transition out) and move on to a more productive situation. There will always be newness to experience, for the variables of "life" are truly infinite and evolving. You can neither grow too much, nor too fast. The greater the rate of growth, the greater the rate of change, and thus the subsequent awareness of new variables or possibilities.

There will always come the next challenge. It is by design and universal desire that this fact can be stated as a "universal law". One cannot escape it, for it is the fundamental awareness of The Creation that infuses all life with the Life-Force energy that brings forth consciousness. This is to say that it is a desire that spans all dimensional "realities" and permeates all aspects of all possible electromagnetic frequency spectra.

Learn to embrace the changes that you will inevitably experience, for change is the excitement and newness; it is the Inner Desire that you ones seek. You are all explorers on a journey that is without end. Death (transition) of the physical body is perhaps a resting point for some of you, and yet all the while you are quite busy planning your next great adventure.

Allow for the element of time. It is a buffer for those of you who are experiencing in the physical. You need it so that ones can slow down the creative process enough to truly examine it in great detail, so as to have a unique opportunity to study the energy flows of the creative process itself.

Focus carefully your thoughts, for you create that which you dwell upon. If you wallow in your fears, you will surely find yourself closing off from one another and withdrawing from "life". If you lack excitement, then it is surely because you have disconnected yourself from the inner security of knowing that you are infinite and immortal. This is to say that, out of fearful (or doubtful) thinking is born a desire to be overly cautious. This out-of-balance desire for security is always based upon fear of losing that which you have, or never having that which you think you want.

These are subtle but powerful emotional emanations that will always be a part of your experience. Part of your challenge is to amplify and recognize the subtle habitual thoughts that play in your mind like a "skipping" record, forever repeating the same track on an album. Every now and then some one or some thing will come into your experience and "jar" (or jolt) the record player so that you can move on. This "jarring" will almost always be uncomfortable at first, but the aftermath will always prove to be quite valuable.

The key here is to learn to first recognize for yourself these "stuck" recordings that play continuously within your mind, and then get the "needle" (energy translational device) moving again!

In doing so, you will always find that, after the "chaos" settles, you will have accepted change and moved forward in a new direction, with new experiential knowledge (tools), and new and evolving challenges. THIS WILL ALMOST ALWAYS CURE ANY BOREDOM IN WHICH YOU MAY BE WALLOWING!

You are part of a larger Whole which spans many dimensional "realities" and connects you to one another in a most direct manner. This connection draws you ones, there in the physical at this time, together for common types of experiences and challenges unique to your current environment. This bond also draws many of us, who have agreed to be your Guides, into your experiences as well.

We, in turn, call upon counsel from yet Higher Source

still, as we too are faced with challenging decisions and choices. **The net result is a massive collective experience that causes all beings, everywhere, to expand their awareness.**

Among many ones from many different levels and realms of experience and awareness, this common desire to experience the opportunities that you now have available also can be looked upon as a "planetary karmic-type of connection". This is to say that there will be challenges on all levels of societal structure. You will be faced with personal growth, growth in a family setting, growth in community or group settings, and growth as a planetary species as a whole. There are many aspects to each of these general groupings, and each of them overlap in many ways.

This overlap would be as follows: Let's say that you take the time and effort to go through extensive training to become a skilled healer. You may have to put family concerns aside temporarily while you focus on a "narrow" part of your life experience. As you are going through your training, you will be interacting with others on the same or a similar course, in group types of settings, and in individual settings. Let's say that, when you finish your training, you treat someone who then goes on to discover and share a new method of producing energy that subsequently feeds your starving world.

Do you see the interconnectedness in this example? And how YOU (just one person) could assist in "feeding" the world!

You are ALL part of the planetary condition that has evolved at this time. You both contribute to this condition, and modify it on a DAILY basis.

Most of you will not accept the personal responsibility for your planetary condition, and thus do everything you can to avoid taking an active, CONSCIOUS role in changing it. HOWEVER, on another plane of awareness, you are crying out for balance!

Those of you who are more "in touch" with these other levels and dimensions of awareness will feel a strong desire for balance. This desire, swelling up within much of mankind, is what is summoning forth great global changes (challenges) so that there WILL BE the return to balance. Count on it!

This restlessness is the same reason your dark "elite" controllers do NOT wish to place too many, too fast into a state of feeling desperate and trapped. People feeling desperate and trapped, if they do not become overwhelmed with fear, will most often become VERY focused upon the desire to survive, and will thus create the conditions that will ensure their survival.

This sort of strong emotional desire, coupled with extreme focus, will wreck the suppressive plans of these dark "elite" controllers EVERY TIME! Though they can observe the phenomena, they are powerless to do anything about it, for the energy summoned forth and focused in this manner MUST manifest the desire.

As the people of your world head closer and closer to the point of mass awareness of their "desperate" situation, you ones will find that you are coming closer and closer to great and "catastrophic" events that will cause the ones who survive to be JOLTED into a new mental and emotional attitude and focus. From this new perspective, ones will no longer tolerate the lies and deceit. The house of cards, with all of its illusionary coverings, will crumble as ones demand answers and see Truth.

YOUR WORLD IS WHAT YOU MAKE OF IT AND YOU CREATE YOUR OWN REALITY WITH THE *THOUGHTS* YOU THINK. WHETHER YOU VOICE YOUR THOUGHTS OR NOT, OR EVEN PAY ANY ATTENTION TO THEM AT ALL, THEY STILL AFFECT YOU AND MOLD YOUR EXPERIENCES. *YOUR THOUGHTS ARE PERHAPS THE MOST REAL PART OF YOUR ENTIRE PHYSICAL EXPERIENCE!*

Please give careful thought to these words, for they are in response to your petitions to have the "tools" that you need in order to face and overcome your coming challenges.

I am Ceres Anthonious Soltec. I come in the Light of Creator Source (God of Light). I am a Messenger and Guide to your planet Herself, and to many ones around your globe. Be not mistaken about the Power that lies within you each—it is limitless and infinite!

Salu.

CHAPTER FIFTY-SIX

The Time Is *NOW* For Making A Difference!

Violinio Saint Germain
September 2, 1998

Good day, and thank you for sitting to write for me. It is I, Germain, come in and with the White Light of the One God.

There is much that we could speak on today, as the pace of your world races at an ever-increasing speed. For those who are experiencing in that third-dimensional play, which is so heavily focused upon the material, many things are causing great concern. However, **it is the condition of your souls with which I am concerned at this time!**

With each passing day, you are seeing your world's condition becoming more troublesome. Some have reached the point of saying they hope they do not live through the days ahead, and many are choosing to leave through the process of physical death at this time because the "stress" in their lives completely overwhelms them. Others are numbing themselves with alcohol and drugs, and still others have chosen to bury their heads in the sand, so to speak. These are the ones whose very foundations are being shaken.

BUT, DEAR ONES, YOU HAVE SEEN *NOTHING* YET! IN THE COMING DAYS, YOU ARE GOING TO BE WITNESS TO THE MOST TROUBLESOME TIMES ANY OF YOU HAVE EVER EXPERIENCED. FEAR IS GRIPPING AT THE VERY HEARTS OF PEOPLE, AND IN THIS FEAR LIES THE DESTRUCTIVE POWER PROVIDED THROUGH (AND UTILIZED BY) THE ADVERSARIAL FORCES.

Those who succumb to the temptation to opt-out of experiencing these times will only live to repeat the lessons at another time, in another body. It is none of my business who chooses not to continue, but it IS my business to tell you why it is happening and to expose the author of the lie.

The lie is that through death you are free from that which troubled you in life. That is only true until you reincarnate into your next life, and then you will find yourself right back where you left off.

And, if you went out with fear, that fear will follow you. If you are going to choose to opt-out of the physical experience, then first get past those fears and focus on GOD. The funny thing is, once you get focused on GOD and THE TRUTH, you will see that life is a great gift, and death is not the solution that honors The One who created you.

However, the lie has worked very well, and for the weak-of-heart, the lie feels very comforting. Life may not be the easiest path to take, but you'll get a lot farther and learn a lot more than through dying and trying to escape.

Many thought Esu "Jesus" Sananda very cold when he told the young man, who wanted to follow him but first wanted to attend the burial of his father: "Let the dead bury the dead." Esu's teachings were for the living, as are these messages! There are *plenty* in your world focused on death and dying. They are the weak-of-heart, who have not purged the fear of living from their being.

Now, understand that fear is a natural part of your third-dimensional existence. Everyone is going to suffer from (and need to confront) fears from time to time.

The ones who I am addressing here are those who are so gripped by fear that they won't allow themselves to live and experience!

And that brings us to THE biggest preoccupation of you ones—MONEY. How many of you are so concerned about saving money for your old age that you don't live now? Those who are squirreling away all that financial "security" are in for one tough time when the realization of what's really important hits you!

Many of you lay awake at night worrying about your money. If you have so much that it is a worry, then get rid of it! You'd be better off giving it away to the widows and orphans. Is it not better to store-up your treasures in the kingdom of heaven? *That doesn't mean only after you die, you know!*

For those of you who fear the loss of financial "security", I am sorry to break the news, but YOU ARE IN FOR A *VERY* RUDE AWAKENING! Though your stock market has regained some of its losses the past few days of your counting, KNOW that the gain is going to be very short-lived.

There has been intervention by those who have the most to lose in the game, and that is the *only* reason all the markets world-wide have not collapsed into a heap of dust! Had the situation been left alone, you would be seeing massive sellouts and a catastrophic drop!

The artificial propping-up of the markets cannot go on forever, however, and those who are doing the propping-up are about to run out of options. YOU HAVE SEEN THE SITUATION IN RUSSIA—WELL, IT IS BUT THE PRECURSOR OF DAYS COMING WORLD-WIDE. So, if you are among the numbers of people whose "security" is based upon financial standing, you will have to change the tune to which you are dancing, for the band is about to stop playing FOR GOOD!

When all the counting is done, it won't matter one iota

whether you had a million dollars in the bank or three pennies in your pocket. *IT WILL MATTER, HOWEVER, WHAT YOU HAVE DONE WITH WHAT YOU HAVE!*

I cannot tell you how to spend your money. That is something you will have to determine for yourselves.

It will also matter *how* you went about getting what you have. How many have you hurt as you pushed your way up the ladder to financial success? How many lies have you told to get there and stay there? How many have you trampled upon?

And, above all: what was and is YOUR INTENT? How many have you encouraged, or taken under your tutelage? How have you treated those in the lower ranks, or those who have been of service to you? How have you treated the waitress when you had your business lunches? And then the biggie: how much of your life is *really* honest? These are the things you will get to review, you know.

So, rather than sit and pass judgement on one another, you will do far greater good in the long run to sit in critical analysis of yourself. If you have even one thing in your life for which you are ashamed, then you have no right and no business pointing a finger at anyone else. Very, very few of you qualify. Remember that point the next time you point a finger at another or gossip behind someone's back.

Remember you each have an awful lot of forgiveness to ask for. And, if you are holding ANY unforgiveness toward anyone, including yourself, you are but choking off your own blessings—especially your ability to allow God to work through you!

The sand in the hourglass is rapidly running out. Time to get your houses in order is running out, as well. And there is no time like the present to get your spiritual life in order, because on that day of judgement, it will be too late.

If each of you spent half as much time judging your own lives as you have spent judging President Clinton's life, you would have accomplished a VERY GREAT DEAL, indeed. Though what the man has done may be considered perverted and immoral, be careful that you do not judge. For when you judge another, you are opening up to another judging you.

I have been over this subject with you ones many times before, and I will repeat myself here, because either you did not get it, or you are ignoring it. Either way, it bears repeating: YOU MAY DISCERN THE *ACTIONS* OF ANOTHER, BUT SEE TO IT THAT YOU DO NOT JUDGE THE PERSON! JUDGEMENT IS TO BE LEFT BETWEEN THAT PERSON AND CREATOR. SINCE YOU ARE NOT CREATOR, YOU HAVE BEEN GIVEN NO RIGHTS TO SIT IN JUDGEMENT OF ANOTHER MAN OR WOMAN! ONLY THAT WHICH IS PERFECT MAY JUDGE WHAT IS IMPERFECT.

For those of you who have not gotten yourselves right with GOD, I am here today to tell you that you are out of time. Do it now, or do not do it.

Events are shaping up such that there is no more time to be sitting on the fence waiting to see what happens tomorrow. Tomorrow has arrived!

As the old saying goes, "There is no time like the present." If you do not have YOUR OWN spiritual house in order, you may not have the strength of spirit to make it through the coming days. It is going to be difficult enough for those who have been "training" for these days. The adversarial attacks have increased, and many have already lost the battle. Meanwhile, the adversary promises to make everyone's lives as miserable as possible.

These are the days of testing your resolve and testing your spiritual determination. I cannot stress enough the importance of self-examination. If there is anything within your heart that you have not come to terms with, you better be coming to terms with it NOW.

Whatever your weakness is, that's the place where the adversary will attack. Your only defense is strengthening every fiber of your being—body, mind and spirit. And, if there is a weakness found, recognize it, deal with it openly, and go on. Do not take the time for wallowing in your fears or guilts, for these are weaknesses, and a perfect target for attack.

If you have been carefully watching, you are fully aware that your world is changing very rapidly, and events are accelerating at an unprecedented rate. Many of you complain that there seems to be less time in each day, though mostly you put it off to your ever-increasingly busy lives. And, to some degree, that is what is occurring.

However, time *is* speeding up, as you and your world are making a dimensional transition. Your perception of time is changing, and though your clocks still register 24 hours in a day and the Sun still appears to come up at the proper time, you are losing several hours of that perception.

Once the planetary transition has been completed, and each one who is going to move upward with her has done so, it will all balance itself out. You are in the time of the change now, and it is a time of turmoil all about. What once was a task of thirty minutes, now may take forty-five minutes to an hour, by the clock, to complete.

Remember: time is the invention of third-dimensional man. As you are changing into higher-dimensional beings, you are still living in a third-dimensional perception. You are becoming lighter (less dense), and time does not have the same meaning to you. Your bodies are in preparation for that which is coming shortly. Unless your physical being changes (clarifies), you will not survive.

So, as you are complaining daily about not enough time to take care of things, remember it is happening for a very good reason. You still will not have any more time in a day, but you at least will know it is for a good reason. And this condition DOES cause one to better utilize (focus) what time one does have!

It is most important that you ones not become overwhelmed by daily events and news. The darkness, that seems to have your world in its grip, preys on those who become too involved in the daily concerns of the world.

Watch that which goes on about you; don't bury your head in the sand; but keep things and events in proper perspective. Remember your years of training and remember that becoming weighed down by worldly affairs and events only lowers your frequency and may prevent you from maintaining your focus on the goal, which is serving GOD.

When the attacks of the adversary come, know that you are right on course, and the attacks are attempts to take you off course. Look upon these attacks as mere pesky distractions, and keep your eyes on the goal. Because, dear friends, when all is said and done, you will be most glad you were not dissuaded.

As the Earth shakes, and wars flare up, and winds and rains blow, and governments lie and cheat, and the adversary runs to and fro throughout your world—know that these are but the signals that the clock is running down. As the very elements themselves, of which your body and all physical matter is composed, seem to be heaving, understand that there *IS* a Grand Master Plan.

Hold this knowledge within your very beings, as your Source of Strength in these times of trial and tribulation. There is a great change coming rapidly upon you all, and all will experience it in one form or another.

How you fare through these times, however, is of your own making. Whether you persist and hold-on to the TRUTH and LIGHT, or whether you opt-out of the physical existence because of FEAR and DARKNESS, is totally up to each and every one of you, individually.

No one can make your decisions for you, but each of you who are going to experience that which is upon you will need to lean upon one another. Those who give unselfishly of yourselves are the ones who will make the greatest strides and the greatest difference.

The world *IS* going to be rebuilt—not by the bigwigs and not by the giant corporations, but by each of you "little people" out there, who are in actuality spiritual giants!

Thank you for your time this day. I am Violinio St. Germain, and I leave you with the Light of Holy God about you and yours.

Salu.

CHAPTER FIFTY-SEVEN

Ignoring The Clues Won't Lessen The Lessons

Ceres Anthonious Soltec
September 6, 1998

Good evening, my friend. It is I, Commander Ceres Anthonious "Toniose" Soltec, come in the Radiant One Light of Creator Source. Be at peace.

Many have taken notice of the recent tectonic plate movements around the Pacific "Ring of Fire". In the last week of your counting there have been in excess of 6 large quakes greater than 6.5 in magnitude around the boundaries of that Pacific Plate. (I say "in excess of" because of how your reporting philosophy devalues the actual earthquake intensities.) This last Wednesday there were three such quakes of a greater than 6.5M in one day along the Pacific Rim. The one in the Philippine Islands was reported to you there in the United States as a 6.9M event, while it was locally reported in the Philippines as a 7.4M shaker—this is about 5 times greater in intensity.

There are very good reasons why these numbers are so obscure to you who have ability to reason: You would be in full alert and, for some—IN FULL PANIC! There are but threads holding the fault lines at this time. You will soon see terra firma turning into "terror fury" as your geological stability becomes more and more compromised with each passing day.

These earthquakes should be viewed as signals to you ones, especially those of you who are experiencing them first hand. These areas are the ones which will indeed be the most impacted in the coming days, weeks, and months.

For many this message will simply be discarded as another "fear mongering" attempt to frighten you ones. However, if one can see "around the corner" because of the advantage of their current viewpoint, and that one is able to "radio" down to those who are driving along and cannot see that the "bridge" is out up ahead, is that one doing so in order to frighten and harass those who are on a collision course with pending disaster? Or, is that one merely attempting to assist ones who are asking for assistance?

You see, from my vantage point, I can see that the "bridge" is crumbling beneath your very feet and that what is about to happen is a natural interaction between material physics, thermodynamics, and fluid mechanics. This is not to even complicate the picture by mentioning all of the "etheric" precursors and indicators which have a very real and solid scientific grounding in fact—whether your current science acknowledges same or not.

I can do no more than respond to your inquiries in a manner that is of a logical and caring nature. If that brings discomfort to your weary heart, then you would do well to look within and look at what about this sort of message truly bothers you.

Is the discomfort, perhaps, the fact that you do not want to be reminded that you have continually ignored the clues and indicators all about you? Or maybe your uneasiness swells from procrastination about making the changes you already know you should have made?

Allow me to assure you that there *WILL* be a remnant, and those who are left *WILL* have their hands full with the necessities of survival.

There will be little time to worry about those who chose not to participate in the rebuilding of your world. This is to say that only YOU who do not intend to survive will "suffer" your reluctance to prepare. Your actions indicate your true intent. You can scream from mountain tops that you want to survive, but if you do little more than excessively vibrate your vocal cords, you will surely not be prepared for that which is coming.

It is God's promise to you ones that there would be those sent to assist you in your times of need. THESE ARE THOSE TIMES, and I, Ceres Anthonious Soltec, come with the many Hosts of God as a Messenger, Teacher, and Guide. We of the Hosts are entrusted with the task of giving forth the necessary guidance so that those of you who "have eyes to see" will see and those of you who "have ears to hear" will hear.

It is NOT our job to MAKE you see or MAKE you hear. We have offered—and will continue to offer—our assistance to any and all who wish to have it. We will always provide you with a unique and broader perspective from which to view any given situation. We will also always effort toward that which will enhance YOUR overall growth experience as an Infinite Creative Being.

You are each there in the physical because you have a strong desire to expand your awareness and knowledge about self and Creator Source. The physical experience is "nothing" more than a holographic type of role-playing game. There is nothing about this game to fear! If a building crumbles and falls upon your physical head, then your body may cease to function, but YOU will go on.

I know that, for the majority of you, you wish to keep the body functioning as long as possible so that you can better optimize your growth potential! It is easy to see the "right" answers from a non-physical perspective, looking back. It is not so easy to perceive the "right" answers from where you ones are experiencing at this time, looking forward. This is the wondrous challenge that you ones desire greatly to master.

Many of my fellow Teachers have, in recent weeks in these pages, expanded upon the following point, which I likewise emphasize: **It *IS* possible to connect to Higher Source in a deliberate and continuous manner WHILE REMAINING IN THE PHYSICAL.** However, the desire and self discipline must be strong if you are to achieve such awareness. With desire and persistence on YOUR part, then WE will assist you with this connection—a most worthy goal or skill to develop at this time.

YOU DO NOT NEED WEATHER REPORTS, EARTHQUAKE REPORTS, OR ANY SUCH REPORTS IF YOU BUT LEARN TO LISTEN *WITHIN!* Many of you who are reading this continue to deny that YOU are CREATOR. Regardless, you each have within you a Divine Connection—a "Spark of Light" that *IS* CREATOR within you! You are all efforting continually to actualize this perceptual realization for self.

I tell you now that you need not struggle towards this realization; you only need to *allow* for it to BE! Most often, when you ones struggle over something, you are in actuality pushing it away.

Do NOT dwell upon that which you do not have, but rather be thankful for all that you do have. In the appreciation of that which you do have, you will find that you will have more and more for which to be thankful, and that your life is continually becoming fuller and fuller.

If you continue to dwell upon that which you don't have, you will become more and more miserable, and you will become more and more disconnected from the Inner Infinitely Abundant Energy that IS your God-given "Spark of Life".

When you feel "alive" and "on top of the world", you can *KNOW* that you are allowing this Creative Energy to flow. If you are feeling anything less, then you can know, with equal certainty, that YOU are disallowing this same flow.

I will always strive toward that which will assist you ones the most in your overall experience of growth, for as you each respond to these messages in your own way, we monitor the effectiveness and impact of the energy (the messages) that we send forth. This return flow helps us to see what is then the next best step to take to help you ones.

Many of you have agreed to participate in very daring and elaborate experiments along these lines. This is to say that some of the approaches that we will use to guide you toward your goals of growth would be considered a "long shot". But, as with any "long shot", what comes in the "pay-off" (reward) is usually quite large in terms of movement and growth.

You will see the physical world turned upside-down and inside-out, and you will have reactionary responses to many situations that are coming. You only need to remember that all is part of the "game" of life and living, and that there are perfectly good reasons for all that happens, and that none whose bodies perish are truly "gone", and that the result of these experiences will be a clarifying of the thoughts, priorities, and subsequent "realities" of many ones.

The net result will be for the betterment of all beings, everywhere, for all will grow either directly or indirectly from the experiences of any one. You in the physical are on the leading edge of creative thought, and contrasting experiences offer the greatest potential for new understanding and growth.

Out of pure chaos will be borne a pure desire for balance. As a pure balance is achieved, ones begin to develop a sense of mediocrity and boredom, and thus look for a "problem" to solve, a "challenge" to face, or a new "game" to play. Adventure is often a more desirable experience than is a tranquil and lazy afternoon. This is to say that the cycles of life are infinite and ever changing.

Just as an electromagnetic pulse-wave of energy cycles from a positive potential through a zero point of pure balance, and continues on into a negative potential, only to repeat the cycle again and again, so too are the infinite experiences of life.

So, for those of you who wish to remain stagnated where you are, you don't have to worry, for your next experience will surely pick-up right where you are at right now. For those of you who truly desire a new and evolving experience toward greater understanding of your true creative potential, you will heed these guiding messages and take full advantage of the insights offered herein. Yours will be "the adventure of a lifetime".

I am Ceres Anthonious Soltec; I come with the Hosts of God so that His Will be done.

It is from within this Light that we originate, and it is this same Light that we continue to seek out and understand. Know thyself and you will come to know your Creator. May your journey always be one of excitement and growth, and never be without a good challenge!

Salu.

CHAPTER FIFTY-EIGHT

Creating Your Part In The "Great Awakening"

Esu "Jesus" Sananda
September 13, 1998

Good evening, little one. It is I, Esu "Jesus" Sananda. I come as the golden-white Light of Creator's Divine Will. I am come to you this day that there may be clarification of focus at this time.

Your world is on the brink of very grand events which will become the catalyst for greatness and renewed focus upon the greater importance of the spiritual aspects of your current growth experience. These are TRULY grand times! We of the Hosts have come to assist the few, who are open to our energy, in preparing for this magnificent transformation.

Be not fearful of that which is coming, for there is NOTHING to be frightened of—EVER! If only you would truly understand this one last sentence with HEART KNOWING, then you would indeed rise up out of your lackful beliefs, and the lies and the perception of all pain would leave your aching hearts.

ALL IS TRULY UNFOLDING IN PERFECTION! The

opportunity for creative growth is quite unique at this time, and all you need to do is accept your place and part in this most wondrous "drama" of creation.

Learn to accept those who oppose you in your beliefs and perceptions of the world, for there cannot be a challenge without the presence of opposing thoughts, ideas, and beliefs. You are all struggling to be "right". You may very well be playing the right part and to the best of your perceived ability, but until you are challenged by those of comparable (or even greater) ability, how will you ever know what is truly the "limit" of your ability.

This is to say that one should be thankful that there are those who are willing to play the role of the "oppressor". There are cases, usually on a personal level, where the one who brings you the most "grief" in your experience is one who is your closest friend when you are not playing the physical game. Who better to draw forth the BEST out of you than someone who knows you quite well?

The key is to not allow these ones to cause you to disconnect from Source! This is perhaps the most tricky challenge to work through, and as one should quickly realize, the most valuable challenge to overcome and master. Learn to truly appreciate your "oppressors", for they are providing you with valuable lessons and unique opportunities.

We monitor closely everything, from the general emotional frequency of your planet, to the individual emotional frequency of you each. We monitor the effectiveness of these words as they are uniquely translated by you each. Each of you will perceive the meaning and significance of these words in your own unique way, and often the Greater Message within the message is overlooked.

Let me offer to you an example: Take the word "desire". What does it mean to YOU? What are all of the possible interpretations of this word that you can find? Perhaps you should look it up in the dictionary and see if there are other definitions about which you are not yet aware. If I ask you to go within and monitor how the word makes you feel—good, bad, or indifferent—I would, indeed, get varying responses. If I were to go one step further and say to you that a desire is anything upon which you focus your attention or anything you "think about", then how would you feel?

You are Creator! *YOU ARE CREATOR!* Your thoughts are what summon forth the Creative Energy which then begins to manifest that upon which you hold your attention. Most simply look around and continue to create more of what they already have—and thus the rich get richer, the poor get poorer, the happy get happier, the stuck get more stuck, and those who understand this have an extremely good time.

Your desires, as I here refer to them, are the thoughts you focus upon from moment to moment, day to day. You each are creating (manifesting) in your daily lives the sum total of these desires. If you perceive that you are somehow not getting your fair share of attention or money or love or (you fill in the blank), then let me assure you that you are fixating upon the LACK of same, rather than the having.

Know thyself and you will know your GREATEST enemy! YOU are the only limitation who stands in the pathway between excitement and mediocrity. It is as simple as monitoring, in a deliberate and conscious manner, the thoughts you think.

If someone near you is antagonistic toward you, and you find yourself getting angry or frustrated, then simply stop arguing with that one and say, for instance, "You're probably right, but I derive great satisfaction from considering alternative viewpoints other than the *Associated Press* version of a given story." Or more generally: "Isn't it nice that we are not all the same?"

You see, you need not allow yourself to get angry, and when you quit pushing back against those who try to push on you, then there is quickly a change in focus, for the challenge to determine who is right or who is smarter or stronger is then gone.

When you quit resisting the other, then it is like playing a game without an opponent: You leave them rolling their dice and moving their pieces without any challenge or satisfaction to be gained. They will quickly get bored with the game and simply shift their focus in another direction.

When you stop playing the distracting games that cause you to become upset, then you will find that there are truly better subjects upon which to focus. Effort always to approach a discussion from a point of agreement, rather than from one of who is right and who is wrong.

Productivity in a forward direction is seldom accomplished by winning debates about obscure subjects. Be an example to the ones you feel inclined to help—by such as preparing your emergency food supplies and getting any alternative energy devices you may have installed and operating. Show them with actions taken that you truly believe the ideas and concepts behind your energetic mouthings. Let them each to their own choosing, and honor their choices.

There is nothing that YOU cannot create! You *can* have your cake and eat it too. Will you see, and accept, that you ARE a creator? Will you deny, blame, and make excuses for all of the "hardships" you have endured? What will be is what YOU DECIDE will be.

I showed your world, over two thousand years ago, the potential of your abilities as an extension of The One Source. I also said that, what I put forth as an example, YOU too would do—AND MORE!

Ones are awakening to this realization all around your world. Quit denying who you are and accept the reality, and step forth out of the mind-numbing world of fear and denial.

I am your brother, NOT your God! I am merely more advanced in my understanding of the nature of my being. I have accepted my place as a co-creator, and I have mastered the physical arena. I am merely an example for you ones to focus upon so as to know that there are no limitations that you must accept. Let go of the idea that you "can't" for this is a LIE!

You CAN do anything you can imagine! When the belief is pure enough, all is possible. When you doubt, even for a moment, so too will the manifestation of your desire be diminished or negated by the countering energy set forth by your doubt.

Letting go of past limiting beliefs is the only way to progress forward in understanding and growth. This need not be difficult, and in the mere twinkling of an eye ones can step forth, out of self-imposed limitations, and begin to exercise and utilize their God-empowered right to manifest anything that may be desired.

You have chosen to accept the challenge (game) of coming into a *VERY* manipulated world, wherein you are constantly being swayed through not only direct (mostly electronic) mind-control methods, but through the subtle techniques of advertisers who find it very profitable to sell you fear.

The rules of the game are simple: You create that which you focus your attention upon, regardless of your perception of what is "right" and what is "wrong". This basic and fundamental rule works for everyone, regardless of race, religion, political or sexual orientation, or age. There are no victims or "unfortunate" players in the game. Most importantly there are NO LOSERS, for all grow through experience by just entering the physical arena to "play a part" in the game of "physical life".

Enjoy the unique opportunity for growth that is before you. Know that your life is a reflection of the sum total of your thoughts, beliefs, and ideas. The Great Awakening experience that is now unfolding is part of your desire to experience; it can be one of wondrous achievement or one of horror and disbelief. The only

difference will be in how YOU choose to perceive its unfolding events.

I am Esu "Jesus" Immanuel Sananda. I come to participate in the capacity of the golden-white Light of OUR Father's Creative Energy. I am that which you are: a co-creator on an infinite journey of growth and expansion. I too am exploring the infinite newness, as are ALL.

Be at peace in knowing that you are without end and that all will unfold in PERFECTION according to the One Divine Will.

In Light, BLESSINGS TO YOU ALL!

CHAPTER FIFTY-NINE

What Shall *You* Paint On *Your* Life Canvas?

Sanat Kumara
September 20, 1998

Good morning, little one. It is I, Grandfather. Be at peace, for there is no need for concern. All is well and all will always be well. The physical structure of your entire universe could disintegrate from all around you, and still all would be well!

Yes, indeed I do come in and of The One Light! Thank you for seeking clarification. I go by many names: I am known as Sanat Kumara by some, and as Tonkashila (or Grandfather) by many, especially among your Native American peoples. I am the voice in the wind and I often sing with the wolf and soar with the eagle. I am the representative of Creator's Silver Ray. You know me well, my friend!

I have come at this time so that there will indeed be closure to the current work that you ones are putting forth. I come now in blended form with MANY who have been a part of the ongoing outlay of information which you have been bringing forth at this time. We are of one general purpose and that is to teach those who desire same.

[*Editor's note: Here Grandfather is referring to the current challenge in progress among those of us involved with putting together the second volume of the* WISDOM OF THE RAYS: The Masters Teach *series of collected spiritual writings from the* CONTACT *newspaper. It is always difficult to "draw the line" on what to include and exclude, and when to stop adding more writings, so that the labor of book production can move forward in a timely manner. Naturally the human tendency is to want to defer such "yea or nay" decisions to Higher input. And, thankfully, it was Aton who helped with that decision for volume I, and Grandfather here with volume II.*]

Though we all have our own unique perspectives, talents, and specialties of interest, be assured that there is a strong Common Bond which allows us to focus the collective consciousness of many, largely unnamed beings, so as to provide you ones with a very well orchestrated outlay of information at this time. Never underestimate the role played by EACH participant in this current Great Cycle of experience, for it is often you readers of this information who dictate to us, by your inner desires to KNOW, what the next subject will be and how exactly it will be presented.

The sum total of ALL who partake in this interaction brings forth a constant, forever evolving growth interchange wherein ALL grow in some way. We are as much thankful for those of you who elect to play the physical game of "life" as you are who frequently express your gratitude for our Higher assistance.

This circle of interaction is infinite in its possibilities and without end in its extension, and often, as ones leave behind the physical and re-emerge into the nonphysical, YOU become the Guides for those who are entering into the physical arena. WE ARE ALL BOTH TEACHER AND STUDENT!

The "game of life" can be as big as you like, or as small and simple as you like. The more one grows in understanding, the more one will seek a greater challenge.

This often is reflected in the physical as a "hard" or "harsh" life.

Be assured that, prior to coming into the physical experience, you had a very strong desire to participate in the physical and, as soon as the experience is over, you will most likely have a very strong urge to return again so that you can further experience the wide array of magnified (focused) emotional intensities that the physical experience provides to you.

Many of you are "longing to go home". Your experience is but a brief twinkling of an eye, yet you have already "thrown in the towel".

Quit feeling as though the pressure is somehow too great or that all of the tiny little things somehow actually matter. Let go of the perception that anything really matters beyond the newness (opportunity) which each day brings. Yesterday is gone. ***Today and tomorrow are empty canvases upon which you can paint any picture you desire.*** **Perhaps you should experiment with a different, more vibrant color (tone, emotion, frequency) instead of reliving constantly the same old one you generated yesterday.**

If you are tired of feeling bad or bored or old or tired or..., then simply change the way you are feeling! Learn to see the glass not as half empty, or even as half full, but rather, as a marvel of creative energies coalesced in a very unique manner so as to provide you with a very unique tool to use. How many ways can the same materials of the glass be shaped so as to provide you with infinite variations of form and potential uses?

Learn to see beyond that which you take for granted. The secrets of the universe are locked within the most simple of objects. The tiniest little wildflower you may come across when walking along a country road is bursting with the same intricacies of creative detail as are the galaxies your astronomers strain so hard to observe and understand.

There are infinite paths which lead toward this Greater Understanding. You each are efforting toward allowing more and more of the Infinite Energy of Creation to flow through you in a deliberately focused attempt to combine the sum total of all of the elements of the universe together in a completely new and unique manner that has not ever existed prior.

Quit trying to run away from your perceptions of pain or grief because you will carry them with you until you let them go. There is NOTHING you ones can do that you cannot let go of and "chalk up to experience".

Guilt does not have to be a part of your experience. You cannot hurt someone unless they first accepted you into their experience, and therefore they too must accept that they (or you) are no more a "victim" than is the one who wins the multi-million-dollar lottery.

All is of an experiential nature. There must be opposition for a game condition to exist in the first place; therefore you must have ones willing to play EITHER side of "right" versus "wrong".

There is, in actuality, neither "right" nor "wrong". The closest thing that you ones have to being "wrong" is when you cower and hide and proclaim: "I give up; I want to go 'home' now; just whisk me away or let me die."

This sort of "woe is me" attitude usually comes about after ones get themselves completely "stuck" in a condition of defeat and they have decided (in error) that a situation is somehow hopeless. When this point of view is assumed, the one who holds this belief as true has chosen to disconnect to a very great extent from Creator Source—and thus not allow for the creative, inspirational, and revitalizing energies to come forth and show the way out of the challenge.

The result of the disconnect is a condition of stagnation. Ones are left holding a very dark gray paintbrush, painting the same exact picture for themselves, day after day, year after year.

Only YOU can decide that nothing in the physical experience is "*that* bad". When you finally do come to understand this, you will see that, NO MATTER WHAT, all is still VERY MUCH WELL!!

A loved one died. SO WHAT?! Now they're over here—where most of you are wanting to be anyway. And you're feeling "sorry" for them?

NO! You are feeling sorry, alright, and that is fine—but just remember WHO you're *really* feeling sorry for! Then you'll quickly be able to pull yourself out of your "woe is me" dark hole and begin planning the next day's picture you want to paint.

If you find yourself in a situation that is undesirable to you in any way, then plan a change of routine. Perhaps you could do something that you have not done in awhile, like going down to the library and exploring some of the many books you never knew existed. Many a creative being has poured out their heart and soul into these countless volumes so that others may find value in their experiences.

Or, perhaps you could make a game out of the day and decide that you are going to meet 3 new people today—even if you have to go and introduce yourself to the neighbor two doors down who has lived there for the last ten years, yet you don't even know their name.

Do you see that there are infinite possibilities before you this very moment? You can go about your daily "routine" of something like: up at six a.m., out the door by seven, off work at five p.m., turn the news on at six, watch your favorite TV show at eight, in bed by ten.

Or NOT. Instead of turning on the television, you could choose to go to the park and enjoy Nature, or take a walk around your neighborhood and maybe even meet some of your neighbors, or visit the elderly friend who may need some assistance.

Identify those things which you routinely do on a daily and weekly basis. Do you have to do all of your grocery shopping in the exact same store EVERY week? Do you have to have your coffee in the morning while reading the same newspaper every morning? Do you have to drive the exact same route to work EVERY day?

Learn to allow yourself to be spontaneous. Allow for these subtle differences to be a part of your experience. When you realize that YOU decide whether or not (and how much) to allow the flow of Creative Energy into your experience, you will realize also that you are responsible for all things that "happen" to you.

If you choose to simply let your life canvas sit, and let others splash their paint all over yours, as they wish, and you just "take it as it comes", then recognize that you do so BY CHOICE, and you get what you are "secretly" (subconsciously) desiring.

If you insist that you are a "victim of circumstances" and you always come out on the "short end", then you will most likely ALWAYS come out on the short end. Likewise, the ones who *know* they are a winner will most always come out on top. The "winning" attitude is one of adventure and thankfulness, wherein just being given the opportunity to "play the game" inspires these ones to have a good time and insures they will be better off for just having showed up and played.

You have all heard the infinite variations of the old saying that goes something like this: "Old Jake could have a truckload of manure dumped on him and he still comes out smelling like roses!" What is it about these people which allows them to make the best out of any situation?

First of all, they do not believe that anything truly bad can happen to them. And then, deep down inside, they also know (or simply sense) that they need the "negative" experience in order to see something they are overlooking, or to facilitate a chain of events that will eventually help them to fulfill their desires.

Maybe the person who stops to help you with your flat tire turns out to be just the right business associate you hoped to find from your not-yet-placed newspaper advertisement (because of the flat). Be honest: how many of you view something "negative" like a flat tire as an exciting opportunity to meet new people who may be crossing your path for a good reason?

Let's say that you are desiring a new vehicle. You go down to the new car dealership and spot the vehicle you want. You drive it and really fall in love with the car; you just *have* to have it.

Now you sit down to make the deal. But you realize the automobile salesman is not giving you a fair value for your trade-in, so you decide to go home and think the whole thing over.

Meanwhile, three days later, your car (the one you were going to trade-in) gets stolen. Several weeks go by, yet it is not recovered. Is this a "negative" experience? Maybe it seems so for awhile, but:

Then your insurance company pays the claim for the full (actual) value of the car, and then some. Now you go back to the dealership and purchase the car you wanted. This time there is no "problem" haggling over the price of a trade-in and you are happy with the outcome.

Do you see how the "misfortune" of the stolen car is in DIRECT response to wanting to have your new car, and have it under conditions of fairness to all? It is even fair to the insurance company, whom you pay for their services. It is a risk they have chosen to take. The larger "play" even includes the one who chose YOUR particular automobile to steal at that particular time.

You can choose to smell like roses all the time, or whatever you like—even manure, if that be your choice! We are letting you know that ALL situations you experience are for reason. You can play the one who bobs up and down upon the currents of life, going any old way, or you can take note of what you would like to experience in life and start focusing (flowing) your energy toward it.

This is a very important realization to make, for many

wish to get you to focus your energy upon their "cause"—knowing that if they can get enough people focusing, then eventually their goal will be reached. This is fine when goals are wisely chosen, perhaps by group consensus, for after all, it is the combined goal of we of the Higher Realms to help you in the physical with your next steps forward in the development of your potential.

Problems arise when the goals of another are not very well in alignment with YOUR goals (especially Higher goals), but are motivated by petty matters. This is to say that often ones will, for example, take on a campaign to "save the trees"—as soon as they find out that their biggest competitor wants to build their store across the street where there happens to be a lot of trees and woodlands!

Often ones are motivated more from a fear of losing than from a point of knowing that all is well and there is only prosperity and the excitement of living to be gained each and every day. Discerning which of these motivates YOUR goals is a most important step in understanding how to make your life experience productive and fulfilling.

There is no beginning or end to life. It is a continual journey of exploration. There are no destinies which are absolute. Even the attaining of a goal brings forth a greater awareness that there is always more to look forward to in coming experiences. And always, the "game" gets a little bit bigger from the growth gained from each small step toward any one goal.

As you progress forward, you will begin to see these larger challenges. Someday you may choose to play the role of one who embraces an opportunity to go forth, somewhere in the physical realms, with a blinding desire to infuse into everyone you meet a pure love and acknowledgment of their being. In doing so you become the next great spiritual teacher who is remembered throughout centuries and time as one of the "Great Ones".

You are ALL great and perfect creations, borne of a Perfect Desire and a Perfect Will. Creator God does not

make mistakes! To view yourselves as anything less than a perfect being, with a perfect desire to grow through diversity, is to say that God does not know what He is doing.

LET ME ASSURE YOU THAT *ALL IS WELL* AND GOD *DOES* KNOW WHAT HE IS DOING! He does NOT make mistakes.

Do you not see that there is, in the Larger Picture, a perfect balance maintained on your world? When it begins to get overpopulated and the species has not yet advanced far enough in balanced technological ability to be allowed to spread to neighboring planetary bodies, then there will always manifest the floods, famines, plagues, and related (educational) experiences so as to cause a shift toward a more balanced equilibrium for all involved.

There is no real death of the experiencing beings, and so there is, in the Larger Picture, really no big deal if a planet goes through one of these rebalancing cycles. After all, is it not the collective choices of the experiencing beings which bring about the corrective (rebalancing) events to be experienced as part of the cause-and-effect schoolroom learning cycles?

Be thankful for all of those things which take place each and every day that many of you rarely take the time to even notice, much less consider, such as:

• Isn't it wonderful that you have an ever-replenishing oxygen supply in your atmosphere?

• Isn't it wonderful that the Sun is shining and you didn't have to do a single thing to insure that it continues to do so?

• Isn't it wonderful that the Earth continues to spin in a perfect orbit around the Sun, so as to provide the perfect environment to sustain the countless physical life-forms thereon?

• Isn't it wonderful that there is so much to learn and an infinite possible combination of events, so that every day holds a new mystery to explore, a new person to meet, a new fragrance to smell, or a new adventure to experience?

THERE IS *INFINITE POTENTIAL* AWAITING YOU EACH!

This Potential simply must be recognized. In the recognition comes the understanding of how to use it. You each will utilize it in your own unique way. In the expression of your uniqueness comes the joy you desire.

Joy is not something you should strive for, but rather, a state of experiential awareness that you allow along the way—every day, no matter what you are doing. Life's greatest joys come as a result of allowing the Creative Energies to flow through you in an uninhibited manner, with the least amount of resistance.

Resistance is anything that causes you ones to feel that you must force your desires or will upon another, for any reason. Resistance is that which you believe to be true, and dwell upon, which causes you to feel negative emotional reactionary responses. Resistance is, simply put, any opposition to the natural flow of Creator's Energy within and through your being.

You ALL create your own reality, despite what you may believe is the case. The sooner you come to accept this responsible awareness of self, the sooner you will take control and begin to transform a life of mediocrity into something of GREATNESS.

We are summoned forth at this time and in this manner as a result of the desires of those of you who read these words. Always look beyond the words and seek understanding for yourself, within.

You each have personal Guides who will help provide clarity of thought concerning any part of our messages about which you may have more questions. Seek always clarity of understanding upon any subject that causes you to question.

Test the accuracy of any and all information for yourself. Live the journey of "life" with vigor and zest! If another tries to splatter THEIR paint on YOUR canvas, then welcome the uniqueness of the situation and paint your own picture anyway—just as you want it to be. And IT WILL BE!

I am Grandfather, Sanat Kumara, The Silver Ray of Creation. I place my many identifications upon this writing so that ones will realize that there are as many differing perceptions about any one aspect of Creator's creations as there are differing viewpoints from which to view.

I have a profound love for (and association with) the animal friends. I often will experience briefly with and through them, so as to cause ones to see the INTERCONNECTEDNESS OF ALL THINGS, and to provide you ones, from time to time, with the confirmations that you most enjoy, especially those of you who regularly partake of Nature's many outdoor wonders.

I leave you with the knowing that ALL IS WELL, regardless of the dramas that may unfold in your lives.

Blessings and peace to you all.

Salu!

Appendices

APPENDIX A

Tutorial On Volcanos And Related Geophysics

Ceres Anthonious Soltec
&
Gyeorgos Ceres Hatonn

Editor's note: This appendix has been assembled in response to the recent dramatic increase in earthquake and volcanic activity worldwide. Moreover, Soltec refers us back to his "old" material on this subject in several of his writings in this volume, especially chapter 9.

There have been recurring news stories about the explosive activities of Mt. Popocatepetl near Mexico City, as well as about the frequent rumblings (and volcanic alerts) concerning Mammoth Mountain and Mono Lake near Yosemite National Park in California—with its attendant large skiing and hiking resort communities.

As well, Mount St. Helens and Mount Rainier in the Cascade Mountain Range in west-central Washington State have been periodically rumbling with swarms of nearby earthquakes. This is all prelude to greater activity worldwide as Mother Earth efforts to come back into balance after enduring much unhealthy tampering by man—both out of ignorance and also to advance various political agendas through technological means.

We are not used to thinking in these terms of massive rebalancing reactions to tamperings because, until relatively recently, man on Earth had not advanced enough technically to truly upset the natural planetary balance on such a large scale. However, since approximately the time of the first nuclear detonations in the 1940s, all of that has changed—and not for the better!

Whether we consider the many underground and above-ground nuclear detonations, the modern control of weather by electromagnetic means, the erasing of huge, air-cleaning rain forests almost overnight, or a sickening array of other greedy insults to Mother Earth's balance, it should be clear that she has every right to say "Enough is enough!" and do what is necessary to bring herself back into a state of health. And volcanos play an important role in that rebalancing process.

To quote from Soltec's 5/22/93 writing on this subject: "You ones in California and Nevada, especially, need to be very aware of that old volcano in the Mammoth and Mono Lakes area, because you have been experiencing a great deal of renewed activity there. Not only are there earthquakes, but you also have a lava dome that has been building for quite a few years, and this is not something to be ignored.

"As you should be aware, I have given instruction on this area several times in the recent past, and the information was given for a purpose. This sleeping giant is awakening, chelas, and you ones are most likely going to experience, in your lifetimes, an eruption of this volcano.

"This is not some little insignificant volcano, but one that, during its last eruption, made Mount St. Helens look like a little toy. The ash cloud at that time spread as far east as Nebraska and Kansas, as far south as Old Mexico, and as far north as Wyoming. The ash within a 100-mile radius of the volcano could accumulate to as much as 3 to 4 feet in depth, and there would also, most likely, be hot

pyroclastic ash flows, which could extend as far as 150 to 200 miles from the volcano itself. So, as you can see, this is not a volcano to be taken lightly, and this new flurry of seismic activity is symptomatic of magma movement below the surface.

"The Long Valley Caldera is approximately 20 miles in diameter, and the area of magma uplift within the caldera is approximately 7-1/2 miles in diameter. The magma chamber lies at a depth of approximately 5 miles, but it is rising continually. The new round of earthquakes recently is cause for concern in this place, as the area is riddled with many faults as well. As your part of the world moves into its 'vacation' time of year, the concern for this area should be ringing loudly, as this is a very popular vacation site, and many could be caught there unaware of the potential hazard that exists."

We are in serious times these days, as the signs of building pressures within Mother Earth continue to announce what lies ahead. Thus it is most appropriate to share this very readable tutorial on the subject of volcanos and related volcanic activities.

Perceptive readers will note that the writings which make up this appendix exhibit a much more scientific tone (as we presently understand science) than many of Soltec's writings elsewhere in this volume, wherein he efforts to help us understand the spiritual "physics" at work in our lives. Thus, while this appendix is Soltec, the geophysicist, at his finest for a general audience, even in this context there still flows, as an undercurrent, his perennial theme of our intimate connection with Mother Earth—a theme our Native American brothers and sisters have long attempted to teach.

The first writing below originally appeared in the older Phoenix Journal #21, called Creation, The Sacred Universe, *as there had been, according to the usual media understatement, an "insignificant" rash of small earthquakes in this same Long Valley Caldera area at that late-October 1990 time frame. Soltec obviously decided this was a good opportunity to provide a major geophysics lesson, which then was expanded in a writing of a few years later. The seriousness of this discussion is related to the fact that the "stuff" (magma and gases) released from some volcanic locations is going to be not just hot and widespread, but "hot" due to the mixing-in of nearby man-generated underground radioactivity. No matter how you look at it, THAT kind of "stuff" raining down upon us does not lend to the painting of a very pretty picture!*

October 24, 1990

Hatonn present in service unto God and Man—within the Light of Truth. So be it. I ask, Dharma, that you avail yourself and service, briefly, to Commander Ceres Anthonious Soltec for, before we write this day, I must call urgent attention to you ones. There has been a rather small earthquake within the past 12 hours in Northern California which bears great importance. It is a sign to you ones who will "see" and "hear". The quake itself is not of great importance; it is the fact that it is in the area of Lee Vining (close to Yosemite), but that is not the point. It epicenters in the area where the radioactive "bulge" of molten matter made radioactive by your Nevada testing is "coming to a head". This quake has two points of interest—it tells you where first the toxic material might surface and also relieves a bit of pressure from the "cone" itself. I move to stand-by, thank you.

* * * * *

Soltec present to speak of general information regarding the type of quake just experienced in this most important area. I am responsible for the Command following most closely your Earth changes in a "geophysical" attitude and, hopefully, allow you ones to have knowledge regarding these changes and "possibilities" involved. I can also tell you what to look for, relative to a given action, as follow-on. Please do not ask me to define explicitly in "Earth-time-frame". We calculate possibilities and probabilities by "sequence of events". I shall also make it as simple for general understanding as I can find words to fit descriptions.

The relatively small quake in point was experienced in California to the coastal area near and around San Francisco as well as throughout portions of Nevada (most important indeed). To allow understanding to the "lay" public, I must first speak of vulcanism in general. Therefore, I ask ones who know all this information to please be patient, for we find that 99.9% of the human masses do not have the foggiest idea of that which we outlay unto you.

VULCANISM

The term "vulcanism" implies volcanos—and they are, to be sure, a spectacular product of it. But vulcanism involves much more than mere volcanos. *Any invasion of the Earth's crustal zone by magma from below is properly called vulcanism.* If the magma pushes its way far up into the crustal strata, but does not reach the surface, it is termed ***intrusive*** vulcanism; but if the magma flows out onto the surface, via volcanic or other vents, it is called ***extrusive*** vulcanism. (These, of course, are Earth-English words and will need translation for other language groups.)

The question may well be asked, "Why does molten material from the Earth's interior force its way into and through the hard rock of the crust?" This is one of the questions that has vexed your geologists for many years—not only: "Why does magma invade the crust?" but, "Where precisely does the magma originate?" It is obvious to you "close" observers that release of pressure on the interior of the Earth by deformation and fracturing of the crust triggers the outward movement of magma, but whether it originates initially at the Earth's core, the mantle, or even the crust itself, is difficult for you to determine, for you have not enough knowledge or ability to research those pressures and temperatures to reach valid, provable conclusions.

It depends on the TYPE of volcanic activity. Most volcanos tap only relatively shallow source regions; however, this does not obviate the deep-seated sources for certain types of volcanic activity.

Nearly all major mountain masses are underlain by intrusive masses, and frequently there is some sort of extrusive vulcanism in evidence as well—simply through visual observation. Mountain-building mechanisms, such as folding and faulting, cause vulcanism, but vulcanism, once set in motion, can be a potent mountain-building mechanism in its own right. Massive intrusions may lift and warp the surface layers, and extrusive magma, finding its way to the surface through faults, can build huge piles of volcanic rock. Also, intrusions may be exposed by the wearing away of the softer overlying strata by erosion, and the hard igneous mass will stand up as highlands. The Adirondacks and mountains of New England, for instance, are of this type.

Please understand that I am speaking of the United States in this instance, for this is where the scribe can have association and this is where the subject in point has and is occurring. The information is valid for all Earth locations geographically.

Other examples are the smooth lava flows in Alaska's Valley of the Ten Thousand Smokes, which poured out of a volcanic vent just a few of your decades past and still have the appearance of motion as observed. Today the area, Katmai National Monument, as you have named it, has only about 100 smokes active. It is, however, an area only in the "sleeping".

Another great example of a landscape filled with volcanic plugs, the Kapsiki Mountains in Cameroon [*west-central Africa*], is far different in visualization. There, each great "protrusion" (plug of rock lava) was once a live volcano, its vent filled with molten lava. As the volcano expired and eventually eroded away, only the solidified igneous rock, relatively harder and more resistant, has survived for your modern-day viewing.

INTRUSIVE VULCANISM

BATHOLITHS AND STOCKS:

The largest of the intrusive masses is the ***batholith***, found to underlie every major mountain system and frequently exposed at the surface as the roots or cores of ancient mountains that have eroded away. But the batholith is not merely the upper margin of the monolithic Sima volcanics. It is a lobe that has forced its way well beyond that into the sedimentary (or altered rock) layers that form the continental epidermis, because of lessened pressure as a result of diastrophism. As for size, a ***stock*** is simply indication of "size". There is not "reason" of two terms other than somebody felt it helpful to describe the "bulging" or "hat" under the surface as a ***batholith*** if over 40 square miles in area and a ***stock*** if smaller. Both will be found in the same "bulge".

The batholith and stock are coarse-grained igneous or plutonic rock that has obviously cooled slowly deep underground. At their point of contact with the stratum above is a metamorphosed aureole or baked zone where the combination of heat, pressure, magmatic fluids, and gases have commonly given rise to concentrations of useful minerals.

For practical Earth purposes, you may as well regard these as essentially "bottomless" structures, and intrusive rock has not been "seen" to actually crystallize as extrusive lavas have. You are, as usual, dealing again with conjecture on your placement and it serves well enough in concept.

LACCOLITHS:

On a much smaller scale than the batholith are several

other kinds of magmatic intrusions. One of these, the ***laccolith***, has some of the character of a small batholith or stock—except that it is fed from below by a tube cutting across the overlying strata like the conduit of a volcano. However, where the volcanic bore gets into the surface rocks, magma rising up the laccolith feedpipe loses some of its impetus and spreads out between two flat-lying rock layers, eventually forming a lens-shaped mass that lifts and bows the surface into a dome—and this is indeed most important to the subject in point.

SILLS:

Similar to the laccolith but much more common is the ***sill***. In this case the invading magma spreads out as a flat sheet, often for many miles, but does not throw up the overlying layers. Sills come to your attention when erosion exposes an edge as a sheer wall, often darker and harder than the surrounding rock. The down-cutting Hudson River, as example, has revealed a sill in the Palisades that is particularly striking because of the columnar jointing of the cooling magma. Another major feature standing out in a moderately subdued landscape is the Great Whin sill of Northumberland, England. The black escarpment describes a 100-mile crescent from the Pennines to the sea, and since its steep side faces northward, it was seized on by the Romans as the foundation for Hadrian's wall. Again, within the U.S., you will have a good example in the Black Canyon of the Gunnison [*river in west-central Colorado*].

DIKES:

If the invasion of the surface layers is in the form of a thin sheet cutting sharply across all horizontal strata but falling short of intersecting the surface, then you have a ***dike***. Visualize a sill turned on edge, except in the case of a dike it draws magma from its entire lower edge rather than from a bore or conduit. Dikes often occur in swarms, most frequently radiating from a volcanic vent. If the resulting igneous rock is harder than that which surrounds it, erosion may lay bare the solidified magma in the volcano conduit as a ***neck*** or ***plug***, and the radiating dikes as long narrow ridges. Ship Rock, New Mexico, is an outstanding example. One can see the radiating dikes exposed at the surface and Ship Rock itself is a volcanic ***plug***.

PEGMATITES:

Note that although the originally molten rocks involved in intrusives are properly classified as plutonics and should therefore display a coarse granularity, only the batholith or thick sill is highly typical. Generally, the smaller intrusives isolate the magmatic melt into such thin or limited quantities that cooling is quite rapid and crystal formation is impaired. However, it is possible that a long, intrusive finger may keep its contact with the molten mass below and selected gases and fluids will find their way into this backwater (***pegmatite***). Occasionally crystals will grow to huge size under these unusual conditions. In South Africa, mica crystals have been encountered measuring 10 to 15 feet in width.

EXTRUSIVE VULCANISM

VOLCANOS:

Volcanos are, of course, of particular interest not only because of their unpredictable explosive habits, but also because of their impressive structure. They tend to follow fault lines, and thus the world's great seismic zones. Faulting, earthquakes, and volcanos go together, and faulting is the basic cause for the other two. The Pacific Ocean's unstable margin is often popularly referred to as the "Ring of Fire" because of its extensive volcanic activity.

Everywhere, cones of all sizes, both active and dormant, are evidence of continuing vulcanism.

It is foolish indeed to ever refer to any volcano as "dead". Dormant is your word most suitable for use and should be used if there has been no eruptive activity in historical time. Even historic time is not sufficient. For instance, in 79 A.D., your labeled Vesuvius was not even a very imposing landform which was half hidden inside the broken remnant of the older Monte Somma and had never erupted in the memory of human inhabitation. There were not even any fanciful legends of vulcanism, so long ago had been its most recent activity.

Yet, in that fateful year, Pompeii was buried in a great blast of fiery ash and Herculaneum was overrun by repeated flows of hot mud. Then, for sixteen centuries, there were only ten additional major eruptions. But in 1631, after 130 years of quiescence, Vesuvius began its modern, more frequent eruptive cycle, marked by increased lava flows that had been of little consequence earlier.

So today, Vesuvius is by any measurement active, its personality changed considerably from its former self; and if Somma is any evidence, there have been many times in the distant past when Vesuvius and its precursors have surprised the sleepy folks along the Bay of Naples.

The northwestern United States' own Cascade Mountains, pimpled with 600 miles of snow-capped cones, must be regarded as merely dormant. Lassen Peak, the least spectacular of the lot, was active in 1914-15, but there has been a tendency to think of the others as "scenery". All are very new, geologically speaking, scarcely mutilated by erosion, and this, of course, is why they make such outstanding scenery.

But by the same token, dear friends, they are more likely to be alive than dead after such a short time span. Evidences pointing to just such a likelihood are very modern cinder cones all around the base of Mt. Shasta, another in Crater Lake, and recently discovered by your own geologists, hot spots high on the slope of Mt. Rainier and Mt. Baker, and Mt. Lassen itself.

VARIATIONS IN ERUPTION

No two volcanos are alike in their eruptive habits, and as you have seen from the Vesuvian example, an individual volcano is often capricious. Some are spewers of ash, like Irazu in Costa Rica, which erupted continuously for almost two years (1966-1968), subjecting the residents of the capital city, San José, to a seemingly endless rain of thick dust.

Others eject lava, but with variation: Vesuvius goes off violently with loud explosions and gushes of lava streaming down its flanks; Kilauea, the Hawaiian crater, quietly spills lava over its lip with a minimum of fireworks; Strombolian lava, cooling and crusting over lightly in the crater, traps gases beneath it, which explode every half-hour, throwing incandescent clots high into the air.

Then there are the spasmodic eruptors whose conduit becomes clogged with hardened igneous rock between eruptions. With a cork in the bottle, so to speak, it is not uncommon for the increasing pressures to blow out suddenly through a weak spot on the side of the mountain. This is what happened to Mt. Pelé on Martinique in 1902. Internal pressure started moving the cork, pushing it out of the vent tube in the form of a high spire, but before it could wholly clear the passage, the side of the passage blew out. A dense cloud of intensely hot gases and self-exploding lava mist swept down the slope to the sea, completely wiping out the town of St. Pierre in an instant.

CALDERAS

There is yet another kind of happening that involves the reverse of eruption—that is, a sudden emptying of the magma chamber. When this occurs, the entire top of the mountain, lacking support, collapses and is engulfed into itself. The end result is a huge crater-like pit called a ***caldera***.

Crater Lake, Oregon, is one of these. It is not a true crater because glacial evidences on the contemporary slopes indicate that a peak of over 12,000 feet must have existed to support full-blown glaciers. This reconstructed volcano, dating back probably some 8000 years, has been named posthumously Mt. Mazama.

But volcanos can blow their tops, so how do you know that it collapsed rather than blew up? You can know because the entire surrounding countryside would have to have been covered with debris from the old peak and there simply is none. So now you are faced with the question: what causes the abrupt evacuation of a magma chamber? And you have no certain, finite answer.

Of more recent origin than Crater Lake is the caldera of Krakatau, an island just off western Java [*in Indonesia*]. On August 27, 1883 there were four tremendous explosions, the last of which was heard 3000 miles away, in Australia. A towering dust cloud was thrown up, noticeable around the world for two years, and a great tidal wave drowned 36,000 people. Subsequent investigation revealed that a deep pit had replaced two-thirds of the island, but despite the dust and ash ejected, the bulk of the island had collapsed and the sea had rushed into the resultant caldera. The area is still indeed active.

A new volcanic island is building, called by you Anak Krakatau (child of Krakatau). But even the original Krakatau was merely a remnant of an earlier, much larger island. Like Vesuvius, standing in the breached caldera of Somma, generations of crustal ulcers appear on occasion to be healing, but the infection distressingly reasserts itself again and again when least expected. [*Editor's note: This sleepy volcano started to come to life again in 1994. One of its more spectacular recent eruptions occurred in April of 1996, a clue to what's yet to happen.*]

LOSS OF LIFE

On recounting the loss of human life from volcanic disaster through the centuries, one might be inclined to wonder why anyone would choose to live with volcanos as neighbors. But if a given cone can be classified conveniently as “extinct”, then local residents come to love it and are inspired by its majesty, or even regard it as divine. That “the mountain” could be venomous and turn on its friends is unthinkable until, of course, it does so!

Agricultural people are drawn to the frequently fertile lava soils, willing to take an unknown risk to derive a known livelihood. And, if the giant should cough-up rejuvenating showers of ash periodically, so much the better. Anyway, absolute security is not a guarantee of living anywhere. Why would anyone choose to live in earthquake country, tornado alley, or along hurricane coasts? The law calls these “acts of God”, and God seems, in the short run, less lethal than midtown or freeway traffic, which threatens you all on a daily basis.

CLASSIFICATION BY CONE SHAPE

The simplest classification of volcanos is on the basis of the shape of the cone. Most of them fall generally into one of three types that are easily recognizable, and the cone shape also gives some indication of the type of ejecta and the eruptive habits of the volcano.

First, there is the ***cinder cone***. This is the product of a violently explosive volcano where the lava has solidified in the vent, forming a plug. The accumulation of steam and magmatic gases gradually develops sufficient pressure to blow the plug with such force as to shatter it into tiny fragments (called ***cinders*** and ***ash***), and these are deposited in a symmetrical pile around the vent, the larger particles nearest the vent and the finer ones farther away.

The resulting cinder cone is steep sided (around 37

degrees, the maximum angle of repose of unconsolidated material) and usually symmetrical (Mt. Asmara in Ethiopia). Although evident in many parts of the world, the cinder cone seldom achieves any great size, as erosion rapidly wears away what is essentially merely a pile of loose material. The disappearing islands of the Pacific are often mere cinder cones, where an eruption may throw-up a pile of solid ejecta above the ocean level, to be visible for a few days or months until wave action removes it.

The second type of volcanic cone is called a ***shield*** or ***dome***. Here a quiet flow of fairly fluid lava issues from the vent, forming a vast low-angle cone as it cools. Mauna Loa-Mauna Kea, whose 13,000-foot tips form the island of Hawaii, is an excellent example of this type of cone, and if the low angle of the island's slope is traced to the sea bottom, some five miles deep, the true size of this twin cone becomes apparent!

As often as not, however, a volcano passes through several stages in its history, alternating between explosive eruptions and lava flows. The resulting cone develops a combination of the low-angle shield and the high-angle cinder cone. These are ***composite*** or ***strata*** cones and display concave slopes with a sharp peak. Imagine first a cinder cone, but before it can erode away, it is overlain by lava flows. Then, built on top of this, is another cinder cone, followed again by lava.

The end product looks like Fujiyama, Shasta, Rainier, or Egmont, the world-famous volcanos that inspire poets and legends. The most tell-tale concave slope development, however, is shown by Mt. Shishaldin in the Aleutians, which is smoking and active today. Its classic shape is totally unscarred by any type of erosion as it continues to build. Currently, Shishaldin towers well over 9000 feet above sea level and almost 40,000 feet above the ocean floor—and growing!

The four formerly mentioned volcanos are considered dormant, but El Misti in Peru is equally as impressive and still active, as is Mayon in the Philippines. Mayon, despite its generally low elevation and lack of picturesque snowcap, is reputed to be the most perfectly shaped of the world's composite volcanos. ***I URGE YOU TO NOT BE FOOLISH IN YOUR ATTITUDE THAT THESE "DORMANT" GIANTS ARE CONTINUING IN DORMANCY. THE ENTIRE OF THE CASCADE CHAIN IS AWAKENING.***

Now, let us turn to a most important link-up with information regarding the current quake in point.

FISSURE FLOWS

Lava, in pouring out onto the Earth's surface, does not always issue from volcanic vents; it may well out of faults or fissures many miles in length. If the lava is highly liquid and the terrain fairly subdued, such ***fissure flows*** have been known to cover thousands of square miles and build up extensive plateaus, as in Eastern Washington, Eastern Oregon, Southern Idaho, and Northern California, U.S.A. The bulk of peninsular India is also of this origin.

In Washington, the Columbia River Gorge and the Grand Coulee reveal along their sides a banded layering of differing colors and textures, each of which represents a separate flow. On occasion, the hot lava will be heavily charged with gases, and as the lava cools, the escaping gases leave holes in the rock, making it extremely porous. Water will occasionally flow through the permeable **(scoriaceous)** rock as though it were a pipe. It is also possible that, in a moderately viscous flow, with the surface cooling and congealing through contact with the atmosphere, the hot, still liquid, lava underneath will run on and out leaving an igneous cave.

SO WHAT, SOLTEC?

If you reason carefully regarding the quake in point, you can determine the situation and watch for further

examples or increased activity—in any and all directions. This can allow you to begin to determine likelihood of damage and EXTENT OF PASSAGE OF *RADIOACTIVE* MATERIAL from the Nevada testing site. Because of underlying strata, the flow will be toward the Pacific Ocean and will, obviously, affect the immediate areas around the site of the "caldera" container and the direct fissure network radiating to the sea.

It would be expected, then, that material flowing from the nuclear testing center in Yucca Flats outside of and north of Las Vegas would flow along fissure lines into Death Valley and thus and so; however, this is a false premise.

A brief and general outlay of descriptive flow from Yucca Flats test grounds would be between the Spring Mountains to the west and the Spotted Range and Sheep Range to the east, moving through and into "Devil's Hole" which I believe is one of your National Monuments north of the town of Pahrump, Nevada, on the south edge of the Amargosa Desert, east of the Amargosa Mountain Range and scattering in all directions.

The most open and active fissure, however, runs on through (under) Sarcobatus Flat, between the Inyo and Toiyabe National Forests and pools in the major underground-to-surface cauldrons beneath Mono Lake. Mono Lake is not formed for no reason, dear friends, and it is quite a toxic lake in its already pristine state. ***Lee Vining is at Mono Lake!***

Does this mean the only danger from radioactive material problems would be along that route, then scattering out from the Mono Lake Bulge (which, by the way, is under water for the most part)? No, it means that the danger is where the weakest surface portion of the landscape lies.

The fissures running into Southern California are much more extensive, but are deeper and less likely to show surface bulging. The flow, however, is much easier with much less interference from strata mass.

THE MAJOR FISSURES ALL END UP AT THE SAN ANDREAS FAULT!

When you hear of the prophecies expecting death from open fissures exuding death-causing vapors—it will be from toxic substances, yes, but deadly because of radiation from foolish man-made experiments of nuclear materials.

How much will surface, if it surfaces? I cannot answer, for it depends upon pressure buildup, pressure slippage versus man-caused slippage, and extent of flow.

You can expect deadly gases to spring from what you call Lake Elsinore and on down to the Salton Sea. These gases may or may not be radioactive. Watch the type of tremors, for you can know, if a quake is felt over a large area, it is a bit deeper than a little surface jolt. It means a lot of deep churning and activity in radiating fissures.

Since you do not YET show surface fissures to any great extent, and very little surfacing material at this point, you can surmise it is still in the "***intrusive***" stage and moved into the "***sill***" stage from and forming additional "***laccoliths***". ***The area at Mono Lake represents a batholithic stock in a location not noticed easily through visualization***. The lake is not "just getting lower from depletion of water" but is also more shallow from the "rising" of the lake floor.

I am not here to argue points of physical geology or geography. We have great difficulty with your new names for everything; the entire area described was once at the bottom of the sea, and my vision and instrumentations recognize no difference except for isolating the identification of markers for you ones.

The quake in point is of little notice except for the massive information it should be telling you. More important substance is coming forth along the New Madrid Fault, but the toxic quality of the California tremor bears more destructive potential from that aspect.

The widespread activity is indeed important, but I have not the facility, nor you the understanding, to outlay it all.

I just ask that you be at alert. If you can understand the functioning of your "Mother's" circulatory system, you can better know where safety can be found in order to continue service in this time of transition and upheaval.

You, in contact and counsel with the Higher Energies, will be given to know if you but listen. You who just desire to save your assets (of all types) will likely not hear, and thus discount much of this information. So be it, for it is most certainly up to your own acceptance.

Thank you, Dharma, for scribing this information. I realize you have neither the time nor the interest in these matters, but your service is greatly appreciated, for I have no receiver, regarding these matters, in this location. Much, much focus is given to this area geographically, and I am greatly appreciative of your willingness to entertain my input.

I ask the blessings of Understanding on behalf of you ones awakening from the confusion of the sleep, and I am most grateful to be of whatever service I might project.

I take leave in salute unto you of our "land-locked" fellow-man. Saalomé and Salu!

Soltec to clear.

Hatonn returned to sign-off for this session, as it has grown quite lengthy—being that Soltec has not been subjected to having to reduce a chapter to a page, or a page to a paragraph, as has been jested upon Hatonn.

When we come back I will continue with items of "TODAY'S WATCH" and shake you up a bit with Quantum Cosmic Code.

I shall at first reduce the paragraph to a sentence, but as you might guess, the subject is technical indeed and may require a bit more in-depth projection of wordiness as we move into the subject of GENETIC DOUBLES abounding upon your place these days of political and technical chaos.

So be it.

Let us close this segment and take rest.

Salu.

May 29, 1993

Toniose Soltec present. I come with the Hosts of God, and in the Light and Love of God of Creation, during this time of transition for planet Earth-Shan. We take this time and space to bring, unto you ones of Earth, information regarding that which is taking place within and upon your planet regarding what has come to be known as Earth changes. These changes come in many forms, yet all is interconnected and interrelated; therefore, nothing which takes place within the confines of your world can be omitted when dealing with this subject matter.

It is difficult to put into words, given your limited expression of language, the full impact of that which is taking place with your world, and there are so very many aspects to tie-in together that, without writing entire volumes of text, you have received but a mere smattering of the facts thus far. Keep in mind, also, that our main focus is to inform you ones, on a timely basis, of those events which affect your world on a day-to-day basis, and of those things which have been presented in misinformation—be it on purpose or through ignorance—and to bring basic education about your world to those who lack same.

Either way, we must at all times remember first the purpose of this Earth Transition Mission, and that is to get a remnant through all the upheaval of politics, economics, and geologic changes that are upon you ones of Earth-Shan.

The best defense that you ones have at this time is to be informed and armed with THE TRUTH, which has become a very precious commodity in your world. Yet, this truth is the only chance you ones have for survival. Without it, you too would be following all the other lost lambs unto the slaughter which the Adversary has planned for your world.

You are in the final counting of time as you perceive such, and the Adversary understands this fact quite fully. It is because of this that the battle has grown so fierce of late and you ones are experiencing attacks from all sides.

You see, if the Adversary can cause you ones to become fragmented in your purpose, and cause you to become side-tracked, then you can be defeated. Yet, if you stand united, stay on course, keep yourselves right with God, and one in your purpose, armed with the truth, *nothing* can defeat you!

As soon as you take your sights off God, the Adversary will slip in so quickly that you will not even be aware. This is no small enemy you ones are dealing with, and not one to be taken lightly and, for Heaven's sake, this is not one to be taken on without the Shield of God about you!

Ones become tired of our badgering to continually clear your space, yet it is of absolute necessity during these times. You ones are here for lessons, and you shall have many opportunities for learning, for it is the reason that you CHOSE to participate in this mission. This current mission is the greatest opportunity you ones shall have, in your present dimensional expression, to learn.

Yes, the lessons may seem difficult, and many times you may perceive that you have failed. But believe me when I tell you that each one of you are making giant strides in your own development, and it is only through such seeming "adversity" as has been experienced that you ones experience the most growth.

So, when you reach a point of wanting to give up and not participate any further, keep in mind that you are never given more than you are able to handle. And, the more you are given, the more you have grown. So look upon each "obstacle" with joy and understanding of what it represents.

We understand that you grow weary, but you are never alone so long as you request our presence about you. And, should you stumble along the way, pick yourself up, dust yourself off, and go on—and learn from the stumbling, for in the learning you will have grown stronger.

In our writing of last week, we discussed volcanic activity upon your world and, during this writing, I shall continue this discussion. Commander Hatonn has requested that my dissertation on volcanism, which was scribed by

Dharma previously, be rerun in this edition of the *CONTACT*, as it is a very good primer for the information I have been giving forth of late. I would therefore urge each of you to read that article prior to delving into this article, for it provides a good foundation. [*Editor's note: That earlier lecture by "Professor" Soltec, on matters related to volcanism and Mother Earth's circulatory system, is the writing immediately preceding this one. Note the almost three-year time gap between these two important writings.*]

PHYSICS ON A PLANETARY SCALE

Your Earth is constructed of several different layers, or strata. They are: the continental crust, oceanic crust, uppermost mantle, asthenosphere, mantle, outer core, and the inner core. The crust and uppermost part of the mantle are relatively rigid. Collectively, they make up the **lithosphere.** The upper mantle underlying the lithosphere behaves plastically (a semi-fluid state), and is known as the **asthenosphere.**

Convection takes place within the asthenosphere, as well as within the lower mantle. The lithosphere is moving, as a result of the underlying mantle convection, and the internal processes of the crust are significant to understanding geology.

The tectonic forces are those generated from within the Earth and cause deformation of rock, as well as vertical and horizontal movement of portions of your planet's crust. Mountain ranges are created by tectonic forces stronger than the gravitational forces.

Mountain ranges are built over long periods of time as portions of the planet's crust are compressed and raised. Most of these tectonic forces are mechanical in nature and some of the energy is put to work deforming rock, bending and breaking it, and raising these mountain ranges.

This mechanical energy may be stored or converted to heat energy. An earthquake is a sudden release of this stored mechanical energy, while melting rock, resulting in volcanic eruptions, is another type of release of this same stored energy. By your scientific definition, the machinery of the Earth works by what is called "Plate Tectonics".

Volcanic activity is directly related to Plate Tectonics and most active volcanos are located near plate junctions, where magma is produced as spreading or sinking lithospheric plates interact with other Earth materials. Approximately 80% of all active volcanos are located around the Ring of Fire, which circumscribes the Pacific Ocean. This area essentially corresponds to the Pacific Plate. In the United States, several volcanos in Hawaii, Alaska, and the Cascade Mountain Range are considered, by your scientists, as active.

The Hawaiian volcanos are of interest due to their location, well within the Pacific Plate, rather than near a plate boundary. Below the Pacific Plate, where magma is generated, are what are known as "hot spots". Magma pushes upward through the fissures and fractures in the plate and vents to the surface, producing a volcano on the bottom of the sea floor that eventually may become an island.

At the Hawaiian Islands, the Pacific Plate is moving in a northwest direction and passing over one of these so-called "hot spots", and so a chain of volcanos has formed. The island of Hawaii is, at this point, near one of these "hot spots" and is presently experiencing active volcanism and land-mass formation from the active volcanos.

Other islands to the northwest are off this "hot spot" and volcanos on these islands are no longer active. In time, the larger island of Hawaii will also pass from over this "hot spot" and its volcanic activity will also move into a quiet or inactive stage.

Magma, which becomes lava if it reaches the surface, forms locally within the outer 100 kilometers (approximately 62 miles) of the Earth's surface. Pockets of magma form from the melting of rock within the crust or uppermost part of the mantle.

LONG VALLEY CALDERA

We have been discussing the area in California known to you ones as the Long Valley Caldera, a volcano that erupted some 700,000 years ago, and one that is exhibiting signs of renewed activity in recent years. Let me first give explanation of a caldera for you who may be unaware of this term. A caldera, or crater, is a large volcanic depression formed by the explosive disruption of a volcanic cone or by the collapse of a volcanic crater floor. The explosive eruptions are rather rare, but usually extremely violent.

A large caldera-forming eruption may explosively extrude 1000 cubic kilometers of pyroclastic debris, mostly ash. [*Editor's note: "pyro" = hot, "clastic" = broken; thus "pyroclastic debris" can be pictured to mean small rock chunks and other lumpy magma fragments formed during the cooling down into solid material after being hurled as hot, chunky "liquid" from the volcano.*] This would be about 1000 times that which was ejected by the eruption of Mount St. Helens in 1980. The most recent caldera forming eruptions on the North American Continent occurred between 600,000 and 700,000 years ago in Yellowstone National Park in Wyoming and in the Owens Valley in east-central California (known as the Long Valley Caldera).

The main explosive eruptions are over very quickly—within a few days or a few weeks—but intermittent and lesser magnitude volcanic activity can linger on for millions of years. In Yellowstone, the original event left the result of hot springs and geysers. The Owens Valley event (Long Valley Caldera) is still producing volcanic and seismic potential hazards.

Both the Yellowstone and Long Valley sites are still capable of producing future volcanic activity because magma is still present at variable depths beneath the caldera floors. Both are what your scientists refer to as *resurgent calderas*, because the floors of the calderas have slowly domed upward since the explosive eruptions that originally formed them.

The concern, however, with the Long Valley Caldera, as I have written on before, is that the rate of uplift has been accelerating, and there have been swarms of earthquakes in the area with magnitudes of 5 to 6, which became harmonic, and this is symptomatic of magma moving closer to the surface. **It was considered, by your own scientists, enough of a potential hazard that a notice of potential volcanic hazard was issued in 1982.**

At present, the notice has been lifted, but the future situation there is still deemed "uncertain" by your scientists, so they are continually keeping a watchful eye on this place. With the recent renewed earthquake activity in this area, you can rest assured that they are once again taking a very close look at this area.

[*Editor's note: It was only about a year after Soltec's writing of the above that worried scientists had to begin to issue a now-ongoing series of volcanic alerts concerning Mammoth and the Long Valley Caldera. It has been almost comical (if that's really a good word to use for such a serious situation) to watch these scientists struggle with their ethics on the one hand, and the tourist economics of the area on the other. One particularly memorable recent alert window was kept off the greater Los Angeles area news programs until local-area skiers were all "safely" checked-in for a long holiday weekend; then the news programs all of a sudden "discovered" an alert that had been in progress for about four days.*]

When a volcano, such as the Long Valley Caldera, erupts, it is the explosive type of eruption which spreads ash for literally hundreds of miles in all directions, and produces an ash cloud that can spread for thousands of miles.

In a normal eruption, in addition to the ash itself, various gases are also released. These gases include: water vapor, carbon dioxide, carbon monoxide, sulfur dioxide and hydrogen sulfide. Even some thought-to-be-dormant volcanoes emit gases for very long periods following eruptions.

DEADLY RADIOACTIVE GASES

Although these natural escaped gases produce some hazard, the greater hazard in the Long Valley Caldera scenario is that of ***radioactive gases,*** which would be released if this old giant should come to life.

These radioactive gases present are due to all the fissures and fractures that extend over into the State of Nevada (where shaking has been felt as far away as Las Vegas in the recent series of earthquakes associated with this situation). All areas of land mass have a certain amount of natural fissures and fractures created by the continual moving, grinding, folding, and separating actions of the Tectonic Plates.

Nevada, however, has experienced a tremendous amount of tampering by man—because of all the underground nuclear testing that has taken place there over the years. So, here in this place you have natural fractures and fissures, but these have been enlarged by man's interference, and new fractures and fissures have been created by the same man-caused interference. ***There are also underground storage areas of hazardous waste of the most insidious kinds—genetically altered life forms, radioactive waste, and the like. Yet, your new President has given the go-ahead to continue, for a "limited" time, the ridiculous practice of underground testing.***

These underground storage facilities are of grave concern at this point due to all the seismic and potential volcanic activity from that Long Valley Caldera area. If that volcano goes, there will be even more new fissures and fractures, and you can bet that all those nice little surprises stored belowground will end up in the atmosphere and spread worldwide. That is in addition to the mass destruction which would take place from the resultant volcanic ash that would be naturally produced by this sleeping giant.

Let me take a few lines to summarize the different types of volcanos you will find on your planet. **Shield Volcanos** by far are the largest volcanos and are characterized by relatively non-explosive activity, resulting from the low silica content of the magma. They are broad, gently sloping, cone-shaped, and are built-up almost entirely from solidified lava flows. During eruptions, the lava spreads widely and thinly due to its low viscosity. Because the lava flows from a central vent, without much lava build-up around the vent, the slopes are usually in the shape of a flattened dome or shield.

The Hawaiian Islands are essentially a series of Shield Volcanos, built upward from the ocean floor by intermittent eruptions over millions of years. They are spectacular to observe, and the eruptions are relatively non-violent because the lava is generally fluid (less viscous). The Hawaiian Islands, then, are composed of a series of layers of basalt (low in silica and relatively high in iron, magnesium, and calcium oxides).

Cinder Cones are volcanos constructed of loose rock fragments which have been ejected from a central vent. In contrast to the gentle sloping sides of Shield Volcanos, Cinder Cones commonly have steep-sided slopes (approximately 30 degrees). Most of the ejected material lands near the vent during an eruption and builds up the cone to a peak. The steepness of slopes of accumulating loose material is limited by gravity to approximately 33 degrees. Cinder Cones tend to be much smaller than Shield Volcanos. Most Cinder Cones are in the area of 1500 feet in height.

The fragments of volcanic rock ejected from Cinder Cones range in size from 1.5 to 13 inches. Dust and ash are the finest particles emitted. When solid rock has been blasted apart by volcanic explosion, the fragments are angular and have no rounded edges or corners. If lava is ejected into the air, a molten blob becomes streamlined during flight, solidifies, and falls to the ground in a spindle or lens shape. Local concentrations of gas in magma cause eruptions that build Cinder Cones. They are not necessarily related to the silica content of the extrusive rock lava. Some Cinder Cones are found in Hawaii, on the flanks of much larger Shield Volcanos. The lifespan of an active Cinder Cone tends to be short, as the local concentration of gas is depleted rather quickly during the period of eruption.

Composite Volcanos are constructed of alternating layers of pyroclastics and rock solidified from lava flows. They are known for their cone shapes and are associated with a magma of intermediate silica content, which is more viscous (less easily flowing) than the low-silica magma of Shield Volcanos.

Volcanic activity characteristic with this type of volcano is a mixture of explosive activity and lava flow. Composite Volcanos are built-up over long time spans. Eruption is intermittent, with hundreds or even thousands of years between eruptions.

During the quiet intervals, Composite Volcanos may be eroded by running water, landslides, or glaciers. These processes tend to alter the surface, shape, and form of the cone, but due to their long lives and relative resistance to erosion, Composite Volcanos can become extremely large. Also, because of the sometimes long periods of quiet between eruptions, populations tend to ignore their potential hazards. They are normally quite beautiful and majestic-looking mountains, and this can tend to deceive people.

Mount St. Helens and Mount Rainier are examples of Composite Volcanos. Nearly all the larger and better known volcanos of the world are Composite Volcanos and these tend to align around (1) the Pacific Ocean's "Ring of Fire", which includes the Cascade Mountain Range, and (2) the Mediterranean Belt, which is home to the legendary Mt. Vesuvius.

Several Composite Volcanos are in Mexico, among which is El Chichon, which erupted in 1982. The towns near this volcano were buried by the heavy ash and ash flows, leaving thousands dead in the small towns and villages.

Volcanic domes are steep-sided, dome, or spine-shaped masses of volcanic rock formed from viscous lava that solidifies in or immediately above a volcanic vent. A volcanic dome grew within the caldera of Mount St. Helens after the climactic eruption in 1980. Mt. Lassen in Northeastern California is a good example of a volcanic dome. One previous eruption of this volcano blew out horizontally and destroyed a very large area. A group of volcanic domes, known as the Chaos Crags, are located just north of Lassen Peak. These domes have a recent history of explosive activity and large rockfall debris avalanches.

The alignment of Composite Volcanos around the perimeter of the Pacific Ocean's "Ring of Fire" is due to subduction at converging plate boundaries. For example, the source of magma for Mount St. Helens and Mount Rainier is the Juan de Fuca Plate, whose spreading center is in the Pacific just a little west of the Washington and Oregon coastline. This plate moves eastward and is subducting beneath the North American Plate, which is moving westward.

As this Juan de Fuca Plate descends, it is the upper portion of the plate which, of course, tilts forward as it is going downward, and thus that "leading" surface of the plate comes into contact with increasingly hotter material. Once it has slid beneath the continental lithosphere, it continues under the asthenosphere. At that point, temperatures are high enough to cause partial melting of the upper portion of the descending plate. The magma, being less dense than the surrounding rocks, then rises toward the surface, eventually erupting and building these composite volcanic domes of the Cascade Mountain Range.

Let us draw this writing to a close, as we have given quite a lesson on volcanos and volcanic events. Thank you for your attention, and we shall continue this lesson in basic geology.

As always, you are held in the Light of God and with our blessings. Toniose to standby. Salu.

APPENDIX B

72-Hour Kit Checklist

Editor's note: Since there are many places within the writings of this volume where we are urged to gather together emergency supplies, we present the following.

Everyone knows that the time to plan for an emergency is *before* the emergency occurs. Unfortunately, few people have taken the time to plan and make emergency preparations. Most people don't even have an evacuation plan in case of a fire in their home.

Thinking about emergency preparedness is not pleasant, but it could save the lives of you and your family, or at least make getting along a lot more pleasant during an emergency. Sometimes it is the fear associated with unpleasant happenings that keeps people from even considering how they would handle such events as natural disaster emergencies. Sometimes it is simple laziness.

At best these are excuses to procrastinate; at worst they are disasters in the making, with ones running away from responsibility—responsibility that may include the care of a family, some members of which may be dependent upon someone(s) in that nucleus of interaction having good sense and a level head.

You need only talk to any of those people who were directly affected in recent-years' earthquakes, hurricanes, floods, or tornados, and they will be the first to tell you that some items are ESSENTIAL. When they were left without shelter, food, clothing, water, or cash, many wished they had taken the time, prior to the emergency, to put together a kit of survival items.

Even if you do not have to leave your residence, having some basic essentials will make the difference between being miserable, cold, hungry, thirsty, etc., and being able to satisfy these basic needs. And, should you have to leave your home in a hurry, having a pack pre-prepared allows you more time and peace of mind to plan your journey.

It is only common sense to plan for your own survival. Your neighbors, nearby friends and relatives, etc., will be more than busy taking care of themselves in a large-scale emergency, and do not need any other burdens. So, you can't expect to depend upon anyone but yourself and maybe your immediate family.

However, if several families elected to get together in an organized way, then you could pool your supplies. Moreover, it can be quite helpful to be able to draw upon the moral support of others in any type of emergency. Thus, should you find yourself together with some others, then recognize the possibilities of cooperative action and sharing of resources—so long as ALL are "BRINGING something to the party" rather than simply TAKING.

On the following pages is listed a 72-Hour Kit Checklist of items you may wish to consider assembling together in some form of a portable pack. These items are basic bare essentials, and you may add to them as you have space and funds. Each family will have their own specific, personal needs to customize this general list.

With any luck, you will never need these all-important items; but isn't it better to be prepared and not need them, than to be unprepared and left stranded, wishing you did have them?! Will it be the ounce of prevention, or the pound of cure?

We are in a time of massive changes everywhere upon our beautiful little planet, and you do not need to be a psychic or "receiver of Higher Sources" to be aware that something unprecedented is occurring upon our world. These changes are only going to continue to accelerate, the further we proceed into the planetary transformation, and we would all be wise to get ready and remain in a state of preparedness. Some of the things that are likely to happen can be merely a minor inconvenience if one is prepared with the essentials; but without such preparation, even something as simple as a drink of water can be a major challenge.

REMEMBER, IT'S TOO LATE TO PREPARE *AFTER* THE EMERGENCY! SO TAKE RESPONSIBLE ACTION NOW!

Water:
Stored in a portable container; at least three gallons per person (for a three-day supply). Rotate regularly. Have water purification method(s) such as 10-12 drops (per gallon of stored water) of 35% food-grade hydrogen peroxide, plus water filtration equipment.

Food:
This should be suitably packaged for long-term storage. Also cups, utensils, paper plates, can opener if needed.

Extra Clothing:
A complete outfit of extra (maybe heavy) clothing for each family member. Include socks, underwear, walking shoes.

Warmth and Shelter:
Coats, hats, scarves, and gloves for everyone. Include warm blankets (wool and emergency blankets are best). Rain ponchos, plastic garbage bags, umbrellas and boots are helpful to keep dry from rain. Warm packs or other heat sources. Tent or tarp and sleeping bags.

Light Sources:
Flashlights with extra batteries, chemical lightsticks. Flames from candles, kerosene or propane lanterns, and large propane heaters require caution. Have at least two quick and safe light sources.

Tools:
Pocket knife, camping shovel, duct tape, waterproof matches, pocket sewing kit, screwdriver, pry bar, hammer, etc. Compact tool kit for minor automobile repairs.

Important Papers:
Copies of important documents (birth and marriage certificates, insurance forms, wills, etc.), addresses and phone numbers of relatives, and places to meet if separated.

Money:
Store at least $50.00 (CASH) per person. Be sure to include change, such as quarters for phone calls, etc. Don't expect credit cards to be useful under emergency conditions.

First Aid Supplies:
Pain relievers, bandages, antiseptics, clean cloths, burn ointment, rubbing alcohol, first-aid instruction manual. Include personal medications and prescriptions.

Special Needs:
For babies: diapers, ointments, bottles, pacifiers, hand towels, special foods and medicines. Consider needs of elderly, handicapped, or other special cases. Don't forget pets. Include pet foods and any medications they need. A pet carrier will be handy.

Stress Relievers:
Card games, books, small hobbies, audio (music) tapes and player. For children: small toys, paper and pen, and favorite security items (blanket, stuffed toy or doll).

Communications:
Portable radio with batteries (one requiring no batteries is best), signal mirrors, whistles, red flags, signal flares. Consider having a portable CB (citizen's band) two-way radio and a portable (battery operated) communications scanner if your budget permits.

Personal Sanitation:
Toothbrushes, mouth wash, antibacterial hand soap, dish soap, razors, sanitary napkins, towels, toilet paper.

Portable Container(s):
Backpacks and duffel bags are ideal. Containers should be lightweight, sturdy, waterproof, and easy to carry. Shoulder straps are best for traveling longer distances.

Additional Items:
Add as carrying weight and budget will allow. Extra food, camp stove, cooking equipment, tents, sleeping bags, Sun block, insect repellant, portable toilet, additional tools (like axe for clearing fallen branches) and more sophisticated first-aid items. The *U.S. Army Survival Manual* (FM 21-76, available from Barnes & Noble Books) is an excellent resource of information and suggestions covering an extensive array of emergency conditions.

Sense of Humor:
More than anything, try to keep your wits about you in an emergency. Even a simple pocket knife or match can cause dangerous wounds in nervous hands. Moreover, everyone near you will respond much more helpfully and favorably to a kind word than to a temper tantrum. And above all, cultivate a sense of humor! Sometimes it is just the release of stress, through humor, that frees up the mind enough to think clearly and see a way out of an emergency situation that otherwise seems impossible. At the very least you will help to ease the fears of those around you.

transcontinental
PRINTING
IMPRIMERIE GAGNÉ

PRINTED IN CANADA